PRENTICE-HALL
HISTORY OF MUSIC SERIES
H. WILEY HITCHCOCK, editor

MUSIC
IN THE
RENAISSANCE

MUSIC
IN THE
RENAISSANCE

HOWARD MAYER BROWN

Department of Music
University of Chicago

PRENTICE-HALL, INC., ENGLEWOOD CLIFFS, NEW JERSEY

Library of Congress Cataloging in Publication Data

BROWN, HOWARD MAYER.
　Music in the Renaissance.

　(Prentice-Hall history of music series)
　Includes bibliographies and index.
　　1. Music—History and criticism—Medieval, 400–
1500.　2. Music—History and criticism—16th cen-
tury.　I. Title.
ML172.B86　　　780′.9031　　　75-28352
ISBN 0-13-608505-9
ISBN 0-13-608497-4 pbk.

FOR R.W.W.

Printed in the United States of America

10　9　8　7　6　5　4　3

© 1976 by Prentice-Hall, Inc.
Englewood Cliffs, New Jersey

PRENTICE-HALL INTERNATIONAL, INC., *London*
PRENTICE-HALL OF AUSTRALIA, PTY. LIMITED, *Sydney*
PRENTICE-HALL OF CANADA, LTD., *Toronto*
PRENTICE-HALL OF INDIA PRIVATE LIMITED, *New Delhi*
PRENTICE-HALL OF JAPAN, INC., *Tokyo*
PRENTICE-HALL OF SOUTHEAST ASIA PTE. LTD., *Singapore*

CONTENTS

1425-1475   *1400-1474*   *1400-1460*

FOREWORD

Students and informed amateurs of the history of music have long needed a series of books that are comprehensive, authoritative, and engagingly written. They have needed books written by specialists—but specialists interested in communicating vividly. The Prentice-Hall History of Music Series aims at filling these needs.

Six books in the series present a panoramic view of the history of Western music, divided among the major historical periods—Medieval, Renaissance, Baroque, Classic, Romantic, and Contemporary. The musical culture of the United States, viewed historically as an independent development within the larger western tradition, is discussed in another book, and forthcoming will be similar books on the music of Latin America and Russia. In yet another pair, the rich yet neglected folk and traditional music of both hemispheres is treated. Taken together, the eleven volumes of the series will be a distinctive and, we hope, distinguished

Foreword, continued

contribution to the history of the music of the world's peoples. Each volume, moreover, may be read singly as a substantial account of the music of its period or area.

The authors of the series are scholars of national and international repute—musicologists, critics, and teachers of acknowledged stature in their respective fields of specialization. In their contributions to the Prentice-Hall History of Music Series their goal has been to present works of solid scholarship that are eminently readable, with significant insights into music as a part of the general intellectual and cultural life of man.

H. WILEY HITCHCOCK, *Editor*

PREFACE

Quite simply, I wished to write a book that would introduce university students as well as my colleagues in other disciplines and interested laymen to the music of the Renaissance, a book that would answer several fundamental questions: What were the most significant features of Renaissance music? Who were its greatest composers? How were they great? In short, what is there about this music that still makes it meaningful for us today?

I have placed much emphasis on the contributions of the greatest composers for two reasons. The first is that many (though by no means all) musical scholars in the past have tended to stress secondary figures of the fifteenth and sixteenth centuries almost as much as the principal composers. We have studied the Renaissance differently from almost every other period in music history, and hence we know more about Palestrina's lesser contemporaries, say, than about Beethoven's. Consequently, the contribution of the most important composers has not always been as sharply focussed in the minds of music students as it should be. I hope that this book may help to reverse that trend. More important, the history of an art is in the first instance the history of great achievements by individuals. At least a part of the task of conceiving of our past has to do with judging those great achievements against the conventions of an age.

I have been encouraged to stress major composers and great accomplishments rather than genres, conventions, and lesser figures by the existence of Gustave Reese's *Music in the Renaissance* (rev. ed., New York, W. W. Norton, 1959). Reese has been so thorough that I felt more free to omit whatever I wished than I might otherwise have felt, since I could comfort myself with the certainty that interested readers could find whatever information they needed by consulting Reese's book. I do not mean thereby to imply a criticism of Reese. On the contrary, his magnificent achievement has already given several generations of students, myself included, their most precise notions about the music of the period, and it has shaped our conception of this music more than any other single work.

In the course of my book I have assumed on the part of the reader an elementary knowledge of the church modes—Dorian, Phrygian, Mixolydian, and Lydian—and I have therefore felt free to discuss the music in slightly broader conceptual terms. Those who are uncertain of the character of the modes should consult any standard dictionary of music, for example, the article, "Modes," in *Grove's Dictionary of Music and Musicians*, 5th edition. I have referred to note values and time signatures by modern terms, a practice that seemed to me to help our understanding of the musical style more than it would confuse the unwary reader. Most, if by no means all, modern editions translate the note values of the fifteenth and sixteenth centuries—breve (□), semibreve (◇), minim (♩), semiminim (♩), and so on—into modern values that imply a reduction by half, into whole notes (o), half notes (♩), quarter notes (♩), and eighth notes (♪). Moreover, earlier mensuration signs do not mean precisely the same thing as modern time signatures; the differences are explained in Willi Apel's *The Notation of Polyphonic Music, 900–1600*, 5th ed. (Cambridge, Mass., 1961), as well as in various other standard reference books.

A number of people have read parts of the manuscript, and offered valuable suggestions and criticisms. I am especially grateful to Daniel Heartz, O. W. Neighbour, Jeremy Noble, Leeman Perkins, and H. Colin Slim. And a number of people have given me invaluable help in turning my manuscript into a book, among them, Kaye Clements, who copied the musical examples with admirable accuracy; Patrick Gallagher, who typed the final copy and improved the punctuation; Genevieve Libin and Carole Richardson of Prentice-Hall, who copyedited the manuscript and saw to the innumerable details with unfailing kindness and efficiency; and the Series editor, H. Wiley Hitchcock, whose patience, encouragement, and advice were badly needed more than once.

HOWARD MAYER BROWN

MUSIC
IN THE
RENAISSANCE

INTRODUCTION
MUSIC IN THE RENAISSANCE

Masses, motets, and settings of secular lyric poetry were the chief kinds of music written in the fifteenth and sixteenth centuries. The first task of this book is simply to describe how composers' attitudes changed in the course of two hundred years towards each of these genres. I shall enumerate the diverse ways of approaching the invariable words of the Mass, the musical solutions devised for setting many kinds of motet texts, and the process by which national dialects gradually fragmented the one universal language of music in settings of secular poetry. Only during the fifteenth century did musicians begin to conceive all five sections of the Mass Ordinary—Kyrie, Gloria, Credo, Sanctus, and Agnus Dei—as a cycle by basing each movement on the same musical material. Whereas motets had existed since the thirteenth century, their character had changed over the years, and many major developments of style between 1430 and 1600 can best be examined by studying this genre. Chansons—settings of stereotyped French courtly lyrics—constituted the principal sort of secular music in the fifteenth century, regardless of the composers' nationalities. The sixteenth century saw a flowering of compositions in other languages, the Italian madrigal above all, but also settings of Spanish, German, Dutch, and finally English poems.

Historians, however, do not describe the past merely to picture it as it really was so much as they attempt to impose some order on intransigent reality to comprehend it better. Were we ever able to reconstruct the continuum of daily events we might even be tempted to argue that the Renaissance never really existed: the fifteenth century was simply a continuation of the Middle Ages, and the sixteenth century, without any sharp break with the past, prepared the way for the Baroque era. Similar statements might be made about any period, but they are not satisfactory. In order to understand the past we must continue to try to find characteristics common to many diverse phenomena and to decide which events were most significant or typical.

The past may be divided into comprehensible segments by singling out the greatest achievements of individuals, those original inventions and magnificent accomplishments that influenced future generations and raised musical geniuses above their contemporaries. Dufay's brilliant realization of the possibilities for organizing gigantic musical structures around borrowed melodies and his consummate skill in using the mellifluous English sonorities, for example, bespeak a genuinely new attitude toward the art of music. So also do Josquin's amalgamation of Italianate and Netherlandish traits into a highly supple and expressive texture and Monteverdi's stunning demonstration of the musical and dramatic potentials of the new techniques of *basso continuo* and recitative, invented by lesser musicians. These are the great achievements that carried in themselves the seeds of further development. Because they shaped the age they have determined the major divisions of this book.

The invention of a new technique has no importance unless a great composer demonstrates its artistic significance, or unless it raises aesthetic problems and implies technical possibilities that challenge the best efforts of a whole generation of musicians. The historian, then, seeks the most influential as well as the best music as a focus around which to group related compositions in order to determine the specific shape of a period. In singling out the most novel and characteristic features of the music of these two centuries, the historian in effect outlines the history of the art during the Renaissance, a necessary preliminary step toward understanding the term "Renaissance" as it applies to music. By explaining how the fifteenth and sixteenth centuries differ from earlier and later times he can, then, approach a reasonably meaningful definition of the Renaissance that is yet broad enough to tolerate the notion that conflicting and contrasting elements do in fact co-exist.

The fifteenth century saw a last great flowering of older musicial techniques based on pre-formed patterns and formal outlines—cantus firmi, *formes fixes,* and isorhythm. Some of these practices, though, underwent important transformations. Earlier composers, for example, often placed a borrowed melody in long notes in an inner voice to serve as a structural foundation; but the practice of basing all five movements of a Mass Ordinary on a single rationally disposed cantus firmus extends the older technique on an altogether different and larger scale. Since the cyclic Mass clearly places aesthetic above liturgical laws, its invention suggests that composers were beginning to see themselves as creative artists and not mere servants of the Church.

In the course of two centuries, composers emancipated themselves from many of these pre-determined strictures. They freed themselves from the shackles of medieval authority by inventing a more flexible and musically self-sufficient technique of organizing form by means of thematic manipulation. Writing music by creating a series of points of imitation went hand in hand with the change from successive to simultaneous composition. Music based on a cantus firmus was conceived one line at a time, but the intricate web of thematically interrelated melodies that constitutes a point of imitation had to be woven all at once by a composer working with one section at a time. Even though composers of the sixteenth century still based new compositions on old—by using Gregorian chant as building material, for example, or by parodying a pre-existent motet, chanson, or madrigal—the new techniques enabled them to shape and transform their borrowed material more freely than had the old, and they could and did construct large musical structures completely free of borrowings, generated entirely by their own imagination.

The imitative polyphony of the sixteenth century was greatly enriched and, indeed, partly determined by the new notion that music ought to reflect the text it set. The desire to write a kind of music inspired by words, a contribution of the generation working between about 1490 and 1520, marks the influence of the humanists. Composers wished to mirror not only the external characteristics of the words—their syntax, grammar, and accentuation—but also their meaning. The relationship of text to music preoccupied composers throughout the sixteenth century, as they sought ways to achieve a new level of expressiveness.

The emancipation from medieval ways of thought and the restrictions of pre-formed structure meant that music became for the first time a self-sufficient, self-generated art. It is no coincidence, then, that the rise of abstract instrumental music—an "absolute art" not related to literary meanings and preconceived patterns—coincides with the invention of these new techniques in the sixteenth century.

During the fifteenth and sixteenth centuries the dominion of the church modes over melody and harmony was threatened and finally overcome by a number of forces, chief among them the growth and development of new concepts of functional tonality with its orientation around the cadential formula V–I, dominant to tonic. Dufay's music, permeated with the new sounds of full triads, already recognizes this central principle. Later composers began to explore musical space, expanding the range of usable notes from low to high, and probing the furthermost reaches of chromaticism. Composers during the later sixteenth century worked with a well-developed tonal system, although different in important ways from the tonality of the seventeenth century and still relatively little studied.

All of these features—freedom from medieval authority, preoccupation with text expression, the invention of instrumental music, and the development of tonality—lead to the conclusion that music during the fifteenth and sixteenth centuries became a more personal and expressive art, with man at its center. This truism about the Renaissance, then, applies as well to music as to every other product of human endeavor during the period.

On the other hand, the primary meaning of the term "Renaissance," a rebirth from classical models, is not so easily applied to music. Although descriptions of the effects music produced in the ancient world played a role in forming composers' attitudes, few actual examples from Greece and none from Rome survived. Most of the extant fragments of Greek music were discovered during the sixteenth century; they were avidly discussed in some circles but remained antiquarian curiosities without influence on the styles of the major composers.

Studies of the Renaissance, from the time of Burckhardt and Huizinga on, have rightly centered on artistic, intellectual, and philosophical events in Italy. Music in the Renaissance, on the other hand, is a northern art, or at least an art by northerners. All of the great composers of the fifteenth and early sixteenth centuries were born in what is today northern France, Belgium, and Holland. But it does not follow that Italy was a provincial backwater; on the contrary, Italy was the center of a brilliant and flourishing musical culture. Curiously, though, few if any of the composers working there after about 1420—by which time the burst of energy of the *trecento* had finally died down—were native-born. And even if a few Italian composers do emerge about 1490 they do not threaten the artistic hegemony of the *oltremontani*. Flanders, Burgundy, and Italy were the centers of musical life in the fifteenth and sixteenth centuries. Northern composers all flocked to the elegant Italian courts, and, for most of our period, music in Spain, France,

England, and Germany must definitely take second place. In the course of the sixteenth century the relationship between north and south was reversed, and by 1600 Italian composers were acknowledged supreme.

BIBLIOGRAPHICAL NOTES

In the Preface I have already mentioned the standard work on the period, Gustave Reese's *Music in the Renaissance*. A more concise survey may be found in Donald Jay Grout, *A History of Western Music* (New York, 1960). Students should also consult *The New Oxford History of Music*, ed. Dom Anselm Hughes and Gerald Abraham (London, 1960–68), especially vol. 3, *Ars Nova and the Renaissance, 1300–1540*, and vol. 4, *The Age of Humanism, 1540–1630*.

Although out of date, Hugo Riemann, *Geschichte der Musiktheorie im IX.–XIX. Jahrhundert*, 2nd ed. (Berlin, 1920), is still the most comprehensive survey of music theory during the Renaissance. Its first two books, on polyphonic theory from the ninth to the sixteenth centuries, have been translated into English by Raymond Haggh (Lincoln, Nebraska, 1962). Oliver Strunk, *Source Readings in Music History* (New York, 1950), contains translations from many of the most important theoretical treatises; those from the Renaissance are available separately as a paperback.

For information on unfamiliar instruments used during the period, the student should consult Anthony Baines, ed., *Musical Instruments Through the Ages* (Penguin Books, 1961).

For chronologically arranged examples of the music of the period, see *Historical Anthology of Music*, ed. Archibald T. Davison and Willi Apel, vol. 1, rev. ed. (Cambridge, Mass., 1964); Arnold Schering, *Geschichte der Musik in Beispielen* (Leipzig, 1931); Carl Parrish and John F. Ohl, *Masterpieces of Music Before 1750* (New York, 1951); Carl Parrish, *A Treasury of Early Music* (New York, 1958); and the various volumes in the series *Das Musikwerk* (in English translations as well, under the title *Anthology of Music*), published by the Arno Volk Verlag in Cologne. Students will also find useful and convenient the series of small volumes called *Das Chorwerk* (Wolfenbüttel, 1929–), published under the general editorship of Friedrich Blume.

My exposition of the most significant innovations of the Renaissance is much indebted to Edward E. Lowinsky, "Music in the Culture of the Renaissance," in *Renaissance Essays from the Journal of the History of Ideas*, ed. Paul Oskar Kristeller and Philip P. Wiener (New York, 1968), and to various other essays by Lowinsky.

Music students should also read discussions of the concept of the Renaissance written by historians in other fields, among them Paul Oskar Kristeller, *Renaissance Thought* (New York, 1961–65, 2 vols.); Erwin Panofsky, " 'Renaissance'—Self-Definition or Self-Deception?," in his *Renaissance and Renascences in Western Art* (London, 1965); and Michael Levey, *Early Renaissance* (Penguin Books, 1967).

A number of scholars have begun to apply the term "mannerism" to certain trends in sixteenth-century music. But the concept, problematic in art history and even more troublesome in its application to music, needs to be thoroughly studied by music historians before it can be accepted. See John Shearman, *Mannerism* (Penguin Books, 1967), for a recent and excellent treatment of the subject in art history with some mention of music (especially pp. 96–104). For three recent discussions in English of mannerism in music, see Robert Wolf, "Renaissance, Mannerism, Baroque: Three Styles, Three Periods," in *Les Colloques de Wégimont*, 4 (1963); Don Harran, " 'Mannerism' in the Cinquecento Madrigali," *Musical Quarterly*, 55 (1969); and James Haar, "Classicism and Mannerism in 16th-Century Music," *International Review of Music Aesthetics and Sociology*, 1 (1971).

part one

The Early Renaissance:

1420-1490

ONE

THE BEGINNINGS:
DUNSTABLE AND
THE CONTENANCE ANGLOISE

"Although it seems beyond belief, there does not exist a single piece of music, not composed within the last forty years, that is regarded by the learned as worth hearing." In 1477 Johannes Tinctoris, chapelmaster to the King of Naples, acknowledged the beginning of the Renaissance with that sentence in the introduction to his treatise on counterpoint. He identifies the Englishman John Dunstable (ca. 1380/90–1453) and the Burgundians Guillaume Dufay (ca. 1400–1474) and Gilles Binchois (ca. 1400–ca. 1460) as the founders of a new musical style, and Johannes Ockeghem (ca. 1420–97) and Antoine Busnois (ca. 1430–92) as the most distinguished heirs of the tradition. Tinctoris's historical judgement seems as valid today as when he made it 500 years ago; we still associate the early musical Renaissance with Dunstable, Dufay, and Binchois, and recognize Ockeghem and Busnois as the best composers of the following generation.

The relationship among the composers of the first generation is made clear in a poem, *Le Champion des dames,* written by the Burgundian Martin le Franc about 1441. Dufay and Binchois, wrote Le Franc, have found a new way to make lively consonances *("frisque concordance").* They wear the English guise *("la contenance angloise"),* and in following Dunstable they have made their music *"joyeux et notable."* To the men of the fifteenth century, then, something new in music began with Dunstable and was then taken up by continental composers.

To the modern listener, early fifteenth-century English music sounds sweeter and fuller than continental music of the same period, and this great euphony undoubtedly constitutes the greater part of what Le Franc meant by *la contenance angloise.* Three technical features explain the sound: full triads, that is, those which regularly include the third; block chords or else lightly ornamented homorhythmic passages; and bland, uniformly consonant harmonies that avoid dissonances on strong beats, or indeed anywhere save as inconspicuous passing notes. Compare Leonel Power's simple setting of the antiphon *Beata progenies* (Example 1–1), in which the undecorated chant is sung by the middle voice, or even his more complicated *Gloriose Virginis* (Example 1–2), which sets an antiphon text without any reference to the chant melody, with a roughly contemporary isorhythmic motet, *Ut te per omnes* (Example

EXAMPLE 1–1. Leonel Power, *Beata progenies,* mm. 1–14. Used by permission of the American Institute of Musicology.

EXAMPLE 1–2. Power, *Gloriose Virginis,* mm. 1–18. Used by permission of the American Institute of Musicology.

1–3), by Johannes Ciconia, an Italianized Franco-Netherlandish composer of the same period. All three "English" features, absent from the composition by Ciconia, instantly identify the nationality of Power.

EXAMPLE 1–3. Johannes Ciconia, *Ut te per omnes,* mm. 1–12.

To furnish textural contrast and to give their music some formal design, English composers of the early fifteenth century frequently interrupted the characteristically full sound of all three, four, or even five voices singing together by introducing duets for two equally melodious voices. Both voices in these duos, as well as the upper voice (and sometimes the upper two voices) in the full sections, are written as graceful arches of melody in fluid rhythms that seem always to push forward towards their cadential goals. While the rhythms are conceived within a metrical framework—that is, the barlines of the modern editions often coincide with the real musical subdivisions of the melodic lines—accents are displaced within each bar, syncopations across the barline are frequent, and the melodies are often phrased in irregular groupings of two, three, or four measures. English compositions frequently begin with a characteristic figure or its inversion (Examples 1–4a and b), revealing the triadic orientation of the melodic lines. This supple English melodic style contrasts strikingly with the highly decorated yet static melodic cells in nervous, disjointed rhythms that are found in Italian and French fourteenth-century music.

EXAMPLE 1–4. Some examples of the "English figure," after Charles Hamm, "A Catalogue of Anonymous English Music in Fifteenth-Century Continental Manuscripts," *Musica Disciplina*, 22 (1968), pp. 58–59.

Leonel Power, *Et in terra*

Dunstable, *Specialis virgo*

Besides its full sound (characteristic also of later English music) and its graceful melodic style, insular music of the early fifteenth century was distinguished for its formal experiments. English composers tried in various ways to relate the various movements of the Mass Ordinary to one another. Pairing two movements together—Gloria with Credo, or Sanctus with Agnus Dei—led eventually to the establishment of the cyclic Mass in which each movement is organized by means of the same structural melody, a formal ground plan that became one of the great musical conventions of the fifteenth and sixteenth centuries.

Like the continental composers of the late fourteenth and early fifteenth centuries, English musicians turned away from setting the Proper of the Mass—those sections proper only to special occasions during the church year—in favor of setting the Ordinary, the five sections that are an invariable part of the Mass each time it is sung. Similarly, the English as well as the Europeans gradually ceased to write motets that were sophisticated secular pieces (like those by Guillaume de Machaut in the fourteenth century) or that formed a part of the responsorial sections of the Mass Proper. Instead they cultivated the votive antiphon, especially the antiphons devoted to the Virgin Mary. In the course of the first half of the fifteenth century, English composers came to depend less and less on plainchant models in setting antiphon texts. The English composers, then, freed themselves from the restraints imposed by the practice of harmonizing a given plainchant. At the same time they developed a keener sense of large-scale musical form by devising techniques for unifying long compositions by means of a cantus firmus.

LEONEL POWER AND
THE OLD HALL MANUSCRIPT

To understand precisely how the English influenced European music in the early fifteenth century, we must first look at the music by Dunstable's immediate predecessors and older contemporaries—the music, that is, contained in the most important English musical source of the period, the Old Hall Manuscript, especially the music by the leading composer in that anthology, Leonel Power. The Old Hall Manuscript is not the only source of English music from the period. Besides various fragments and smaller insular sources, there are a number of large continental manuscripts—the great Trent Codices and manuscripts in Aosta and Modena come to mind immediately—which contain among them some 200 English pieces; many of the English compositions are copied out one after another in special sections of these anthologies, as if the continental scribes wished to signal the differences between their own and English music. In spite of persistent efforts to establish two separate English traditions, one narrowly insular and the other expatriate, scholars now seem to agree that all of these compositions reflect the same stylistic outlook; thus the Old Hall Manuscript can be considered a representative source for English music from the late fourteenth and early fifteenth centuries.

The Old Hall Manuscript was named for the Roman Catholic

seminary in England where it was kept until recently. It was compiled about 1410—possibly for the king's Chapel of the Royal Household, or for the Chapel of St. George at Windsor. The main portion of the anthology consists of sections devoted to settings of single movements from the Mass Ordinary; since the beginning of the manuscript is now lost, it opens with a series of Glorias, followed by one of Credos, and so on. Where space permits, scribes have interpolated a few motets and movements from the Proper. Aside from a single piece by Dunstable, two pieces by "Roy Henry" (either Henry IV or Henry V), and a number of works by Power, the composers represented in Old Hall are minor figures: Aleyn, Bittering, Burell, Chirbury, Cooke, Damett, Excetre, Fonteyns, Forest, and others.

The fact that the Old Hall contains no Kyries seems to be simple historical accident: all those originally in the manuscript were lost when its first section became detached from the rest. But English cyclic Masses often lack their Kyries, especially when they are preserved in continental sources. In fact, the English may have preferred to hear the Kyrie sung as chant rather than polyphony, or else they chose to set Kyries to which tropes—textual interpolations appropriate to a particular liturgical occasion—had been added, making them unsuitable for general use. The recent discovery of a number of Kyries by Dunstable does not substantially alter the conclusion that the four-movement polyphonic Mass, lacking a Kyrie, is a common English convention. Moreover, the English sometimes omitted portions of the Credo, especially the clause beginning "Et in Spiritum Sanctum Dominum," or they telescoped the text so that more than one portion of it was heard simultaneously, apparently in order to get through as quickly as possible the Mass movement with the greatest number of words.

Some of the Old Hall Manuscript is notated in score, an arrangement already out of date in most continental manuscripts of the time. Some is notated in the more conventional "choirbook format," or *cantus collateralis*—that is, with each voice written out separately, two (one above the other) on the left- and two on the right-hand side of each opening (for compositions *a* 4). This difference in notation reflects a difference in musical style. The Old Hall contains, in fact, a mixture of styles, some deriving from French and Italian fourteenth-century music and some from earlier native elements. There are simple homorhythmic discant settings; compositions in which the top voice predominates as in the continental chanson; those pieces using canon in a manner reminiscent of the *trecento* caccia; and works based on the central French technique of isorhythm. Old Hall presents all of the discant settings in score, and most of the contrapuntally complex pieces in *cantus collateralis*.

The discant settings (Example 1–1 is a classic example) are un-complicated and generally note-against-note harmonizations of a plain-chant, which is most often to be found undecorated in the middle voice, although on occasion it appears also in one of the outer voices or even migrates from voice to voice. These simple polyphonic compositions may well represent the everyday "service music" of the later Middle Ages.

Late medieval theorists describe discant as the technique of adding a second voice against a tenor in note-against-note counterpoint, for the most part in contrary motion. Learning to improvise this second voice above a chant must have constituted an important part of the elementary training of singers and composers alike. English theorists of the early fifteenth century describe another kind of improvisation as well, "faburden" in three parts, in which the plainsong cantus firmus appears in the middle voice (the "mean"), a lower voice accompanies it in thirds and fifths, and a treble moves in fourths above the mean. Its realization was made easier by a system of "sights" or "sighting," a technique of transposition that enabled the singers to imagine their added voices on a single four-line staff. (Some slightly later pieces are said to be "on the faburden," meaning that they use the counterpoint to the chant rather than the chant itself as the cantus firmus in a new composition.) English faburden is clearly distinguishable from continental fauxbourdon, a semi-improvised music in which the chant appears in the top (not the middle) voice in a more or less decorated version and in a fluid rhythm rather like that of a freely composed treble. The bottom voice in fauxbourdon moves partly in parallel and partly in contrary motion against the treble, while the middle voice, which was not written down, follows the treble, always exactly a fourth below it. Both faburden and fauxbourdon pro-duce many parallel $^6_3$ chords. Hence early fifteenth-century music which includes such parallelisms—for example, at the approach to cadences—is thought to be influenced by fauxbourdon, but the term in its strictest usage should be reserved for compositions which adhere strictly to the technique of semi-improvisation, like the hymn settings of Dufay.

The second category of compositions in the Old Hall consists of works written in chanson style, like Example 1–5a, a Sanctus by Leonel Power, in which the top voice moves more quickly and with more melodic ornaments and greater rhythmic fluidity than the lower two voices. This dominating treble sometimes paraphrases a chant, as Ex-ample 1–5a does with the Sarum chant shown in Example 1–5b. The two slower-moving lower voices share the same range, generally about a fifth below that of the treble. The tenor acts as a supporting voice to the treble, usually cadencing with it and supplying either the root or the third of the appropriate chord. The contratenor, presumably composed after the other two voices, complements them, filling out bare harmonies

EXAMPLE 1–5a. Power, *Sanctus* from Old Hall Manuscript, No. 115, mm. 1–6. Used by permission of the American Institute of Musicology.

EXAMPLE 1–5b. The Sarum chant Power paraphrases.

and providing rhythmic movement when they stop; because it plays a subservient role in the texture, the contratenor could not be written with careful regard for the fine contours of its melodic shape, and so it often seems ungainly or fragmentary. Although the style apparently derived from the fourteenth-century French chanson, it was by no means restricted to that genre in the following century. As we shall see, many composers throughout the fifteenth century, and not just English ones, wrote in this treble-dominated texture, with its closely related tenor and superius. In the Old Hall Manuscript the style was modified in any one of several ways. If four voices take part, the upper two both usually move at the same fast pace. And composers sometimes combined chanson style with discant technique to produce compositions with more nearly equal voices.

Movements in discant or chanson style, or in some combination of the two, comprise the major portion of Old Hall, but there are also isorhythmic Mass movements as well as some with canonic upper parts. Composers constructed their isorhythmic movements in the fourteenth-century manner, save that the style of their upper voices is closer to that of the rest of Old Hall rather than to the nervous, static, highly decorative lines of Guillaume de Machaut and his contemporaries. In the Old Hall pieces, the plainsong cantus firmus in the tenor is invariably isorhythmic and the upper voices often repeat their rhythms each time the tenor repeats. Other Mass movements seem to modern ears oddly inappropriate for a liturgical service because of their jaunty rhythms and their two or sometimes three canonic upper parts. These movements were apparently modelled on the *trecento* caccie, Italian hunting songs, in which the second and third canonic voices enter after relatively long time-intervals and are supported by one or two slower-moving lower voices.

Almost nothing is known about the life of the best and most important composer in Old Hall, Leonel Power, the first great name in English music. The archives reveal only that he died at Canterbury in 1445 and that he was associated with Christ Church there during his last years. All of his fifty or so compositions are sacred: Mass movements and motets. He arouses our interest not only because of the quantity and high quality of his music but also because of its varied character; he does not fit neatly into any historical scheme. Some of his music includes dissonance handled as freely as any in fourteenth-century music; and some of his music anticipates developments of the late fifteenth century in its use of imitation and its attempt to make all three voices equal in importance and function. Most of his music, however, displays the English features, especially the euphonious sweetness and grace of melody, that so attracted continental composers of the time.

Power's motets can be grouped into three overlapping categories: simple harmonizations of plainchant in discant style, like Example 1–1, with more or less note-against-note counterpoint; treble-dominated motets for three voices (although two are *a 4*), like Example 1–2, in which full sections alternate with duos for two equally important voices; and a handful of presumably late works in which all voices approach equality, panconsonance prevails, passages of rhythmic and melodic imitation occur, and the text is set with a care unusual for the time. A discant setting by definition employs a plainchant as the basis for a new composition. Some but not all of Power's treble-dominated motets incorporate a paraphrased plainsong into the fluid rhythms and arched melodies of the upper voice. In his latest works, however, he seems to have abandoned altogether the practice of basing a new composition on chant. The music is entirely original, its formal shape being determined by a free alternation of tuttis and duos.

In setting the more formalistic texts of the Mass Ordinary, Power made use of a greater variety of techniques including isorhythm. But perhaps most important are the attempts he (and his contemporaries) made to relate two Mass movements to each other and, eventually, to unify all four or five movements of the Mass Ordinary by basing them on a single cantus firmus. The relationship between paired Mass movements—normally Gloria and Credo or Sanctus and Agnus Dei—took many different forms. In some cases both movements use the same plainsong cantus firmus in the tenor; in other pairs the tenors are related liturgically rather than musically (for example, where the two musically unrelated cantus firmi are taken from the same plainsong Mass). Some Mass pairs are connected by a "head motive," a melodic incipit that begins both movements. The relationship between some Mass pairs is even looser, consisting merely of laying out both movements in the same way—for example, by dividing the movements into two roughly equal parts, the first in triple and the second in duple meter, or by using the same pattern of tuttis and duos in both, or the same techniques such as canon or isorhythm. Some Mass pairs seem not to have any musical or liturgical connection with one another, but apparently the scribes who wrote them down thought they belonged together for reasons now unknown. While continental composers of Power's generation were also experimenting with ways of relating two Mass movements to one another, it was apparently an English invention to unite them in a musically audible and structurally important way by basing both on the same plainsong tenor. Insular composers seem also to have been the first to see the greater possibilities of this technique by applying it to a whole Mass.

The earliest cyclic Masses built on a single cantus firmus were composed by Power, his slightly younger contemporary Dunstable, and their contemporaries. Power's *Missa Alma redemptoris mater* is, in effect, a gigantic series of isorhythmic motets, for the tenor appears in the same rhythmic shape in each movement. The *Missa Rex seculorum,* attributed both to Power and to Dunstable, abandons the isorhythmic principle. The long plainsong antiphon that underlies this Mass is stated complete once in every movement, but each time in changed rhythms and with notes or even whole phrases interpolated. The composer has not even attempted to preserve the original phrasing of the chant; he treats the borrowed melody with the utmost flexibility. The rhythmic pace of every movement is approximately the same: each begins with a long section in triple meter, changes to duple, and then, towards the end, changes back again to triple (the scheme in the Credo is similar to the others, though slightly more complex). On the other hand, the vocal scoring varies. Although both Gloria and Credo resemble each other in beginning with extended duos, the placement of tuttis and duos changes in each movement, giving each its own distinctive shape and sound. Form is determined largely by the predominant top voice, which is joined by an equally melodious contratenor during the duets and supported during the tuttis by the structural tenor.

Tenors in the earliest cyclic Masses can, then, be either isorhythmic or without a predetermined and repeating pattern. Some Masses of the time are built either on a freely composed tenor or on one stemming from a chant or other borrowed melody as yet unidentified. Other Masses use more extensive borrowing from polyphonic models, like Bedingham's *Missa Dueil angoisseux* and Frye's *Missa Summe Trinitati*, although neither can be called a parody Mass, an important technique of the sixteenth century. However used, structural tenors enabled composers to build longer and more imposing musical structures than any previously possible. The importance of this technique, then, can hardly be overemphasized.

JOHN DUNSTABLE

That Martin le Franc should single out John Dunstable (d. 1453) in praising English musicians is scarcely surprising, for Dunstable was not only the best composer of his generation but also very probably the one who had the most contact with, and therefore the most influence on, continental musicians. While his epitaph describes him as a mathematician and an astronomer as well as a musician, his principal occupation seems to have been as a singer in the Duke of Bedford's chapel. Thus he may have spent many years in France while the Duke was regent of Paris (1423–29) and governor of Normandy (1429–35), and he could, then, have known both Dufay and Binchois personally.

Dunstable belongs among those great composers who accept their stylistic heritage and refine and polish it to a high degree. The attribution of the *Missa Rex seculorum* and many other pieces both to him and to others is perhaps symptomatic. The difficulty of reaching a decision on stylistic evidence alone may suggest that Dunstable's music differs not so much in kind as in degree from that by his contemporaries. He is better rather than different, and his music shows none of the stylistic changes and "developments" that are so obvious in that by Power; it is all of a piece. If Dunstable is distinguished by one quality alone, it is the incredible sweetness that Le Franc emphasized. Dunstable avoided altogether the freely handled dissonances characteristic of music in the fourteenth century and present to some extent even in the Mass movements of Old Hall. Indeed, in a few pieces, like his famous *Quam pulchra es,* he eliminated almost entirely any dissonances save an occasional passing tone and one or two suspensions at cadences. Careful control of dissonance is an extremely important feature of Dunstable's style, which Dufay and his continental contemporaries may well have learned from him. And this panconsonance, combined with an insistence on full triads, gives to Dunstable's music its characteristically agreeable sound.

Like most major figures of the Renaissance, Dunstable composed Mass movements, motets, and secular pieces. The least important part of his *oeuvre*, by far, consists of two secular pieces, even though they are both very beautiful. It would be difficult to say how *Puisque m'amour,* a rondeau setting, differs from a chanson by Gilles Binchois. And *O rosa bella,* the setting of an Italian ballata presumably written by Leonardo Giustiniani, may not even be by Dunstable; in any case, the composer seems to have misunderstood the form of the poem. Both *Puisque m'amour* and *O rosa bella* survive also in arrangements for solo keyboard, which are interesting for the way they demonstrate the freedom of performers in the fifteenth century to elaborate melodic ornamentation and add accidentals.

Dunstable's motets, which include some of his loveliest and most immediately accessible music, may be divided into three large categories: the most complex and elaborate motets, which are isorhythmic; a few that incorporate a plainsong into the top voice; and others, the largest group, which make no use at all of chant. Only one motet, *Crux fidelis,* does not fall into any of those categories; its *cantus prius factus,* a processional antiphon, appears in the middle voice except in the duet section. The isorhythmic motets have a special texture derived from their distinctive structure. Almost all the rest, whether or not they make reference to a borrowed chant, alternate between sections *a 3,* in which the top voice predominates, and equal-voiced duets. In the full sections the tenor supports the faster-moving treble melody; the contratenor completes the triads, keeps the motion going when the outer voices pause, and acts as a counterbalance, sometimes to the treble but mostly to the tenor. Dunstable seems to make more effort than Power to equalize the pace of all three voices; the treble never dominates quite so much as in some of the Power motets. Some passages, and even some complete pieces, move in lightly decorated blocks of chords, a texture that goes along with a clear and precise declamation of the words unusual at this time.

Most of Dunstable's isorhythmic motets, which are written in praise of a particular saint or of the Virgin, follow the same general structural outline. All voices, not just the tenor, are isorhythmic, or nearly so. In most motets, one statement of the complete chant in the tenor involves two or three repetitions of the rhythmic pattern (the *talea*); the complete pitch-pattern (the *color*) is stated three times in note values that get progressively faster by simple arithmetical proportion, for example, 3:2:1. A drive to the final cadence is thus built into the structure itself. That this complicated, mathematical means of constructing a piece of music can yield graceful and apparently spontaneous results is a tribute indeed to Dunstable's superb melodic gift. The motet *Veni sancte spiritus / Veni creator* is even more ingenious in that it incorporates as well a paraphrased chant into the top voice; it is the only one of Dunstable's isorhythmic motets to do so.

The overall structure of Dunstable's treble-dominated motets, whether or not they are based on a chant melody, depends on textural and metrical contrast. Long duets for varied combinations of voices interrupt the tutti passages; and most motets are divided into several sections in contrasting meters. But it is Dunstable's melodic gift that brings these structures to life—his ability to spin out long sustained melodies without breaking them into small units by means of intermediate cadences. The treble of his *Ave Regina caelorum,* for example, displays this admirable feature, even though it is derived from chant.

Dunstable's single and paired Mass movements reveal the same stylistic traits as his motets. Whether isorhythmic or treble-dominated, and whether or not they make reference to a chant, these movements pour forth a seemingly endless flow of melody harmonized by full triads. Some of the Mass pairs reveal Dunstable's clear and obvious intent to relate two movements to one another by musical means, either by basing each on the same chant (the Gloria–Credo pair based on *Jesu Christe Fili Dei,* in his *Works* nos. 15 and 16) or by using the same overall structure and scoring in each (the Gloria–Credo, nos. 11 and 12). One pair uses different tenors in each movement, though they are related liturgically (the Sanctus–Agnus Dei, nos. 13 and 14). But several pairs (for example, nos. 7–8 and 9–10) exhibit no musical relationships; although they were copied side by side by fifteenth-century scribes, they may actually have been intended as separate movements.

Dunstable may have written as many as three cyclic Masses. I have already discussed the *Missa Rex seculorum,* attributed to Power as well as to Dunstable. The identity of the composer of the *Missa sine nomine* is even more ambiguous; various sources ascribe it to Power, Dunstable, or Benet. Only the *Missa Da gaudiorum premia,* based on an isorhythmic tenor, is surely by Dunstable, and it is incompletely preserved, for the Agnus Dei has not come down to us.

Dunstable may be the best of a large school of English composers of the first half of the fifteenth century, but he was not the only good composer of the time. A fuller view of the English contribution to the history of music would have to take into account not only Power and Dunstable but also John Pyamour, John Forest, John Benet, John Bedingham, John Plummer, Robert Morton, and the slightly later Walter Frye (d. 1475), as well as a host of lesser musicians. Some of their music is contained in two manuscripts of the mid-fifteenth century: British Museum, MS Egerton 3307, available in a modern edition by Gwynn S. McPeek (London, 1963); and Cambridge, Magdalene College, MS Pepys 1236, available in a modern edition by Sydney Robinson Charles (American Institute of Musicology, 1967). Already by the third quarter of the century interchange between insular and continental musicians had begun to wane, and by the time of the Eton Choirbook, copied between ca. 1490 and 1502 and available in a modern edition by Frank Ll. Harrison as vols. 10–12 of *Musica Britannica*, English composers seem to have gone their own way, largely independent of continental developments.

ENGLISH SECULAR MUSIC

If the surviving sources reflect a true picture of their output, most major English composers of the early fifteenth century concentrated almost exclusively on sacred music. A native secular musical tradition did exist in England at the time, however, in the form of carols. Most of them are preserved anonymously in a handful of manuscript anthologies. No polyphonic settings of carols, and only a single monophonic setting (*Lullay, lullay,* probably composed in the fourteenth century), can be dated before the fifteenth century. Thus the early history of the genre, and its origin as a monophonic dancing song, can only be guessed at. By the fifteenth century, carols no longer served as accompaniment to the dance. They were simply secular songs of a popular character. They were popular not by origin but by destination, to paraphrase R. L. Greene, editor of the definitive collection of carol texts, *The Early English Carols* (Oxford, 1935). Sometimes they were used as optional parts of the liturgy and, especially, as processional songs, perhaps for civic and courtly processions as well as those in church.

Carols, with texts in English, Latin, or a mixture of the two, consist of a refrain (the "burden") and a series of uniform stanzas (often rhyming a a a b). The burden begins the carol and is repeated after each stanza. Composers commonly scored the burden for three voices (sometimes in fauxbourdon) and the stanzas for two. Some carols have a slightly more complicated formal scheme in that two versions of the burden (or occasionally of the stanza) were composed. A few explanatory rubrics suggest that the burden could be sung by full choir, the stanzas by soloists. While the texts deal with many subjects—moral, political, and religious—most of them praise the Virgin Mary or celebrate the birth of Christ. Their religious orientation notwithstanding, the stereotyped repetition patterns, similar to the French virelai and the Italian ballata, make them the English equivalents of the continental secular *formes fixes*.

The best known carol is doubtless the rousing *Deo gracias, Anglia,* written in honor of the battle of Agincourt. But the gentle, lyrical *There is no rose* (Example 1–6) may be more typical. Directness and simplicity in harmony, in melodic outline, and in the markedly metrical rhythms (varied chiefly by the frequent hemiolas) characterize the carol and explain its great popularity.

A mere handful of English secular songs that are not carols found their way into early fifteenth-century manuscripts; some of them may be seen in *Early Bodleian Music,* edited by John, J.F.R., and C. Stainer (London, 1901). The examples from the first half of the century are written in a remarkably clumsy and old-fashioned two- or three-part counterpoint. Composers after mid-century seem to have followed continental models. The chansons on French texts by John Bedingham, Robert Morton, and Walter Frye resemble those by Burgundian composers in every way, as do Walter Frye's *Alas, alas* and *So ys emprentid,* Bedingham's *Myn hertis lust,* and several other English songs found in continental manuscripts. The English texts, doubtless unfamiliar to continental singers, are often omitted in these sources and French ones substituted; this technique of contrafactum may hide yet other songs by English

EXAMPLE 1–6. Anonymous English carol. By permission of the Royal Musical Association, London.

composers. The difficulty of distinguishing between English and French chansons written during the second half of the fifteenth century reveals the changed position of the English. They had forged a distinctive style that had an important influence on their continental colleagues during the early years of the century. After 1450 the expatriate composers were completely assimilated into foreign cultures, and those who stayed at home continued to refine and polish older techniques and to devise new techniques without regard for developments on the continent.

BIBLIOGRAPHICAL NOTES

Frank Ll. Harrison, *Music in Medieval Britain* (London, 1958), surveys plainsong and polyphony from about 1100 to the Reformation. Sylvia W. Kenney, *Walter Frye and the contenance angloise* (New Haven and London, 1964), includes an extensive discussion of early fifteenth-century English style, discant, and the music of Frye. On English style, see also Charles Hamm, "A Catalogue of Anonymous English Music in Fifteenth-Century Continental Manuscripts," *Musica Disciplina*, 22 (1968).

On faburden and fauxbourdon, see especially Brian L. Trowell, "Faburden and Fauxbourdon," *Musica Disciplina*, 13 (1959), with references to most of the recent debates on the subject. See also Ann B. Scott, "The Beginnings of Fauxbourdon: A New Interpretation," *Journal of the American Musicological Society*, 24 (1971).

The Old Hall Manuscript, now in the British Museum, is available in a modern edition made by Andrew Hughes and Margaret Bent (3 vols. in 4, American Institute of Musicology, 1969–73) which is much more reliable than that by A. Ramsbotham, H. B. Collins, and Dom Anselm Hughes (Plainsong and Medieval Music Society, 1933–38, 3 vols.). See also Andrew Hughes and Margaret Bent, "The Old Hall Manuscript—A Re-Appraisal and an Inventory," *Musica Disciplina*, 21 (1967).

The complete works of Leonel Power are being edited by Charles Hamm (American Institute of Musicology, 1969–), and the complete works of John Dunstable have been published by Manfred Bukofzer (2nd rev. ed. by Brian L. Trowell, Margaret Bent, and Ian D. Bent, *Musica Britannica*, vol. 8; London, 1969). On Dunstable, see also Manfred Bukofzer, "John Dunstable and the Music of His Time," *Proceedings of the Royal Musical Association*, 65 (1938); and "John Dunstable: A Quincentenary Report," *Musical Quarterly*, 40 (1954). The corpus of carols is published in *Mediaeval Carols*, ed. John Stevens (*Musica Britannica*, vol. 4; London, 1958). For chansons by Morton, see Jeanne Marix, ed., *Les musiciens de la cour de Bourgogne au XVe siècle* (Paris, 1937); for music by Plummer, *Four Motets by John Plummer*, ed. Brian L. Trowell (Banbury, 1968); and for further examples of fifteenth-century English music, H. E. Wooldridge, *Early English Harmony* (London, 1897).

TWO

DUFAY AND BINCHOIS

During the first half of the fifteenth century, English composers, as we have seen, created a musical style that was highly influential but different in some respects from the continental mainstream. Although Italy, acknowledged as the birthplace of the Renaissance in the other arts, possessed a brilliant and flourishing cultural life, its music was dominated by foreigners, northern *oltremontani*, for most of the century. By about 1420 the great flowering of the *trecento* had withered away, and the rich, strange, and overly subtle style of the mannerists, which had attracted some Italian as well as many French composers (especially those under the cultural domination of Avignon during the Papal Schism), seemed to have reached a dead end. For one reason or another, then, Italy failed to produce any significant composers at all between about 1420 and 1490, although the country welcomed and supported many of the most important musicians of the time. Germany in the earlier fifteenth century remained a cultural province, content to follow the fashions of its more sophisticated neighbors. And France lacked a major composer around whom musical forces could rally. Perhaps the country was too debilitated from the Hundred Years War. Whatever the reason, Paris was no longer the musical capital of the world.

Although Italy was extraordinarily generous in fostering composers, the leading role in training them fell to the newly important duchy of Burgundy. By one of those curious historical coincidences—or perhaps because the cultural forces were right—most of the major composers of the fifteenth and early sixteenth centuries—Dufay, Binchois, Ockeghem, Busnois, Josquin, and Isaac, to name but a few—were born in Burgundy or, to be precise, in that part of it which is now northern France and Belgium. Burgundy itself, in the northeastern part of France with Dijon as its capital city, comprised only a portion of the lands ruled by the dukes. By marriage, purchase, and conquest, the four dukes of Burgundy—Philip the Bold (d. 1404), John the Fearless (d. 1419), Philip the Good (d. 1467), and Charles the Bold (d. 1477)—had put together a kingdom that included Burgundy itself, northern France, Belgium, and Holland, which they hoped to forge into a major power, a buffer state between France and the Holy Roman Empire. Their hope, as it happened, was vain. When Charles died in a battle undertaken in the continuing effort to unite geographically the disparate parts of the duchy, the Burgundian threat to France ended for all time.

The dukes were not only politically ambitious but also avid in their support of the arts. Their court became one of the most brilliant in western Europe. In *The Waning of the Middle Ages,* Huizinga describes the fairy-tale atmosphere of Burgundian courtly life, with its exaggerated costumes—peaked hats with veils, long pointed shoes, and so on—polished gemlike paintings and illuminations, and fanciful poetic conceits. The well-known descriptions (by two chroniclers from the court) of the Banquet of the Oath of the Pheasant given by Philip the Good at Lille in 1454 reveal the extravagant spirit of the Burgundians. The banquet was planned to celebrate the vows undertaken, but never fulfilled, to lead a new Crusade against the Turks, who had the year before captured Constantinople. The hall was elegantly decorated with tapestries; wine flowed from fountains, and music sounded from within a mock pastry large enough to hold twenty-eight performers, and from within a model church. Allegorical tableaux related, among other things, the adventures of Jason seeking the Golden Fleece. At one point, Mother Church, dressed in black, mourned the fall of Constantinople from her castle atop an elephant. The banquet provides in microcosm a view of the elegance and the extravagant fancy that made the Burgundians the cultural leaders of the early fifteenth century.

Music at their court, and indeed at all the princely courts of western Europe, centered on the chapel choir and its organist, a small band of virtuoso instrumentalists for chamber music (that is, *basse musique* or soft music), and the players of *hauts* (that is, loud) *instruments* who accompanied dancing and outdoor entertainments. The singers were the intellectual leaders of these musical establishments; indeed, singing in a princely chapel or a cathedral choir became the principal occupation of composers throughout the fifteenth and sixteenth centuries.

Most composers received their initial musical training as choirboys at cathedral schools, where they undoubtedly learned counterpoint, sight-singing, musical notation, and the liturgy. Virtually every cathedral had a school, but those in Cambrai and Liége were especially famous. A number of fine musicians throughout the century studied in Cambrai, including Dufay. After their voices changed, some young musicians went on to the University, and many took clerical orders before joining a cathedral *maîtrise* or a prince's chapel as full-fledged members. Their professional careers explain why most of them reserved their best or most ambitious efforts for sacred music, even though these were the same men who provided chansons and secular motets for courtly entertainments, state occasions, and private enjoyment.

In contemporary accounts these musicians, trained in the most complex aspects of their art, are sometimes contrasted with *ménétriers* (minstrels), who were primarily instrumentalists (although there were some *ménétriers de bouche*, or "popular singers"). Aspiring young professional instrumentalists were apprenticed to a master player. Since their training was strictly regulated by the musicians' guild and the guilds maintained a medieval tradition of secretiveness, we know very little about their methods of education. Certainly most apprentices learned to play more than one instrument; many seem to have specialized in one range, studying treble cornetto, for example, as well as treble recorder, treble shawm, and so on. They may have spent much of their time learning one by one a vast repertory of melodies along with ways to improvise polyphonic parts around them. But they also probably played composed, non-improvised polyphony, even though they themselves almost never became composers. Once admitted to the guild as journeymen or master players, they either formed small bands to supply music for civic occasions as well as private entertainments or, if they were very proficient or very fortunate, they joined a prince's musical establishment as one of the small group of virtuosi. These two kinds of professional training—at a cathedral school or through apprenticeship to a master player—constituted the principal means of acquiring a thorough musical education throughout the fifteenth and sixteenth centuries.

GUILLAUME DUFAY

It is no exaggeration to say that Guillaume Dufay (ca. 1400–1474) formed the central musical language of the Renaissance. Even a superficial comparison of, say, his youthful isorhythmic motet, *Vasilissa ergo gaude*, with his last Mass, that on *Ave Regina caelorum*, reveals the great changes in style that took place during his long lifetime. He led the way in giving to Franco-Netherlandish music a new sonority based on full triads, harmonic direction, and a careful control of dissonance; a new kind of melody composed in freely flowing rhythms and gently curving arches; newly homogeneous textures; and new methods for achieving formal grandeur. Dufay was without doubt the greatest of the early fifteenth-century Burgundian composers and one of the great figures in the history of western European music.

Dufay's career, though more brilliant than most, was not atypical for a composer of his age. It led him frequently to Italy and exposed him to the most advanced musical thinking of his time. It differed, perhaps, chiefly in that the city where he was educated, Cambrai, played such a central role. He returned there often from his travels and eventually settled there. While the place of his birth is not known, it may well have been in the vicinity of Cambrai, where he was enrolled as a choirboy in 1409. His tombstone describes him as a bachelor of law (a degree he may, however, have taken late in life). Dufay left Cambrai sometime after 1414, and by 1420 he was already established in Italy as a member of the chapel at the court of the Malatesta family in Pesaro and Rimini. They had enough confidence in the young composer to commission from him works commemorating important events in the family: the isorhythmic motet *Vasilissa ergo gaude* and the chanson *Resvellies vous* to celebrate marriages; and the isorhythmic motet *Apostolo glorioso* to dedicate the Church of St. Andrew in Greece, restored in 1426 by the Archbishop of Patras, Pandolfo Malatesta.

Dufay returned home to Cambrai between about 1426 and 1428. It was probably then that he first became acquainted with English music and that he probably composed his chanson *Adieu ces bons vins de Lannoy* (dated 1426 in one manuscript) and the *Missa Sancti Jacobi*. But he left again for Italy in 1428, became a singer in the Papal chapel and remained there until 1437 (with a leave of absence from 1433 to 1435). He joined this distinguished organization just after Pierre Fontaine and Nicolas Grenon had resigned, and he belonged to it at a time when

Philippe de la Folie, Barthélemy Poignare, Gaultier Libert, Guillaume Malbecque, Jean Brassart, and Arnold de Lantins were all fellow members. For the election of Pope Eugene IV in 1431, Dufay wrote the isorhythmic motet *Ecclesie militantis;* another isorhythmic motet, *Supremum est mortalibus,* celebrates the peace of Viterbo in 1433; and the chanson *C'est bien raison* marks the peace of Ferrara in the same year. By the time Dufay returned to the Papal chapel in 1435, Pope Eugene had had to flee Rome, settling first in Florence and then in Bologna. Two of Dufay's motets from this period praise Florence and its citizens, *Mirandas parit haec urbs* and *Salve flos Tuscae;* and his magnificent isorhythmic motet *Nuper rosarum flores* was composed and first performed for the dedication in 1436 of the architect Brunelleschi's superb masterpiece, the cathedral of Florence. During his years in the Papal chapel, Dufay also undoubtedly composed many of his single Mass movements (the *Sanctus papale,* for example) and, very probably, his collection of hymn settings.

During the 1440's and from 1558 until his death, Dufay worked in Cambrai, as a canon of the cathedral there. He left his native city for about seven years—from 1452 to 1458—to reside at the court of Savoy, where he had established cordial relations with Duke Louis and his wife, Anne of Cyprus. During these years he composed some of his finest music: the lament on the fall of Constantinople (probably the lament sung at the Banquet of the Oath of the Pheasant in 1454), *O très piteux de tout espoir fontaine;* a motet in praise of St. John, *Moribus et genere,* which refers to Dijon, capital city of Burgundy; the moving antiphon-motet *Ave Regina caelorum,* which the composer asked to have sung to him during his last moments; and four of his best Masses, those on *L'homme armé, Se la face ay pale, Ecce ancilla Domini,* and *Ave Regina caelorum.*

Dufay's Chansons

Dufay composed over seventy chansons and a handful of songs on Italian texts. Their lyrical qualities, refinement, and delicacy make them an appropriate reflection of the Burgundian civilization that produced them. Most of the chansons celebrate love, especially the sort of frustrated love embodied in the dying ideals of chivalry. The poems are written in the stilted and artificial language characteristic of the courtly *rhétoriqueurs* of the fifteenth century. Dufay's settings invariably overshadow them in artistic significance.

In the fourteenth century only a few fixed poetic schemes (*formes fixes*) were thought appropriate for polyphonic chansons. Most of Machaut's chansons, for example, are either ballades, virelais, or rondeaux. Dufay continued this late medieval tradition, but with a decided preference for rondeaux. And rondeaux continued to be the favorite poems for composers to set throughout the fifteenth century; the hegemony of the *formes fixes* was not threatened until about 1500. Rondeaux, in fact, make up by far the largest number of Dufay's chansons; he composed almost sixty of them. The poems consist of a refrain, part of which alternates with a stanza. Only the refrain need be set—to two sections of music, which are then used also for the stanza, according to the following pattern: AB a A ab AB (the captial letter signifies the refrain, that is, the section in which the same text is set to the same music each time it recurs). Dufay set rondeaux with four-line refrains (*rondeaux quatrains* with the repetition scheme ABCD ab AB abcd ABCD), some with five-line refrains (*rondeaux cinquains*, with the repetition scheme ABCDE abc ABC abcde ABCDE), and even one or two *rondeaux sixains*.

The longest and most serious poems set by Dufay were ballades, strophic poems in which the first two couplets of each strophe were both set to the same music, while the remaining lines—including the refrain that ends the strophe—received different music. Thus the musical form of the ballade is a a bC or, if a letter is assigned to each phrase of music, ab ab cdE, or ab ab cdeF, or whatever, depending on the number of lines in each strophe. Sometimes in a ballade there is musical rhyme between the end of the first section and the end of the refrain (that is, the last few measures before the first double bar are the same as the last few measures of the chanson); and sometimes the traditional three strophes (not all of Dufay's ballades have been preserved with complete text) are followed by a shorter envoi, addressed to a prince. Whereas the majority of Machaut's chansons are ballades, Dufay set but ten, and two of them are exceptional; *Se la face ay pale* is through-composed (that is, without any repetition within a strophe), and *La belle se siet* seems to be based on a pre-existent popular tune.

The virelai is often less serious in content than the ballade; in poetic tone it still preserves something of its medieval origin as a dance song. Like the rondeau, the virelai alternates repetitions of a refrain with stanzas. A refrain opens the song; Dufay's refrains invariably contain five lines (ABCDE). The refrain is followed by a stanza which consists of a pair of couplets or tercets each set to the same music (fg fg, or fgh fgh), then a series of lines equal in number and similar in structure to the refrain and set to its music (abcde). The repeated middle section (fg fg) is sometimes supplied with first and second, or *ouvert* and *clos,* endings; it sometimes contrasts in meter and texture with the refrain. The refrain recurs between each stanza. Thus the musical form of a virelai of three stanzas is: A bba A bba A bba A or, if the refrain consists of five lines and the first part of the stanza of two couplets, ABCDE fg fg abcde ABCDE, and so on. Virelais of one stanza (A bba A) are called berger-ettes. Like Machaut, Dufay set very few of such poems, a single virelai (of three stanzas) and three bergerettes.

By their number as well as by their high quality, Dufay's chansons constitute a significant portion of his *oeuvre*. Spanning his entire career, they reveal the characteristic features of his style at varying times during his life. As a young man Dufay forged a personal style amalgamating elements from the French Gothic music of his immediate predecessors with Italian and English elements. During his middle years, from about 1435 to about 1450, he produced a series of mature works. And his latest, and in some ways greatest, chansons date from his final years in Savoy and Cambrai, from about 1450 to his death in 1474.

Most of Dufay's chansons combine three voices, although a few are for four. A more or less elaborate top voice carefully planned in balancing arches of melody is usually accompanied by a simpler but equally finely worked tenor and a contratenor that fills in (or sometimes determines) the harmonies and keeps the motion moving forward at cadences. Dufay, in other words, inherited the treble-dominated texture, based on a superius-tenor duet, from his immediate predecessors. During the course of his lifetime Dufay revised and refined his style, partly in order to make the rhythm of his melodies flow more smoothly and to bring the various strands in the texture closer together. But he never abandoned completely the concept of song as accompanied melody. Which is not to say that all of Dufay's chansons were intended to be performed by a solo voice with two instruments. Composers in the Renaissance did not conceive their music with specific sonorities in mind; they gave the performer freedom to adapt the written notes to various combinations of voices and instruments. Thus many of Dufay's chansons might well be performed with two voices (presumably singing superius and tenor) and one instrument, or even with three voices with or without instrumental doubling. And many songs (see Example 2–1, for instance) include introductory, intermediate, and closing phrases which suggest that instruments played some or all of the top line as well.

The melodic style of Dufay's early chansons is metrically simpler than that of his predecessors or, indeed, than that of his own later music. Most of these early works can be transcribed in 3/4 or 6/8 with very few or no syncopations over barlines. Some of them are as straight-forward as *Adieu ces bons vins de Lannoy* (Example 2–1). The melody of the top voice, ascending from D to A and then gradually descending a whole octave, shows Dufay's careful concern for architectonic planning. The tenor and contratenor, as in many of Dufay's chansons, share the same range, but the contratenor often supplies the roots of triads, and its contours emphasize the tonic and dominant notes (D and A). Contratenors such as this that "carry the harmony" (*Harmonieträger*, in Heinrich Besseler's somewhat awkward term) show that Dufay had absorbed in Italy the southern predilection for a kind of tonality which Ciconia's music also reveals. Even in his early years Dufay demonstrates an awareness of the special function of tonic and dominant in determining the keynote of a composition. Some of his early chansons are filled with hemiola (that is, the juxtaposition of 6/8 and 3/4), the chief rhythmic effect Dufay produced in his metrically regular compositions.

EXAMPLE 2–1. Guillaume Dufay, *Adieu ces bons vins de Lannoy*, mm. 1–13. Used by permission of the American Institute of Musicology.

The pace of *Mille bonjours* (Example 2–2) is apparently slower than that in the preceding example; motion by half note and quarter note (instead of quarter note and eighth note) characterizes many of the chansons from Dufay's middle years. Typical of this period, too, are the syncopations, especially those at the beginning in the top voice. Dufay had begun to break loose from the shackles of regular metrical stress and to conceive of his melodies in irregular groupings of two or three beats independent of metrical units (that is, measures of a modern transcription), a feature that gives to his melodies their floating quality. Besseler, in his edition of Dufay's complete works, makes a distinction between the earlier chansons, which he transcribes with regular bar lines, and those with free prose rhythms, which he transcribes with *Mensurstriche* (lines that go between rather than through the staves and thus more clearly reveal the rhythmic independence of the individual parts).

EXAMPLE 2–2. Dufay, *Mille bonjours,* mm. 1–20. Used by permission of the American Institute of Musicology.

Dufay's rhythmic freedom is even more prominent in his sacred than in his secular music; he seems to have adopted this technique relatively late in his chansons and it is only barely suggested in *Mille bonjours*. Composers after Dufay took up this feature; throughout the fifteenth and, indeed, the sixteenth centuries they continued to write melodies that unfolded in irregular rhythmic groupings.

In his middle years Dufay abandoned the ballade; he seems to have composed none after about 1440. He worked at refining his control of dissonance and tonality. And, while never abandoning the layered structure of treble-dominated texture, he took ever greater care to integrate the various strands of his texture into a homogeneous whole. In *Mille bonjours*, for example, all three voices move at about the same rate of speed; the top voice is not strikingly faster, as those in his earlier chansons are apt to be. And in several structurally important places (for example, in bars 13–15), the tenor imitates the superius.

These same traits—rhythmic independence of the voices and the integration of the texture by imitation and other means—distinguish Dufay's late chansons as well as those from his middle years, but in the late works the techniques of composition are handled with an ease that bespeaks complete mastery. In *Adieu m'amour* (Example 2–3), for instance, the melody in the top voice proceeds with complete freedom from metrical restrictions; it has a memorable quality that stems from the careful way the phrases are shaped, which gives form to the constantly

EXAMPLE 2–3. Dufay, *Adieu m'amour*, mm. 1–6. Used by permission of the American Institute of Musicology.

changing rhythms. (By this time, by the way, compositions in duple meter were as common as those in 6/4 or 3/4.) And to be noted is the skill with which the tonality is established in the first phrase by the simple alternation of dominant and tonic harmonies. Even though it may have been written as early as the 1440's, *Adieu m'amour* typifies Dufay's later chanson style; it is a miniature masterpiece with few equals in the entire fifteenth century.

In addition to French chansons, Dufay also wrote several Italian songs that seem to be in rondeau form (they may be contrafacta, originally composed in French but adapted to Italian words); some Italian ballate (a form more closely related to the virelai than to the ballade, in spite of its name); a superb setting of Petrarch's canzone to the Virgin Mary, *Vergine bella,* which should perhaps be considered a song-motet; and a handful of other shorter secular pieces in French or Latin.

The new sense of tonality in Dufay's music, exemplified by *Adieu m'amour* as well as the other chansons we have examined, does not depend merely on building individual phrases largely from tonic and dominant harmonies. Dufay connected each phrase to the structure of the whole piece by controlling the scale degrees on which the cadences occur. Most fall on important notes, and especially, of course, on I and

V, but enough occur on other degrees to provide contrast and variety and to give the music a sense of forward motion. It is in Dufay's music, perhaps for the first time, that we see such a conscious attempt at overall tonal planning.

The cadences by which Dufay realizes a larger musical structure are, for the most part, those he inherited from his fourteenth-century predecessors. Most phrases end with the harmonic pattern VII⁶–I, with a double leading tone (that is, a raised fourth as well as seventh degree in the penultimate chord, a mannerism that gradually disappeared in the course of the fifteenth century). This cadence is usually decorated with a melodic ornament (on the scale degrees 7–6–8) that explains why it is called an "under-third cadence." Example 2–4 shows such cadences in their simplest form for each mode.

The more modern V–I cadence (with or without a 4–3 suspension in the top voice) also sometimes occurs in Dufay's music, especially that of his middle and later years. More often than not this cadence is partially disguised as an "octave-leap cadence." In such a cadence, the stepwise contrary motion that leads to an octave between superius and tenor is harmonized by the contratenor leaping up an octave from the root of the first triad to the fifth of the second (Example 2–5). This trick manages to preserve the traditional part-writing of the structural voices while avoiding undesirable parallelisms that would occur between the lower voices if both leapt up a fourth to the final note.

EXAMPLE 2–4. Under-third cadences in each mode.

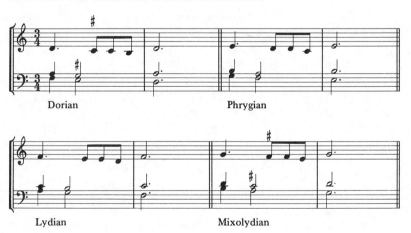

Dorian   Phrygian

Lydian   Mixolydian

EXAMPLE 2–5. An octave-leap V–I cadence in the Dorian mode with 4–3 suspension.

Any of these cadences can occur on scale degrees other than the ones shown, but transpositions were most commonly made by fourths or fifths. By a convention of the time such transpositions are indicated by a flat in the key signature. Thus a composition on G with one flat in the key signature is said to be in transposed Dorian mode, a composition on C with one flat in transposed Mixolydian mode, and so on. Two flats indicate a transposition by two fourths or fifths; thus a composition on C with two flats in the signature is said to be in twice transposed Dorian mode. Two of our examples (Examples 2–2 and 2–3) have only partial key signatures; the first two have a flat in the lower two voices, the last only in the lowest voice.

Dufay's Motets

Dufay composed a number of relatively short pieces—most of them harmonizations of plainchant—to accompany the liturgical service. And he wrote some rather more elaborate motets based on cantus firmi or paraphrasing the chant in the top voice. Some of his most elegant Latin compositions fall into this last category; most of them are dedicated to the Virgin Mary, and their treble-dominated texture and lyrical charm —they resemble chansons in many ways—explain why they are called song-motets. But until the mid 1440's, when his attention turned to Mass cycles, by far his most impressive and most complex compositions were isorhythmic motets, many of them written, as we have seen, for a particular historical occasion.

Fourteenth-century composers found in isorhythm a compositional technique on which they could base their most ambitious and complicated musical structures; Machaut's most elaborate secular compositions, for example, are isorhythmic motets. In taking over the technique, Dufay realized that like all ancient rituals, hallowed by tradition and constant use, isorhythm was especially appropriate for official state occasions and other great events. Thus, the isorhythmic motet, slightly anachronistic even in Dufay's own time, flourished in spectacular fashion for the last time under his care. Although one might say that in this respect Dufay ended rather than began a tradition, that would be an oversimple statement, for, as we shall see, his Mass cycles do carry on the older principles of the isorhythmic motet—but in a completely new and unexpected manner.

Dufay worked out the complex structures of isorhythmic motets in a variety of ways. For them he generally preferred a texture of four voices, though two have three and two have five voices. In two (*Apostolo glorioso* and *Rite maiorem*) he arranged the compositions so that they can be performed either with four or five parts, or with only the two top voices accompanied by a *solus tenor* (a lower part that can substitute for the original tenor and contratenors). All of the isorhythmic motets combine a slow-moving tenor—a cantus firmus almost invariably based on plainchant—with faster-moving upper voices singing one or sometimes more texts simultaneously with the cantus firmus. In some motets only the tenor is isorhythmic; that is, it is composed of a rhythmic pattern— if an extended rhythm sometimes lasting more than forty measures can be called a pattern—which is repeated literally one or more times, on occasion in diminution or augmentation. In some, all the voices are isorhythmic. In some, Dufay added to his already elaborate design a second isorhythmic tenor also based on chant. In some, the isorhythmic voices are constructed not only with a *talea* (the rhythmic pattern), but also with a *color* (a pitch-pattern that repeats, but not necessarily in phase with the repetitions of the rhythm). And some have introits, interludes, or postludes independent of any isorhythm.

The earliest motet by Dufay, *Vasilissa ergo gaude* (Example 2–6), composed in 1420, resembles in many ways the mature motet of Ciconia shown in Example 1–3. In both, all voices are isorhythmic, with one repetition of the *talea* (and no *color*); Dufay's motet differs from Ciconia's in beginning with a canonic introit independent of the isorhythmic design. The texture in both consists of two slower-moving lower voices and two faster melody-bearing upper voices; the mature Ciconia, however, has a sharper sense of tonality than the young Dufay. And in both, the two upper voices imitate each other frequently, though even the young Dufay writes longer-breathed and more directional melodies.

EXAMPLE 2–6. Dufay, *Vasilissa ergo gaude*, mm. 1–40. Used by permission of the American Institute of Musicology.

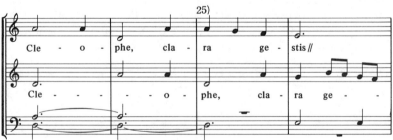

Tenor: Concupiuit rex decorem tuum

The organization of *Supremum est mortalibus,* one of Dufay's most beautiful and most accessible isorhythmic motets, is at once slightly more complex and freer than that of *Vasilissa ergo gaude.* In *Supremum est mortalibus,* only the tenor (apparently not based on a plainchant) is isorhythmic. The *color* in the tenor is stated twice; each statement coincides with three statements of the *talea.* The mensuration changes when the *color* is repeated, a change which seems to require a new tempo, even though it is not indicated in the modern edition of Dufay's complete works. Thus, the basic organization of the tenor is:

color: A B C A B C
talea: x x x x′ x′ x′

But the motet is freer than most in a number of ways. It opens with a non-isorhythmic introit in fauxbourdon, the earliest datable composition in which that technique is specifically demanded. It closes with a similarly free postlude in which the names of Pope Eugene and Emperor Sigismund are underlined by being sung in block chords marked with fermatas. The upper voices are not isorhythmic. And the statements of the *talea* are interrupted each time by free interludes while the tenor is silent.

The most impressive motet of all, and one of Dufay's most complex, is *Nuper rosarum flores,* commissioned for the dedication of the cathedral of Florence in 1436. The lower of the two melody-bearing highest voices sometimes splits into two to reinforce the sonority, increasing the sense of grandeur. The two slower-moving tenors are both derived from the same chant, *Terribilis est locus iste* ("Awesome is this place"), the Introit for the Mass at the dedication of a church. Tenor I states the chant a fifth lower than Tenor II and in a different rhythm, so that a free canon results. The *talea* and the *color* coincide; the isorhythmic tenors are stated four times in tempos which vary in the proportions 6:4:2:3. Between each full section with all four parts, the two equally melodious upper voices sing a rhythmically free duet. Each section of duet plus tutti corresponds with a strophe of the text. But the most remarkable formal device of the motet stems from the elaboration by the upper voices of the same melodic material in each full section (Example 2–7). The motet is thus a free set of variations based on a free canon controlled by isorhythm. The formal ground plans of this and the other isorhythmic motets are in fact their most impressive feature; in making number audible they reflect the waning of the Middle Ages far more than the birth of new ideas.

Dufay's shorter and simpler Latin pieces include those written for use in the liturgy: antiphons and sequences, for example, as well as hymns. While cantus-firmus technique remained Dufay's principal means of constructing sacred compositions, in almost all of his hymns (readily available in a modern edition in *Das Chorwerk,* vol. 49) he paraphrased the borrowed chant by presenting it in a more or less ornamented version in the top voice. His collection of hymns, all for three voices, consists of a cycle for the whole liturgical year, composed very probably while he was at the Papal chapel in the 1430's. They are simple unpretentious harmonizations of the decorated chant. Four of them are written in fauxbourdon, that is, with the inner part not written out but intended to be sung a fourth below the superius. Two of these exist also in alternative versions in regular three-part counterpoint. Like various other liturgical pieces of the fifteenth and sixteenth centuries, Dufay's hymns were intended for *alternatim* performance. That is, the even-numbered strophes of the hymn were sung to a single polyphonic setting supplied by Dufay, while the odd-numbered strophes were performed in plainchant.

Cantus-firmus technique is abandoned, too, in some of Dufay's

EXAMPLE 2–7. Dufay, *Nuper rosarum flores,* upper voices, mm. 34–43, 90–99, 129–134, 157–162. Used by permission of the American Institute of Musicology.

song-motets, shorter and more lyrical Latin compositions in treble-dominated texture, many of them honoring the Virgin Mary. The well-known and very beautiful *Alma redemptoris mater*—with its surprisingly effective ending in block chords—paraphrases a chant in the top voice. The very florid superius turns out, in fact, to be a remarkably literal version of the chant, transformed rhythmically and with a few ornamental notes added. Other Marian song-motets, like *Flos florum*, were composed apparently without any borrowed material.

　　Dufay's four-part setting of the Marian antiphon *Ave Regina caelorum*, on the other hand, uses a cantus firmus. But how different it sounds from the more conventional long slow notes of many a structural voice. Everything in the motet supports Dufay's evident desire to achieve a homogeneous texture. He gave the chant a rhythmic shape—and decorated it—so that it is indistinguishable from any of the other voices. They sometimes take up parts of the tenor's melody, either in imitation or in the duets and trios that vary the texture. The formal divisions of the piece are very clear—it is divided into two *partes*, the first in triple, the second in duple meter, and each *pars* is subdivided according to the phrases of the original chant—but the music flows along smoothly in that free prose rhythm that characterizes Dufay's late works. Since a second contratenor moves for the most part below the tenor, the composer can control the harmonic movement more closely than he could if the chant were the lowest voice. And there is one stunning expressive effect, a sudden minor chord at the textual interpolation "have mercy on thy dying Dufay," which strikes the ear as surprisingly modern. All in all, *Ave Regina caelorum* is a most remarkable composition; it can truly be said to be in advance of its age, for in many ways it reminds the listener more of Ockeghem, and even Josquin, than of Dufay. It is easy to understand why Dufay wished to hear it during his dying moments.

Dufay's Masses

Dufay himself did not invent the cyclic Mass, in which all five movements of the Ordinary are based on a single cantus firmus. He took over this technique for unifying the central musical portion of the liturgy from the English composers of the early fifteenth century. But Dufay realized brilliantly the musical possibilities of this convention and brought it into the mainstream of Franco-Netherlandish polyphony. He was apparently the first composer to use a secular melody as chief structural member in a Mass; he adapted the four-part texture of the motet to the Mass; and he was the first regularly to write a contratenor beneath the borrowed tenor, in order to furnish a strong bass and to free himself from the harmonic restrictions imposed by a given melody stated in the lowest voice. In a sense Dufay continued in his cantus-firmus Masses the tradition of the isorhythmic motet. Although some of his borrowed tenors —like those of his English contemporaries—are presented in new rhythmic guises each time they appear, others keep the same rhythmic identity through all five movements. The latter Masses are in effect gigantic isorhythmic motets, except for the possibility that the Mass tenor may have been intended to have an audible effect on the listener's perception of the form. One of the great formal conventions in the history of Western polyphony, comparable in importance and in its flexibility to sonata-allegro form, the cantus-firmus Mass became the vehicle for a composer's most serious and large-scale musical thought in the fifteenth and through much of the sixteenth centuries. If Dufay's isorhythmic motets are, as Besseler says, the musical equivalents of Jan van Eyck's altarpieces, then the Masses by him and his successors may be compared to great fifteenth-century buildings or, to stick to purely musical forms, to the symphonies of the eighteenth and nineteenth centuries.

Dufay did not write cantus-firmus Masses, however, until after he had come into contact with English music in the late 1420's and

1430's. His earlier efforts at Mass compositions, between about 1420 and 1440, resulted in single movements, paired movements (Gloria–Credo and Sanctus–Agnus), two short Masses of three movements each (Kyrie–Gloria–Credo and Kyrie–Sanctus–Agnus), and three Mass cycles without a unifying cantus firmus (*Missa sine nomine, Missa Sancti Antonii Viennensis,* and *Missa Sancti Jacobi,* the last including some movements of the Proper as well as the Ordinary). Most of the individual movements are composed for three voices in treble-dominated style, as often as not without a borrowed chant, although there are some with chant (paraphrased) in the top voice. The *Missa Sancti Jacobi* includes what is probably the oldest surviving passage in fauxbourdon (although, as we have seen, the fauxbourdon in *Supremum est mortalibus* is the oldest example that can be securely dated). Some movements were intended for *alternatim* performance, with a part of the text sung as chant and the rest in the polyphony supplied by Dufay. Some movements are troped, and one Gloria–Credo pair in four-part motet texture (with two upper melody-bearing voices and two slower-moving lower voices) incorporates snatches of French and Italian popular melodies into the music set to the tropes. And the delightful *Gloria ad modum tubae* resembles a caccia, with a rousing canon between the top two voices and a series of fanfare-like ostinati alternating between the lower two voices, which lead the piece to a smashing climax by means of stretto and hocket.

The Mass pairs, three-movement Masses, and Mass cycles are unified in various ways. In some, each movement begins with the same phrase in one or more voices (a so-called "motto opening"). A distinctive final cadence ends each of the movements of one of the short Masses. The sections within many of the movements of the *Missa sine nomine* and the Ordinary of the *Missa Sancti Jacobi* follow each other with the same sequence of time signatures. But some of the multi-movement works are not unified by any discernible musical means; they are joined together in modern editions only because the original scribes did so in the manuscripts that preserve them. In short, in his earlier years Dufay experimented with a number of devices for relating one Mass movement to another. He had no fixed concept of the musically unified Mass Ordinary, nor indeed was there any need for such a concept from a strictly liturgical point of view.

Missa Caput, the earliest of the cantus firmus Masses attributed to Dufay, may not be by him at all. Several enigmas surround the work. The central mystery, the origin of its cantus firmus, was solved by Bukofzer, who discovered that the tenor was taken from a melisma in the antiphon *Venit ad Petrum,* used in the English (Sarum) service—but not in the Roman liturgy—for the ritual washing of the feet during Holy Week. Its "Englishness" seems to be confirmed by the fact that it appears in several insular manuscripts (if it is by Dufay, it is the only continental

Mass of the time to be found in an English source). Moreover, documentary and possibly musical evidence as well suggest that the troped Kyrie—divided after the English fashion into two rather than three partes —was composed later than the other movements. Ockeghem and Obrecht, who both wrote Masses partly modelled on the earlier work, seem not to have known Dufay's Kyrie. Finally, the attribution to Dufay in the main source refers only to the Kyrie, and his name was at one time erased from the manuscript. No clear documentary evidence links Dufay with a second cantus firmus Mass, on a French popular tune, *La mort de saint Gothard,* but Besseler was convinced enough that the style was Dufay's to include the Mass in his edition of the composer's complete works. But even if scholars eventually agree that neither the *Missa Caput* nor that on *La mort de saint Gothard* was composed by Dufay, his stature as a Mass composer rests secure on the four magnificent late works firmly attributed to him. Two of them are based on secular cantus firmi, *Se la face ay pale* and *L'homme armé,* and two on plainchant, *Ecce ancilla Domini* and *Ave regina caelorum.*

Missa Se la face ay pale, composed about 1450 and the first of Dufay's Masses to be based on a secular tenor (unless *La mort de saint Gothard* is earlier and genuine), demonstrates very well Dufay's genius in planning a large-scale musical structure. He took the cantus firmus from his own three-voiced ballade, *Se la face ay pale,* where it also serves as tenor (Example 2–8). As in some earlier works, the Mass has a

EXAMPLE 2–8. Tenor of Dufay's ballade, *Se la face ay pale.* Used by permission of the American Institute of Musicology.

motto opening, in this case a bit of two-part counterpoint; the first three measures of Example 2–9 show the motto exactly as it appears in all movements but the Kyrie. But it is the thoroughly rational disposition of the cantus firmus that really binds together all five movements as a unit. Dufay's grand design is summarized in the following table, which shows the portion of the tenor used in each section as well as the speed at which it sounds (*integer valor* means the normal time values of notes as distinguished from values reduced or enlarged by diminution or augmentation):

THE FORMAL LAYOUT OF DUFAY'S *MISSA SE LA FACE AY PALE*

	Section of c. f. used	Speed of c. f.
KYRIE		
Kyrie I	AB	2 x *integer valor*
Christe	c. f. omitted	
Kyrie II	C	2 x *integer valor*
GLORIA		
Et in terra pax	Complete	3 x *integer valor*
Qui tollis	Complete	2 x *integer valor*
Cum sancto spiritu	Complete	*integer valor*
CREDO		
Patrem omnipotentem	Complete	3 x *integer valor*
Et iterum venturus est	Complete	2 x *integer valor*
Confiteor	Complete	*integer valor*
SANCTUS		
Sanctus	A	2 x *integer valor*
Pleni sunt caeli	c. f. omitted	
Osanna	B	2 x *integer valor*
Benedictus	c. f. omitted	
Osanna	C	2 x *integer valor*
AGNUS DEI		
Agnus I	AB	2 x *integer valor*
Agnus II	c. f. omitted	
Agnus III	C	2 x *integer valor*

The tenor creates the form of the Mass. Its systematic repetitions impose order on the music. The way it speeds up proportionally produces a sense of climax in the Gloria and the Credo, the two movements with the most text (and the least obvious intrinsic shape). Even by dropping out for particular sections (in the Christe, Pleni, Benedictus, and Agnus II—sections which came traditionally to be set without cantus firmus) the tenor establishes a pattern that determines the overall form. Furthermore, in some passages within each movement the tenor is absent and the counterpoint reduced to two equally melodious voices. These changes in texture further clarify the shape of the music. Each movement except the Kyrie opens with an extended duet. In the Gloria and Credo, extended duets precede each statement of the cantus firmus, reinforcing the larger design by the alternating densities of sound, duet-tutti-duet-tutti-duet-tutti; and within each tutti the bipartite shape of the tenor melody is made clear by inserting a brief duet just before phrase C.

On a more detailed level the form of the music is determined by the length of each phrase, and especially by the placing of the cadences. Example 2–9, the beginning of the Gloria, illustrates well how Dufay built up his grand structures from smaller units. The clarity of the melodic design is especially apparent in the superius during the opening duet. Its gentle arch rises several times to E before cadencing on C, and its divisions into segments are marked by strong and obvious cadences, some (at mm. 13 and 19) more important than others (m. 6). After the entrance of the cantus firmus in m. 19, the next important cadence occurs at m. 31. It coincides with the end of the first phrase of the tenor (mm. 31–33 function as a codetta), and thus the force of the structural voice in determining the form is confirmed by the behavior of the other voices; the details of form reinforce the overall plan.

Neatly balanced as it is, the musical structure does not, however, necessarily coincide closely with the rhetoric of the text. Thus, for example, the entrance of the cantus firmus, clearly an important point of articulation in the musical form, occurs on the third of the four acclamations, "Laudamus te. Benedicimus te. Adoramus te. Glorificamus te." Typically, Dufay here valued abstract musical design more than the projection—one cannot yet speak of expression—of the text.

Dufay was an Apollonian composer, not a Dionysian one, and it is not too strong to say that in his music the words usually play a subservient role to the notes (some exceptions, like the block chords to stress important phrases in several motets, and the wonderfully expressive minor triads in *Ave Regina caelorum,* have already been mentioned). Indeed, it is usually impossible to know precisely how Dufay intended individual syllables to be set beneath the music, for the scribes were not careful to indicate such details, and the melodic design and frequent melismas do not usually suggest one obvious and clearly correct manner of performance. Quite possibly text underlay, like instrumentation, was an area where the performer was allowed a certain freedom to seek the solution that suited him best. The composer's duty was done in supplying the notes, to which the appropriate words could be made to fit in more than one way.

EXAMPLE 2–9. Dufay, *Missa Se la face ay pale, Gloria,* mm. 1–34. Used by permission of the American Institute of Musicology.

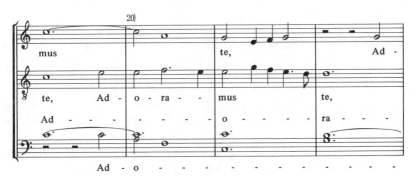

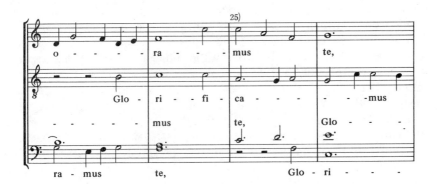

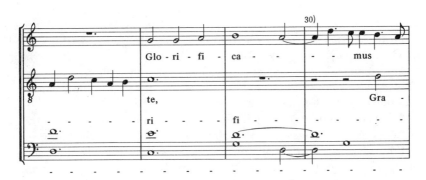

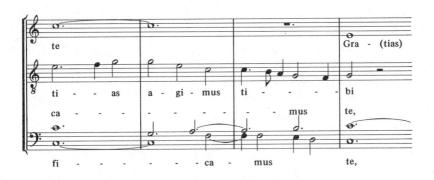

Example 2–9 is also, by the way, an excellent example of the rhythmic style of the mature Dufay. Except for the long notes in the tenor, no two consecutive bars ever present the same rhythms. Moreover, this ever changing succession of note values can be grouped into units of two, three, four, or more beats which frequently do not coincide with the bar line or *Mensurstrich*. Indeed, the tension set up between the free prose rhythms and the implied metrical structure—for the cadences always come out "correctly" on the down beat, and the dissonances always take into account strong and weak beats—gives to Dufay's later music one of its most characteristic and most exciting qualities.

In all of his late Masses Dufay wrote for four voices. To be sure, he does not keep them all active at every moment; aside from the extended duets, which function importantly in creating form, Dufay also wrote much briefer passages for two or three voices in every conceivable combination simply in order to vary the sound and to keep the texture light and transparent. Just as he took over from the isorhythmic motet to his Masses the idea of the repeating cantus firmus, so he adapted the texture of the motets, with their two melodious upper voices and their two slower-moving lower voices, but with one important difference. In the late Masses Dufay invariably kept his second contratenor (whatever he called it: tenor bassus, contra bassus, or simply bassus) below the cantus firmus. The contratenor became, in fact, a real harmonic bass, an important step in the development of "normal" four-part texture. This new arrangement left Dufay free—or more free at any rate—to determine the succession of chords unhampered by the necessity of using the notes of a *cantus prius factus* on which to build each triad. (To write of triads in Dufay's music may well be an anachronism: he surely thought in terms of intervals between voices, in the way that all treatises of the time explain counterpoint; and yet triads are in fact the basic harmonic unit out of which his phrases grow.)

The harmonic style of Dufay's Masses is partly determined by the careful way in which he handled dissonances. Bukofzer calls his "normalization of dissonance treatment . . . one of the outstanding accomplishments of Renaissance music." Intervals and chords are normally consonant on strong beats, unless a suspension creates a dissonance which quickly resolves (see, for instance, Example 2–9, mm. 9, 12, 15, and 18). For the most part, dissonances occur on weak beats or subdivisions of the beat, frequently only in passing. This regularity gives to Dufay's music its characteristic sound, so much "sweeter" than that of fourteenth-century French composers and yet with a high enough level of dissonance to keep the motion flowing smoothly forward. Controlled dissonance became a hallmark of music throughout the Renaissance. If

Dufay's counterpoint is not quite as rigorously purified of unusual dissonances as, say, Palestrina's in the sixteenth century, it is nevertheless the
earlier composer who established the normal practice and who made it a
principle of style that was to be maintained through almost two centuries.

The *Missa Se la face ay pale* is, in short, a monument to ration-
ality and order. It stands both as the beginning and as a high point in
the history of the cyclic Mass with unifying cantus firmus. In all of
Dufay's other late Masses he used borrowed material with more rhythmic
freedom, changing and elaborating the tenor each time it recurs. Dufay
probably wrote the *Missa Ave Regina caelorum* in the last decade or so
of his life. It appears, at least, to be the work of an old and very wise
musician, and it shares many stylistic features with the motet Dufay
composed on the same Marian antiphon. Its most distinctive trait is the
way in which all four voices begin to resemble one another. The top
voice does not assert its dominance quite as much as in Dufay's earlier
music, nor does the lowest voice distort its melodic line for the sake of
harmonic clarity. The tenor, which states a pre-existent melody, has
exactly the same contours and moves exactly as fast as the other voices,
who imitate it. But the amount of imitation in the *Missa Ave Regina
caelorum*—the extent to which the cantus firmus permeates the other
voices—as remarkable as it is, should perhaps be emphasized less than
the fact that all four voices have melodic lines which seem to be
designed for singers who are all equally important. This is the texture
that Dufay's successors were to adopt.

In these four late Masses as well as in his motets and chansons,
Dufay not only established the norms of style for the music of the Renaissance but also, in his latest works, pointed the way to the future. He
literally created the musical Renaissance. His method of writing melodies
in free prose rhythms was taken up and refined over the next hundred
or so years. His techniques for underpinning the structure of a composition by carefully planned networks of tonal cadences were widely imitated and eventually led the way to full-blown sixteenth-century tonality.
His chaste regulation of dissonance gave to music a characteristic sound
widely adopted throughout the period. In some of his later works the
hierarchical, layered texture of the Middle Ages began to be modified in
favor of a homogeneous sound that later composers came to prefer.
Above all, his music is distinguished for its formal clarity. In bringing
the cantus-firmus Mass into the mainstream of Franco-Netherlandish
polyphony and demonstrating how gigantic musical structures could be
created, Dufay gave his successors one of the great formal conventions
in the history of Western music.

GILLES BINCHOIS

Dufay was one of the great international figures of his time; his music was known and admired everywhere in western Europe. His most distinguished contemporary, Gilles Binchois (ca. 1400–1460), led a much less cosmopolitan life; he spent most of his mature working years, from about 1430 onwards, as a chaplain at the court of the dukes of Burgundy. Save for his years of service under Philip the Good, we know relatively little about Binchois's life. He grew up at the court of William IV, ruler of Hainaut. Ockeghem, in his lament on Binchois's death, reports that the Burgundian composer served as a soldier when a young man, before he took clerical orders. And he spent some of the decade of the 1420's in Paris and elsewhere working for William de la Pole, the Earl (and later Duke) of Suffolk, who was himself both poet and musician.

To measure the degree of greatness of a composer is always difficult and sometimes pointless. Many of Binchois's chansons are as rich and elegant as any by his contemporaries, even those by Dufay. Others merely string clichés together. But a deeper evaluation of his contribution must also take into account his versatility and his breadth. Some of Binchois's motets and Mass movements have the charm and sweetness of sonority that characterize much music of this epoch, though few aspire to the heights reached by Dufay. Compare, for instance, the beginning of a Gloria by Binchois (Example 2–10) with Example 2–9, from Dufay's *Missa Se la face ay pale*. The underlying melodic design in the superius of Binchois's opening duet is much simpler; it descends an octave from A to A and then, after a diversion, cadences on G. Moreover this straightforward descent is not elaborated with nearly the complexity and richness of melodic and rhythmic invention of Dufay's more eloquent opening. Throughout, Binchois's melodies are short-breathed and disconnected. He evidently desired to weld the strands of the texture into a homogeneous sound, at least partly by an unusually large amount of imitation. But he could not sustain his musical thought; he stopped the motion completely at regular intervals; the part writing is far from elegant; and the composition grows merely as a cumulation of shorter segments.

Much of Binchois's sacred music smacks of work done in daily service, to fulfill a particular set of liturgical needs. Thus many of his motets, hymns, and Magnificats are created largely from formulae or move in plain (or only slightly embellished) three-part chords. Binchois composed some music in fauxbourdon; his setting of the psalm *In exitu*

EXAMPLE 2–10. Gilles Binchois, *Gloria,* mm. 1–23. Used by permission of Oiseau Lyre.

Israel is virtually in fauxbourdon and moves almost entirely in $\frac{6}{3}$ chords, even though all three voices are written out. The rhythmic interest of the music depends entirely on text accents that do not correspond with the bar lines. More typical of his simple chordal style is a setting of the hymn *Quem terra,* which mixes parallel $\frac{6}{3}$ chords with slightly more independent part writing and adds some melodic embellishments; the chant is paraphrased in the top voice.

Aside from one incompletely preserved isorhythmic motet (*Nove cantum melodie,* written for the birth of Philip the Good's son, Antoine, in 1430, and including in its text the names of many of Binchois's colleagues among the court singers), the most elaborate of his sacred compositions are written in treble-dominated style, with or without a para- phrase of a pre-existent plainchant in the top voice. In his setting of the Marian antiphon *Ave Regina caelorum, mater regis angelorum* (Example 2–11), Binchois, exceptionally, paraphrased the chant both in the superius and the tenor, creating thereby a series of points of imitation that contrast with several quite simple chordal passages. The example gives a fair impression of Binchois's treble-dominated compositions, in which the top voice is seldom as florid or as clearly distinguished from the others as in most of Dufay's comparable works. Binchois seems not to have composed cantus firmus Masses; at least, no tenor in any of his Mass movements has yet been identified as a transformed plainchant.

EXAMPLE 2–11. Binchois, *Ave Regina caelorum, mater regis angelorum,* mm. 1–12. Used by permission of Oiseau Lyre.

Nor do cyclic Masses of any sort survive by him; at most, he created a liturgical but not a musical relationship between two movements by basing both members of the pair on chants taken from the same Gregorian Ordinary. But his most attractive sacred compositions are those single Mass movements that most closely resemble chansons, the genre in which he excelled.

Binchois pieced together some of his chansons from musical formulae in much the same way he composed his simpler sacred music. A rondeau like *Adieu m'amour et ma maistresse* is in this respect highly instructive, for the stereotyped nature of much of the material enables us to see how the composer planned his chanson. The refrain of the rondeau consists of four lines of poetry, each set to a single phrase of music. A highly conventional cadential formula ends each phrase. These cadences plainly articulate the form; there can be no doubt about how each part relates to the whole. In *Adieu m'amour,* cadential formulae occupy an unusually large number of measures, and they are all harmonized in similar fashion, with parallel sixths between superius and tenor leading to an octave. Each phrase begins with a distinctive melodic gesture; these memorable beginnings cannot be called motives, for they never return and play no part in the formal process of the composition. They are often constructed of thirds (sometimes filled in or embellished) or outline a triad; Example 2–12 shows a characteristic sample.

EXAMPLE 2–12. Binchois, *De plus en plus,* superius, mm. 1–4. Used by permission of B. Schott's Söhne, Mainz/BRD.

The melody of a Binchois chanson—or indeed of any Franco-Netherlandish chanson in the fifteenth century—is seldom constructed in a way that reveals or demands a single particular solution to the problem of joining the words to the notes. Nevertheless most phrases seem to begin syllabically, the distinctive opening gesture carrying most of the syllables of the poetic line—and then they broaden out into a melisma on the penultimate or antepenultimate syllable (whichever gets more stress), which leads directly to the cadential formula. Exceptionally, in *Adieu m'amour* instrumental interludes, separated from the main phrases by passing cadences, have been substituted for the well-nigh inevitable closing melismas. Since the phrases in this chanson are all so short, they scarcely consist of more than an opening gesture and a closing cadential formula.

Adieu m'amour reveals itself as an early chanson of Binchois by its rhythmic style and its texture. In the early works, the superius moves largely in eighth notes and seldom conflicts with the 6/8 time signature. The tenor is still usually the lowest voice. The contratenor's role is slightly ambiguous; it sometimes acts as a harmonic bass (for example, at the final cadence and the end of the first phrase), but it often serves merely as a filler voice. Both lower lines merely support the superius and take little part in the significant melodic activity of the chanson.

The ballade *Dueil angoisseux* (Example 2–13), on the other hand, shows signs of being one of Binchois's late works. Characteristically, it is written in 3/4, with movement largely in quarter notes. The melody does not run its course with the same degree of flexibility as in Dufay's late chansons with their free prose rhythms, and yet Binchois's superius exhibits a pleasing variety of rhythms and carefully planned contours. In the first phrase the melody descends gradually from F to C (after the opening "motive") and then rises an octave before cadencing on A, staking out the musical space to be explored. The second phrase pulls the extremes together but leaves the listener suspended on the leading tone, E, which is resolved immediately after the first ending by a return to the beginning (and after the second ending by an instrumental coda cadencing on the keynote, F). This kind of careful balance and ultimate repose gives to Binchois's chanons their "classical" grace, but it would be more difficult to explain their slightly melancholy charm. *Dueil angoisseux* exists in three- and four-part versions, the latter with two contratenors. In both, the tenor is principally an inner voice (though occasionally it goes below the others). The contratenor in the three-part version (or the lowest of the two in the four-part version) thus serves mostly as a harmonic bass; at some cadences, for example, the contratenor moves from V to I, in some it leaps an octave from V to the fifth of the tonic chord, and in some it preserves its older function of filling out the sonority while the superius and tenor resolve into an octave. The emphasis on I and V at the beginning of *Dueil angoisseux* solidly establishes F as the tonal center and reveals the inroads that tonal thinking had made on musical style by the second quarter of the fifteenth century. Little more can be claimed for fifteenth-century tonality than that it emphasized the two most important tonal degrees at significant places in a form. In any case Binchois did not always harness the unifying force of tonality. In *Se je souspire*, for example, a late rondeau in G-Mixolydian, all of the important cadences except the last one are on D or A, and the final resolution on G comes as something of a surprise.

Not all of Binchois's chansons express the ornate and rather artificial sentiments of courtly love. *Filles à marier* wittily admonishes young girls not to marry lest jealousy destroy their love. But it is exceptional

EXAMPLE 2–13. Binchois, *Dueil angoisseux,* mm. 1–15. Used by permission of B. Schott's Söhne, Mainz/BRD.

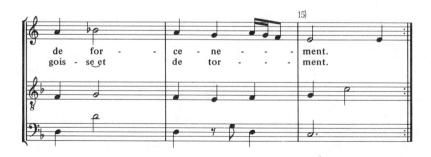

in more ways than that. Binchois wrote most of his chansons for three voices, whereas *Filles à marier* has four; the two upper voices quite unusually chase after one another in free canon (or, perhaps more accurately, highly imitative dialogue). And it, alone of all his songs, is based on a pre-existent melody—most likely a popular tune—which appears in the tenor.

All the rest of Binchois's chansons set poems in one of the *formes fixes*. The vast majority are rondeaux—forty-seven of the fifty-five chansons firmly attributed to him. He composed no virelais and only seven ballades. That he wrote three chansons based on texts by the greatest poets of his time, Charles d'Orléans (*Mon cuer chante*), Christine de Pisan (*Dueil angoisseux*), and Alain Chartier (*Triste plaisir*), may suggest that his literary tastes were more highly developed than those of his fellow musicians.

Taken as a whole, Binchois's chansons include many real masterpieces and reveal a distinct musical personality. Elegant and sophisticated musical gems, they are ornaments worthy of the most brilliant court in western Europe.

CONTEMPORARIES OF DUFAY AND BINCHOIS

Our knowledge of music by the contemporaries of Dufay and Binchois comes largely from a number of vast manuscript anthologies containing pieces by English as well as Franco-Netherlandish composers. More than 800 compositions are preserved in the three manuscripts of Italian origin that constitute the most important sources of early fifteenth-century music—the Aosta Manuscript (Aosta is a small town in northern Italy); Bologna, Civico Museo Bibliografico Musicale, MS Q 15; and Oxford, Bodleian Library, MS Canonici misc. 213. (Since there are many concordances among the three, however, the total number of separate and distinct pieces is considerably smaller.) The 129 Mass movements (out of a total of 180 pieces) in the Aosta Manuscript constitute its most important part, but it also includes motets and smaller liturgical pieces such as antiphons and hymns. The absence of secular music suggests that the manuscript was used by chapel singers; other evidence indicates that it was compiled towards the middle of the century, perhaps in some part of the Holy Roman Empire close to the Italian border. Bologna Q 15—with its 325 compositions a much larger source than Aosta—was likewise intended for a church or chapel; its main part was probably copied in Piacenza about 1430, though further compositions continued to be added during the next decade. Its importance stems partly from the fact that it offers the largest collection of motets from the period, as well as the largest anthology of paired Mass movements and partial, composite, and complete Mass cycles. Single Mass movements and cycles of smaller pieces for office hours (hymns, Magnificats, and sequences) are also included, and, where space permitted, scribes inserted some secular music, mostly French chansons but also two Italian laude. The Oxford manuscript complements the other two. It is about the same size and date as the Bologna manuscript and appears also to have been written in northern Italy, almost certainly in Venice. It contains many more chansons than any other genre, although the scribe added almost sixty motets and Mass movements, plus a handful of Italian ballate and laude. Together, these manuscripts offer a representative cross-section of early fifteenth-century music in every genre: Masses, motets, smaller liturgical forms, and chansons. The quality and character of this repertory can easily be studied in the four volumes of *Early Fifteenth-Century Music*, edited by Gilbert Reaney for the American Institute of Musicology.

In addition to these three central sources, a number of smaller fragments and also a few major sources compiled at a slightly earlier or later date preserve music of Dufay's generation. The seven gigantic Trent Codices (Trent, Castello del Buon Consiglio, MSS 87–93), compiled between about 1440 and 1480, must be the largest anthology of the century. Together the seven manuscripts contain almost 1900 compositions of all sorts (with many concordances among them), including compositions by Dufay and his contemporaries as well as music by composers of a later generation. Some earlier sources also contain music from the first years of the fifteenth century. The Reina Codex (in the Bibliothèque nationale in Paris), two manuscripts in Modena, and the Chantilly and Apt manuscripts (both of which preserve works written for the papal court at Avignon, 1309–1376, and afterwards) are described briefly in Albert Seay's *Music in the Medieval World*. Along with mannered compositions of great rhythmic complexity and late fourteenth-century French and Italian music, these manuscripts also present some compositions by Franco-Netherlandish musicians from the very beginning of the fifteenth century.

Martin le Franc, whose poem in defense of women has already been cited for its allusion to *la contenance angloise* (see pp. 7–12), names the most important composers of the early fifteenth century when he describes how much better the Parisians of about 1440 thought the songs of Dufay and Binchois in comparison with those by their recent predecessors, Tapissier, Carmen, and Césaris. These three, together with Baude Cordier from Rheims, Johannes Ciconia from Liége, and perhaps the few Italians whose work ended the great efflorescence of the *trecento* by a rapprochement with Franco-Netherlandish style (for example, Bartolomeo da Bologna, Bartolomeo Brolo, and Antonio Zachara da Teramo), were writing the best music of their time when Binchois and Dufay were growing up.

The composers more nearly contemporary with Dufay and Binchois moved around so much from position to position that it is difficult to group them by city, region, or even country. A surprising number of them were associated at one time in their careers with one of the two great choir schools at Cambrai and Liége. Besides Dufay, Cambrai could boast of having employed or trained Franchois Lebertoul, Reginald Libert, Richard de Locqueville, and Nicolas Grenon, the last two possibly being teachers of Dufay. Even more composers had worked or studied in Liége—among others, Johannes Ciconia, H. Battre, Jean Brassart, Johannes Franchois of Gembloux, Hugho and Arnold de Lantins, Johannes de Limburgia, and Johannes de Sarto.

The leading composers at the Burgundian court during the first half of the fifteenth century included (besides Binchois) Richard de Bellengues (called Cardot), Philippe de la Folie, Pierre Fontaine, Grenon, Guillaume Ruby, Tapissier, and Jacques Vide. The other great musical establishment of the period, the Papal choir in Rome, included among its members Brassart, Cameraco, Cardot, Dufay, Fontaine, Grenon, Hugho and Arnold de Lantins, Guillaume Legrant, Gualtier Libert, Guillaume Malbecque, Jean de Pullois, and Gilet Velut. About some of the secondary figures of the period, like Johannes Reson, Estienne Grossin, and Benoit, we have no biographical information whatsoever.

Most of these musicians have left us only a handful of their works —a few chansons perhaps, several motets, one or two Mass movements, or, exceptionally, a Mass cycle. Johannes de Limburgia and Hugho and Arnold de Lantins stand out from the rest simply because more of their music survives—some fifty compositions by Limburgia and thirty by each of the Lantins. Because of the paucity of material, then, if for no other reason, it would be almost impossible to draw a musical profile for each of these composers as distinct as those for Dufay and Binchois. Among the works of these lesser musicians, there are, of course, some compositions of great beauty—I think immediately of Brassart's *O flos fragrans,* Hugho de Lantins's *Ce j'eusse fait,* Pierre Fontaine's *Sans faire de vous departie* (with its basse-dance tenor), and his *J'ayme bien celuy qui s'en va* (with its contratenor for slide trumpet)—while some compositions are quite pedestrian.

These composers set almost no virelais to music, and very few ballades. Most early fifteenth-century chansons are settings of rondeaux, and most are written in treble-dominated style, often with textless (that is, apparently instrumental) preludes, interludes, and postludes framing the sung phrases of the top voice. In the works of the older composers like Cordier, Césaris, and the Avignonese Johannes Simon de Haspre and Haucourt, the mannered rhythmic intricacies characteristic of the late fourteenth century and present in their presumably early chansons were replaced in their late works by simpler, more metrical melodic lines that give to the music an altogether more lyrical sound. But in general the chansons of the early fifteenth century exhibit a remarkable uniformity of style, even though many of them deviate in one way or another from the norm. Most of them, for example, are written for three voices; but there are some like Reson's charming *Ce rondelet je vous envoye* for two equally melodious voices moving in the same range, and some like Jacques Vide's *Amans doublés* for four voices, in which the two top voices are equally important, after the manner of a tenor motet. Most early fifteenth-century chansons consist of a more or less florid top line and two slower-moving lower lines; a tenor that forms a self-sufficient duet with the superius (and may or may not be florid enough itself and divided into sufficiently clear phrases to carry the text easily); and a contratenor which, less elegant in melodic shape than the other two voices, either fills in the gaps between the tenor and the superius and keeps the motion going forward at cadences, or else, in the chansons written after 1430, functions as a harmonic bass and moves for the most part below the tenor. But there are also chansons in which superius and tenor sing different texts, like Gaultier Libert's *Belle, plaisant / Puisque je sui de vous;* chansons in which all three voices move together more or less homorhythmically, like Grenon's *La plus jolie et la plus belle;* and chansons, like Hugho de Lantins's A *madamme playsant,* in which the imitation between superius and tenor is so consistent and so exact that the top voice can scarcely be said to dominate.

When an early fifteenth-century composer wished to write a large and important motet, he naturally chose to organize it according to isorhythmic principles, following the traditions established in the fourteenth century and continued, as we have seen, by Dufay. Many of these isorhythmic motets were written to honor a particular saint, like Locqueville's *O flos in divo / Sacris pignoribus* for St. Yvo of Britanny, or Grenon's *Ad honorem / Caelorum / Isti semper* for St. Catherine. Some are less local in their application, like Grossin's *Mater dulcis* for the Blessed Virgin Mary and Césaris's *A virtutis / Ergo beata nascio / Benedicta filia tua* for the Assumption. And some refer to contemporary events, like Velut's *Benedicta viscera / Ave mater gratie / Ora pro nobis,* and Carmen's *Salve pater / Felix et beata,* both of which mention the Papal schism. Some are isorhythmic only in the tenor, or in the two lower voices, while in others the rhythm of all the voices repeats according to a predetermined scheme.

But while isorhythmic motets took pride of place, composers also wrote treble-dominated motets (song-motets), like Locqueville's *O regina clementissima,* which may in fact be a contrafactum of a rondeau, as well as simple settings of texts from the Office Hours and the Mass Proper, like Benoit's *Virgo Maria, Puer qui natus, Lucis creator optime,* and *Tibi Christe splendor patris,* all of them composed either of a slightly embellished series of chords or in fauxbourdon. Some non-isorhythmic motets use a pre-existent plainchant as a structural tenor or paraphrase a chant in the top voice. Others are apparently free of borrowed material, like Arnold de Lantins's two superb settings of verses from the Song of Solomon (a comparatively rare instance of motets on Biblical texts so early in the century), *Tota pulchra es* (for four voices in "motet texture") and *O pulcherrima mulierum* (for three voices in a treble-dominated style that often reverts to simple chords).

Like non-isorhythmic motets, single Mass movements were composed by early fifteenth-century composers in all of the textures in common use at the time—simple homophony, treble-dominated style, four-voiced motet texture, and even with the upper two voices in canon in the manner of an Italian caccia. And composers gave even more formal definition to many of their single Mass movements by prefacing full sections with extended duets. Performing directions—*solo, unus, duo,* or *chorus*—appear in some Mass movements, suggesting that groups of soloists alternated with a full choir. And some lower voices are marked *trompetta* (or something similar), indicating that instruments—especially slide trumpets or trombones—sometimes played tenor and contratenor lines.

The most important innovation in early fifteenth-century polyphonic settings of the Ordinary of the Mass involved, of course, composers' attempts to link movements together to form larger units, Mass pairs, or partial or complete cycles. The solution that ultimately dominated—unifying movements by basing them all on the same chant used as a cantus firmus in the tenor—was only one of the methods tried by Dufay's immediate predecessors and contemporaries, and it was by no means the most common. Composers were much more apt to begin each movement with a melodic "motto," or to base each movement on the liturgically appropriate chant from a single Gregorian Mass (which, however, fails to establish any aurally intelligible musical relationship among the movements), or even merely to lay out the movements in the same way (that is, by using the same clefs, the same sequence of mensuration signs, or the same pattern of duos alternating with full sections, or simply by ending each movement with the same cadential formula).

And there are several paired movements which seem to be based on pre-existent musical material recomposed in a way that predates in astonishing fashion sixteenth-century parody technique.

Very few Mass cycles by Franco-Netherlandish composers survive from before mid-century, and none uses a recurring tenor cantus firmus. Reginald Libert's *Missa de beata virgine,* partly in fauxbourdon, includes settings of both the Proper and the Ordinary. In some movements the liturgically appropriate chant is paraphrased in the top voice (occasionally it migrates to another voice), but other movements seem to be composed without reference to borrowed material. The chant is very freely paraphrased, if it appears at all, in Arnold de Lantins's *Missa Verbum incarnatum,* in which several movements are adorned with tropes. Whatever real connection exists among the movements stems almost entirely from Lantins's use of à motto. Grossin's *Missa Trompetta* (which lacks an Agnus Dei) seems to hang together merely because of its sonority: the contratenor for slide trumpet recurs at regular intervals. In short, early fifteenth-century composers were clearly seeking ways to create large multi-movement works unified by some readily perceptible musical principle. It took a Dufay, however, to realize the potentialities of the tenor cantus firmus Mass and thus to establish it as a central genre of the musical Renaissance.

BIBLIOGRAPHICAL NOTES

An important but difficult book on Dufay's music is Heinrich Besseler, *Bourdon und Fauxbourdon* (Leipzig, 1950). See also Charles van den Borren, *Études sur le XVe siècle musical* (Antwerp, 1941).

Dufay's complete works have been edited by Guillaume de Van and Heinrich Besseler in six volumes (American Institute of Musicology, 1948–64). On Dufay see also Charles van den Borren, *Guillaume Dufay* (Brussels, 1926); the essay on the Caput mass in Manfred Bukofzer, *Studies in Medieval and Renaissance Music* (New York, 1950); Charles Hamm, *A Chronology of the Works of Guillaume Dufay* (Princeton, New Jersey, 1964); Alejandro Enrique Planchart, "Guillaume Dufay's Masses: Notes and Revisions," *Musical Quarterly,* 58 (1972); and Charles Warren, "Brunelleschi's Dome and Dufay's Motet," *Musical Quarterly,* 59 (1973).

Binchois's complete chansons have been edited by Wolfgang Rehm (Mainz, 1957). Some of his sacred music along with music by other composers appears in Jeanne Marix, ed., *Les Musiciens de la cour de Bourgogne au XVe siècle* (Paris, 1937), and in J. F. R. Stainer and C.

Stainer, eds., *Dufay and his Contemporaries* (London, 1898; repr. 1963), which contains selections from the Oxford manuscript, Canonici misc. 213. On the Aosta manuscript, see Guillaume de Van, "A Recently Discovered Source of Early Fifteenth-Century Polyphonic Music, the Aosta Manuscript," *Music Disciplina*, 2 (1948). On Bologna Q 15, see Guillaume de Van, "Inventory of Manuscript Bologna Liceo Musicale Q 15," *Musica Disciplina*, 2 (1948). Selections from the Trent Codices are printed in modern editions in the following volumes of the *Denkmäler der Tonkunst in Oesterreich:* 14/15, 22, 38, 53, 61, and 76; and the manuscripts are also available in facsimile published by Bibliopola in Rome. For other early fifteenth-century music, see Charles van den Borren, ed., *Polyphonia Sacra* (London, 1932; repr. 1962); Charles van den Borren, ed., *Pièces polyphoniques profanes de provenance liègoise* (Brussels, 1950); Gilbert Reaney, ed., *Early Fifteenth-Century Music* (American Institute of Musicology, 1955–69, 4 vols.); Laurence Feininger, ed., *Documenta polyphoniae liturgicae* (Rome, 1947–51); and Laurence Feininger, ed., *Monumenta polyphoniae liturgicae* (Rome, 1947–53).

On music at the Burgundian court under Philip the Good, see Jeanne Marix, *Histoire de la musique et des musiciens de la cour de Bourgogne sous le règne de Philippe le Bon (1420–1467)* (Strasbourg, 1939; repr. 1972), which includes a description of the Banquet of the Oath of the Pheasant. It explains the organization of music at courts and cathedrals, as do a number of other local histories, for example, Antoine Auda, *La Musique et les musiciens de l'ancien pays de Liége* (Brussels, Paris and Liége, 1930) and G. van Doorslaer, "La Chapelle musicale de Philippe le Beau," *Revue belge d'archéologie et d'histoire de l'art*, 4 (1934). The most complete work to date on minstrels is B. Bernhard, "Recherches sur l'histoire de la corporation des ménétriers ou joueurs d'instruments de la ville de Paris," *Bibliothèque de l'école des chartes*, First Series, 3 (1841–42): 377–404; 4 (1842–43): 525–48; 5 (1843): 254–84; and 5 (1844): 339–72; see also François Lesure, "La Communauté des 'joueurs d'instruments' au XVIe siècle," *Revue historique de droit français et étranger*, Fourth Series, 31 (1953).

THREE
OCKEGHEM AND BUSNOIS

No great technical innovations comparable to the rise and development of the cyclic Mass mark the music of the Franco-Netherlandish composers born in the 1420's and 1430's. They adopted the forms and procedures of the preceding generation, and forged their own musical style from what they had learned from the mature Dufay and Binchois. Some great composers invent new things, while others, accepting the conventions of their time, assimilate what they wish from the novelties of the immediate past while developing and refining the style of their teachers. Busnois and, especially, Ockeghem reveal their importance and imaginativeness, at least in part, in the ways in which they worked out the technical questions and problems posed by an older generation. In truth, it is oversimple to regard Ockeghem merely as a follower of Dufay, for he created a musical world of his own quite unlike that of any of his contemporaries. He is a difficult, even an enigmatic composer, whose music is neither immediately accessible nor easy to fit into a historical context. Some of Ockeghem's greatest works may, in fact, have been written before those of Dufay's last period.

A partial explanation for the special quality of Ockeghem's music, and to a lesser extent Busnois's, may lie in the fact that neither imitated their many contemporaries who spent large amounts of time in Italy. Indeed, no documentary evidence indicates that they ever visited that country. Ockeghem and Busnois were both Flemish. Busnois spent most of his life in the service of the dukes of Burgundy, and Ockeghem worked at the royal court of France. Unlike many other composers of the Renaissance, then, they cultivated their musical personalities at home, or at least close to it. As Reese writes, "Ockeghem's spirit is more that of the north, less that of Italy; more that of developed flamboyant architecture, less that of Santa Maria del Fiore."

JOHANNES OCKEGHEM

Johannes Ockeghem (ca. 1420–97) may have been born in Dendermonde in East Flanders. Perhaps he studied with Binchois at the Burgundian court; no documents reveal information about his musical education, but he did compose a lament on the older composer's death in 1460. As a young man, at least from 1443 to 1444, Ockeghem sang under Jean Pullois at the Church of Our Lady in Antwerp. His whereabouts for the next few years are unknown. By 1448 he had become a member of the twelve-man chapel choir of Duke Charles I of Bourbon in Moulins.

From the early 1450's—his name is cited in French court records for the first time in 1452–53—until his death more than forty years later, Ockeghem served successively three French kings—Charles VII, Louis XI, and Charles VIII—as chaplain, composer, and chapelmaster. By the late 1450's he was highly enough esteemed to be appointed treasurer of the royal abbey of St. Martin in Tours, where the king himself was abbot. For Ockeghem this was a position of great honor. He was charged with caring for the incredibly rich treasury, and in return he was given an elegant house and a number of generous benefices. It was a position he could hold, apparently, without continuous residence in Tours, for he continued to be first chaplain in the royal musical establishment. Except for a trip to Spain in 1470, possibly on a mission for the king, Ockeghem spent the remainder of his life attached to the royal court, honored as a singer, choirmaster, composer, and teacher. Among his students may have been the incomparable Josquin des Prez. When he died in 1497 an unusually large number of laments appeared, one by Guillaume Crétin and two by the poet and musician, Jean Molinet, one in French, set to music by Josquin, and another in Latin; even the great humanist Erasmus composed a *Naenia*, which was later set by Johannes Lupi.

For such a distinguished musician, Ockeghem composed but little music. Ten complete Masses survive, along with the earliest extant polyphonic Requiem, a handful of partial Masses and Mass fragments, fewer than ten motets, and some twenty chansons. Though their number is not large, these compositions are fine enough to have sustained his reputation over the centuries. His fame is based on his Masses, partly for the simple reason that his motets are not all easily accessible in modern editions, but mostly because the Masses do in fact form a magnificent and intriguing group of masterpieces. Ockeghem apparently responded better to the traditional and ritualistic (hence more abstract) words of the Mass Ordinary than to the shorter motet texts that he could choose himself and which were therefore more personal. Ockeghem based about half of his complete and partial Masses on the cantus-firmus technique he inherited from Dufay (though he transformed it for his own aesthetic goals); his Requiem paraphrases plainchant; the remaining Masses are, quite unusually, apparently free of borrowed material.

Ockeghem's four great cantus-firmus Masses for four voices—those based on the *Caput* melisma, the plainchant *Ecce ancilla Domini*, the popular tune *L'homme armé*, and the tenor of Binchois's chanson *De plus en plus*—reveal their relationship with Dufay's procedures in their overall formal design. That is, the *cantus prius factus* is the prime agent in creating the formal structure, for it is stated completely one or more times in each movement. In the *Missa Ecce ancilla Domini*, the rational disposition of the cantus firmus is even made explicit by a pattern of alternating duets and tuttis that reinforces the formal plan, as in a Dufay Mass. Unlike Dufay, Ockeghem sometimes places the borrowed melody in the lowest voice, an indication that he is less concerned than the older musician with harmonic clarity and tonal planning. (The obvious corollary, that Ockeghem must then be more concerned with the independence of voices and contrapuntal complexity, is patently true and reflects his Gothic heritage and lack of contact with Italy.)

Ockeghem usually prefers to vary the rhythmic shape of the structural voice each time it appears. The *Missa Caput* is an exception to his normal practice, since it presents the chant in the same form in each movement; paradoxically this Mass differs in style from Dufay's music more sharply than any of Ockeghem's other cantus-firmus Masses, although it is the only one closely based on a particular Dufay work. Ockeghem does not construct the highly rational systems of proportional relationships among statements of the cantus firmus that distinguish some Dufay Masses and inevitably make audible the underlying structure through their clear differentiation of the structural voice. On the contrary, Ockeghem usually prefers to transform his borrowed melody rhythmically so that it resembles the other voices in its melodic contours and pace. Thus the texture of his music is apt to consist of four seemingly independent voices, equally fast-moving and equally florid. But, however hidden, it is the borrowed material and its repetitions that give to these works their basic structure. "Hidden structure," in fact, may fairly be said to characterize Ockeghem's attitude towards form. Even on those few occasions when he used mottoes to link one movement to another (for example, in the *Missa Caput*) he disguised the relationship by varying each statement of the recurring melody.

At the beginning of the second Kyrie in Ockeghem's *Missa L'homme armé* (Example 3–1) the texture resembles relatively clearly that in Dufay's music: the upper two predominantly melodic voices are supported by two slightly slower-moving lower voices, one of which states the cantus firmus. By the end of the short movement all four voices approach equality; the bass speeds up in m. 34, and from m. 38 onwards the tenor states free material unrelated to the *L'homme armé* tune in rhythms like those of the other voices.

The impression that Ockeghem's voices are all equal in importance stems partly from the nature of his melodies. Individual lines are often so non-imitative and non-repetitive that they seem more continuous, more independent of one another, and more non-structured than they sometimes really are. In the first section of the Gloria of the *Missa L'homme armé* (Example 3–2), for instance, the cantus firmus is clearly differentiated from the other voices. Quite exceptionally, the section ends (in m. 15) with a cadence in all voices (typically one based on a VII⁶–I progression). There is even a relatively clear-cut point of articulation in mm. 6–7 after the opening statement of the text and before the series of exhortations "Laudamus te. Benedicimus te. Adoramus te. Glorificamus te," a caesura that is disguised by the overlapped contratenor, the lack of rests in the outer voices, and the absence of unambiguous cadence formulas. Within the section (mm. 1–15) the music appears to move forward without breaks and without apparent subdivisions into phrases. Save for the tenor, the individual voices proceed without obvious cadences and, indeed, without motives that relate one line to another (except for the contratenor in mm. 4–5, which echoes the cantus firmus). Instead, the endless melody flows along without pause, at a relatively steady pace, and for the most part without rational controls like imitation, sequence, or motivic work to clarify the structure and the relationships between one part and another. In this Mass, to a much greater extent than in Ockeghem's free Masses, the top voice still seems to predominate. It grows "organically," as it were, in long and gently arching

EXAMPLE 3–1. Johannes Ockeghem, *Missa L'homme armé, Kyrie II.* Used by permission of the American Musicological Society.

strands of melody. The superius in Example 3-2 reaches its high point in m. 3, for instance, and gradually descends to the cadence in m. 15 in a series of curves that does not disturb the even flow. But if the endless melody hides the points of articulation, the structure of this Mass is still fairly easily visible beneath the skin.

A few of Ockeghem's cantus-firmus Masses depart more radically than the *Missa L'homme armé* from the procedures and style he inherited from Dufay. The *Missa Caput* assimilates the cantus firmus completely into the rest of the texture, and the top voice has scarcely more importance than the others. One voice and then another take turns in drawing our momentary attention, and this constantly shifting contrapuntal fabric appears to be built without any seams or joins. Ockeghem placed the tenor of his own (or Barbingant's?) chanson in the tenor of the Kyrie of his *Missa Au travail suis*, but in the following four movements the

EXAMPLE 3-2. Ockeghem, *Missa L'homme armé, Gloria,* mm. 1–15. Used by permission of the American Musicological Society.

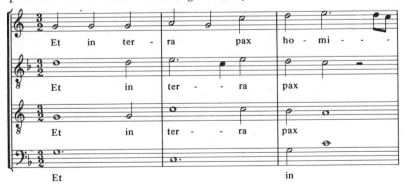

cantus firmus appears only at the beginning, in an unusually imitative texture in which some or all of the voices share the opening motive of the borrowed melody. Thereafter the music unfolds freely, without any reference to the chanson tenor. In his five-voiced *Missa Fors seulement,* which includes but three movements (Kyrie, Gloria, and Credo), Ockeghem did derive the well-hidden scaffolding voice from his own chanson; but he incorporated elements from both the superius and the tenor of the model into the structural line and changed it for each movement, not only its melodic and rhythmic shape but also the voice in which it appears. Moreover, he introduced from time to time more than one voice from the model. If the *Missa Fors seulement* is still far from being a parody Mass, it nevertheless shows that Ockeghem was exploring various means for using cantus-firmus technique in new and imaginative ways.

In his free Masses, *Missa Mi-Mi, Missa Quinti toni,* and *Missa sine nomine* (No. 2 in his *Complete Works*), Ockeghem's style unfolds at its most irrational and enigmatic, revealing his full command of non-imitative counterpoint made up of strands of endless melody. In these Masses no cantus firmus, paraphrased chant, or borrowed material of any kind gives rise to a pre-determined schema. At least no one has yet succeeded in identifying in them thematic material modeled on any other music; apparently they are from beginning to end entirely the product of Ockeghem's own musical invention. Their style is difficult to describe precisely, because no one contrapuntal technique underlies the music. The texture constantly shifts its emphasis and changes its orientation, and the absence of systematic imitation, sequence, and motivic work prevents the listener from anticipating what musical events will happen next. The music is always new and always changing—Ockeghem's inventiveness is astonishing—and yet he gave to every movement a unity of mood that belies the apparent inconsistencies and imposes a shape unique to each work, and hence is incapable of serving for generalizations about his complete *oeuvre*.

The final section of the Gloria from the *Missa Mi-Mi* (Example 3–3) exemplifies Ockeghem's most mature contrapuntal technique, in which individual lines are subordinate to the total effect of the interplay among all voices. As Bukofzer writes about the *Missa Caput*, "the voices are very nearly equivalent with regard to contrapuntal texture and rhythmic pace. While Dufay keeps the leading voice florid and sets it off against cantus firmus and bass, Ockeghem distributes florid passages more evenly over all free voices. . . . The voices serve each other mutually as springboards for counterpoints, so that it becomes impossible to say which is the 'melody' and which the 'counterpoint' or countersubject." And because the voices are nearly equivalent to each other in speed, floridness, and function, the bass does not stand out as the voice which determines and controls the harmonic movement. Ockeghem's music seems much less tonally oriented than Dufay's for this reason, and also because it so effectively avoids prominent cadences with their propensity for establishing tonality. Example 3–3 illustrates Ockeghem's modal harmonic style especially well, since the Phrygian mode, in which it is written, does not use the fifth degree as dominant.

At the smallest level of detail, of course, Ockeghem relied on various traditional techniques to make the texture hold together and to help the listener hear what is going on in the music. In Example 3–3, for instance, there is imitative dialogue among the tenor in mm. 105–6, the bass and contratenor in mm. 107–8, and the superius in m. 109 (on the words "miserere nobis"); there are brief imitations between tenor and superius at both "Tu solus Dominus" and "Tu solus Altissimus"; and there is parallel motion in tenths between tenor and superius in mm. 141–42, and imitation between bass and superius in mm. 144–47. But these techniques are not used systematically to illuminate the structure. They vary within any one section of music so much and so quickly that

EXAMPLE 3–3. Ockeghem, *Missa Mi-Mi, Gloria*, mm. 97–162. Used by permission of the American Musicological Society.

they scarcely can be said to constitute the formal principle of the work, even though they do aid the listener immensely to penetrate the difficult and concentrated combination of strands of melody.

Like other fifteenth-century composers, Ockeghem subdivided larger sections of music into smaller units—phrases and half-phrases —each contrasted with the others by thematic material, texture, speed, or some other distinguishing feature. Example 3–3, for instance, might be divided into the following segments, each of them setting a single phrase of the text:

1. Qui sedes ad dexteram Patris, miserere nobis.
2. Quoniam tu solus sanctus. Tu solus Dominus. Tu solus Altissimus, Jesu Christe.
3. Cum Sancto Spiritu, in gloria Dei Patris.
4. Amen.

The second of these sections might further be subdivided into three phrases, each identified with a clause of the text. But the sections are not clearly marked off from one another by cadences, as they would be in a Dufay Mass. On the contrary, some of them flow into the next ones almost imperceptibly; in some, the cadence is overlapped and disguised (as in m. 111); and in some, a new section begins precisely at the moment the preceding one cadences (as in m. 144, which is also overlapped).

Ockeghem built complete movements in this way, by writing a series of sections that meld into one another but that can be separated for the purposes of analysis and to make easier the task of hearing and understanding the way the music is constructed. The Gloria of the *Missa Mi-Mi*, for example, divides into two large parts, marked off by a complete stop in all voices and a double bar. Ockeghem uses one of the two or three traditional ground plans in making this bipartite division and in beginning the second part at "Qui tollis peccata mundi." The first part can then be subdivided into the following sections, which quite rationally correspond with the clauses of the text and are either articulated by a disguised cadence or else overlapped with their neighbors:

1. *Et in terra pax hominibus bonae voluntatis.*
2. *Laudamus te. Benedicimus te. Adoramus te. Glorificamus te.*
3. *Gratias agimus tibi propter magnam gloriam tuam.*
4. *Domine Deus, Rex coelestis, Deus Pater omnipotens,*
   which overlaps with
5. *Domine Fili unigenite Jesu Christe,*
   which overlaps with
6. *Domine Deus, Agnus Dei, Filius Patris.*

That Ockeghem's schemas for every movement unfold freely and in an *ad hoc* manner so that each is different from the others explains why generalizations about his formal principles are so difficult to formulate. On the other hand we can easily grasp the way in which he so often achieved a sense of climax and gave shape to a number of movements: by devising a drive to the final cadence. The end of the Gloria from the *Missa Mi-Mi* (Example 3–3) illustrates this technique well. Starting with the Amen in m. 144 (or, indeed, even two measures before the entrance of the bass) the motion speeds up in all voices—the number of eighth as well as quarter notes increases markedly—and so the music drives forward suddenly to the final cadence.

While eschewing any predetermined schemas to unify his free Masses, Ockeghem did have recourse to the traditional means of identifying each movement as belonging to a larger unit by writing motto beginnings. The melodic tag that connects the various sections of the *Missa Mi-Mi* consists of a descending fifth, E to A, heard at the beginning of each movement in the bass. The interval would have been sung to the solmization syllables "mi, mi" (the third degree of the natural hexachord on C, followed by the third degree of the soft hexachord on F), a circumstance that has given the Mass its sobriquet. Similarly, the *Missa Quinti toni* and the *Missa sine nomine* (No. 2) both include mottoes that recur, although each time in the typically disguised manner of Ockeghem. These latter two Masses are both written for three voices and hence may be among his earliest compositions; if they were written as early as the 1440's, with their motto beginnings and no cantus firmus or other borrowed material, they may relate directly to the early stage of cyclic Mass settings, before the English composers and Dufay had yet established the cantus-firmus technique as the central means of building gigantic musical structures.

In two of his free Masses, the *Missa Cuiusvis toni* and the *Missa Prolationum*, Ockeghem set himself technical hurdles of the utmost complexity. As its name suggests, the *Missa Cuiusvis toni* ("Mass in any mode") is written in such a way that by changing the combination of clefs it can be sung in any one of four modes, Dorian, Phrygian, Lydian, or Mixolydian. The *Missa Prolationum,* on the other hand, consists of a series of complicated double canons. They are mostly mensuration canons. Mensuration (or *prolatio*) is a general term for the relationships of smaller to larger time values. Mensuration signs, the predecessors of modern time signatures, explain the number of breves in a long, the number of semibreves in a breve, or the number of minims in a semibreve. In the *Missa Prolationum* all the voices begin simultaneously in many of the movements, each with a different mensuration and thus moving at a rate of speed unlike that of its canonic partner. In overcoming the immense conceptual problems posed by the technical demands he placed on himself in these Masses, Ockeghem displayed compositional virtuosity of the highest order. What is even more remarkable, he managed at the same time to write superb music.

Ockeghem is also known to have composed a canon for thirty-six voices, which has been identified as a setting of *Deo gratias* published for the first time in 1542. This canon and the two Masses based on ingenious compositional programs have given Ockeghem the reputation of being a Gothic contrapuntist, a lover of puzzles and intricacies for their own sakes. We have already seen, though, that the composer was no mere crabbed artificer but a musician working intensely to produce a series of individual works, each of them unique. These three works are not exceptions; they present a somewhat more extreme view of the disguised and often inaudible order found in all of Ockeghem's music. More convincing are the attempts by Bukofzer and others to identify Ockeghem's difficult and seamless style as a manifestation of the same pious mysticism, the *devotio moderna,* that had earlier produced Johannes Ruysbroeck's fervent philosophy, the Flemish (and German) Brethren of the Common Life, and Thomas à Kempis's *Imitation of Christ.* No one has yet been able to connect Ockeghem in any tangible way with the Flemish mystics, although Lowinsky has made a convincing case for the symbolic significance of the thirty-six-voice canon that relates the music directly to a philosophical tradition. Nonetheless Ockeghem's "far-reaching renunciation of rational organization in music" (Bukofzer's phrase) does indeed constitute a musical mysticism that distinguishes Ockeghem's work from that of his contemporaries.

An elegantly decorated manuscript in the Vatican Library (Chigiana, C. VIII.234, the so-called "Chigi Codex") contains more of Ockeghem's Masses than any other source. The music is written out in the typical "choirbook format" of the time, not in score but with the individual voices following one after another on facing pages, the superius and tenor on the left hand side of the opening, and the contratenor and bass on the right. Besides Masses, the Chigi Codex includes also one of

Ockeghem's longest and most striking motets, *Intemerata Dei mater*. Its five voices create a most solemn and majestic flow of sound, especially since they lie rather low; the bass at one point reaches the C below the staff in the bass clef. Ockeghem seems not to have used borrowed material. Instead he adopted the same technique as in his free Masses: he set each clause of the text to long, irregularly shaped melodies combined into a rich non-imitative texture, and each phrase was then overlapped with the others to make a continuous stream of music. In the second of the three *partes* he exploited choral sonority to shape his music, writing a series of trios leading to a final section for all five voices. And in the third part, after an opening duet and an unusually declamatory sequence of chords, he built up to the end by increasing the speed of each voice in his characteristic "drive to the cadence."

Intemerata Dei mater is thought to be free of borrowed material because no chant has been discovered that sets the text, and because no one voice in Ockeghem's setting differs from the others so strikingly that it could be singled out as cantus firmus or paraphrased *cantus prius factus*. In some of Ockeghem's other Marian motets the chant is well known and his paraphrase of it in a single voice is therefore obvious; yet if the chant were unknown no one would suspect its presence in the polyphony, since the voice carrying it is completely absorbed into the contrapuntal texture. In *Alma redemptoris mater,* for example, the next-to-highest voice paraphrases the well-known Marian antiphon, but the texture sounds as though it were composed of four equally important strands of melody, each as "organic" and freely developing as in any of Ockeghem's music without pre-existing material. *Alma redemptoris mater* has an unusually bright and clear sound, partly because it is pitched so high (for Ockeghem) and partly because the tutti sections are interrupted from time to time by duets for varying combinations of voices. In this motet the other voices, too, occasionally paraphrase the chant, but they usually do so without producing imitation. Ockeghem wrote several other Marian motets as well, some with paraphrased chant and some apparently without. And one of his motets, *Ut heremita solus,* is preserved without text in the only two printed sixteenth-century sources that contain it, but with a complicated set of instructions (a "canon") explaining how to sing its tenor, by no means obvious from the arcane way in which it is notated.

Ockeghem's beautiful lament on the death of Binchois is really a chanson rather than a motet, in spite of the Latin cantus firmus in the tenor, since the French ballade text, beginning "Mort, tu as navré de ton dart," which the top voice sings, governs the work's repetition scheme. The superius dominates the four-voiced texture, too, by having the most active and the most carefully wrought melody. With its treble-dominated texture and its succession of $\frac{6}{3}$ chords in the lower voices, this is a rather old-fashioned work, doubtless because Ockeghem paid homage to the dead master by imitating his style. Ockeghem wrote one other cantus-firmus chanson, also for four voices, but of a very different sort. While the tenor sings the popular tune *Petite camusette*, imitated by the contratenor and the bass, the superius, which shares melodic material with the other voices, is set to a conventional love lyric in rondeau form, *S'elle m'amera je ne scay.* (The piece has been published several times without the rondeau text in the superius.)

Most of Ockeghem's chansons are three-voiced settings of ron-deaux, though a few are virelais (or, to be more precise, one-stanza bergerettes), and several have four voices. In addition to the twenty-odd chansons entirely of his own composition, Ockeghem also re-arranged Juan Cornago's *Qu'es mi vida* (in Spanish) and added a new top line to an older arrangement of the Italian *O rosa bella*, incorporating Dun-stable's superius. And he wrote to a French text one *catholicon* (that is, a piece like the *Missa Cuiusvis toni*, capable of being performed in more than one mode), the famous three-voiced canon *Prenez sur moy votre example*, cited by various theorists into the sixteenth century and even worked in intarsia (wooden inlay) for Isabella d'Este's study in the ducal palace at Mantua.

His chansons reveal a slightly simpler and more traditional side to Ockeghem's musical personality. In most of them, as in the chansons of Dufay's generation, the top voice predominates and the tenor sings an equally good counter-melody against it, so that together they make self-sufficient two-part counterpoint. The contratenor may be better integrated into the texture than in many chansons from the first half of the century, and imitation may play a greater role in enriching the texture; but the earlier principle still holds good that form in chansons is determined largely by the repetition scheme of the poem and by the carefully controlled network of cadences on important scale degrees. The melodies themselves generally avoid constructive devices like sequences, sharply profiled motives, and other repetitive elements; they unfold as complete pieces rather than as series of isolated phrases because Ocke-ghem took such care to balance high points against low points, and be-cause he built into his complex arches of melody a long-range sense of directional thrust towards a final goal. The first two phrases of *Ma bouche rit* (Example 3–4), for instance, while tracing a satisfying curve in rising to high D and then gradually descending through a series of looped curves down to the final C, nevertheless leave several gaps in the middle range to be filled in by later phrases. (The chanson begins with an uncharacteristic sequence in the superius that propels the motion forward.) Ockeghem's chansons are subtle and delicate miniatures; taken as a group, they modify somewhat our conception of one of the greatest composers of the fifteenth century, whom we might otherwise consider a more austere figure than he evidently really was.

EXAMPLE 3–4. Ockeghem, *Ma bouche rit,* mm. 1–10. Used by permission of Mediaeval Academy of America.

ANTOINE BUSNOIS

The musical personality of Antoine Busnois (ca. 1430–1492), so different from that of Ockeghem, was undoubtedly formed by his long association with the Burgundian court. He worked for Charles the Bold both before and after Charles became duke. He served Charles's duchess, Margaret of York. And he sang in the chapel of their daughter, Mary of Burgundy, during the last five years of her life, after her father had died in battle in 1477 and she had married Archduke (later Emperor) Maximilian and become Duchess of Burgundy herself. Busnois also apparently had some contact with Parisian circles. Several of his chansons allude by acrostic or pun to Jacqueline d'Hacqueville, the wife of a Parisian parliamentarian, as his beloved. Like Ockeghem, Busnois never worked in Italy, though he may have visited that country. No document records a trip south of the Alps, but Busnois did set a ballata, *Con tutta gentilezza*, a text he is not likely to have chosen had he never left the north. He spent his last years at the Church of Saint Sauveur in Bruges, and died there in 1492.

Busnois wrote poetry as well as music and exchanged poems with the Burgundian court chronicler, Jean Molinet, a poet who also wrote some music. Perhaps this versatility is not as unusual as it seems. Very few of the poems set to music in the fifteenth century can be identified as the work of recognized poets; most are anonymous, and many, therefore, may have been written by the men who subsequently composed the music for them.

Whoever were the authors of his texts, Busnois, like Binchois, was pre-eminently a composer of chansons. He wrote at least one Mass and a handful of motets, but his more than sixty-five chansons comprise the corpus of works by which he is rightly best remembered. Most of them set rondeau or bergerette texts, the two most common *formes fixes* by the second half of the fifteenth century, but a few are polyphonic arrangements of popular tunes and, in some, one or two popular tunes serve as cantus firmi. Normally, three voices sufficed to set these stereotyped love poems to music, but in about a third of his chansons Busnois wrote for four voices, a texture that was to become standard for secular as well as sacred music by 1500. Some chansons, like *Je ne fay plus* (Example 3–5), were originally conceived for three voices, but at a later time Busnois or another musician added a fourth, optional (*si placet*) voice to bring the texture up to date. (*Je ne fay plus* is published in its four-voiced version in Helen Hewitt's edition of the *Odhecaton* of 1501.)

EXAMPLE 3-5. Antoine Busnois, *Je ne fay plus*, mm. 1-18. Used by permission of Mediaeval Academy of America.

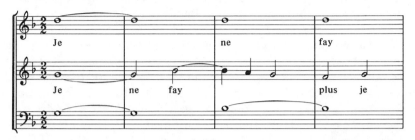

Je ne fay plus (Example 3–5) was almost certainly composed by Busnois, even though it is attributed to a minor composer, Gilles Mureau, in some sources. Indeed, it resembles Busnois's other chansons so closely that it can serve as a representative example of his style. It reveals him to be a great melodist, not a composer of catchy tunes but of long and elaborately shaped vocal lines. Often, it is true, they are composed of melodic clichés, cadence formulae, and turns of phrase common to all Franco-Netherlandish composers of his time. But Busnois filled his melodies with finely wrought details and organized them in carefully balanced segments. Many of his chansons open, like *Je ne fay plus,* with the first phrase of the superius divided into two parts by a rest which coincides with the poetic caesura in the middle of the first line of text. The distinctive opening motive, thus isolated from its continuation, sets the first four syllables of the poem syllabically, and moves more slowly and with greater metric emphasis than the remainder of the phrase. The second half acts as a melodic extension; it moves in smaller note values than the opening, includes syncopations and rhythmic figures that conflict with a regular metric pulse, and ends with a long melisma on the penultimate syllable. Busnois's technique of beginning each phrase syllabically and with a clear-cut motive and continuing with faster motion and a long melisma on the penultimate or antepenultimate syllable derives from earlier masters. But he normally took greater pains than they to contrast the differing formal and melodic functions of phrase beginnings and endings. In so doing, he demonstrated his awareness of the possibility of writing melodies that reflect in detail the metrical structure and the accent pattern of the text. That he was not greatly concerned with reflecting the emotional content of the words is suggested by the tenor's melisma on "ne" in m. 5f, a neutral word that is given such emphasis for purely formal, that is, musical reasons.

The way Busnois linked the first two phrases of *Je ne fay plus* exemplifies his method of achieving formal clarity without sacrificing continuity. The superius and tenor cadence together, so that the overall formal outline of the composition is crystal clear; the contratenor keeps the motion going by imitating rhythmically the opening motive of the second line. *Je ne fay plus* is a *rondeau layé,* that is, one with short lines of text alternating with longer ones. As an exception to the rule that each poetic verse gets a separate phrase of music, the short second line, "En mains escripts," serves as the opening motive for the longer third line, beginning "L'on trouvera." On the other hand, the short fourth line (which begins the second half of the composition), is set as a full-fledged phrase, doubtless for purely formal reasons; the composition as a whole has the proportions and balance among phrases typical of a normal *rondeau quatrain.*

If the logic of a composition by Busnois reveals itself in its melodic construction, he nevertheless made an effort to weld the three voices together into a homogeneous texture, understating the conventional hierarchy of principal melody (superius), supporting melody (tenor), and filler voice (contratenor). Not infrequently two of the three voices move in parallel thirds or tenths, a mannerism associated with Busnois as well as his younger contemporaries, Obrecht and Agricola. Both the tenor and the contratenor of *Je ne fay plus* imitate the superius from time to time (for example, the tenor in mm. 5–6 and the contratenor in mm. 13–14), but seldom at the beginnings of phrases, where the technique would draw most attention to itself. The amount of imitation Busnois wrote in any one chanson varies greatly. Some have as little as *Je ne fay plus;* others, such as *Cent mille escus,* include fully developed points of imitation between two or even all three voices at the beginnings of each or nearly every phrase. In *Ha que ville et habominable* (one of the chansons that alludes to Jacqueline d'Hacqueville), the superius may either be accompanied by two freely invented lower voices or may be set to itself as a three-part canon, the ultimate stage of imitation. The consonant, almost bland, harmonies of *Je ne fay plus,* with 4–3 or 7–6 suspensions furnishing the only dissonances, typify Busnois's style, as does its clear scheme of tonal cadences exclusively on I and V.

The voices in *Je ne fay plus* seldom cross; each voice operates in its own territory. Busnois and his contemporaries extended the range downwards even to notes below gamma ut (the G at the bottom of the stave in the bass clef) and they also extended it upwards to the top of the stave in the treble clef, in effect distributing the melodic lines more evenly over the whole available compass.

Along with delicate and refined courtly lyrics, Busnois also set rather more earthy and direct poems, the popular songs of their day, associated then, as now, with relatively simple monophonic melodies. Sometimes he used one of these melodies as a cantus firmus for a rondeau setting. In *Mon mignault musequin / Gracieuse plaisant munière,* the rondeau in the superius is perhaps more explicitly amorous than usual, but with a completely different tone from the wryly equivocal cantus firmus extolling the virtues of the milleress's mill. The imitation between the tenor (stating the cantus firmus) and the contratenor might more accurately be called free canon, so closely do the two voices resemble each other. In *Amour fait moult tant que argent dure / Il est de bonne heure né / Tant que nostre argent dura,* two popular cantus firmi are combined beneath a rondeau setting without destroying the elegance of the counterpoint. In other chansons, like *On a grant mal par trop aimer* and *Vous marchez au bout du pied,* Busnois set popular tunes more simply and without any interference from a second text. In these four-part popular arrangements, the tune appears in its simplest form in the tenor; the other voices imitate it and also sing rhythmically complex counterpoints around it.

Busnois made use of cantus-firmus technique, too, in most of his sacred music. The *Missa L'homme armé* presents the popular melody once or twice in each movement; each is also related to the others by means of a motto beginning. The motet *Anima mea liquefacta est* is built on the plainsong tenor *Stirps Jesse,* and one of Busnois's two settings of *Regina coeli laetare* presents the Gregorian chant in a free canon at the fourth in the lower two of the four voices. In his *Magnificat* and his relatively short but rhythmically complicated setting of *Conditor alme siderum,* Busnois paraphrased the chant in his superius. And some of his motets, notably the short and unpretentious *Alleluia. Verbum caro factum est* and *Noel noel,* seem to have been freely invented without any reference at all to pre-existing melodies. Two of the presumably free motets are, however, based on cantus firmi apparently of Busnois's own invention. *In hydraulis,* with a curious Pythagorean text in praise of Ockeghem, is organized around a simple ostinato figure, D–C–D, presented repeatedly at pitch and transposed a fifth or an octave higher. The text of *Anthoni usque limina* alludes to the composer, who must have chosen it himself to link his name with that of his patron saint, St. Anthony Abbot. In the manuscript which preserves the motet, a scroll with an image of a bell, one of St. Anthony's attributes, explains in an obscure fashion that the tenor consists of the single note, D, possibly intended to be sounded at various times in the motet on an actual bell.

The sacred music of Busnois exhibits the same delicacy, refinement, and great melodic gifts that mark his chansons. But his few motets and single Mass cannot compare in breadth of conception or depth of realization with Ockeghem's greater achievement in this field. Perhaps Busnois's brilliance in creating chansons that are exquisite gems reflects the predilections of the hedonistic court of Burgundy. In any case Busnois is one of the great masters of the fifteenth-century chanson, whom even Ockeghem can scarcely rival.

CONTEMPORARIES OF BUSNOIS AND OCKEGHEM

Large choir books that stood on lecterns supplied church choirs in the fifteenth century with the music they sang. A number of small and precious songbooks, most of them scarcely large enough for two people to sing from, survive from the second half of the century and contain the secular music of Busnois and his contemporaries. Some of these "chansonniers" are elegantly illuminated; most of them once belonged to princes or rich collectors and have been saved because they are handsome examples of book-making, not because they preserve an important part of our musical heritage. Nor were they manuscripts from which courtly musicians sang and played daily, but rather deluxe editions, collectors' treasures, or presentation copies.

Chansonniers adorned rich libraries everywhere in western Europe, and especially in France, Burgundy, and Italy. A few that survive can be associated with the court of Burgundy or with the central Burgundian tradition: the Copenhagen Chansonnier (edited in a modern edition by Knud Jeppesen); the Dijon Manuscript (Dijon, Bibliothèque publique, MS 517, recently published in facsimile by Dragan Plamenac); the Laborde Chansonnier in the Library of Congress in Washington; the Wolfenbüttel Chansonnier (Wolfenbüttel, Herzog-August-Bibliothek, MS 287 extrav.); and the Nivelle de la Chaussée Manuscript (belonging to Mme. H. de Chambure in Paris). One of the most beautiful of all is the Chansonnier Cordiforme (Paris, Bibliothèque nationale, Collection Rothschild, MS I.5.13), so-called because the manuscript itself takes the shape of a heart; it was prepared in Savoy about 1470. Some of the chansonniers from Italy are equally elegant. A Florentine chansonnier from the time of Lorenzo de' Medici, "the Magnificent" (Florence, Biblioteca Nazionale Centrale, MS Banco rari 229, to be published in a modern edition by H. M. Brown), is sumptuously decorated with miniatures; it is only slightly more beautiful, though, than two other Florentine chansonniers from the last quarter of the fifteenth century, the Pixérécourt Manuscript (Paris, Bibliothèque nationale, MS fonds fr. 15123) and the Medici Chansonnier (Vatican City, Cappella Giulia, MS XIII.27). Several chansonniers were probably prepared in Naples, among them the Escorial Manuscript (El Escorial, Biblioteca de S. Lorenzo, MS IV.a.24) and the Mellon Chansonnier (Yale University Library, soon to be published in facsimile and a modern edition by Leeman Perkins). And one (Rome, Biblioteca Casanatense, MS 2856) comes from the Este court at Ferrara; it was intended for Isabella d'Este's wedding to Francesco Gonzaga in 1490. Also of Italian origin is the Seville Chansonnier (Seville, Biblioteca Colombina, MS 5-I-43, to which was originally joined Paris, Bibliothèque nationale, MS nouv. acq. fr. 4379, both parts of which are now available in a facsimile edited by Dragan Plamenac). And there are even some German chansonniers, notably the Glogauer Liederbuch (partly published in a modern edition in *Das Erbe deutscher Musik*, vols. 4 and 8) and the Schedelsches Liederbuch (Munich, Bayerische Staatsbibliothek, MS 3232), written down in the 1460's by a doctor and historian, Hartmann Schedel.

No matter where they were written, these anthologies contain mostly French chansons. Obviously French culture was foremost in courtly circles everywhere in western Europe at the time, at least so far as secular music was concerned. But the chansonniers are true miscellanies and also reflect local tastes and customs. Along with chansons they include song-motets in Latin; compositions with Italian, German, Spanish, English, or Dutch texts; and even a few compositions apparently originally conceived for instruments.

Chansonniers and manuscripts prepared for use in churches, cathedrals and princely chapels include music by the great composers of the century—Dufay and Binchois, Ockeghem and Busnois, and their younger contemporaries like Agricola, Obrecht, Isaac, and Josquin—as well as compositions by a host of minor composers about whom little is known and whose compositions do not survive in sufficient quantity or do not reflect sufficiently distinctive quality for us to be able to draw for them any very precise stylistic profile. Fifteenth-century manuscript sources preserve, for example, music by some of the composers who worked with Busnois at the Burgundian court—his slightly older colleagues, Gilles Joye and the Englishman Robert Morton, and his friend, Jean Molinet, the court chronicler. Chansonniers include a number of chansons by Hayne van Ghizeghem, a Burgundian composer of considerable charm, whose *De tous biens plaine est ma maistresse,* along with the anonymous *J'ay pris amours en ma devise,* is among the best loved and most widely distributed chansons of the entire fifteenth century.

Johannes Tinctoris (ca. 1435–1511), associated in his younger days with both the cathedrals of Cambrai and Chartres, settled in the 1470's in Naples, where he worked for King Ferrante, taught the king's daughter, Beatrice of Aragon, before she became Queen of Hungary, and wrote a series of treatises that forms the most substantial corpus of theoretical work we possess from the fifteenth century. Less important as a composer than as a writer on music, Tinctoris nevertheless composed at least four Masses, two motets, and a handful of chansons.

Like Tinctoris, Philippe (or Firmin?) Caron, Jean Cornuel (called Verjust), and Johannes Regis were all associated with Cambrai at some time in their lives. Caron seems to have spent much of his life in Italy, where he composed some charming chansons—among them *Helas que pourra devenir* and *Accueillie m'a la belle,* which were widely distributed throughout western Europe—as well as longer and more ambitious works. Regis stayed north, working in Soignies, Antwerp, and Mons, and acting for a time as Dufay's secretary. His *Missa L'homme armé* uses the cantus firmus to illustrate the liturgical occasion for which the work was intended, the Feast of St. Michael the Archangel, the "armed man" in this context.

Tinctoris certainly knew Johannes Stokhem, Beatrice of Aragon's chapelmaster in Budapest, for the theorist sent the composer one section of his treatise *De inventione et usu musicae* (the only section that now survives). In another treatise, Tinctoris cited with admiration the work of Guillaume Faugues, who composed, among other things, several Masses of considerable interest. One is based on a basse dance tenor; another uses as its cantus firmus the tenor of Dufay's chanson *Le serviteur* and also quotes other voices of the model, at times all three voices simultaneously. And Tinctoris surely knew Gilles Mureau, since both worked at the cathedral in Chartres at the same time.

Of the Papal singers during the second half of the fifteenth century, Bertrand de Vaqueras, who had spent some time in Liége, and Jean Sohier (called Fedé), a native of Douai who also sang for a while at the Sainte Chapelle in Paris, won considerable fame as composers. Among the many other contemporaries of Busnois and Ockeghem, the "three B's" —Barbingant, Jacob Barbireau, and Philippe Basiron ("Philippon")—are easily confused because of their names. Collinet de Lannoy, a northerner who worked in Italy, achieved notoriety because he left Isabella d'Este's service without her permission, as correspondence between the Marchesa and her music teacher, Johannes Martini, makes clear. Collinet's chanson *Cela sans plus*, though it seems to modern ears thin and lacking in invention, appealed to contemporary musicians enough to find its way into numerous sources and inspired Pope Leo X to write a five-voice version around the original tenor. And Cornelius Heyn's *Missa Pour quelque paine* is of high enough quality to have been mistaken in one source for a work by Ockeghem.

BIBLIOGRAPHICAL NOTES

The complete works of Johannes Ockeghem are in process of publication, edited by Dragan Plamenac (Vol. 1: Leipzig, 1927/2nd rev. ed., American Musicological Society, 1959; Vol. II: American Musicological Society, 1947). Some of his motets, along with examples of Franco-Netherlandish music by other composers, can be found in Albert Smijers, ed., *Van Ockeghem tot Sweelinck*, 6 vols. (Amsterdam, 1939–52), and in Heinrich Besseler, ed., *Altniederländische Motetten* (Cassel, 1929). The best essay on Ockeghem's style is that on the *Caput* Mass in Manfred Bukofzer, *Studies in Medieval and Renaissance Music* (New York, 1950). See also Edward E. Lowinsky, "Ockeghem's Canon for Thirty-six Voices: An Essay in Musical Iconography," *Essays in Musicology in Honor of Dragan Plamenac on his 70th Birthday*, ed. Gustave Reese and Robert J. Snow (Pittsburgh, 1969); and Ernst Křenek, *Johannes Ockeghem* (New York, 1953). An exhibition catalogue, in Dutch and French, *Johannes*

Ockeghem en zijn tijd (Dendermonde, 1970), published by the Oud-heidkundige Kring van het Land van Dendermonde, summarizes all the available documentary evidence, and supplies much useful information about the composer and his music.

On Busnois, see Catherine Brooks, "Antoine Busnois, Chanson Composer," *Journal of the American Musicological Society*, 6 (1953); Edgar H. Sparks, "The Motets of Antoine Busnois," *Journal of the American Musicological Society*, 6 (1953); and George Perle, "The Chansons of Antoine Busnois," *Music Review*, 11 (1950). Some of his chansons are published in the chansonnier editions cited in the text above and in the supplementary list given below. Several motets appear in Smijers, *Van Ockeghem tot Sweelinck*.

For additional editions of chansonniers, see also Eugénie Droz, Yvonne Rokseth, and G. Thibault, eds., *Trois chansonniers français du XVe siècle* (Paris, 1927); E. Droz and G. Thibault, eds., *Poètes et musiciens du XVe siècle* (Paris, 1924); and Helen Hewitt, ed., *Harmonice Musices Odhecaton A* (Cambridge, Mass., 1942). On motets of this period see Wolfgang Stephan, *Die burgundisch-niederländische Motette zur Zeit Ockeghems* (Cassel, 1937; repr. 1973).

part two

The High Renaissance:

1490-1520

FOUR

ITALIAN MUSIC, 1490-1520

Foreign composers, *oltremontani*, dominated the musical life of the Italian courts throughout the fifteenth century and during the first part of the sixteenth century. By 1474, for example, Galeazzo Maria Sforza, Duke of Milan, had assembled a brilliant group of musicians that included Gaspar van Weerbecke, Johannes Martini, Loyset Compère, Alexander Agricola, and the young Josquin des Prez. Martini also worked in Ferrara for many years, but he was only one of the many northerners —among them Jacob Obrecht, Josquin, Collinet de Lannoy, Antoine Brumel, and Johannes Ghiselin (called Verbonnet)—who came to the city while Hercules d'Este I was duke (1431–1505). Agricola, Collinet, Ghiselin, Johannes Stokhem, and others spent some time in Florence, where Heinrich Isaac, the most distinguished composer in the city, had settled about 1484. The Papal chapel in Rome, not surprisingly one of the leading musical centers in all of Italy, boasted among its singers a number of accomplished foreigners—Josquin, Weerbecke, Marbriano de

Orto, Johannes Prioris, and, under Leo X, Antoine Bruhier and Elzéar Genet (called Carpentras), among many others.

It is one of the greatest oddities of musical history that so few Italian composers were active during the century that saw in that country the birth of the Renaissance in painting, sculpture, and architecture. Yet the fact remains that after about 1420, when the great musical efflorescence of the *trecento* had died down, no native-born composers could compare in stature and achievement with Alberti, Fra Angelico, Brunelleschi, Donatello, Filippo Lippi, Masaccio, and other artists. Even after 1490, when some Italian composers finally began to make a name for themselves—Tromboncino, Cara, and the other frottolists in northern Italy, for example, and Coppini, Bartolomeo degli Organi, and others in Florence—Franco-Netherlandish musicians still held the most important positions in courts and cathedrals. Italian princes, in fact, vied with one another to secure for themselves the best foreign talent they could afford. Perhaps this situation developed simply because it was fashionable to import musicians from the north. Perhaps Italian cathedral schools could no longer train young musicians for important positions. Or perhaps the prejudices of Italian humanists against elaborate "Gothic" polyphony discouraged native-born composers from developing their talents. The reasons why Italian composers largely disappear from view between 1420 and 1490 are by no means obvious.

The importance of the *oltremontani* explains why French musical culture had such a central place in Italian courts and why chansons predominate to such an extent even in the secular collections prepared in Italy. But late fifteenth-century chansonniers also contain some compositions with Italian texts or titles, many of them written by northern composers. Some Italian incipits turn out to be garbled versions of French titles; thus Busnois's rondeau *Cent mille escus* is called in one source *Cento milia scuti*. In some manuscripts, Italian incipits begin compositions that can be identified as French chansons; the incipits apparently refer to contrafacta, Italian texts that replaced the original French in performance. Thus Caron's *Le despourveu infortuné* is labeled in one manuscript *Tanto è l'affanno* (no further text is given), and Busnois's *M'a vostre cueur* is called *Terribile fortuna*. On closer examination even more of the Italian compositions in chansonniers will doubtless turn out to be French chansons in disguise. Some compositions in late fifteenth-century manuscript anthologies have Italian titles rather than text incipits, and some of these seem to be compositions originally conceived for instruments and written in more or less the same style as chansons. Many of the titles allude to people's names—for example, Ghiselin's *La Alfonsina*, Josquin's *La Bernardina*, Martini's *La Martinella* (a title used by several other composers as well), and perhaps even Isaac's *La Morra*. These compositions pay homage to the composer's friends or patrons.

The fifteenth-century chansonniers also include some original settings of Italian poems. A few are based on popular monophonic tunes, which the northern composers worked into elaborate polyphonic arrangements; both Josquin and Compère, for example, perhaps in competition, devised witty contrapuntal versions of *Scaramella va alla guerra*. And a few fifteenth-century Italian songs are altogether exceptional, compositions that do not follow any established tradition, like Dufay's extraordinary setting of the first stanza of Petrarch's canzone *Vergine bella* and Dunstable's setting of Giustiniani's *O rosa bella*. But many of the Italian songs in secular anthologies do relate to an older convention in that they are ballate, one of the chief forms of secular music carried over from the *trecento* into the *quattrocento*. The repetition scheme of the ballata, A b b a A, resembles that of the virelai. Composers as early as Dufay composed Italian songs in this form, and settings of ballate or closely related poems comprise most of the Italian compositions in a number of later fifteenth-century chansonniers, like the Neapolitan anthology now at El Escorial in Spain.

A few Italian songs in the Escorial chansonnier and other fifteenth-century anthologies are strambotti, poems in *ottava rima* (eight-line stanzas rhyming abababcc or abababab). This verse form was adopted for the epic poetry of Ariosto and Tasso and also for the improvised, semi-popular narratives and lyrics performed at courts and in Italian cities from the very beginning of the fifteenth century. The improvisers were poet-musicians whose reputations were based neither on their compositional skill alone nor on the brilliance of their instrumental technique, but rather on their ability to declaim improvised poems while accompanying themselves on the lute or the *lira da braccio*. The Brandolini brothers, Leonardo Giustiniani in Venice, Pietro Bono in Ferrara, Serafino dall'Aquila in the service of Cardinal Ascanio Sforza in Rome, the Spaniard Il Chariteo (Benedetto Gareth) in Naples, Ugo Baciolini in Florence (who sang the title role in Poliziano's *Orfeo* in the 1470's), and even Marsilio Ficino, the great philosopher, who claimed his invention of Orphic singing to the lyre as one of the great achievements of the age—all of these men and more were the great native Italian musicians of their day. Many of their poems survive, not only strambotti but also capitoli and other narratives in *terza rima* (see p. 102), odes, sonnets, ballate, and so on. And there are many extravagant descriptions of their talent in improvising music to these texts. But, since the music was composed extempore, it was almost never written down; hence it is largely lost to us today.

A few chansonniers include isolated examples of strambotti, among them some by northern composers that combine a very simple melody with fairly elaborate counterpoint. The character of pieces like Japart's *Nenciozza mia*, Johannes Martini's *Fortuna d'un gran tempo*, and

Obrecht's *La tortorella* suggests that strambotti were associated with monophonic formulae repeated for each couplet in a stanza. (Example 4–1 shows one such setting, with the chanting formula in the tenor; in the second half of the piece, the same formula appears in the superius.) Although the counterpoint in these arrangements is Franco-Netherlandish, the stereotyped and conventional nature of the Italian formulae which inspired the composers is clear. We can get a further idea of the style of fifteenth-century improvised music by examining carefully the few straightforward settings of strambotti that do survive, and also by inferring it from literary descriptions and by extrapolating backwards from the style of the slightly later Italian repertory of Mantuan frottole, Florentine canti carnascialeschi and other songs, and Latin laude.

EXAMPLE 4–1. Japart, *Nenciozza mia,* mm. 1–9. Used by permission of Mediaeval Academy of America.

One important clue to the nature of the Italians' improvisations comes from the fact that we know they accompanied themselves on the lute or, more characteristically, on the *lira da braccio,* a violin-like fiddle with seven strings (five on the fingerboard and two drones off the fingerboard) that was adept at playing chords. The number of strings on the *lira da braccio* is the only feature that resembles the ancient lyre, and yet the name was given to the instrument because it was associated with the declamation of epic and narrative poems in a style that apparently reminded fifteenth-century listeners of the ancient world. When the instrument is shown in fifteenth-century Italian art it is often seen in the hands of Orpheus, Apollo, or another of the more musical ancient gods or heroes.

Aside from a few musical examples in theoretical treatises, the only source of actual *lira* music, a late sixteenth-century manuscript in Pesaro (Biblioteca Oliveriana, MS 1144), reveals that when the *lira da braccio* was used as a solo instrument it played melodies accompanied by relatively simple chords, as in the Romanesca setting shown in Example 4–2. That the Pesaro manuscript should offer as its two specimens of *lira* music a Romanesca and a Passamezzo—two of the most common series of chord progressions that underlie many compositions throughout the sixteenth century—is itself significant, for these chordal patterns may originally have been invented for Italian improvisers as early as the fifteenth century. What little evidence exists certainly suggests that these poet-musicians worked with standard patterns of chords—like twentieth-century jazz musicians.

EXAMPLE 4–2. *Romanesca* for the lira da braccio (Pesaro, Biblioteca Oliveriana, MS 1144, p. 174), mm. 1–9.

Occasionally a formula for singing all Italian poems in a given form appears in the musical sources. The *modus dicendi capitula,* for example, taken from the first book of printed frottole of 1504 (Example 4–3), consists simply of a skeletal melody and a pattern of chords. To sing a complete narrative capitolo consisting of many stanzas using this formula without variation would be aesthetically intolerable. The art of the *improvvisatori* must partly have consisted in the skill with which they

EXAMPLE 4–3. Michele Pesenti, *Modus dicendi Capitula.*

Ben mil - le vol - te al | di me di - ce a - mo - re

Non la lau - dar ser - ví con - fe - de e ta - ce

Che ques - te lau - de a te cres - con l'ar - do - re

could vary and embellish the bare outline from which they began. But however much these poet-musicians decorated the basic formula, they would have wished to project the words. The syllabic, declamatory style as well as the chordal orientation of the texture exemplified in Example 4–3 and, indeed, in the entire frottola repertory sharply distinguish Italian fifteenth-century improvised music from the highly melismatic and contrapuntal inventions of the Franco-Netherlanders.

The music of the courtly poet-musicians must have been a revelation to the northern composers of the fifteenth century coming to Italy for the first time, for almost nothing in their own training within the Franco-Netherlandish tradition would have prepared them for these formulaic chord patterns, clearly declaimed texts, and *fioriture*. These two cultures —improvisatory southern song and refined northern polyphony—existed side by side in Italy throughout the fifteenth century.

THE FROTTOLA AND RELATED TYPES

The Italian composers who began to appear on the musical scene in great numbers in the last decade of the fifteenth century set the sort of poetry declaimed by the improvisers—strambotti, odes, and capitoli, for example—as well as barzellette, lyrical strophic poems with refrains not unlike the older ballate. All of these kinds of songs are called, rather loosely, frottole, a word that refers more particularly to the barzelletta. Most of the frottolists came from northern Italy: Francesco d'Ana, for example, from Venice, Michele Pesenti and Giovanni Brocco from Verona, and Antonio Caprioli from Brescia. But the frottola was identified especially with the small court of Mantua, partly because the enlightened patronage of Isabella d'Este (1474–1539), marchioness of Mantua, greatly stimulated the development of the genre, and partly because the two most distinguished composers of frottole, Bartolomeo Tromboncino (died ca. 1535) and Marco Cara (died ca. 1530), both established their reputations in that city and worked there for long periods in their lives.

As a young girl in Ferrara, Isabella d'Este studied music with the Netherlander Johannes Martini. But her cultural interests were broad, and she exemplifies the enlightened patron of the Italian Renaissance. After she moved to Mantua as the bride of Francesco Gonzaga, she began commissioning works of art and corresponding, in letters distinguished for their wit and intelligence, with painters, poets, and musicians. She had contact with most of the greatest artists of her time, including Leonardo da Vinci, Titian, Castiglione, and Ariosto. In pursuing her musical interests she dealt not only with instrument makers and performers, but also with poets like Galeotto del Carretto and Serafino dall'Aquila, encouraging them to supply poems to be set to music. And she kept in her employ the tempestuous Tromboncino even after he had murdered his unfaithful wife and escaped punishment for the crime, as well as the calmer and more dependable Cara, who spent his entire career working for her and her husband. Isabella may have sponsored these Italian musicians because she could not afford to hire the great international figures for her court; she may have wished to foster a national style; or she may simply have been intelligent enough to cultivate the best work being done around her regardless of the pressures of fashion. Whatever the reasons, her active support of the frottolists substantially aided their efforts to establish a truly Italian style of composition.

Frottole survive in a number of manuscripts and printed books from the first quarter of the sixteenth century. The largest corpus of them is contained in the eleven volumes of frottole published in Venice between 1504 and 1514 by the first great printer of music, Ottaviano Petrucci. Books of plainchant and isolated examples of polyphony had been printed before 1500, and Michel Toulouze of Paris had issued a collection of basse-dance tenors set in movable type; but Petrucci was the first to perfect the techniques necessary for publishing complete collections of polyphonic music set in movable type and printed by multiple impression —that is, with the staves printed separately from the note heads, stems, and texts, a procedure requiring very precise control over registration (the exact correspondence of the position of the sheets when they are put through the presses a second time). Petrucci's first book, issued in 1501, *Harmonice musices Odhecaton A* (the title, a mixture of words derived from Latin and Greek, means simply "One hundred songs of harmonic music," though in fact the volume includes only ninety-six), is the first of a three-volume set comprising in addition *Canti B* and *Canti C*. The collection represents both an end and a beginning. While it is the first printed anthology of polyphonic music, it is one of the last great chansonniers containing a comprehensive and diverse cross-section of all of the kinds of secular music current in the late fifteenth century, though its emphasis is on French chansons. Thereafter anthologies tended to cater to slightly more specialized tastes. Petrucci went on to produce a large number of luxurious volumes of motets and Masses and collections devoted to individual composers—among them Josquin, Obrecht, Brumel, Pierre de la Rue, Ghiselin, Agricola, Marbriano de Orto, Isaac, Weerbecke, Févin, and Mouton—as well as laude, frottole, and volumes of music for lute, lute and voice, and keyboard.

Petrucci's eleven books of frottole (only a few fragments of Book X survive) appeared more than a decade after the genre began in and around Mantua in the 1490's. The volumes should be regarded, then, as a slightly retrospective view of the new music and perhaps, as Einstein suggests, as the musical equivalents of epistolary guides for the composition of letters. The frottola books offer to the courtier "suitable compositions for all occasions and situations of amorous and courtly life"; they furnish excellent examples of the genre, models to follow in constructing similar pieces, and, not least of all, formulae on which improvisations can be based. The utilitarian nature of the volumes explains why much of the poetry has but little literary value—it is mere *poesia per musica*—and also why the volumes are so miscellaneous in character. They contain not only frottole in the narrowest sense of the word but also settings of all the other sorts of poems in common use at the time—strambotti, capitoli, odes, sonnets, canzoni, and so on.

The frottola proper or barzelletta, as it is sometimes called, is a fixed lyrical form much like the French virelai or, more to the point, like the older Italian ballata. Typically it consists of a four-line refrain (called the *ripresa*) and a six-line stanza. Four phrases of music (ABCD) are supplied for the *ripresa*. The first quatrain of the six-line stanza is sung to the first two phrases of music and their repetition, and the final couplet to the second half of the music, as the following diagram makes clear:

	Ripresa	*Stanza*
Music:	A B C D	a b a b c d
Rhyme scheme:	a b b a	c d c d d a

The number of stanzas in a frottola is not fixed. Between each the refrain is repeated in whole or in part. If only a part of the refrain is to be sung between stanzas, the composer often supplies a special version of the truncated part consisting of the first two phrases of music plus a more or less extended coda (AB + x), and this shortened refrain is given in the sources immediately following the complete version.

Thus the performance of a typical frottola results in the repetition scheme ABCD ababcd AB + x ababcd AB + x, and so on, ending with a complete statement of the refrain.

These barzellette, charming, unpretentious settings of stereotyped lyrical poems dealing chiefly with love, make up the major part of the earlier Petrucci books of frottole. From the fourth volume onwards other forms of poetry take an ever greater share of space. Even the most complex settings of strambotti, odes, capitoli, and sonnets are often little more than patterns to follow, formulas to use in declaiming poetry, or bare frameworks on which to base presumably more elaborate semi-improvisations. The simplest are no more than a few chord progressions harmonizing a melodic formula.

The odes of the frottolists deal with a variety of subjects, moralistic or amorous, usually in a series of quatrains. They are modeled on similar poems by Horace and other classical Latin poets. In Petrucci's first book, there is even a setting by Michele Pesenti of Horace's *Integer vitae,* one of the barest of all the patterns in the frottola books, scarcely more interesting musically than some of the contemporary experiments by German humanists in setting Latin odes for use in schools. Marco Cara's ode *Udite voi finestre* (Example 4–4) is hardly more complicated than

EXAMPLE 4–4. Cara, *Udite voi finestre*, mm. 1–12.

the capitolo by Pesenti. The composer's emphatic repetition of the last lines of each quatrain is unusual, but the interlocking rhyme scheme (abbc cdde effg, and so on) in this slightly melancholy serenade is a feature common to the form.

Interlocking rhymes are also frequently found in capitoli, in which the middle rhyme in one three-line strophe continues over into the next (aba bcb cdc, and so on, as in Example 4–3). Called *terza rima*, this is the verse form Dante chose for his *Divine Comedy*. Capitoli are associated with lyrical or dramatic eclogues—pastoral poems, often pathetic in tone. Sonnets are set by the frottolists as schematically as the other poetic types. The composers often use the same four phrases of music for both quatrains of the poem, and three contrasting phrases for both tercets, while some sonnet settings consist simply of three phrases of music, the first two repeated over and over again for successive couplets, and the last phrase reserved for the final line of the poem.

Of all the poetic forms used by the frottolists, the canzone shows the greatest degree of structural irregularity and the highest literary standards. Strophic like most of the other forms—though often only one strophe of poetry is included in the frottola books—canzoni consist of a varying number of alternating seven- and eleven-syllable lines in irregular rhyme schemes. The frottolists began to set these more sophisticated poems, including the magnificent canzoni by the great fourteenth-century Italian poet Francesco Petrarch, in the first decades of the sixteenth century. For these poems the musicians did not change their simple and often declamatory manner, as the excerpt from Tromboncino's setting of Petrarch's *Sì è debile il filo* (Example 4–5) makes clear; but the irregular nature of the poetry at least forced them to write through-composed music, lacking the patterned and stereotyped features that characterize most frottole. In addition to all these poetic types, Petrucci also included some examples of other sorts of music in his volumes of frottole: contrapuntal, even highly imitative settings of villotte, or popular songs, like Michele Pesenti's *Dal lecto me levava* in the first book and Compère's *Che fa la ramacina* in Book IV; classical Latin texts, as we have seen; a few quodlibets; and various irregular forms like Josquin's *El grillo*.

EXAMPLE 4–5. Bartolomeo Tromboncino, *Sì è debile il filo*, mm. 1–9. From Disertori, ed., *Le Frottole per canto e liuto intabulate da Franciscus Bossinensis.* © Copyright 1964 by G. Ricordi & C.s.p.a. Milan. By kind permission of the owner G. Ricordi & C.s.p.a. Milan.

The style of the frottole differs markedly from that of Franco-
Netherlandish polyphony of the late fifteenth century, above all in its
chordal orientation and in its use of patterned rhythms. Frottole are often
strongly metrical, even though the mensuration sign sometimes implies a
meter different from that required by the music (as in Examples 4–4,
published by Petrucci in triple mensuration, and 4–6, published in duple
mensuration). A rhythmic pattern once established is apt to be repeated
over and over again throughout most of a composition. When the meter
is triple the patterns almost always involve hemiola, the juxtaposition and
combination of rhythms in 6/8 and 3/4 (or 6/4 and 3/2). Tromboncino's
Chi se fida de fortuna (Example 4–6) displays the characteristic dance
rhythms and hemiola of frottole in triple time (and its repeated notes at
cadences echo the feminine ending so typical of Italian poetry).

A frottola melody is usually set to its text syllabically or with a few
short melismas to accentuate stressed syllables; it cadences regularly on
feminine endings; and it is supported by a bass line that usually supplies

EXAMPLE 4–6. Tromboncino, *Chi se fida de fortuna*, mm. 1–5. From Disertori, ed., *Le Frottole per canto e liuto intabulate da Franciscus Bossinensis.*
© Copyright 1964 by G. Ricordi & C.s.p.a. Milan. By kind permission of the
owner G. Ricordi & C.s.p.a. Milan.

4

the roots of triads formed into surprisingly tonal progressions. Patterns of chords underlie the harmony of frottole in the same way that patterns of note values determine their rhythm. Chords built on tonal degrees of the scale—I, IV, and V—generally predominate over others (Example 4–4 in G-Dorian, for instance, is almost entirely based on those three chords except at the very beginning, where a progression of chords built on F, G, and D establishes the key nonetheless clearly for being "modal" rather than "tonal"). Final cadences are more apt to involve an octave leap in the bass, while an inner voice supplies the last root, than the more modern I–V–I bass movement of Example 4–4.

5

Between the principal melody in the top voice and the harmonically oriented bass line, the inner voices act as harmonic filler and keep the rhythmic motion moving forward. The special relationship between superius and tenor so often found in Franco-Netherlandish polyphony— the two-part counterpoint that forms the basis for the entire contrapuntal fabric—is absent from these Italian songs. Even when the inner voices furnish imitations or other contrapuntal refinements, their primary function is simply to fill out the texture and to keep the sound from being unpleasantly thin. They often share the same range; they are frequently written in the same clefs and cross each other regularly. In short, the texture of frottole has much in common with that of Baroque songs with *basso continuo,* though in the earlier music the realization is superficially contrapuntal rather than purely chordal.

This distinctive texture with its strong chordal orientation explains why frottole often seem to be so apt for solo singing with an accompaniment of a lute or an instrumental ensemble. That Italian musicians in the late fifteenth and early sixteenth centuries often performed them in this way is not surprising in view of the connection between this repertory and that of the earlier fifteenth-century courtly improvisers who accompanied themselves on lute or *lira.* Nor is it then surprising that Franciscus Bossinensis published two volumes of frottole (in 1509 and 1511) arranged for solo voice and lute; a third volume, featuring works by Tromboncino and Cara, was issued in the 1520's. (In almost all of the songs the voice sings the superius and the lute plays the tenor and bass, so that the alto line of the four-part "original" is simply omitted in the arrangement.) Frottole were also sometimes sung a cappella, a method that poses some problems: the text fits the lower voices very awkwardly, because many of the bass lines are continuous and the inner voices filled with busy passagework. Almost certainly, then, the versions of frottole published by Petrucci do not represent the music in its fixed and immutable state; rather, they present material in a manner that is most convenient for musicians to arrange in as many differing ways as they can invent.

Within a comparatively narrow range of style, frottole offer a surprising amount of contrast in mood and technique. Some are charming and delicate lyrics; others are so declamatory that they seem mere excuses for reciting the poetry, or perhaps for displaying the performer's skill at improvisation; and quite a few are dance songs set out in lively rhythmic patterns. There are, perhaps, few compositions in the volumes published by Petrucci that can be described as great masterpieces in the sense that they are impressively complex or intellectually demanding. But the collections are filled with music of great charm, much of which reveals itself fully only in performances that take account of the fact that the printed versions merely indicate a bare framework which the singers and instrumentalists must fill in by using their creative imagination.

By the second decade of the sixteenth century, Italian composers had begun to take the frottola more seriously as a vehicle for intensifying by music their perception of great poems. More and more they chose to set texts of high literary merit, especially canzoni and sonnets. Petrucci's eleventh book of frottole (1514) contains as many as twenty poems by Petrarch. And an important stage in the transition from frottola to madrigal was reached when Petrucci published in 1520 a whole volume of settings of Petrarch's canzoni by the Tuscan Bernardo Pisano. In short, the frottola began to lose its concentration on courtly trifles and its connections with the world of the improvisers as it came to serve more serious artistic aims. Little by little it gave way to the madrigal.

CANTI CARNASCIALESCHI
AND OTHER FLORENTINE MUSIC

Like nineteenth-century Vienna or present-day New Orleans, Florence in the late fifteenth century celebrated the carnival time just before Lent with special intensity. Both then and during the Calendi-maggio, the period between May 1 and the Feast of St. John the Baptist, the city's patron, on June 24, the citizens of Florence organized a number of festivities, especially torchlight parades with cars, floats, masked musicians singing carnival songs ("canti carnascialeschi"), and dancing in the streets. Some of the cars or floats were sponsored by trade guilds; others satirized one or another of the groups that made up the colorful life of the city. There were songs by tailors, oil makers, used clothing dealers, and bird sellers; songs by poor pensioners, beggars, widows, gypsies, Jews, and German soldiers (*Landsknechte*, whose songs were written in heavily accented Italian). The singers almost always identify themselves at the beginning of their song, and then proceed to poke fun at their own customs, their dialects, or their station in life. Political as well as social satire sometimes enters in, and the second meaning of the double entendres is often obscene.

The celebration of carnival and the songs associated with it flourished especially during the time of Lorenzo de' Medici, "the Magnificent," who ruled in Florence from 1469 until his death in 1492. He himself wrote *canzoni a ballo* (dancing songs) as well as some of the best known canti carnascialeschi, including the mythological song of Bacchus which begins "Quant'è bella giovinezza, Che si fugge tuttavia" ("How beautiful is youth, though it vanishes all too quickly"), one of the freshest of all the poems exhorting the young to enjoy themselves while they can. And Lorenzo encouraged his courtiers and the city's poets to write similar poems for carnival, or at least for setting to music. Cynical modern historians have suggested that Lorenzo arranged lavish entertainments to make the Florentine people forget their oppressed state. Whatever his motives, Lorenzo did play the same role that Isabella d'Este had in Mantua; he furthered the cause of vernacular poetry and stimulated the formation of an Italian musical style distinct from that of the Franco-Netherlanders.

The tradition of celebrating carnival with extravagant entertainments declined after Lorenzo's death in 1492, when the city fell into the grip of the reforming friar, Girolamo Savonarola. In his puritanical zeal he argued eloquently against foolish ornament and worldly frivolity, and secular songbooks joined playing cards, trivial literature, fans, and immodest articles of clothing on the bonfires of vanities that he organized in the city. But opposition to his ideas soon grew, and in 1498 he was hanged and then burned in the Piazza della Signoria. The Medici were restored in 1512, expelled in 1527 when the republic was re-established, and restored again in 1530, this time as hereditary rulers and, eventually, as Grand Dukes of Tuscany. These civic disturbances help to explain why so few sources of carnival songs survive. Our knowledge of the repertory comes from a few manuscripts dating from after Lorenzo's death, and mostly from a retrospective collection of texts, *Tutti i trionfi, carri, mascherate e canti carnascialeschi dal tempo del Magnifico Lorenzo Vecchio de' Medici*, edited by Anton Francesco Grazzini, called Il Lasca, and published in Florence in 1559.

The two best-known composers of carnival songs during the time of Lorenzo the Magnificent were foreigners: Heinrich Isaac, who had settled in the city in 1484, and Alexander Agricola, who spent long periods in Florence from the 1470's onwards. But the largest number of surviving examples were written by Alessandro Coppini (ca. 1465–1527), a native Florentine, monk, Doctor of Sacred Theology, and composer and organist who worked at various Florentine churches, including the prestigious Santissima Annunziata and the Medici family's favorite, San Lorenzo. Only a few others among the many anonymous canti carna-scialeschi are attributed to composers, among them the slightly younger Bartolomeo degli Organi (1474–1539), called Baccio by his contemporaries, and Ser Giovanni Serragli (fl. 1502–27).

A few canti carnascialeschi are simple strophic songs in which the through-composed music set to the first strophe is repeated *in toto* for all subsequent ones. But most of the carnival songs resemble ballate, with a two-, three-, or four-line refrain (the *ripresa*) and a series of complex strophes, each of which consists of two alternately rhyming couplets (the *piedi*) and a closing section with a variable number of lines (the *volta*). The music composed to fit this poetic form does not follow a predetermined repetition scheme as rigid as those devised for the French *formes fixes* or the northern Italian barzellette. The refrain is almost always marked off by a double bar. Often the two *piedi* are sung to the same music, which contrasts with that for the refrain, and the *volta* is set to a third section of music. But some canti carnascialeschi do not include any repeated phrases—each strophe is through-composed—and others repeat phrases according to no preconceived pattern. Thus in his song of the bird-catchers, *Canzona degli uccellatori alle starne* (Example 4–7), Coppini used the same music for the two middle lines of the refrain (mm. 7–12 and 12–17), and he began the *volta* ("Vuolsi dunque aristiare") with a phrase he had previously set to the third line of the *piedi* ("Ci poteva insegnare").

Along with its ad hoc pattern of repetition—by no means an unusual feature of the canti carnascialeschi—Coppini's *Canzona degli uccellatori* displays certain other mannerisms characteristic of carnival songs. Most of them, for example, include brief sections in triple meter, either at the beginning of the *piedi*, as in Coppini's piece, or at the end of the *volta*. Most of them reduce the standard number of four voices to two or three for at least one passage in imitative counterpoint. And Coppini's composition is written in the typically homophonic texture of the canti carnascialeschi, even though the middle phrases of its *ripresa* are unusually contrapuntal. Florentine carnival songs differ from Mantuan frottole in many ways. For one thing, the style of the carnival songs does not show any clear-cut relationship with the techniques of the earlier fifteenth-century improvisers. And their texture, in spite of excursions into triple meter and passages in two- or three-part imitative counterpoint, is usually much plainer than that of frottole, with their polarized sopranos and basses held together by busy inner voices. Many sections of the carnival songs are almost completely homorhythmic; their inner voices are not nearly so active as those in frottole; and in many the superius and tenor might almost form self-sufficient two-part counterpoint, an indication that in some ways Florentine music was closer than the frottole to Franco-Netherlandish polyphony.

EXAMPLE 4–7. Alessandro Coppini, *Canzona degli ucellatori alle starne*, mm. 1–47. Used by permission of the American Institute of Musicology.

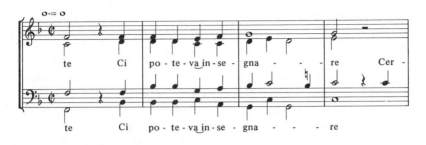

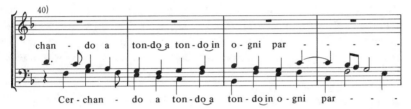

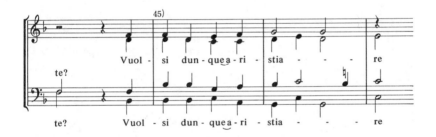

No one could mistake Bartolomeo degli Organi's three-part setting of *Un dì lieto già mai* (Example 4–8), a ballata attributed to Lorenzo the Magnificent, either for a Mantuan frottola or for a French chanson. Yet it partakes of some of the features of both, with, on the one hand, its clear chordal orientation, and, on the other, its sensitively shaped melodic lines. The settings by Bartolomeo and other Florentine composers of ballate and closely related kinds of poetry, more serious in tone than carnival songs, are by no means models of complex and highly refined contrapuntal technique. Bartolomeo's setting is fundamentally as chordal as any frottola and, indeed, more obviously so, since it is more starkly homorhythmic. In this respect it is not dissimilar to the setting of the same poem by the Netherlander Heinrich Isaac. And yet the words of Bartolomeo's song, unlike those in frottole, can be added to the three lower voices without any difficulty at all; they were obviously intended to be sung. A four-part or even five-part texture in which all of the melodic lines are vocally conceived became a hallmark of early sixteenth-century

Franco-Netherlandish music, as we shall see. Albeit with very different effect, the Florentines adopted the same techniques in elaborating their simple harmonic schemes.

The kind of interpenetration between Italianate harmony and Franco-Netherlandish polyphony that was to characterize the sixteenth century Italian madrigal can already be seen in Bernardo Pisano's settings, published in 1520, of Petrarch's canzoni, one of the first volumes printed by Petrucci to be devoted to a single Italian composer. The volume reflects the interest of early sixteenth-century Italian musicians in poetry of high literary quality, and it reveals how they came to give up their schematic settings of predetermined poetic forms in favor of freer kinds of poems (canzoni and madrigals) which they could treat phrase by phrase, in through-composed settings that attempt to reflect the special shape or character of each line of verse.

EXAMPLE 4–8. Bartolomeo degli Organi, *Un dì lieto già mai*, mm. 1–10. Used by permission of the American Institute of Musicology.

LAUDE AND
OTHER ITALIAN SACRED MUSIC

Many Italian composers of the late fifteenth and early sixteenth centuries worked in princely courts where their principal responsibilities were to supply secular music for the enjoyment of the courtiers. Some, notably the Florentines Coppini and Bartolomeo degli Organi, held positions at churches as choirmasters, organists, or singers. They certainly wrote sacred music as a part of their duties, but much of it is now lost. The fragments that survive do not suggest that any Italian composers of the time could rival in the quality of their achievement the great Franco-Netherlanders then employed in most of the leading churches and cathedrals. Petrucci published two volumes of Lamentations of Jeremiah in 1506 and included in them several predominantly chordal settings by Italians, among them one by Tromboncino and a *Passio sacra* by Francesco d'Ana that is surprisingly expressive considering its economy of means. Manuscript sources contain several late fifteenth-century Italian passions in which the dramatic story is told in a mixture of chant and simple polyphony. Coppini and Bartolomeo degli Organi composed motets in a polyphonic style not unlike that of the Franco-Netherlanders, and Coppini even wrote a Mass based on Alexander Agricola's three-part motet *Si dedero*. And Knud Jeppesen in his three volumes of *Italia sacra musica* (Copenhagen, 1962) supplies examples of sacred music written by Italian composers during the first half of the sixteenth century.

The largest corpus of Italian sacred music written about 1500, however, consists of laude. These hymns of praise and devotion, most of them set to Italian words though some are in Latin, were intended for performance by laymen and especially by members of *Compagnie de Laudesi* (companies of lauda singers), which existed everywhere in Italy at that time, but particularly in Florence. St. Francis of Assisi wrote laude as early as the thirteenth century, and they were sung by the numerous penitential fraternities of the fourteenth century. But by 1500 companies of lauda singers were simply groups that met regularly for devotional purposes and for singing, especially hymns of praise to the Virgin Mary. An account from mid-sixteenth-century Florence describes how one society, made up mostly of artisans, met in a church every Saturday after nones. Their procedures were probably quite typical. After singing a number of laude, their simple ceremony concluded when a picture of the Virgin was unveiled to the accompaniment of song and organ music.

In keeping with their homely social function, laude were sung to simple poems that resemble folk songs, popular songs, or fundamentalist hymns. Some are enthusiastically devotional:

> Senza te, sacra regina,
> Non si pò in ciel salire,
> L'alma sua non pò perire
> Che a te serve, a te s'inclina . . .

("Without you, sacred queen, we cannot go to heaven; if we serve you and bow before you, our souls will not die.") Others have a fresh naïveté characteristic of popular poetry:

> Ognun driza al ciel el viso
> E comenza a caminare.
> Su su su, che stiam a fare,
> Su su, tutti al paradiso!

("Everyone should turn his gaze to heaven and start to walk; up, up, you laggards, let's all go to paradise!") Many laude borrow the formal schemes of their secular counterparts—barzellette, strambotti, odes, capitoli, and so on—while some are uncomplicated strophic poems.

Many monophonic laude survive from the later Middle Ages, and it seems likely that they continued to be sung as unaccompanied melodies throughout the fifteenth century. Indeed, lauda texts were imposed on secular songs, both monophonic and polyphonic, throughout the sixteenth century. Several sixteenth-century collections of lauda texts exist, and they indicate the secular tunes to which the poems were meant to be sung. But polyphonic laude, either newly composed or based on pre-existing melodies, began to be written in the fifteenth century. The largest collections of them are two volumes published by Petrucci in 1507 and 1508, the first composed entirely by an otherwise unknown composer, Innocentius Dammonis, and the second consisting of works by musicians familiar to us from Petrucci's frottola books, not only Tromboncino and Cara, but also Giacomo Fogliano, Paulus Scotus, Piero da Lodi, Josquin, and others.

Musically the laude are as simple as their texts. Those based on secular forms resemble frottole in every way. For instance, *Vengo a te, madre Maria* (Example 4–9) by Giacomo Fogliano (or Don Nicolo?) even uses the typical dance rhythms of the frottola, though the triple meter with hemiola is interrupted at some cadences by one bar in duple meter which breaks the forward motion. Like a frottola, too, the inner voices of *Vengo a te* are more active than the soprano or bass. Some laude, on the other hand, are much more strictly homorhythmic; all the voices move together, generally at a slightly slower pace than the more frottolistic examples—that is, mostly in whole or half notes. And the greater solemnity of their rhythm is usually matched by the greater piety of their texts.

EXAMPLE 4–9. Giacomo Fogliano (or Don Nicolo?), *Vengo a te, madre Maria*, mm. 1–4. Used by permission of Mrs. Alice Jeppesen.

BIBLIOGRAPHICAL NOTES

On the musical institutions of fifteenth-century Italy and the interplay between Flemish and Italian musicians, see Nanie Bridgman, *La vie musicale au quattrocento* (Paris, 1964); and Nino Pirrotta, "Music and Cultural Tendencies in 15th-Century Italy," *Journal of the American Musicological Society*, 19 (1966). On courtly improvisers, see Walter Rubsamen, *Literary Sources of Secular Music in Italy (ca. 1500)* (Berkeley and Los Angeles, 1943); Walter Rubsamen, "The Justiniane or Viniziane of the 15th Century," *Acta musicologica*, 29 (1957); and Emile Haraszti, "La technique des improvisateurs latins et de langue vulgaire au XVe siècle," *Revue belge de musicologie*, 9 (1955). Music for the *lira da braccio* is discussed in Howard Mayer Brown, *Sixteenth-Century Instrumentation: The Music for the Florentine Intermedii* (American Institute of Musicology, 1974).

Petrucci's first three books of frottole are reprinted in Gaetano Cesari, Raffaello Monterosso, and Benvenuto Disertori, eds., *Le Frottole nell'edizione principe di Ottaviano Petrucci* (Cremona, 1954). The first and fourth books are reprinted in Rudolf Schwartz, ed., *Ottaviano Petrucci: Frottole I und IV* (Leipzig, 1935). Another volume of frottole has been published in modern edition as Alfred Einstein, ed., *Canzoni Sonetti*

Strambotti e Frottole, Libro Tertio (Andrea Antico, 1517), Smith College *Music Archives*, vol. 4 (Northampton, Mass., 1941). The best summary of the frottola repertory is still that in Einstein, *The Italian Madrigal* (Princeton, 1949, 3 vols.). See also Knud Jeppesen, *La Frottola* (Copenhagen, 1968–70, 3 vols.); and, on the transition from frottola to madrigal, Rubsamen, "From Frottola to Madrigal," in *Chanson and Madrigal, 1480–1530*, ed. James Haar (Cambridge, Mass., 1964). Franciscus Bossinensis's arrangements of frottole for voice and lute have been reprinted in Benvenuto Disertori, ed., *Le Frottole per canto e liuto intabulate da Franciscus Bossinensis* (Milan, 1964).

The standard work on canti carnascialeschi remains Federico Ghisi, *I canti carnascialeschi nelle fonti musicali del XV e XVI secoli* (Florence, 1937). All extant texts are published in *Canti Carnascialeschi del Rinascimento*, ed. Charles S. Singleton (Bari, 1936, 2 vols.). A substantial number of examples appear in Paul-Marie Masson, ed., *Chants de carnaval florentins* (Paris, 1913), and K. Westphal, ed., *Karnevalslieder der Renaissance, Das Chorwerk*, vol. 43 (Wolfenbüttel, 1936). The series *Music of the Florentine Renaissance*, ed. Frank A. D'Accone, *Corpus Mensurabilis Musicae*, series 32 (American Institute of Musicology, 1966–   ), includes as its first volume the collected works of Bernardo Pisano and as its second volume the collected works of Alessandro Coppini, Bartolomeo degli Organi, and Giovanni Serragli, plus three anonymous works. On Florentine musicians, see also Frank A. D'Accone, "Alessandro Coppini and Bartolomeo degli Organi—two Florentine composers of the Renaissance," *Analecta musicologica*, 4 (1967), and D'Accone, "Bernardo Pisano, an Introduction to his Life and Works," *Musica Disciplina*, 17 (1963).

On laude, see Knud Jeppesen, *Die mehrstimmige italienische Laude um 1500* (Leipzig, 1935), which includes a representative selection of works from Petrucci's two volumes of laude.

FIVE

JOSQUIN DES PREZ

If Dufay formed the central musical language of the Renaissance, Josquin des Prez and his contemporaries—the composers born in the 1440's, 1450's and 1460's—modified it in significant ways and created thereby an infinitely sensitive means of communication—more flexible, more expressive, and more adaptable to composers' ideas than music had ever been before. The incredibly productive generation of northern musicians whose careers span the several decades before and after 1500 —in the first place Josquin, but also Obrecht, Isaac, Agricola, Compère, Pierre de la Rue, and many others—transformed music by the force of their creative energy and by forging new techniques whose implications were not fully worked out until the very end of the sixteenth century. The years about 1500 are a watershed in the history of music. The High Renaissance was the age of Josquin.

The new style came about by means of a series of interrelated factors. The confrontation between Franco-Netherlandish and Italian musical cultures resulted in a greater chordal orientation in northern polyphony and a new awareness on the part of the northerners of harmonic possibilities and of the organizing force of tonality. For the first time, Franco-Netherlandish composers took a serious interest in the relationship between text and music. They began to explore the ways in which their melodies could reflect the shape and even the meanings of the words set to them. This lesson, too, they may have learned from Italian musicians.

Although the use of cantus firmi remained a central technical resource of composers throughout the sixteenth century and even later, musicians about 1500 made a decisive step forward in liberating themselves from the scaffolding techniques of the later Middle Ages, which forced upon them predetermined elements of design in planning their compositions. They began to work with motives as the smallest units of musical construction. By this means they could create long movements which consisted of chains of interlocked phrases, each of them devoted to the manipulation of a single motive. In its classical formulation in the sixteenth century, this technique of creating musical form produces a series of "points of imitation," interrupted for variety and contrast by occasional chordal passages. Freed from the need to base his structure on a pre-existing melody, the composer could plan his composition without recourse to any predetermined scheme, and he could vary the texture and change the character of the music at will, shifting from full sounds to thin and from strict imitative counterpoint to dialogue among parts of the choir to thickly scored chords as his mood and the musical requirements dictated. It is no exaggeration to say that the new technique of interlocked phrases, each of them unified motivically, emancipated music; for the first time the art was fully autonomous, its basic organizing principle purely musical and generated by the medium itself rather than by formal convention or by the constricting demands of a pre-existing melody.

Before composers could exercise this new freedom to control at will the details of form and texture, they needed to abandon the accepted medieval method of composing one line at a time, building up the voices around the cantus firmus, and writing each out from beginning to end before the next was conceived. They needed to be able to work with all levels and all voices at once. Successive composition probably gave way to simultaneous composition in the middle of the fifteenth century; the Italian theorist Pietro Aaron was the first person to recommend the new method, in a book published during the first quarter of the sixteenth century.

These new techniques radically changed the way individual voices related to one another and hence the way music actually sounded. As we have seen, both Dufay (especially in his later years) and Ockeghem tended to de-emphasize the differences among various voices. But each strand in the contrapuntal fabric did not become fully equal until the very end of the century, in the music of Josquin and his contemporaries. Perhaps the most obvious result of the innovations of this generation of composers was the change from a hierarchical texture, in which each voice has a special function, to a texture in which all the voices, while independent, are equal in importance and in melodic style. This new sonority is sometimes described as a combination of melodic lines that are all vocal in conception. But though each line can in fact easily be sung—a feature that distinguishes the new music from many earlier compositions—pieces in the new style were not always performed exclusively by *a cappella* choirs. Some organizations, like the Sistine Chapel in Rome, did exclude instruments from the performance of sacred music, but in all probability most choirs sometimes sang with instruments and sometimes without. The "*a cappella* ideal" (a term that used to be associated with sixteenth-century music) has, then, little or no historical validity, even though it does draw attention to the homogeneous texture of much of this music, a texture that sounds well, it must be admitted, whether played by groups of like instruments—consorts of flutes, recorders, or viols, for example—or sung by consorts of unaccompanied voices.

An unusually large number of distinguished composers worked during the last several decades of the fifteenth and the first several of the sixteenth centuries. Of these, the greatest was Josquin des Prez. This was recognized by his contemporaries. Martin Luther, for example, wrote that Josquin alone was master of the notes, which must do as he wishes; other composers do as the notes wish. And the Florentine writer Cosimo Bartoli, in recounting in 1543 the recent history of music, compares Ockeghem to Donatello, both of whom rediscovered an art that was almost dead, whereas Josquin is likened to Michelangelo: they are both wonders of nature who have brought their art to such a peak of perfection that they have no rivals. A letter dated September 2, 1495, and addressed to Duke Hercules d'Este I of Ferrara by his secretary acknowledges backhandedly the high esteem in which Josquin was held while at the same time revealing something of the composer's personality. The Duke was seeking a composer for his court, and his secretary urged him to hire Isaac rather than Josquin, because Isaac "is able to get on better with his colleagues and composes new pieces quicker. It is true, Josquin composes better, but he does it only when it suits him and not when it is requested. More than this, Josquin asks 200 ducats while Isaac is pleased with 120." (It speaks well for the Duke that he ignored his secretary's advice and hired Josquin.)

But for all that his genius was properly recognized, in his own lifetime and later, Josquin has not been studied as thoroughly as many other great masters, and some basic questions about his life and works remain unanswered. We do not know, for example, what part he himself took in forging the new style during its formative years at the end of the fifteenth century. We do not know precisely where he worked during various periods of his life. And we cannot yet arrange his works in chronological order with any degree of assurance. A part of the problem of constucting a chronology for Josquin's works is that we cannot associate many works with specific events in his life, and there seem to be relatively few compositions by him in sources before 1500. We are particularly ignorant, then, about his earliest works, perhaps because so many manuscripts have been lost, or perhaps because he himself was extremely self-critical and destroyed or otherwise prevented his early compositions from being circulated. Petrucci printed some of them in his publications after 1501, and he devoted three volumes exclusively to Josquin's Masses. But many of his works, most unusually, were printed for the first time some years after his death. Beginning in the 1530's, Josquin's Masses, motets, and chansons appeared in publications everywhere in northern Europe. These late sources give us many compositions by Josquin that would otherwise be lost to us, though unfortunately they do not always offer the most trustworthy readings. That musicians throughout the century were obviously still so deeply interested in Josquin's music is a very remarkable tribute to the composer in an age when music went out of fashion rapidly; compositions twenty or more years old were normally considered unworthy of performance.

One of the great international figures of his time, Josquin cannot be associated with a single court, a single ruler, or a single locality, unless it be the land of his birthplace, Picardy, to which he returned as an old man. He traveled extensively and worked in various cities during his long and productive life. Neither the place nor the date of his birth is known precisely. He was probably born in the province of Vermandois in Picardy about 1440, and he may have been a choirboy in the capital city of Vermandois, at the collegiate church in St. Quentin. It is possible, too, that he studied with Ockeghem; he certainly felt close ties with the older composer, since he based several compositions on melodies by Ockeghem and wrote a lament on his death.

The first solidly documented event in Josquin's career dates from 1459, when the young man was appointed a singer at the Cathedral of Santa Maria Maggiore in Milan, a position he held until 1472. The Duke of Milan, Galeazzo Maria Sforza, had assembled a brilliant group of musicians at his court, including, as we have seen, Agricola, Weerbecke, Compère, and Johannes Martini. Josquin joined them and stayed on after Galeazzo Maria was murdered in 1476.

During his years in Milan Josquin had come to know Galeazzo Maria's younger brother Cardinal Ascanio Sforza, and he may have joined the cardinal's entourage after leaving Milan about 1479. Several frottole printed by Petrucci are attributed to "Jusquin d'Ascanio," and the poet-musician Serafino dall'Aquila addressed a poem to Josquin, his companion in service, in which he alludes to their difficulties in getting paid by the cardinal. The Swiss theorist Glareanus reports, too, that Josquin's *Missa La sol fa re mi* was written on a cantus firmus derived from the first line of one of Serafino's satirical poems on the same subject, beginning "Lassa far a mi" ("Leave it to me"). Ascanio introduced the composer to Roman musical circles, and subsequently Josquin joined the Papal chapel, where he sang intermittently from about 1486 until at least 1494, serving under two Popes, Innocent VIII and the Borgia, Alexander VI, and perhaps keeping close contact with Ascanio, for whom he may even have worked during his frequent absences from the Papal payroll.

Eventually Josquin left Rome. He may have gone to Ferrara to work for Duke Hercules d'Este I, for whom he wrote his *Missa Hercules Dux Ferrariae,* but no documents record his arrival in Ferrara. We have seen that the Duke was interested in him as early as 1495, and Josquin is known to have made a trip to Flanders from 1501 to 1503 to recruit singers for the Duke's chapel. The Burgundian Duke, Philip the Handsome, tried unsuccessfully to get Josquin to accompany him on a trip to Spain in 1501. And Josquin visited the court of France during that year: the Ferrarese ambassador reports speaking with him at Blois, and Glareanus recounts two anecdotes involving King Louis XII which may date from this period. Josquin is said to have composed his Psalm setting, *Memor esto verbi tui,* to remind the king of a prebend that had been promised him. And when the king asked for a song in which he could join, Josquin wrote *Guillaume s'en va chauffer,* with a drone for his royal patron.

Josquin seems to have left Ferrara even before Duke Hercules died in 1505, and he spent most of his last fifteen years or so in or near his homeland. He may not actually have been in the service of the French king about 1512, but he almost certainly had some connection with the court. Many of his melancholy chansons, especially those in five and six parts, may have been written for Marguerite of Austria, after he had become provost of the chapter in the small town of Condé-sur-l'Escaut, where he spent his last years and where he died, probably on August 27, 1521. Less than a year before his death he had personally presented Marguerite of Austria's nephew, the Emperor Charles V, with some "*chansons nouvelles,*" including perhaps *Mille regretz,* which was labeled "*La canción del Emperador*" when it was published in 1538 in an arrangement for vihuela by Luis de Narváez.

JOSQUIN'S MOTETS

About twenty Masses, seventy-five secular pieces, and one hundred motets by Josquin survive. In many ways his greatness and individuality are displayed more clearly in his motets than in the other genres. Unhampered by the unchanging words of the Mass Ordinary and thus free to choose the texts that most stimulated his imagination, Josquin could display in his motets his boldest compositional inventiveness and sustain a level of expressive intensity altogether new in the history of music. Josquin's motets embody the innovations of his distinguished generation at their very best. Here the new equal-voiced polyphony built in interlocked phrases took root and flowered in its freshest and finest form. Moreover, Josquin cultivated the motet throughout his long and productive life. By examining a few examples from his early, middle, and late years we can gain some impression of his development as a composer, even though the details of his chronology have yet to be worked out.

It is clear from the few motets that can safely be assigned to his Milanese years (1459–ca. 79) that Josquin began his career by writing music in the tradition of Dufay and Ockeghem. Dufay, for example, might almost have composed the duos formed of long melismatic lines that open *Illibata Dei virgo nutrix,* a rhymed prayer to the Virgin Mary for which Josquin possibly wrote the words as well as the music, since they reveal his name in an acrostic; the motet is built over a cantus firmus that translates "Maria" into musical terms by assigning a solmization syllable to each vowel, la mi la (A E A, or, as transposed in the motet, D A D and G D G). In *Alma redemptoris mater / Ave Regina caelorum,* a motet which paraphrases one Marian antiphon in the outer voices and another in the inner voices, Josquin may actually quote Ockeghem, who began his paraphrase of *Alma redemptoris* in exactly the same way. Josquin's motet starts with three long melismatic duos, but in the middle of the third the other voices enter and lead to a tutti cadence which divides the first part into two halves. The high proportion of two- and three-part writing produces an open texture filled, as it were, with light and air, a texture characteristic of much of Josquin's music. Even in these early pieces, the melodic relationships among voices—in *Alma redemptoris mater* notably the imitations between each of the pairs of voices sharing the same antiphon—create a texture unified motivically to some extent, though the voices often move at varying rates of speed and thus sound "layered." The individual lines are so melismatic that the words can be added to them in more than one stylistically acceptable way. Josquin had not yet begun to explore ways of connecting the text closely with its music. In short, *Alma redemptoris mater / Ave Regina caelorum* displays some of Josquin's characteristic mannerisms while still reflecting the compositional techniques of an earlier generation.

It is the music of Josquin's middle years, during the time he was in Rome (ca. 1480–ca. 94) and Ferrara (until about 1505) that he revealed his true greatness in a series of motets that represent the "classical" formulation of his style. Perhaps no motet better exemplifies Josquin's mastery than his setting of a rhymed prayer to the Virgin Mary, *Ave Maria . . . virgo serena* (Example 5–1), which is one of the best known of all his works. On the lowest level of detail the form of the piece is crystal clear, for each line of the text receives new music, which is composed in points of imitation (each of the first four lines of the poem); in paired duets with or without imitation (the fifth line, "Ave cujus conceptio," set as non-imitative duets with a third voice added in the answer); or in homorhythmic or nearly homorhythmic style (the final three lines of the example, beginning "Solemni plena gaudio"). Indeed, the opening points of imitation are striking (and unusual) in their classic simplicity, each voice singing little more than the motive shared by all the other voices. Even in this short example the flexibility of the imitative technique is obvious. The order of entries and the time interval between them, the ways in which each voice continues the head motive, the way in which each set of entries is overlapped, and so on, can all be modified or changed for each new section; the use of interlocking sections in imitation provides a groundplan capable of almost infinite variety.

A succession of unrelated phrases, however, does not make a well-formed piece of music. In *Ave Maria* Josquin took care to impose a shape that follows the quatrains into which the text falls. The first quatrain ends in m. 30 with a deceptive cadence after a brief section in which all four voices sing simultaneously for the first time. That cadence, however, is merely a passing point of articulation before the first major cadence in the piece, that in m. 53, the importance of which is underscored by several features: it is the first full V–I cadence (with 4–3 suspension) in the motet; a strong drive to this point of repose has been created by the sequence that builds up to a peak just before, and it occurs after the first extensive chordal section in the motet. Notable, too, is the way Josquin strove for melodic coherence by making the second couplet ("Dominus tecum," in m. 16ff) a melodic variant of the first couplet; both paraphrase the same chant in different ways.

The second quatrain ("Ave cujus," in m. 31ff) opens with a paired duet (albeit one in which the answer has a third voice added), one of the hallmarks of Josquin's style, and one of the chief ways by which he created open and spacious textures. Similarly, the remainder of the motet contains many such antiphonal passages, in which two of the voices are answered by two others. This stylistic mannerism, which led in the later sixteenth century to a more systematic exploration of antiphonal effects by *cori spezzati* (divided choirs), is but one of the ways in which Josquin worked with choral sonority, pitting low sounds against high, full against half choirs, and imitative polyphony against simple chords. A new interest in the sound of music—in its sensuous surface—marks the work of Josquin and his contemporaries.

EXAMPLE 5–1. Josquin, *Ave Maria,* mm. 1–53.

Perhaps, though, the first thing to strike the ear in hearing *Ave Maria* is the easy and natural way the words fit the music. There can be no doubt, for example, how the syllables of "Ave Maria" are to be sung to the notes intended for them, and the notes reinforce the natural text accents. Compared with the individual lines in *Alma redemptoris mater*

/ *Ave Regina caelorum,* those in *Ave Maria* are simple, straightforward, and eminently vocal in conception; they lack the extravagant melismas of the earlier motet and reflect Josquin's growing concern for the relationship between words and music. An interest in text declamation and a clarity of form engendered both by the technique of pervading imitation and by the use of cadential patterns and choral sonorities to shape isolated phrases into larger units characterize many of Josquin's mature works; these features help to explain why this music has lost none of its power and charm after more than 400 years.

Even the most contrapuntal sections of *Ave Maria* seem to be influenced by harmonic considerations (if only because the composer has taken such great care to prepare each cadence carefully). The chordal texture and clear tonal orientation of some passages inevitably remind the listener of Italian music of Josquin's time. But these same traits can be heard more clearly in those motets from Josquin's middle years that follow almost exactly the model of Italian laude—for example, *Tu solus qui facis mirabilia* and the Passion motets *O Domine Jesu Christe* and *Qui velatus facis fuisti.* The first named (Example 5–2) was even published as a contrafactum (that is, with a new text in Italian replacing the Latin) in one of Petrucci's volumes of laude (and it appeared, too, in place of a Mass movement in a "substitute Mass," a curious liturgical form associated particularly with Milan, in which motets replace the fixed and immutable words of the Mass Ordinary). *Tu solus* furnishes a striking contrast with other Netherlandish music of the time, even though the almost unrelieved chordal texture is interrupted from time to time by contrapuntal passages including paired duets and imitation. Almost every sonority in the motet is a full triad; almost all of its cadences are based on the progressions IV–I or V–I; and its melodic interest is subjugated almost completely to the harmonies. The conclusion is therefore inescapable that Josquin composed *Tu solus* under the influence of Italian musicians, who apparently began to compose in the new style about 1490. But Josquin may have learned to appreciate chordal harmony by listening to the same improvised music out of which frottole and laude developed; perhaps, then, Italian and Netherlandish cultures began to fuse at the same time that a nationalistic style grew up in the south.

Along with motets of great formal clarity and elegance, like *Ave Maria,* and those made up for the most part of simple successions of chords, like *Tu solus,* Josquin also composed in his middle or later years a series of long motets in five or six voices in which contrapuntal and harmonic elements are in perfect balance. The architectural quality of some of these impressive compositions manifests itself especially in the way the structure is planned around a cantus firmus. In *Praeter rerum seriem,* for example, the tenor and superius alternate phrases of the

EXAMPLE 5–2. Josquin, *Tu solus qui facis mirabilia*, mm. 1–15.

strophic sequence-like poem on which the motet is based. In *Domine Dominus noster* the short motto repeated five times in the tenor grows longer at each appearance (it is stated first in whole notes, then in dotted whole notes, double whole notes, and so on), perhaps to symbolize the way in which the praise of God grows in heaven and on earth. And Josquin's setting of the Marian sequence *Inviolata, integra et casta es* employs a canonic cantus firmus, one of his favorite scaffolding devices, in which the time of canonic entry decreases by one measure in each of the three parts. But these constructivist devices do not produce rigid and mechanical examples of number made audible; instead, the accompanying voices seem as free to expand and develop with irregular and subtle rhythms, contrasting melodies, and ever-changing contrapuntal combinations as though they were not controlled by the progress of the structural voices, and chordal passages interrupt the counterpoint from time to time to make their effective point. At the beginning of *Inviolata,* for example, the slow, metrical head motive of the cantus firmus contrasts strikingly with the exuberant downward run in the superius that traverses a tenth and appears with a slightly different accompaniment each time it repeats (Example 5–3). The third part of the motet, on the other hand, opens in near homophony with a chordal progression that is stated three times to invoke the Virgin ("O benigna, o regina, o Maria") before

EXAMPLE 5–3. Josquin, *Inviolata, integra et casta es, Maria,* mm. 1–16.

it broadens out into a fast-moving finale. Josquin's motets of this period demonstrate the myriad ways in which his imitative counterpoint is manipulated in the service of the texts.

The desire to express the text was surely Josquin's starting point in *Planxit autem David* (Motet 20 of the *Complete Works*), a setting of David's moving lament for Saul and Jonathan (2 Samuel 1) and one of the great masterpieces of the High Renaissance. No scaffolding device determines its structure. At most, some of the melody in the superius is derived from the chanting tone for the Lamentations in Holy Week. At the beginning, the subject is boldly announced like a title, in a harmonically static point of imitation, "Planxit autem David" ("Thus lamented David"). From there the music flows out in a series of phrases, often punctuated by pauses, in which sections of eminently harmonic counterpoint spiced with simple yet tellingly expressive dissonances are contrasted with chordal and declamatory passages and points of imitation. The shifting patterns of texture and choral sonority play a larger role in giving shape to David's words than does any more traditional musical technique.

Planxit autem David was first published in 1504, although it was probably written somewhat earlier. From about that time and through his later years Josquin produced a series of masterly motets that are the crowning achievements of his life. Among them are the earliest settings of complete psalms on such a grand scale, works like *Miserere mei, Deus* (Psalm 50) and *Memor esto verbi tui* (from Psalm 118), both composed in the first decade of the sixteenth century, the latter for King Louis XII of France, and *De profundis clamavi* (Psalm 129), the five-voiced motet that Josquin may have written for Louis's funeral in 1515. These and magnificent works like the sequence setting *Benedicta es, caelorum regina* and the Lord's Prayer, *Pater noster* (with *Ave Maria* as its secunda pars), display the composer's complete mastery of technique, the consummation of the marriage between Netherlandish counterpoint and Italianate harmony.

These late motets do not reflect any sharp break with Josquin's past. Rather, they extend and develop tendencies found in the earlier works. Above all, they are distinguished for their expressiveness and for the way text and music are inextricably bound together. As Lowinsky writes in his commentary on the *Miserere mei, Deus* found in the Medici Codex, "Josquin has arrived at a new concept: music as an artistic projection, elevation, and intensification of the spoken word."

In *Miserere mei, Deus,* Josquin's involvement with the text is revealed even in the motto which underlies the composition and serves both as cantus firmus and refrain. A syllabic recitation on two notes, it is in its simplicity a direct cry for mercy. Josquin repeated it over and over again as a cantus firmus on scale degrees that descend stepwise through an octave in the first part, ascend an octave (in rhythmic diminution) in the second part, and descend a fifth in the third part. This scheme is not as rigid as it seems, since the appearances of the motto do not follow a preconceived plan. The tenor states the theme at irregular time intervals, depending on the length of the verses and the emphasis Josquin wished to put on certain parts of the text. Moreover the other voices join the tenor each time in singing "Miserere mei, Deus" either in imitation or in near homophony, and these tutti passages, the only ones in the motet, give the composition a dramatic shape. In short, the compact and elegantly concise melodies in the motet, shorn of extraneous melismas, vividly interpret the text they carry. The rhythms of these melodic lines mirror the accents in individual words, and their overall contours (the way the high points are prepared, for example) throw into relief important words and phrases. A master of vocal sonority, Josquin loved to play off parts of the choir against each other. Much of *Miserere mei, Deus* is written in two- or three-part counterpoint, and this variety of vocal scoring is another element that helps to make the words clearly audible.

Many of the same stylistic traits can be found in other late Josquin motets. *Pater noster,* for example, reveals the same concern for clarity and simplicity. Its text is declaimed with great economy of means and an apparent dramatic freedom that belies the presence of a canonic cantus firmus, which is so well integrated into the texture that it can scarcely be perceived. *Memor esto verbi tui* ends with a recapitulation of the opening material in diminution, a structural pun that underlines the meaning of the first verse, "Remember thy word to thy servant." And the moving lament, *Absalon, fili mi,* reaches new heights of expression, especially in a sequence that moves downwards in a circle of fifths through progressively flatter keys (both D♭ and G♭ are actually signed in the earlier sources, while the later ones transpose the motet up a ninth), a progression that not only demonstrates the composer's success in exploring the outer limits of musical space, but also symbolizes the idea of a descent into hell in an almost physically palpable way.

In his motets Josquin used all of the compositional procedures available to him. As we have seen, he composed many motets over a cantus firmus, the most important structural device he inherited from his predecessors. Others of his compositions paraphrase a plainchant. And still others are completely free of borrowed material; they are organized around successive points of imitation or else they follow the dictates of the text. In some motets the cantus firmus is stated in the "classical" manner by an inner voice, usually the tenor, in note values slower than those of the other voices. Often when Josquin adopted this technique, he devised a rational plan slightly more complicated than a mere single statement of the borrowed material. In *Huc me sydereo* for example, the plainchant *Plangent eum* occurs three times in rhythmic values that decrease with each statement in simple arithmetical proportion. Not infrequently, Josquin's cantus firmus is associated with a text different from that sung by the other voices, as in *Huc me sydereo;* and in some compositions the borrowed voice alludes to a secular melody, as in *Missus est Gabriel* where the tenor sings Latin words to the tenor of Busnois's *A une dame j'ai fait veu*. Many of Josquin's cantus firmi are ostinatos, like those in *Illibata Dei virgo nutrix* and *Miserere mei, Deus,* either strictly or freely handled with regard to the timing of their appearances. And Josquin had a penchant for canonic cantus firmi, like those in *Pater noster* and in *Ut Phoebi radiis*. Some canons support the surrounding luxuriant counterpoint in an obvious way, while others are smoothly incorporated into the texture. Clearly, then, Josquin did not feel himself uncomfortably restricted by the restraints of a cantus firmus.

Josquin seldom paraphrased a chant melody by stating it with ornamental variation complete in one voice of a motet, in the manner of Dufay or Dunstable. Josquin's use of the technique, in fact, often does not actually influence the structure of his composition. More often than not, he used the chant as a repository, as it were, for melodic ideas, and borrowed whatever fragments he wished to serve as points of imitation or as motives that dominate single sections of a work, as, for example, in *Domine non secundum peccata* and *Liber generationis*. In *Alma redemptoris mater / Ave Regina caelorum* he paraphrased the two chants in a variety of ways, while in *Ave Maria* he departed from the chant paraphrase after the first few phrases and continued his music without reference to borrowed material. In other settings of sequence-like texts, built in double versicles, he sometimes varied the paraphrase of each melodic phrase that is repeated, to produce a so-called variation-chain sequence, as in *Inviolata integra* and *Victimae paschali laudes*. And in some motets, like *Planxit autem David,* and especially his psalm settings, he merely alluded to chant for a few sections in each work.

Imitative technique, or rather the technique of organizing a long composition as a series of interlocked sections, enabled Josquin to abandon older devices of basing new music on pre-existing melodies. Many of his motets, like *Dominus regnavit, Absalon, fili mi,* and most of his psalm settings, are wholly or mostly free of any borrowed material. Form and shape are given to the music by the relationship of sections to each other or by the way in which the text is declaimed in a quasi-dramatic manner. In some of these motets, order is imposed on the music by formally significant repetitions of material, as in *Memor esto verbi tui,* with its recapitulation, or the long *Qui velatus facie fuisti* in six *partes,* with the endings of *partes* 1 and 2, and 4 and 6, being musically alike.

The texts Josquin chose for his motets can be divided roughly into three large categories: those taken from liturgical books and thus prescribed for the Mass or Canonical Hours; those taken from the Bible; and a miscellaneous group neither liturgical nor Biblical that includes prayers, poems of devotion, songs of praise, and the like, many of them addressed to or in honor of Christ or the Virgin Mary. The third category is necessarily the least well defined. Even its extent can scarcely be described with precision, since the liturgical uses of motet texts in the Renaissance have not yet been fully investigated. Perhaps we shall eventually discover that all of Josquin's motets were intended for performance in ritual or votive services in royal chapels or collegiate churches. In the meantime, though, we must recognize that a group of Josquin's motets seem to be based on devotional (rather than liturgical) poems, some of them newly composed, like the two Marian compositions *Illibata Dei virgo nutrix* and *O Virgo prudentissima,* the latter a rhymed prayer by the Florentine poet Angelo Poliziano.

More than half of Josquin's 100-odd motet texts have been found in early liturgical books. Some of them were intended for performance as a part of the Mass Proper, especially as gospel lessons or as sequences. But most of them, including those for some twenty-five psalm settings and thirteen Marian antiphons, belong to those shorter, votive services (such as matins and lauds) that consist of psalms, antiphons, responsories, lessons, and prayers and that comprise the Canonical Hours or Divine Offices. And many or all of the psalm settings may have been simply devotional and extra-liturgical. Besides these, Josquin also composed music for a handful of prayers to be said before or during the Mass or Offices. The composer's concern to relate his music closely to the text extended even to placing the motets firmly within their liturgical context by means of their cantus firmi. Without exception, whenever Josquin set a liturgical text that was associated with its own plainchant, he used the sacred melody as a cantus firmus on which to base his own polyphony.

Some of Josquin's Biblical texts quote scripture verbatim, and others put together fragments from various parts of the Bible. Many of them were used because they had a place in the liturgy. Of his relatively few works based on New Testament texts, for example, *In illo tempore stetit Jesu in medio discipulorum* was intended as the gospel on the Tuesday after Easter, *In principio erat verbum* for the third Mass on Christmas day as well as various other feasts, and *Missus est Gabriel* for the Feast of the Annunciation. The greater number of Old Testament texts were mostly chosen for similar reasons, though the occasion is not always obvious, and some may have been inspired by particular events. It has been suggested, for example, that *Absalon, fili mi* may have been written either for the Emperor Maximilian I of Austria after his son,

Philip the Handsome, died in 1506, or for Pope Alexander VI when his favorite son, Juan, Duke of Gandia, was murdered in 1497. Among the motets based on Old Testament texts, the twenty-five psalm settings hold the place of honor, both numerically and for their general excellence. That Josquin was among the first to set psalms polyphonically may merely reflect the changing liturgical practices of the time, but possibly he was attracted to them for purely subjective reasons. The highly poetic, emotional, and colorful language of David's songs of praise must have appealed to Josquin for the opportunities they afforded him to invent an extraordinarily expressive music, human and personal, that was in every way worthy of the exalted words it set.

JOSQUIN'S MASSES

If Josquin's motets reveal him to be a composer intent above all else on reflecting in his music both the outward form and the inner meaning of the words he set—he was the first composer fully aware that music can be the art that most directly touches human sensibilities—his Masses show off his consummate craftsmanship, his incredible ability to build vast and magnificent structures of sound. The ritual character of the Mass Ordinary must inevitably have suggested to a Renaissance musician that he should put little stress on a subjective interpretation of the text. And the very length of the Mass seldom allowed a composer to lavish on single words and idiosyncratic readings of their meanings the sort of care that he could give in shorter motets. Josquin's Masses, then, display more obviously than do his motets the musically constructivist side of his personality.

We have seen that Josquin's art became simpler, terser, and more eloquent as he grew older. It may be, then, that the complex structures of his Masses reflect the fact that they occupied the center of his attention in his middle years. But that hypothesis still needs to be thoroughly tested. The chronology of Josquin's Masses is a subject still being debated, and even the authenticity of some of the works ascribed to him has recently been successfully challenged. For example, the *Missa Da pacem* may more convincingly be attributed to Noel Bauldewyn, and Josquin probably did not compose the *Missa Allez regretz* given him in the edition of his complete works. Both Masses are found only in sources prepared long after the composer's death. Neither appears, for example, among the three volumes containing seventeen Masses by Josquin first published by Petrucci in 1502, 1505, and 1514 (and reprinted several times thereafter), collections that testify to the esteem in which the composer was held even during his own lifetime. Petrucci issued very few books devoted to the music of a single composer, and no more than one such volume for any musician except Josquin.

The Masses can conveniently be divided into three categories according to the compositional process involved. Josquin wrote some of them around cantus firmi; in others he paraphrased a pre-existing melody; and he organized two, the *Missa Ad fugam* and the *Missa Sine nomine*, around cycles of canons. The cantus-firmus Masses make up the largest group. As scaffolding he chose secular melodies slightly more often than sacred, perhaps because the clear phrase divisions of chansons served better to support large structures. Some of these secular melodies were apparently originally monophonic popular tunes, like *L'Ami Baudichon*, which appears as a cantus firmus in what seems to be Josquin's earliest Mass. But at other times he used single voices from polyphonic compositions, like the tenor of Robert Morton's chanson *N'auray je jamais mieulx*, which underlies the *Missa Di dadi*, so-called because the earliest edition indicated the mensural proportion governing the relationship of the cantus firmus to the other voices by reproducing before each movement dice faces (*dadi*, in Italian) with varying numbers of dots. Most of Josquin's sacred cantus firmi derive from plainchant, as in *Missa Gaudeamus*, *Missa Ave maris stella*, and *Missa De beata vergine*, the last based not on a single melody but on a series of chants that originally set the various movements of the Gregorian Ordinary (the Kyrie and Gloria come from the present-day plainchant Mass IX in the *Liber Usualis*, the Credo from Credo I, and the Sanctus and Agnus from Mass IV). And two of Josquin's cantus firmi involve musical puns on solmization syllables. The *Missa Hercules Dux Ferrariae* is built on the vowels of the title in the following manner:

Her-	cu-	les	Dux	Fer-	ra-	ri-	(a)e	
re	ut	re	ut	re	fa	mi	re	
D	C	D	C	D	F	E	D	(and its transpositions).

And the *Missa La sol fa re mi* unfolds over the ostinato A G F D E and its transpositions, which may ultimately refer, as we have seen, to a line of Italian poetry, "Lassa far a mi."

In some of the Masses, Josquin lays out the cantus firmus following a strictly rational plan in the manner of Dufay, with rigid mensural relationships governing the time values in the recurring statements of the borrowed melody. In the *Missa Hercules Dux Ferrariae*, for example, the subject derived from the vowels (that is, the *soggetto cavato dalle vocali*, or, more simply, the *soggetto cavato*) appears three times during each movement or section of a movement, first on d, then a fifth higher on a, and lastly an octave above the original statement, on d'. The only exceptions to this arrangement occur on the several occasions where the groups of three statements are presented in retrograde motion and in descending order, on d', a and d; and at the beginning of the Sanctus, where the subject is given only once. The speed of each group of subjects is regulated by a simple proportional scheme. Four groups of subjects appear, for instance, in the Credo (the third group in retrograde motion), and they move in progressively smaller (that is, faster) note values, in the relationship 3:2:2:1. Similarly, the *Missa L'homme armé super voces musicales* is organized around a rational and preconceived cantus firmus. The long secular melody is sung at least once complete in each movement, but on ascending scale degrees (that is, "super voces musicales"): the *L'homme armé* tune appears on C in the Kyrie, on D (in both normal and retrograde form) in the Gloria, on E (both normal and retrograde) in the Credo, and so on. Interestingly, the mode of the Mass remains the same throughout; Josquin composed accompanying polyphony in the Dorian mode regardless of the changing pitch level of the scaffolding voice. On the other hand, his other setting of a Mass Ordinary based on the same melody, the *Missa L'Homme armé sexti toni* (that is, in the sixth or Hypolydian mode on F), employs a much more informal structural plan. The borrowed melody appears either in the tenor, the bass, or the superius, but not always in the same rhythmic shape (which changes according to the dictates of the polyphony rather than following a preconceived plan), and free melodic material is sometimes interpolated between statements of the cantus firmus. While the borrowed melody is usually clearly distinguishable from the other voices, it does not control the structure of the music to nearly the same extent as do the more rigidly predetermined cantus firmi. In fact, this rather informal attitude towards the disposition of his borrowed material characterizes many of Josquin's Masses, for example, *Missa Ave maris stella, Missa Malheur me bat,* and *Missa Una musque de Buscaya.* It may be that his attitude towards cantus-firmus technique changed with the years and that we can, therefore, date his Masses approximately on that basis. Perhaps he devised the more rigid schemes early in his career and felt free to vary the way they were used during his middle years.

In planning his Masses, Josquin followed certain formal conventions that had been established by his time and continued more or less unchanged throughout the sixteenth century. For example, the Christe sections in most Masses contrast markedly with the Kyries that surround them—often the Christe is much more transparent in texture, with a greater proportion of two- and three-part counterpoint; sometimes it proceeds under a different mensuration sign. The first phrase in both the Gloria and the Credo movements is invariably intoned in chant by the officiating priest before the polyphony begins, a carryover from the manner of performing the Gregorian Mass. The Gloria is almost always divided into two parts (the second generally beginning at "Qui tollis peccata mundi") and the Credo into three (the second often but not always beginning at "Et incarnatus est" and the third at "Et in spiritum sanctum"). Moreover, Josquin, like other Renaissance composers, often singled out for special treatment the solemn moment of the Credo which describes Christ's incarnation, by setting, for example, the words "Et incarnatus est" or "Et homo factus est" to block chords or in slower note values, or (less often) by writing music for the "Crucifixus" that differs strikingly from the "Et resurrexit." In the Sanctus movement, the "Pleni" and "Benedictus" sections are almost always scored for a reduced number of voices, usually two or three, and the cantus firmus (in Masses based on one) is omitted. The tutti "Osanna"—often in triple meter and set only once so that the same music is sung after both the "Pleni" and the "Benedictus"—furnishes strong contrast to the two- or three-voiced interludes. Similarly, when there are three Agnus Dei settings (for sometimes the Renaissance composer included only one or two settings of the words), the second is often scored for fewer voices than the full complement, while the third occasionally has extra voices added to it to create a final burst of sound that serves as a fitting conclusion to the whole vast musical structure.

Josquin's technique of composing these long ritual texts can best be demonstrated by considering briefly a section of one movement, the beginning of the Gloria from his *Missa L'homme armé sexti toni* (Example 5–4). Superficially it resembles one of Dufay's Masses (discussed above on pp. 43–51) in that after the chanted intonation it begins with a duet; and further duets interrupt the texture from time to time to give the movement shape. Moreover, Josquin writes long sweeps of melody—for example, the first three bars of the superius, which rises elegantly through an octave and then gently settles down. But the character of Josquin's melodies differs significantly from those by Dufay. In this example, the role of melodic motives is crucial in carrying the motion forward and giving to the music the exciting impetus that is one of the most characteristic traits of Josquin's style. The motives themselves are often short and simple, like those in the superius in mm. 5–8, where they are arranged to lead up to the highest point in the line and then down again to its starting pitch. Josquin's compact motives often contradict the underlying regular metrical pulse, as they do in this passage (mm. 5–8). As a consequence the rhythm unfolds in irregular units of two or three beats each; since the units are independent of the bar lines, the music takes on a marvelous disembodied floating quality. Many of these simple motives, like those that set the series of acclamations ("Benedicimus te. Adoramus te," and so on) and those that lead up to the climax in mm. 19–20, are treated as sequences, a technique that gives an even more compelling push to the forward motion.

EXAMPLE 5–4. Josquin, *Missa L'homme armé sexti toni, Gloria,* mm. 1–30.

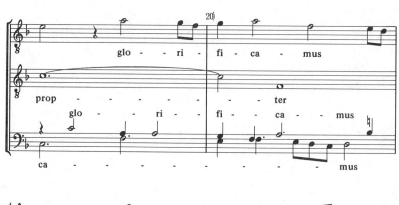

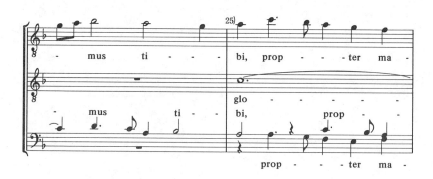

Perhaps the most impressive feature of Example 5–4, though, is the careful formal control that it exhibits. The cadence at m. 29 marks the midpoint of the first main section of the Gloria, a fact that explains why it is the first prominent V–I cadence (with 4–3 suspension) for all voices in the movement. The most important previous cadence occurs on the fifth scale degree in m. 21. A simple description of the first three phrases of the movement (mm. 1–9, 9–21, and 21–29) as (1) an introduction for two voices, (2) a first tutti leading to a half cadence, and (3) a duet and second tutti leading to a full cadence, suggests not only the shape of the music, but also the formal function of each passage and the relationship of each to the whole. The half cadence at m. 21 is prepared by the sequences that lead up to it. The third phrase (mm. 21–29) achieves a sense of climax and of arrival at a goal by repeating in a much more compressed time span the gestures of the first two phrases (that is, a duet followed by a tutti) and by reaching the highest point in the melody (m. 26) with a dramatic sweep upwards from f to c″ (almost the entire range of the superius)—accomplished within the space of two measures and a half by means of a melodic line filled with repeated motives and near sequences. Moreover the structure parallels the syntax of the words it sets; new sections of music begin with new clauses of text. In short, Josquin created an autonomous musical structure in which the relationship of each phrase to the others and to the whole is revealed by a carefully maintained cadential hierarchy, by a network of motives, and by long-range planning of the overall melodic contours; at the same time the music follows closely the form, and hence the meaning, of the words it carries.

The cantus firmus, then, is not really the single most important factor (as it had been in many Masses by earlier composers) in controlling the overall organization of the form in this Mass. In another way, though, the *L'homme armé* melody has far greater impact on the sound of the music than do cantus firmi in most earlier Masses, since all of the parts are sometimes melodically derived from it. Josquin was not consistent throughout his life in the extent to which he used the structural voice as a repository of thematic material for the strands of the polyphony. In works like the *Missa Hercules Dux Ferrariae,* the melody derived from the vowels of the title is invariably kept separate from the melodies in the other voices. In the *Missa L'homme armé sexti toni,* the pre-existent melody influences the other voices in some sections but not in all. And in some Masses, like that based on the Gregorian hymn *Ave maris stella,* the melodic ideas of the cantus firmus so dominate the texture that an unsuspecting listener might suppose it to be a paraphrase Mass. Closer study, however, reveals that the chant melody functions as a cantus firmus; that is, it is stated completely in a single voice at a time, even though it is often accompanied by fragments of itself in imitation.

In cantus firmus Masses in which Josquin borrowed his material from a polyphonic composition, he sometimes quoted more than a single line of the model. In other words, he occasionally approached parody technique, the practice of basing a new composition on all voices of a pre-existent polyphonic piece, which became one of the central procedures of the sixteenth century. In both his *Missa Malheur me bat* (based on a chanson by Ockeghem) and the rather more ingeniously organized *Missa Fortuna desperata* (based on an anonymous setting of the Italian text), Josquin borrowed various single voices of the model to use as cantus firmi for different sections of his new composition (for example, the tenor of the Kyrie in *Missa Malheur me bat* reproduces the tenor of the chanson, while the Credo is based on its superius); he sometimes accompanied the borrowed melody with material derived from the other voices of the model (as he did throughout the *Missa Fortuna desperata*); and he sometimes quoted all voices of the polyphonic model more or less literally in their original relationship to one another (as at the beginning of the Sanctus of the *Missa Malheur me bat* and of each movement in *Missa Fortuna desperata*).

Two of Josquin's Masses (possibly among the earliest he wrote) are based on cycles of canons: the *Missa Ad fugam* and the *Missa Sine nomine.* The canons in the *Missa Ad fugam* are presented at the fifth below between the superius and the tenor. Variants of the same melody, apparently of Josquin's own invention, open each movement and hence unify the Mass thematically. In the *Missa Sine nomine,* on the other hand, the melodic material and the interval between *dux* and *comes* change, as do the pairs of voices which state the canon. It is merely the idea of canon as structural device that binds the Mass together.

Josquin's magnificent *Missa Pange lingua,* a late work and perhaps his only Mass that corresponds in grandeur and greatness with the splendid series of motets composed towards the end of his life, foregoes completely any rigid scaffolding device, either cantus firmus or canonic cycle. Instead, it is a paraphrase Mass using the Gregorian hymn on which it is based merely as a source for thematic material. The chant is never stated complete in any one voice. Some quotations from it are quite literal. In other passages Josquin abandoned the chant, merely alluded vaguely to it, or derived his music from it in a way that is not immediately apparent. Josquin's variety in paraphrasing the plainsong demonstrates how little he depended on pre-existing musical material in planning his grand structure and at the same time shows how completely he had assimilated the chant and how skilfully he could absorb it into his overall musical conception.

Josquin wrote the *Missa Pange lingua,* like so much of his music, in a predominantly open texture, filled with two- and three-part counterpoint. Tuttis are in general reserved for important moments of structural articulation or at the most solemn moments, like the simple and eloquent setting of "Et incarnatus est" in the Credo. Some motives in the Mass are repeated over and over again, a procedure that Josquin customarily adopted to build up a powerful drive to the cadence. As in so much of Josquin's late music, the text of the *Missa Pange lingua* is set in largely syllabic fashion in order to project the words convincingly (though with some misaccentuations); he incorporated just enough melismas to avoid austerity and to give an impressive sweep to his melodic lines.

JOSQUIN'S SECULAR MUSIC

Like composers earlier in the fifteenth century, Josquin and his contemporaries everywhere in western Europe still thought of the chanson as the principal sort of secular music. Although Josquin composed some Italian frottole and instrumental pieces, the largest number of his works besides motets consists of settings of French lyrical poems. As much a master in this as in other fields, he was equally expert at writing chansons for three, four, five, or six voices. In applying the new techniques of imitative counterpoint to equal but independent melodic lines, all of which could easily be sung, Josquin freed himself from the invariable repetition schemes of the *formes fixes.* In doing so, he transformed the chanson from a genre limited by its conventional texture of continuous layers of sound to one capable of so much greater variety in techniques and textures that it could express more moods and shades of thought than ever before, and attain a much greater depth and richness of effect.

We cannot establish with confidence a chronology of Josquin's chansons any more than we can know in what order he composed his motets and Masses. Petrucci published some of his chansons in Venice between 1501 and 1503, but the main corpus did not appear in print until 1545, when the Flemish publisher Tielman Susato of Antwerp issued a commemorative edition. But if we cannot be certain about which of Josquin's chansons were composed early in his life and which later, we can at least point out the differing techniques he used in setting lyrical poetry, each of which may well be connected with a particular stage in his development. Thus his few rondeaux and some chansons in a style not totally unlike that of Ockeghem might well have been written in his student days and during his stay in Italy. The many polyphonic arrangements of monophonic popular tunes may date from his Italian years and from the time of his connection with the French royal court, where Louis XII and his courtiers seem to have affected a great regard for popular culture. And a series of somber, melancholy songs may have been written late in Josquin's life for that most unhappy of rulers, Marguerite of Austria, at a time when he may also have been composing a number of other many-voiced and rather densely scored chansons.

Aside from questions of chronology, it is sometimes difficult to determine even quite basic facts about this repertory. Some chansons, for example, are not securely attributed to Josquin, since various sources ascribe them to other composers. And some chansons cannot unambiguously be associated with a particular poem, because the musical sources often give only the first few words; the complete text must therefore be sought in miscellaneous anthologies of poetry. These difficulties can easily be illustrated in considering the number of rondeaux Josquin composed. He may have set only three: *La plus des plus* and *Madame helas* (both in a style virtually indistinguishable from that of Ockeghem and his contemporaries) and *Plusieurs regretz*. But each of the three raises unanswerable questions. A complete poem beginning "La plus des plus" appears only in one poetic anthology of the time, divorced from any musical context; apparently for that reason the music is included in the edition of Josquin's complete works (as chanson no. 45) without words. Josquin's editors do not accept *Madame helas* as genuine, even though it is ascribed to him in one copy of the *Odhecaton* (and published as no. 66 in Helen Hewitt's edition of that work), presumably because one manuscript gives it to "Dux Carlus," possibly Charles the Bold, Duke of Burgundy. In any case, *Madame helas* survives without any text save for its first two words; that it is a rondeau must be inferred from its form, and especially from the prominent cadence at its midpoint. *Plusieurs regretz*, on the other hand, is certainly by Josquin, and one stanza of text, rhyming aabba (the conventional rhyme scheme for the refrain of a *rondeau cinquain*), is securely identified with the music. A poetic anthology of the time includes a complete rondeau beginning "Tous les regretz" but continuing exactly like Josquin's chanson. Probably, then, that text belongs with Josquin's music. But if that is so, perhaps some of the other poems rhyming aabba and set by Josquin are also rondeau refrains for which the complete text has since been lost.

The problems posed by these three chansons should warn us to be cautious in making generalizations. And the case of *Plusieurs regretz* reveals that the absence of poems in *formes fixes* from Josquin's *oeuvre* is not necessarily as radical a change as might at first appear. Indeed, the poets who furnished verses for the composer—among them Jean Molinet, Guillaume Crétin, Jean Lemaire de Belges, and probably Marguerite of Austria herself—are all associated with the last generation of the *grands rhétoriqueurs,* and hence their works relate closely to a passing literary tradition much as Josquin's music does to that of his immediate predecessors. Moreover, the absence of conventional repetition schemes does not mean that Josquin composed through-composed chansons exclusively. On the contrary, he often repeated phrases in patterns that, though untraditional, are easily comprehensible, and he was especially apt to associate musical repetition with poetic lines that rhyme. Thus the music for *Plusieurs regretz* follows the pattern AABBCC, which matches the rhyme scheme, aabba, save that the composer has supplied a new musical phrase for the fifth line of verse and then repeated it.

Josquin mirrored the structure of the poem in his music especially often in chansons which, like *Plusieurs regretz,* were composed around a canon, the structural device that he used more than any other in his settings of serious courtly lyrics. Curiously, though, the scaffolding device is often hidden in the middle of a highly imitative texture that is itself capable of sustaining the musical fabric; in *Plusieurs regretz* (Example 5–5), for instance, the opening double imitation (involving both a subject and its contrapuntal accompaniment) and the clear motive structure separating "plusieurs regretz" from "qui sur la terre sont" not only hide the canon at the fifth between the next-to-lowest and next-to-top voice, but also make such a rigid framework superfluous. Yet Josquin wrote his other canonic chansons, like *Incessament livre suis a martire, Douleur me bat,* and *Plaine de dueil,* in exactly the same imitative style.

In Josquin's through-composed chansons, on the other hand, like *Je ne me puis tenir d'aimer,* the composer, without repeating any passage literally, took full advantage of the possibilities of imitative writing and choral dialogue to vary the texture of the music and to extend each phrase by working with one or more motives, much as in a motet. The opening measures of *Je ne me puis tenir d'aimer* constitute a lengthy point of imitation in which all five voices eventually take part; in the closing phrase, in contrast, sections of the ensemble oppose one another in stating short motives in ever-changing combinations. Josquin ended the chanson with a coda over a double pedal point that eventually leads to the final plagal cadence, one of his most typical mannerisms. Of his other through-composed chansons, *Mille regretz* (one of his last compositions) is among his subtlest and most perfect, as well as simplest.

Some of Josquin's chansons are written over a cantus firmus originally associated with a separate text. His five-voiced setting of *Cueurs*

EXAMPLE 5–5. Josquin, *Plusieurs regretz,* mm. 1–12.

desolez, for example, is based on the plainchant *Plorans ploravit,* and *Fortune d'estrange plummaige* on *Pauper sum ego.* Perhaps, then, Josquin's very moving lament on the death of Ockeghem, the well-known *Déploration* in which the tenor sings the Introit of the Mass for the Dead (*Requiem aeternam*) while the other voices sing "Nymphes des bois, déesses des fontaines . . . ," should be regarded as a cantus-firmus chanson rather than a motet in French. In truth, the distinction is academic, since the composer employed the same techniques in both genres. At least one of Josquin's cantus-firmus chansons uses a popular monophonic melody as its structural voice. The tune, *Adieu mes amours,* is stated as a free canon in the lower two voices while the upper two sing a rondeau also beginning with the words "Adieu mes amours" but composed in an old-fashioned melismatic style suggesting that the composition was written in Josquin's early years.

Popular poems similar to *Adieu mes amours* and intended to be sung circulated apparently everywhere in France during the sixteenth century in cheaply printed books of verse. The melodies for some of them are preserved in several manuscripts prepared for the aristocratic circles around Louis XII, who evidently cultivated for a time this attractive genre, intended in the first place for the amusement and education of the urban lower and middle classes. Composers before Josquin's day had occasionally set such tunes; Dufay, for example, composed an arrangement of *La belle se siet,* and Binchois used *Filles à marier.* But Josquin's generation was the first to use this material extensively, and he himself wrote a substantial number of popular arrangements. It is not always possible to be certain that a particular chanson borrows a popular tune. If the text or melody cannot be traced in any musical or literary anthology and no other composer has based a polyphonic arrangement on it, then the presence of a popular song can only be inferred from the character of the melodic lines or from Josquin's treatment of them. The tenor in *Si*

J'avoye Marion, for instance, is so simple and straightforward—so tuneful and easy to sing—that there can be little doubt that the composer has taken into his polyphonic texture one of the melodies originally sung in the streets of Paris. And the melody is treated in the manner Josquin reserved for three-part popular arrangements: the outer voices imitate the cantus firmus, but the tenor enters last of all, presenting the melody in its simplest and most complete form while the outer voices either continue their imitation or move in parallel motion.

In some of his popular arrangements, however, like the four-part setting of *Bergerette savoyenne,* Josquin paraphrased the borrowed melody rather than presenting it complete. And sometimes he put the popular melodies into canons with themselves to form a solid structural framework around which the other voices could weave their complex and varied webs—as, for example, in *Faulte d'argent,* one of his best known chansons, and *Petite camusette,* based on a melody that Ockeghem had also arranged. The words of these popular songs are usually bucolic or witty, or at any rate less artificial and stilted than the courtly lyrics. But not all of Josquin's witty songs involve borrowed popular melodies. He himself, for example, probably invented all of the musical material in the four-voiced double canon *Basiez moy,* which a later musician less successfully expanded into a six-voiced triple canon.

If chansons constituted by far the largest part of Josquin's secular works, he nevertheless composed several delightful frottole. Both *In te domine speravi* (with mixed Italian and Latin words) and the formally unconventional *El grillo è buon cantore* were published in Petrucci's frottola books as by "Jusquin d'Ascanio," that is, the Josquin in the service of Cardinal Ascanio Sforza—proof, if proof were needed, that they date from the composer's Italian years. And Josquin's contrapuntally witty *Scaramella va alla guerra,* based on a popular tune similar in style to those sung in France, may date from his years in Milan, that is, from before about 1479, since one of his colleagues there, Loyset Compère, wrote a competitive work borrowing the same melody.

Josquin arranged some of his predecessors' chansons in a way that suggests he intended to make them into compositions suitable for instrumental performance. Beneath the superius and tenor of Hayne van Ghizeghem's famous *De tous biens plaine,* for instance, Josquin added a two-part canon at the unison and at the distance of one minim, transforming this lovely lyrical song into an impressive display of compositional ingenuity. Moreover, Josquin also composed some works originally conceived for instruments and not associated with any literary text. His exploration of imitative techniques and his mastery of the art of creating structures from a series of interlocked phrases enabled him to write textless, musically autonomous works. They can be identified as such only tentatively, however, for new concordances may reveal some of them to have been conceived, say, as chansons. Nevertheless, Josquin and his contemporaries seem to have been among the first composers to create an abstract instrumental music, and it seems unlikely that texts will ever be discovered for pieces like *Ile Fantazies de Joskin* or *La Bernardina*. They are surely both instrumental "carmina," for their phrase structure, the pattern of their cadences, and the clear networks of motives in each make them musically self-sufficient. *La Bernardina* seems to be a title rather than the first line of a text. Doubtless it refers to the person for whom it was written or to whom it was dedicated, like similar works by Josquin's contemporaries—for example, Johannes Martini's *La Martinella,* Ghiselin's *La Alfonsina,* and Isaac's *La Morra.* Josquin's works for instruments include as well the brilliant fanfare (perhaps written for the French king) based on a cantus firmus derived from the letters of *Vive le roy*:

U-	i-	u-	e	le	ro-	i
Ut	mi	ut	re	re	sol	mi
C	E	C	D	D	G	E

In sum, Josquin's mastery of every genre cultivated in his time— Masses, motets, chansons, frottole, and instrumental carmina—explains his preeminence in the minds of his contemporaries and his stature today as one of the greatest composers in the history of western Europe.

BIBLIOGRAPHICAL NOTES

The complete works of Josquin des Prez, edited by Albert Smijers, M. Antonowycz, and W. Elders, have been published in fifty-five fascicles by the Vereniging voor Nederlandse Muziekgeschiedenis (Amsterdam, 1921– 69). Selections from his complete works are available in a number of other publications, for example, the series *Das Chorwerk,* edited by Friedrich Blume (Wolfenbüttel, 1929–   ); Helen Hewitt, ed., *Harmonice Musices Odhecaton A* (Cambridge, Mass., 1942); Helen Hewitt, ed., *Ottaviano Petrucci, Canti B numero cinquanta, Venice, 1502* (Chicago and London, 1967); Edward E. Lowinsky, ed., *The Medici Codex of 1518* (Chicago and London, 1968, 3 vols.); and Martin Picker, ed., *The Chanson Albums of Marguerite of Austria* (Berkeley and Los Angeles, 1965); and others.

The one book devoted to Josquin, Helmuth Osthoff, *Josquin Desprez* (Tutzing, 1962–65, 2 vols.) is written in German. For a slightly out-of-date evaluation of the composer in English, see Albert Smijers, "Josquin des Prez," *Proceedings of the Royal Musical Association,* 53 (1927). More up-to-date information will be found in the *Proceedings of the Interna-*

tional Josquin Festival-Conference, New York, 1972 (London, 1975). In addition, on Josquin's sacred music, see Edgar H. Sparks, Cantus Firmus in Mass and Motet, 1450–1520 (Berkeley and Los Angeles, 1963); Edgar H. Sparks, The Music of Noel Bauldeweyn (New York, 1972); Jacquelyn A. Mattfeld, "Some Relationships between Texts and Cantus Firmi in the Liturgical Motets of Josquin des Prez," Journal of the American Musicological Society, 14 (1961); and Leeman L. Perkins, "Mode and Structure in the Masses of Josquin," Journal of the American Musicological Society, 26 (1973). On Josquin's secular music, in addition to the prefaces of the works cited above, see Howard Mayer Brown, Music in the French Secular Theater, 1450–1550 (Cambridge, Mass., 1963); and James Haar, ed., Chanson and Madrigal, 1480–1530 (Cambridge, Mass., 1964).

Kenneth Levy diss.

SIX

JOSQUIN'S CONTEMPORARIES

Few periods in the history of western music have produced so many composers of the first rank as the several decades before and after 1500. If the High Renaissance was the age of Josquin, his contemporaries nevertheless created an extraordinary body of music worthy to be set beside his. Some of the composers born in the late 1440's, 1450's and 1460's—like Alexander Agricola, Jacob Obrecht, and Loyset Compère—wrote in a style that can be related directly to the older Burgundian and Flemish traditions, while others—like Heinrich Isaac, Pierre de la Rue, and Jean Mouton—composed music that more nearly resembles Josquin's and can be seen to lead to the new sounds and styles of the sixteenth century. Josquin is the giant among them, but the others suffer only by comparison with him. Each of them adapted the new techniques of the age to his own goals and ideals, and each expressed a musical personality still capable of touching us today. Josquin's contemporaries can scarcely be studied as a group. They all had individual things to say and unique ways of saying them. If nothing else, their careers were too varied and too peripatetic to allow them to be grouped into a "school." The composite picture that emerges from the following brief summaries of their achievements may, however, give the reader some idea of the most important characteristics of one of the great ages of Western music, as well as an impression of the special qualities of each of its leading representatives.

ALEXANDER AGRICOLA (1446–1506)

By his mid-twenties, Alexander Agricola had left his native Flanders to seek his fortune in Italy, had taken a Florentine wife, and had found a position in the ducal chapel in Milan at a particularly brilliant moment in its musical history. By 1474, however, Agricola had decided to move elsewhere; in that year Duke Galeazzo Maria Sforza gave him both a letter of recommendation to Lorenzo de' Medici in Florence and permission to return to his northern homeland. During the following twenty-six years Agricola divided his activities between Italy and the north, serving at various times in the cathedrals of Cambrai and Florence and at the court of the French king. In 1500 he took up his final post, as chaplain and singer in the chapel of Philip the Handsome, Duke of Burgundy. While in Philip's service, Agricola twice visited Spain; on the second occasion the sixty-year-old composer caught a fever and died within the same year, 1506, as his ducal patron.

A worthy successor to Busnois at the Burgundian court, Agricola excelled above all as a composer of elegant courtly music. His most striking stylistic mannerism, perhaps, is his tendency to forego long lyrical sweeps of floating melody in favor of quick, nervous lines composed of short motives fitted together with great rhythmic subtlety. The florid nature of the counterpoint, and the unexpected turns it sometimes takes, may be the traits that led one sixteenth-century musician to characterize Agricola's music as "strange in manner," a description that still strikes us as apt.

Agricola spent most of his creative energy writing secular music; some eighty-odd chansons and other secular compositions survive by him, as opposed to eight Masses, a few isolated Mass movements, and about twenty-five motets and other smaller sacred pieces. His chansons are closer in style to late fifteenth-century Burgundian songs by Busnois, Ockeghem, and their contemporaries than to the new equal-voiced polyphony of Josquin and his younger colleagues, a fact that is obvious even from considering the most superficial features of the music. Most of Agricola's chansons are cast in one of the *formes fixes*—the majority are either rondeaux or bergerettes—and they are composed for three voices in the conventional texture of the fifteenth-century song. Both its highly sophisticated imitative technique and its texture, enriched by motivic work that remains effective and individual despite its origin in the common store of late fifteenth-century melodic material, identify a chanson like *J'ay beau huer* (Example 6–1) as representing the end rather than the beginning of a tradition. The melismas, which are an inherent part of its melodic style and cause the ambiguous relationship between words and music, resemble those in earlier chansons. And yet the pervasive imitation at the beginning of both phrases of this rondeau, and the delightfully unexpected and rhythmically unsettling canon between superius and tenor at "De celle la," reveal a refinement of technique characteristic of mature, even overripe, styles and bespeak a contrapuntal ingenuity seemingly contradicted by the facility with which Agricola so often moved two of his three voices in parallel motion.

EXAMPLE 6–1. Alexander Agricola, *J'ay beau huer,* mm. 1–18. Used by permission of the American Institute of Musicology.

Several of Agricola's chansons juxtapose poems in *formes fixes* with fragments of chant. The upper two voices of *Belle sur toutes / Tota pulchra es*, for example, express in French the conventional sentiments of the lovesick suitor while the lowest voice states as cantus firmus a passage in Latin from the Song of Songs, used in the liturgy as an antiphon in honor of the Virgin Mary. Such compositions are often called motet-chansons, although they should more accurately be considered cantus-firmus chansons, since they are really French songs built over chants and not motets with vernacular texts. The technique Agricola used to compose them cannot have differed extensively from that involved in making polyphonic settings of popular melodies, save that Agricola's three-part popular arrangements, like those by Josquin which they resemble, employ one set of words in all voices. The simple tune—either with French words, as in *Et qui la dira* and *Par ung jour de matinée*, or with Dutch, as in *O Venus bant, Tandernaken*, and *In minen zin*—is presented in a straight-forward manner, usually by the tenor, and the other two voices weave their counterpoints around it. Fragments of imitation, motives exchanged in dialogue and extended by variation and sequence, and ubiquitous passages in parallel motion transform humble popular songs into elaborate and artful polyphony.

Not all of Agricola's chansons, however, are so unrelievedly contrapuntal in their orientation as the examples discussed thus far. He did attempt to come to grips with the developing harmonic sense of his contemporaries. In a chanson like *Adieu m'amour*, for instance, chordally conceived phrases are combined with old-fashioned melismatic lines in a way that suggests the composer had not completely assimilated the new style. His setting of the strophic poem *Amor, che sospirar,* on the other hand, is indistinguishable from any similarly chordal composition by a native Italian composer, and so, probably, was his incompletely preserved Florentine carnival song.

Agricola's most distinctive secular compositions, though, are his arrangements of older courtly chansons in a style that must have been intended for instrumental performance. His multiple versions of Frye's *Tout a par moy,* Binchois's *Comme femme,* Ockeghem's *D'ung aultre amer,* and Hayne's *De tous biens plaine* all pit one voice of the original (usually the tenor) against two or three newly composed lines that move primarily in smaller note values and cover a far wider range than those in Agricola's other chansons. Even his three-part popular arrangements, written similarly around a pre-existing melody in an inner voice, do not include the fast passagework that occurs, for instance, in his arrangements of Hayne's *De tous biens plaine* (the beginning of one of them is shown in Example 6–2). In the late fifteenth century, instrumentalists could and did play music in every genre; but this group of instrumental chansons instructs us in the musical styles a virtuoso of the time (or at least a professional) found most congenial and illustrates the kinds of figuration

EXAMPLE 6-2. Agricola, *De tous biens plaine,* mm. 1–8. Used by permission of the American Institute of Musicology.

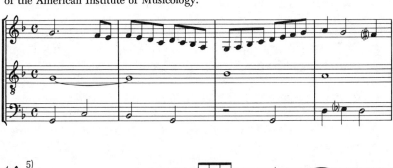

performers improvised over cantus firmi or added as embellishments to melodic lines. Scale fragments (some extending an octave and a fourth or more), stretto-like imitations, brief sections in triplets, and short syncopated figures repeated with little or no variation at the same or different pitches—all of which constantly recur in these pieces—do not differ radically in their nature from the figures Agricola incorporated into his vocal music; they are applied more rigorously, however, without letup and in faster motion over a wider range, than in any of Agricola's other works.

The two simplest of Agricola's eight Masses, the *Missa primi toni* and the *Missa secundi toni,* both evidently intended as relatively straightforward accompaniment to the liturgy, were apparently written without recourse to pre-existing material. His *Missa Sine nomine* uses a chant only in the Credo, and the Easter Mass, *Missa Paschalis,* is based on a succession of Gregorian melodies. The remaining four Masses are composed on cantus firmi derived from polyphonic secular pieces: the chansons *Le serviteur* (attributed to Dufay in some sources), *Malheur me bat* (attributed to Ockeghem), Busnois's *Je ne demande,* and Agricola's own arrangement of the Dutch song *In minen zin.* Agricola generally treated the cantus firmus quite freely. In addition to stating it in long notes in an inner voice, he sometimes speeded it up to make it indistinguishable from the other voices or interpolated newly invented material between phrases of the original; sometimes he omitted it altogether. In one movement of the *Missa Je ne demande* he paraphrased two voices of the polyphonic model simultaneously. Agricola's Masses, save for occasional chordal passages marking off significant words or phrases, are composed in the same contrapuntally elaborate, rhythmically subtle texture that characterizes most of his chansons and, indeed, his hymns, Magnificats, and motets—the lyrical song-motets apparently intended for private devotional use as well as the larger, more impressive compositions written for liturgical and paraliturgical occasions. Only his two sets of Lamentations for Holy Week proceed largely in simple chords or contrapuntally animated homophony, interrupted only occasionally by more complex polyphony.

JACOB OBRECHT (ca. 1450–1505)

Probably the only Dutchman among Josquin's greatest contemporaries, Jacob Obrecht spent the greatest part of his life in his northern homeland. He was born into a family of musicians from Bergen op Zoom. The earliest certain notice of his activities identifies him as a *"zang-*

meester" in Utrecht, where he may have taught the young Erasmus. He was chapelmaster at the cathedral of Cambrai from 1484 to 1485, but when the chapter indicated dissatisfaction with his financial management and evident lack of interest in the training of choirboys, he accepted an appointment as *succentor* at the church of St. Donatien in Bruges. From 1485 until his death he worked mostly in Bruges (1485–1491 and 1498–1500), Antwerp (at the Church of Our Lady, 1492–1496 and 1501–1504), and Bergen op Zoom (1496–1498). His *Missa O beate pater Donatione* may have been written as a parting gift to the church in Bruges in 1491; and his series of great Marian works, *Missa Maria zart, Missa Sub tuum praesidium,* and the motets *Mater patris* and the ambitious setting of *Salve regina* may date from his years in Antwerp. His career in the north was interrupted only twice by important trips to Italy. In 1487 he was granted leave from St. Donatien in Bruges to visit Ferrara, where he had been invited by Duke Hercules d'Este I. Obrecht's fame had preceded him, and he was treated like an honored guest even though he refused the Duke's requests to stay longer. For more than fifteen years, in fact, the Estes tried to lure Obrecht back to Ferrara. He finally accepted their invitation in 1504. While he was visiting the city, plague struck, and he fell a victim to it in 1505.

In assessing Obrecht's music, many critics have stressed the composer's great facility—Glareanus, for example, reported that he could compose a Mass overnight—and his slightly conservative turn of mind, especially as compared with Josquin. In his music, the facile side of his character is perhaps most obviously expressed by his readiness to move contrapuntal lines in parallel motion, especially by tenths in the outer voices; by his penchant for composing sections built from short, succinct motives repeated a number of times with little or no variation; and by his willingness to extend a phrase by means of interminable sequences. Example 6–3, the beginning of the first Kyrie from his *Missa Fortuna desperata,* shows the first of these traits and offers a sample of Obrecht's characteristically busy texture, with nervous and relatively fast-moving melismatic lines combined with slower-moving cantus-firmus-like voices. Typically, the opening point of imitation involves four measures of two-part counterpoint (arranged like a subject and counter-subject) simply transposed up an octave and re-scored upon repetition. The flow of this exuberant polyphony is judiciously controlled, though, by emphatic cadences carefully prepared: Obrecht's clear sense of tonality identifies him as fully aware of the new compositional possibilities of organizing independent melodic lines by vertical, harmonic means. The example reveals, too, why Obrecht is thought to be conservative. The texture of the music preserves many older features of the layered polyphony from the earlier part of the fifteenth century; little attention seems to have been given to sensitive text declamation, that humanistic preoccupation of the northerners who spent most of their careers in Italy; and the movement is organized around a cantus firmus. Indeed, the skill and ingenuity with which Obrecht manipulated cantus-firmus technique constitutes one of the most notable features of his music.

About twenty-five Masses, twenty motets, and thirty secular pieces by Obrecht survive. Thus his Masses bulk far larger in his output than any other genre, and they include some of his best music. Most of them are cantus-firmus Masses in which the structural voice is deployed in several ingenious ways. In the *Missa super Maria zart,* for example, Obrecht divided the monophonic tune on which the work is based into several segments and presented the complete melody only as a structural climax in the Agnus Dei. The cantus firmi in the *Missa Sine nomine* (built on Hayne van Ghizeghem's chanson, *De tous biens plaine*), the *Missa Ave regina caelorum,* and the *Missa Fortuna desperata* are at times combined with material from the other voices of the borrowed polyphonic model. His process of composing approaches sixteenth-century parody technique even more closely in the Kyrie of his *Missa Rose playsante,* in

EXAMPLE 6–3. Jacob Obrecht, *Missa Fortuna desperata, Kyrie,* mm. 1–13.

which he quoted several times all or most of the voices of his model, a chanson by Caron. Obrecht paid homage to Dufay and Ockeghem in *Missa Caput* by quoting and re-arranging passages from the earlier Masses on the same plainsong, and he honored Busnois in a similar way in his *Missa L'Homme armé*. To organize his *Missa diversorum tenorum,* Obrecht used a number of different pre-existing melodies in the manner of a quodlibet. And in the *Missa Sub tuum praesidium,* although one plain-chant is employed as cantus firmus, others are added to it after the first two movements. Moreover, Obrecht created a sense of growing climax in this Mass by adding one additional voice to each succeeding move-ment; three voices sing the Kyrie, four the Gloria, and so on, until the Mass ends with a seven-voice Agnus Dei. In a new edition of the Mass, the editor, Marcus van Crevel, argues that Obrecht built into his work several layers of hidden symbolic meaning, an interpretation that has not won general acceptance.

Like most of Obrecht's Masses, many of his motets are built over cantus firmi. But if this old-fashioned technique serves as a structural basis for his music, the style of some of the motets seems modern insofar as the text is set in a declamatory manner (or in any case more syllabically than in his Masses). Paradoxically, he took special care with setting the words in his five- and six-voiced motets that combine more than one text, such as *Factor orbis*. Written on various Chants (mostly antiphons), this work follows a variant of the standard form for responsories, aBcB; instead of repeating the B section literally, though, Obrecht varied it upon its return at the end. In *Factor orbis,* Obrecht was much more sparing than usual in his use of melisma, and for the verses "Esto refugium pauperum" and "Alleluia, noe noe" he wrote purely chordal settings that throw the words into sharp relief. On the other hand, his Netherlandish artifices tend to obscure the text in another five-voice motet, *Haec Deum coeli,* which combines a chant-derived three-part canon in long notes with fast-moving, newly invented counterpoints. Some of Obrecht's three-part motets, like *Si sumpsero,* are filled with imitative polyphony in which playful exchanges among the equally important voices make the composi-tions as apt for instruments as for voices. In other three-voiced motets, like *O vos omnes* and *Alma redemptoris mater,* one voice usually moves in slow notes while the other two compete in rapid-fire dialogue and duets. In many of Obrecht's four-voiced motets, like the partly poly-textual *Beata es, Maria,* the texture is less transparent than in Josquin's polyphony, partly because of Obrecht's generally full scoring and partly because of the relative absence of imitation; but the lucid way in which the cantus firmus is laid out gives to the music a strong sense of order.

Ingenuity and artifice mark Obrecht's secular as well as his sacred music. His instrumental carmina, including several canonic pieces, are filled with contrapuntal science and wit. He recomposed several older chansons, like *Cela sans plus, Fors seulement,* and *J'ay pris amours,* to make them tonally more focused. And he delighted in placing a borrowed tune in an inner voice and pitting against it quick, nervous, playful lines filled with witty imitations, fragments of canon, motion in parallel tenths, and short motives expanded by repetitions or sequences—as for instance in his three- and four-part arrangements of the Dutch popular songs *Meskin es hu, Rompeltier,* and *Tandernaken* and the Italian strambotto *La tortorella.* Because of the special way cantus-firmus technique was applied to them, Obrecht's popular arrangements, like those by Josquin and Agricola, have a distinctive sound. They differ markedly, for example, from a second group of Dutch songs that Obrecht composed in a much more chordal and tonally oriented style. These latter songs—unusual at a time when French chansons still dominated vocal chamber music everywhere in western Europe—clearly reveal Obrecht's national loyalties and the extent to which he was steeped in local Dutch culture. Unfortunately the songs survive without their complete texts (ten of them are published by Smijers in *Van Ockeghem tot Sweelinck*), and so it is not possible to know what sorts of poems caught the composer's fancy. The music alternates between chordal sections and interludes for reduced forces, often in highly imitative polyphony. In *Laet u ghenoughen,* for example, these interludes take the form of duets that, because of their repeated notes, seem originally to have been syllabic settings, possibly of narrative portions of the poetry. Like many of the other Dutch songs, *Laet u ghenoughen* has a refrain that is varied each time it appears. Perhaps, then, some or all of these Dutch songs are polyphonic arrangements of popular melodies; but Obrecht's technique of harmonizing what may be the pre-existing theme by simple, tonal chords, or of paraphrasing it in witty polyphony, makes the songs totally different in effect from his other, more contrapuntally ingenious but older-fashioned secular compositions.

LOYSET COMPÈRE (ca. 1450–1518)

Aside from the fact that for a year the young Compère sang beside Weerbecke, Martini, Agricola, and Josquin at the ducal court in Milan, little is known of his life. His name appears for the first time in the Milanese records for 1474, the same year that Agricola left the Sforza court. Compère is known to have served the French king, Charles VIII, for he is recorded in Paris in 1486; he held benefices from Cambrai and Douai; and he spent his last years as a canon at the collegiate church of St. Quentin, where he died in 1518. He may have been educated at the famous cathedral school in Cambrai, a hypothesis suggested by the list of men included in the text of one of his earliest surviving compositions, the "singers' prayer," *Omnium bonorum plena* (which begins as a Latin translation of *De tous biens plaine,* the tenor of which serves as cantus firmus). This invocation to the Virgin Mary asks special grace for a number of musicians. Some of them, like Dufay, Ockeghem, Busnois, Molinet, Tinctoris, and Josquin, are among the most famous men of their time, while many among the less well-known figures—Regis, Caron, Faugues, Dussart, Georget de Brelles, Hemart, and Corbet—can be associated with Cambrai.

Like Agricola, Compère was above all a composer of elegant courtly music, but to an even greater extent than his Milanese colleague he specialized in writing small lyric forms like chansons rather than large, expansive structures like Masses. Only two complete Mass cycles by him have survived, along with several isolated or paired Mass movements, three series of motets intended to take the place of the Ordinary and Proper in the liturgical service, some twenty-three motets and Magnificats, and over fifty secular compositions. If he does not quite equal Isaac, Obrecht, and Josquin in stature and achievement, Compère nevertheless wrote music with considerable skill, charm, and wit. And his several diverse manners of composition afford us an unusual opportunity to understand the process by which the new methods of Josquin and his contemporaries were established.

Compère wrote some chansons in which the older Burgundian traditions are modified in ways that suggest he was aware of more modern attitudes towards text setting, melodic planning, harmonic procedures, and textural homogeneity. In other chansons, especially those that reject the outworn ideals of courtly love, he reveals that he had also assimilated completely techniques for writing equal and independent vocal polyphony. These contrasting modes of thought can be differentiated in comparing *Disant adieu* (Example 6–4), a courtly rondeau quatrain, with *Mon père m'a donné mari* (Example 6–5), a saucy popular song doubtless associated originally with a pre-existing melody. Both its texture (with self-sufficient two-part counterpoint between superius and tenor) and its conventional repetition scheme identify *Disant adieu* as a late Burgundian chanson, but it differs significantly from similar songs by, say, Busnois and Ockeghem. Its principal melody in the superius, for example, does not trace a long and complex arch of a sort preferred by those earlier composers, nor is it filled with quick nervous motives after the fashion of Agricola. Instead, Compère writes concise, clear-cut phrases—half-lines of poetry are set to carefully demarcated segments of melody, for example—and for the most part the notes have been devised to fit the words carefully. Much of the text is set syllabically,

EXAMPLE 6–4. Loyset Compère, *Disant adieu,* mm. 1–16. Used by permission of the American Institute of Musicology.

EXAMPLE 6–5. Compère, *Mon père m'a donné mari,* mm. 1–13. Used by permission of the American Institute of Musicology.

although well-planned melismas still have their place in Compère's style, especially at ends of phrases, where the music broadens out before a cadence. And in *Disant adieu* the rhythms are nonetheless metrical for contradicting the barlines. Even if the two upper lines are self-sufficient— and they alone take part in the initial imitation—the contratenor nevertheless plays an important role in stating melodic material in imitation with the other voices and also in clarifying the harmonic progressions. The homorhythm of the beginning throws even more emphasis onto vertical events in the music; even if the harmonies are not dominant-centered, there can be no doubt that G is established and constantly reaffirmed as the tonic. Not all of Compère's rondeaux are so formally compact and melodically succinct as *Disant adieu*. In some, like those built over cantus firmi taken from the Gregorian repertory, the melismatic lines leave text placement ambiguous; in others, like *Mes pensées*, the texture is so transparent that much of the music proceeds in two-part counterpoint. But *Disant adieu* epitomizes one aspect of Compère's work, especially his characteristic way of stating melodies in clear, short segments; it differs not so much in kind as in degree from his other courtly songs.

Mon père m'a donné mari, on the other hand, shows off the even more progressive side of Compère's musical personality. All four voices of the chanson have an almost equal share in stating the important thematic material, mostly as a series of imitative entries. The simple popular character of the tune doubtless explains why it is sung almost entirely syllabically, and why it seems so strongly to imply its own harmonization. The harmonic character of the counterpoint can even be described as "tonal," if that concept can be extended to admit chords on B♭ and F as direct support in establishing the "key" of G-Dorian. The jolly *parlando* style of this narrative chanson can be matched in a number of other compositions by Compère, including *Nous sommes de l'ordre de saint Babouin*, the hilarious invocation to the patron saint of bons vivants; *Je suis amie du fourrier*, which recounts the history of an unrepentant fallen woman; *Lourdault, lourdault*, a mock-stern warning against the dangers of marriage; and his two settings of Italian popular songs, *Che fa la ramacina* and *Scaramella*.

The dichotomy between old-fashioned contrapuntal Burgundian style and the new Italianate harmony and equal-voiced polyphony can be found in Compère's sacred as well as his secular works. *Sola caret monstris*, for example, one of his great ceremonial motets written over a canonic cantus firmus derived from the Gregorian responsory *Videns Jacob* and intended as an attack on the Pope, is austerely contrapuntal in its outlook, whereas *Quis numerare queat*, a similar work based on the antiphon *Da pacem Domine* and composed to celebrate a peace treaty, contains significantly more chordal, syllabically texted passages. Compère's other motets—those with cantus firmus and those without borrowed material—also divide into two large, though overlapping, categories. This contrast may even be found within single large works, such as his two cantus-firmus Masses, *Missa L'homme armé* and *Missa Alles regrets;* the latter is so ingenious in its use of various voices from the chanson by Hayne van Ghizeghem on which it is based that it deserves close study as an important landmark on the way towards the full-fledged parody technique of the sixteenth century. Likewise, in Compère's three substitution Masses (those series of motets intended to replace the usual movements in the Mass Ordinary and Proper), older and newer styles stand side by side: passages in non-imitative counterpoint along with classical points of imitation; sections in discant-tenor technique along with four-part chordal progressions regulated from the bass; continuous layered polyphony along with textures varied by alternating duets and other sorts of choral dialogue; and traditional cantus-firmus technique along with phrases unified by repetitions and transformations of a single motive.

The curious practice of injecting a subjective element into the inviolable ritual of the Mass by substituting motets for some movements was apparently followed only in Milan and other places where Ambrosian rather than Gregorian liturgy held sway. Compère's chapelmaster in Milan, Gaspar van Weerbecke, wrote the earliest examples, and most of the small repertory of such works are preserved together in two manuscripts prepared for the theorist Franchino Gafori, for performance in the Milan Cathedral. Compère's substitution Masses, or *motetti missales* as the Milanese source calls them, each consist of eight motets that were to be sung in place of the following Mass sections: Introit, Gloria, Credo, Offertory, Sanctus, Elevation of the Host, Agnus Dei, and Deo Gratias. Even though there are neither liturgical nor musical reasons for doing so, all the motets in each cycle are written in the same mode, and thematic relationships bind some of the movements even closer together. Although it is tempting to speculate with the editor of Compère's complete works, Ludwig Finscher, that the composer must have written these motets in the 1470's during his year in Milan, there is no compelling reason to suppose that Compère himself conceived them as cycles, nor that he could have been influenced by Italian music so early and before a repertory of frottole and other similar works is known to have existed.

HEINRICH ISAAC (ca. 1450–1517)

Isaac's career centered in Florence, where he was the leading composer during the city's golden age, and the court of the Emperor Maximilian, for whom he worked for many years. The earliest document that unambiguously refers to Heinrich Isaac dates from 1484; it records a payment made to him in Innsbruck, where in all likelihood he had stopped only temporarily en route from his native Flanders to take up a position in Florence at the invitation of the city's ruler, Lorenzo de' Medici, il Magnifico. In Florence Isaac sang in the cathedral choir and at the church of the Santissima Annunziata, and in addition he probably tutored Lorenzo's children in music, including Giovanni, later Pope Leo X. Isaac married a Florentine and stayed on in the city even after Lorenzo's death in 1492. The political turmoil attendant on the downfall of the Medici faction and the rise to power of the puritanical Savonarola made Isaac's livelihood as a musician precarious; already by 1492 Savonarola had had the city's chapels disbanded. Isaac realized that he could no longer work in his adopted city, and so by 1497 he had obtained a post as composer to the Emperor Maximilian, an appointment that apparently did not require his residence at the imperial court. He seems to have traveled fairly extensively during the next dozen or so years, but he still spent much of his time in Florence. He may have worked for periods in Innsbruck, at the Augustinian monastery in Neustift, in Constance, and elsewhere, and he may have negotiated with Duke Hercules d'Este I for a post in Ferrara that never materialized, but he is known to have been in Florence at regular intervals from 1499 on. When the Medici were restored to power in 1512, Isaac petitioned successfully to regain his former position, or at least his former salary; it seems likely that the elderly musician no longer took an active part in liturgical events, but received his income as a retirement benefit in recognition of many years of faithful service. He made a final trip to Vienna in 1515 to seek release from his service to the Emperor, who also granted him a generous pension. Isaac returned to Florence the same year and died there two years later.

Although Isaac is one of Josquin's greatest contemporaries, and some of his compositions, especially his secular works, have been studied and performed widely, there is still no complete edition of his music (though one is finally in progress) nor any detailed study of it. Thus his achievement cannot yet be assessed evenhandedly. His Masses, for example, have not all been published, and scarcely any of his motets, except for those in the *Choralis Constantinus*, are available in modern editions. Moreover, a brief evaluation of his style is made difficult by the fact that no other composer before Lasso was so cosmopolitan in his approach to composition. Isaac seems to have been equally at home writing French chansons, Flemish sacred polyphony, Italian carnival songs, and German tenor lieder. Even if his music were all available, it would not be easy to characterize so many-faceted a body of work. From the nostalgic folk-like hymn of praise to the Emperor's favorite city, *Innsbruck ich muss dich lassen,* to the moving Italianate lament on the death of Lorenzo the Magnificent, to the gothic intricacies of the *Choralis Constantinus,* Isaac reveals that he had understood and mastered all of the regional dialects that were coming to fragment the one central musical language.

In considering Isaac's music as a whole, the *Choralis Constantinus* deserves pride of place, not only for the vastness of its conception but also for the incredibly impressive technical skill the composer exhibits in it. He composed over 300 polyphonic settings of Propers for all Sundays throughout the year and for many major feasts and saints' days, altogether almost 100 occasions from the liturgical calendar. Isaac was the first composer since Léonin and Pérotin in the twelfth and thirteenth centuries to attempt such an ambitious task, and the only composer of the Renaissance to do so except for William Byrd, whose more modest *Gradualia* (published in two volumes in 1605–7) supplied English churches with similar material early in the seventeenth century. The *Choralis Constantinus* is a *summa* of Netherlandish polyphony about 1500, a comprehensive compendium of virtually all devices, manners, and styles prevalent at the time; it is especially illuminating as a summary of the ways cantus-firmus technique could be applied to the new equal-voiced polyphony.

For most Masses, Isaac set polyphonically the Introit, the Alleluia or Tract (depending on the season or feast), the Sequence or Prosa (if one existed for the liturgical occasion in question), and the Communion; left to be performed entirely in plainchant were the Offertory and the Gradual, the remaining two sung portions of the Proper. He usually composed only one of the double versicles in Sequences, and his five settings of the Mass Ordinary appended to the collection also leave out some phrases of the text. The omitted portions of both Sequences and Mass Ordinaries (and various other sections of the Propers) were intended to be performed as plainsong, or else the relevant chant was arranged for solo organ; thus, for much of each Mass, polyphony alternated with plainsong or organ music, a performing convention called *alternatim* practice.

The history of the *Choralis Constantinus* is by no means clear. It was not published until long after Isaac's death; Hieronymus Form-schneider of Nuremberg brought it out in three volumes between 1550 and 1555. In his preface the publisher stated that the diocese of Constance had commissioned the work, but doubts have been cast on the assumption that they had in mind any such ambitious project. Formschneider also reported that Isaac's pupil, Ludwig Senfl, completed the project, left unfinished at the older master's death.

The three volumes differ somewhat from one another in style and arrangement. Book I, for example, contains fewer Sequences, doubtless because they are less appropriate for the liturgical occasions included there. Isaac preferred to paraphrase the chant in the top voice in Book I, whereas in the later volumes he was apt to move it to the tenor or even the bass. Moreover, the polyphony, in from two to six but usually for four voices, grows slightly more complex and florid from one volume to another. This characteristic is explained partly by Isaac's use of complex notation in Book III, which itself constitutes a *summa* of proportional practice and is one of the few sources of the time in which the difficult proportional signs explained by theorists are actually applied in practice.

In some motets from the *Choralis Constantinus* Isaac placed the chant, in long notes or in florid style similar to that of the other voices, in only one part; in others he divided the chant between two or more voices, or developed it in imitation, or combined it with a second borrowed melody. Some impression of the astounding variety of techniques to be found in the work can be gained by comparing briefly merely the opening few bars of each movement from a single Mass from Book II, that for Christmas Day (Example 6–6). The Introit (A) begins with a "classical" point of imitation in four parts; the chant is laid out in its simplest form in the tenor voice in a rhythmic style that makes it identical in character with all the other voices. The Introit verse (B) opens with imitation by duet; the upper voice of each duet paraphrases the chant, which appears in its simplest form in the tenor. The first phrase of the Alleluia (C) sounds less imitative than the preceding movements because of its full sonority; but the upper two voices of the tutti do imitate each other, and the superius paraphrases the chant. The non-imitative duet that begins the Alleluia verse (D)—in which the top voice again paraphrases the chant—soon gives way to a chordal passage on the text "sanctificatus illuxit." The Sequence, like the Introit, opens with a classical point of imitation in four parts. And the Communion (E) contrasts non-imitative counterpoint in the upper two voices with a canon in the lower two.

At first acquaintance rather daunting because of its length and its apparent contrapuntal austerity, the *Choralis Constantinus* repays close study, for it is filled with some of the most magnificent polyphony of the entire period. Similarly, Isaac's Masses (that is, his settings of the Ordinary of the Mass), only now beginning to be rediscovered, deserve more attention. Models of four-part imitative counterpoint, they resemble Obrecht's Masses is some ways, especially in the ingenuity with which fast-moving motive-filled running passages are pitted against slower cantus-firmus-like lines.

If Isaac impresses us in his vast collection of Mass Propers, above all for his dazzling display of contrapuntal mastery, he shows himself capable in motets of writing music that can also touch and move us deeply. For example, his setting of the lament by the Florentine humanist

EXAMPLE 6–6. Heinrich Isaac, *Mass for Christmas Day,* from *Choralis Constantinus.*

(a) Introit

(b) Introit verse

(c) Alleluia

(d) Alleluia verse

(e) Communion

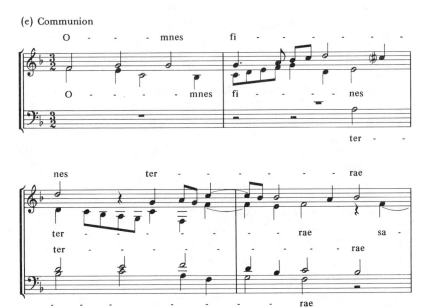

and poet, Angelo Poliziano, on the death of Lorenzo the Magnificent, *Quis dabit capiti meo aquam?*, stands comparison even with Josquin's great lamenting motets. Many details in the composition come together to produce its stunning effect: the austere and mournful beginning, on open fifths and octaves, that only gradually broadens out into a flowing mass of sound; the poignant fragment of canon over a pedal point in an appropriately dark low register at the phrase "ut nocte fleam, ut luce fleam" ("that I may weep by night, that I may weep by day"); the series of nearly symmetrical declamatory statements on the words "Sic turtur viduus solet, sic cygnus moriens solet, sic luscinia conqueri" ("thus the lonely turtle-dove mourned, thus the dying swan, thus the nightingale"), with their lush and unexpected harmonic progressions; or the entire *secunda pars*, built over a descending ostinato on "Et requiescat in pace" and reduced from four to three voices—the tenor is omitted—to signify "the laurel [that is, Lorenzo] suddenly struck down by a thunderbolt."

However impressive as a composer of sacred music, Isaac is best known today for his inventive and diverse secular music. His association with Florence and the Medici resulted in a handful of Italian songs, among the best of their kind, which show that he had assimilated completely the declamatory chordal style of his adopted country. Not only his boisterous carnival songs, but also the more lyrical ballate, like his settings of Poliziano's *Questo mostrarsi adirata* or Lorenzo the Magnificent's *Un di lieto gia mai,* could almost have been written by a native Florentine.

And, doubtless as a consequence of his service to the Emperor Maximilian, Isaac composed a number of German songs in three and four voices, compositions that follow in the footsteps of his northern contemporaries Heinrich Finck and Paul Hofhaimer. Like theirs, most of Isaac's lieder state the principal melody in the tenor and weave an imitative web of counterpoint around it, as in the rather four-square and deceptively naïve *Zwischen perg und tieffen tal* (based, unusually, on a two-part canon in the lowest voices), the melancholy folk narrative *Ich stund an einem Morgen*, or the rollicking and lustily humorous *Es het ein Baur ein Töchterlein.*

Isaac, like Obrecht, neglected the graceful and delicate tradition of the Burgundian chanson in favor of lively songs distinguished for their motivic interplay and rhythmic drive, and arrangements of popular tunes like *Et qui la dira, Par ung jour de matinée* and *Fille vous aves mal gardé.* The few rondeaux attributed to Isaac are mostly recompositions of older songs, such as his version of the anonymous *J'ay pris amours,* in which he used the first few notes of the borrowed melody as an ostinato —repeated incessantly at various pitches in the lowest voice—to accompany its complete statement in the superius, or *Le serviteur,* where he accompanied the elegant curves of the typically Burgundian melody with fast running lines of a sort associated with instruments. A good many of his secular pieces survive without text; although some of them will surely turn out to be chansons, lieder, or Italian songs once their proper words are discovered, others were almost certainly conceived in the first place without words as autonomous instrumental pieces. These include fairly short compositions in sober imitative counterpoint as well as extended pieces in which a singly simple motive is elaborated in witty interplay, as in *La la ho ho,* or in which the elaborate contrapuntal structure is supported by a cantus firmus, derived either from solmization syllables, like *La mi la sol,* or from a simple melodic formula, like the imposing *Palle, palle,* based apparently on the battle cry of the Medici faction (the *palle* being the balls in the Medici coat of arms).

PIERRE DE LA RUE (ca. 1460–1518)

Pierre de la Rue was one of the few major Netherlandish composers who seems never to have visited Italy. Born probably in Tournai about 1460, he spent most of his mature life in Brussels and Malines, at the Burgundian court of the Hapsburgs. Maximilian invited La Rue to join his chapel in 1492, and he stayed on there to serve beside Agricola under Maximilian's son, Philip the Handsome, and, after Philip's death in

1506, under Marguerite of Austria during the years she ruled the Netherlands as regent for the future Charles V. In 1516 La Rue retired from the court to become a canon of the chapter of Notre Dame in Courtrai, where he died two years later. So far as we know, he never left his homeland except for two relatively brief visits to Spain in the entourage of Philip. Marguerite evidently had a high regard for the leading composer at her court. After his death she had two elegant manuscript volumes of his Masses prepared to commemorate his achievements, and her own sumptuously decorated chanson albums contain more compositions by him than by any other composer.

Not surprisingly for a composer who had had no direct contact with humanistic influences in the south, La Rue seldom attempted to match his vocal lines to the way their words might be declaimed, and so his music does not usually project their exact meaning, even though it often expresses their general mood. Nor did he regularly strive for the rich harmonic effects so appreciated by his more Italianate contemporaries. His music is neither as tonally focused nor as rhythmically driving as theirs. His rather sombre counterpoint impresses the listener instead with the great individuality of its single melodic lines and with the complex interaction among them. In Picker's words, La Rue shunned musical rhetoric and sought "expressiveness through the tensions evoked by a linear conception."

The character of La Rue's counterpoint is well illustrated by the opening section of his motet *Lauda anima mea Dominum* (Example 6–7). After the few chords of the beginning the texture is shot through with imitations and, especially, with exchanges of short motives among the voices. But the imitations do not occur as clearly defined expositions of a central body of cogent thematic material, so much as make the continuous flow of music sound more homogeneous than it otherwise would. The same technique often led La Rue to repeat a single motive over and over in one or more voices as a freely recurring ostinato. In most of his twenty-three motets and more than thirty Masses, La Rue interrupted the continuous flow of music fairly frequently for extended passages of duets. And, like Josquin, he was wont to build movements over a canonic substructure, not least of all in his six-voiced *Missa Ave sanctissima Maria,* a triple canon that parodies a motet which is also a triple canon.

No such rigid constructivist device, though, holds together his best known Mass, the Requiem, consisting, like most polyphonic settings of the Mass for the Dead during the Renaissance, of parts of the Proper as well as the Ordinary—here Introit, Kyrie, Tract, Offertory, Sanctus, Agnus Dei, and Communion. La Rue's Requiem is remarkable in the first place for its dark sonorities. Much of the time all the voices sing in their lower registers. The first two movements, Introit and Kyrie, are especially

EXAMPLE 6–7. Pierre de la Rue, *Lauda anima mea Dominum,* mm. 1–16, ed.
Nigel Davison (text ed. R. E. Storrer), in Friedrich Blume (ed.), *Das Chorwerk,*
vol. 91 (Möseler Verlag, Wolfenbüttel and Zürich).

mournful because they are scored for low men's voices and the basses
often descend to the B♭ below the staff in the bass clef. Only the Communion, with its hopeful text "Lux aeterna," makes use of appropriately
bright high voices. Much of the Requiem unfolds in a characteristic full,

even thick, texture, in spite of frequent duets, dialogue between alternating pairs of voices, and passages in imitation.

Sobriety and contrapuntal rigor characterize Pierre de la Rue's secular as well as his sacred music. He wrote chansons over sacred cantus firmi and over canonic or quasi-canonic substructures, and some of his rondeaux demonstrate how the older conventions could be adapted to the new, predominantly four-voiced, vocal polyphony. But those of his thirty-odd chansons that are organized as a series of interlocked phrases without any predetermined scaffolding device or conventional repetition scheme—like *Trop plus secret, Autant en emporte le vent,* and *Pourquoy non* (all of them in the chanson albums of Marguerite of Austria)—best demonstrate his skills at creating musical form by means of motivic imitation. In many ways they resemble those of Josquin's courtly chansons that are not bound by *formes fixes.* Like Josquin, La Rue set poems closely related to older literary traditions by their rhetoric if not by their forms; he repeated musical phrases either to mirror the rhyme scheme of the poetry or merely to round off a closed form; he often overlapped phrases to ensure a continuous texture; and he wrote simpler and less melismatic music as he grew older. Perhaps La Rue's chansons differ most from Josquin's in their more concentrated use of short motives to organize and control the texture, in their high level of dissonance (a characteristic of much of La Rue's music), and in the generally placid character of their rhythm. La Rue's chansons seem to move at a stately pace partly because they are filled with leisurely syncopations, and partly because the composer consistently thwarted metrical stresses without counteracting the resulting loss of vigor by well-defined and sharply profiled rhythmic motives. And this lack of rhythmic drive gives to these highly serious compositions their slightly melancholy calm and their smooth, unbroken flow.

JEAN MOUTON (ca. 1459–1522)

After holding positions in the churches of three provincial cities, Nesle, Amiens and Grenoble, Mouton joined the chapel of Queen Anne of Brittany during the first decade of the sixteenth century. He remained in royal service for most of the rest of his life, working under Francis I after Anne's death. When Compère died in 1518, Mouton was granted that composer's former benefice at the collegiate church of Saint Quentin, and he may have retired there to spend his final years. Mouton was apparently the official court composer, commissioned to write music to celebrate important events both public and private. In his official capacity he probably took part, too, in the conference between Francis and Pope Leo X held at Bologna in 1515, and at Francis's meeting with Henry VIII of England at the Field of the Cloth of Gold in 1520. On both occasions the chapels of the rival heads of state competed with each other; at Bologna, Leo was so impressed with Mouton's genius that he rewarded the composer by appointing him an apostolic notary. Mouton may have composed his motet *Christe redemptor, O rex omnipotens* for the wedding of Anne and Louis XII in 1499, even before he was engaged at court, and a number of other motets by him can be associated with particular occasions: *Non nobis Domine*, for example, with the birth of Renée, the royal couple's second daughter; *Quis dabit oculi* with Anne's death in 1514; *Christus vincit* with Leo X's election as Pope in 1513; *Domine salvum fac Regem* with the coronation of Francis I in 1515; *Exalta Regina Galliae* with Francis's victory at the battle of Marignano, and so on.

Several sixteenth-century critics described Mouton as a pupil of Josquin, but in fact various other composers of the time imitated Josquin's mannerisms more closely than Mouton did. Even though both composers employed many of the same techniques—paired imitation, canonic cantus firmi, and so on—Mouton displayed a musical personality totally unlike that of Josquin. Although his 100-odd motets, approximately fifteen Masses, and twenty chansons at times include brilliant effects, by and large Mouton wrote serene, smoothly flowing polyphony, with great technical finish and superb contrapuntal command but without the flashes of fire of the older and greater master. In short, Mouton's solid steady craftsmanship suited admirably his position as composer for the highest official court occasions.

The smooth flow of Mouton's melody stems in large part from the stately regular pace at which much of his music moves. Short notes are used primarily to break up this slow, regular motion rather than to offer genuine rhythmic contrast. The melodic contours themselves tend to be rather short-spanned, Mouton's penchant for clear, sharply profiled motives perhaps reflecting the rational and precise spirit of his specifically French rather than Flemish heritage. Mouton was often indifferent to good text declamation: his music is filled with incorrect accentuations and other infelicities in the combination of words and notes, a trait that indicates he was more interested in purely musical design than in expression. Yet at times he did take care to match the text carefully to his melodic lines, particularly in his political motets where the words are especially important. In both the motet for Francis's coronation, *Domine salvum fac Regem*, and that celebrating the battle of Marignano, *Exalta Regina Galliae*, for instance, the words can be clearly understood, and the textual and musical accents mostly coincide. Mouton was fond of full sonorities; he consistently brought in all voices soon after the initial point of imitation—although the first entrance of the cantus firmus is often long delayed—and he normally kept all voices active most of the time. In spite of this penchant for continuous full sound, though, the texture of Mouton's music is usually clear and transparent, thanks partly to his care in keeping the voice ranges separate.

Like most of Josquin's contemporaries, Mouton changed his style gradually during his lifetime, the moment of greatest change occurring about the turn of the century, possibly as a result of his confrontation with Italian music. As a young man Mouton was evidently fascinated by purely musical design and constructive elements; as a mature artist he mixed homophony or near-homophony judiciously with passages of imitation and adopted a more humanistic attitude towards the texts he set.

Along with secular motets composed for political or other official events, Mouton set texts appropriate for particular liturgical occasions, such as Sequences (*Ave Maris . . . virgo serena*), responsories (*Antequam comedam*), and antiphons (*Beata Dei genitrix*); verses honoring various saints (*Amicus Dei Nicolas* for St. Nicolas, for example); and Biblical texts that had seldom been set polyphonically before Josquin's time, like psalms and settings of the Epistle or Gospel of the Mass. There are, in addition, a number of Marian texts, several hymns, and various sacred verses not yet identified as belonging to a specific liturgical or para-liturgical occasion. Many of the texts are pieced together from various liturgical or Biblical sources.

Mouton's dazzling contrapuntal skill is shown off in those compositions in which all of the voices are canonic, like *Nesciens Mater Virgo virum*, a quadruple canon partly based on a plainchant. Frequently Mouton constructed his motets around a central canon, either derived from a Gregorian plainsong (*Salva nos, Domine*) or based on apparently free material (*Peccata mea Domine*). Those motets that do not make use of some scaffolding technique sometimes paraphrase a chant (as in *Noli flere, Maria*), but usually quite freely; the composer assimilated the chant so well into his own melodic style that the original is sometimes difficult to disentangle. In those motets which seem to be based entirely on free material, Mouton sometimes repeated sections in a formally significant way: by ending each of the two *partes* with the same music (to produce the standard responsory form, aBcB); by introducing a phrase that returns in the manner of a ritornello; or at the very least by reworking previously introduced thematic material in a later section, using a free variation technique. And, finally, some motets (for example, the brief, lauda-like *In omni tribulatione*) are entirely free of borrowed material, scaffolding techniques, or repetition schemes and depend for their effect on successive points of imitation, on melodic coherence, or simply on the regular and steady rhythmic flow and the interplay between harmony and counterpoint.

Mouton's Masses span the transition from cantus-firmus technique to the newer procedures of paraphrase and parody. Most of the Masses seem to date from his mature years, and especially the decade between 1505 and 1515. Mouton either took his cantus firmi from chant (*Missa Alma redemptoris mater*) or he used one voice from a polyphonic composition (for example, the tenor of Févin's motet *Benedictus Dominus Deus*). More often than not, the cantus firmus is not sharply differentiated rhythmically from the other voices but, rather, is smoothly incorporated into the texture. Some of the Masses paraphrase monophonic material, and one of them, that based on Richafort's motet *Quem dicunt homines*, is a full-fledged parody Mass, one of the earliest using that compositional process.

Like his motets, Mouton's chansons display a variety of styles. Some are canonic, like *En venant de Lyon* and the lament on the death of Févin, *Qui ne regrettoit*. Some are three-part popular arrangements, apparently paraphrasing now-lost popular monophonic tunes. Some, like *Jamais, jamais* (in the *Odhecaton*) and *Resjouissez vous bourgeoises*, are wittily imitative pieces, influenced in their strongly metrical melodic style by popular tunes. Some of those for five and six voices resemble motets in their contrapuntal complexity. And at least one chanson, *De tous regretz*, is not unlike a later Parisian chanson in the manner of Claudin de Sermisy.

OTHER CONTEMPORARIES OF JOSQUIN

Some of the incredibly productive Netherlandish composers whose careers span the decades before and after 1500 have left almost no trace of themselves beyond their musical works. Absolutely nothing is known about the life of Johannes Japart, for example, beyond the surmise that he must have visited Italy since he wrote several Italian songs. In his nineteen secular works, however, he revealed himself to be a lesser master of considerable skill, with a curious penchant for constructing musical collages by combining pre-existing melodies with one another or with music of his own invention. Various other composers in this extraordinary generation were so peripatetic that they can scarcely be associated with one place more than another. As we have seen, Josquin divided his career between northern and southern Europe, and Agricola worked in Milan, Florence, Cambrai, Burgundy, and at the French royal court. But many composers of the High Renaissance, after changing posts several times in their younger years, eventually settled down to a fixed position in a cathedral, church, or princely chapel. The best musicians gravitated towards the richest and most important and active musical centers in western Europe, especially the French royal chapel or the Vatican, or towards one of the smaller but culturally rich city states of northern Italy, or the court of the Burgundian Hapsburgs.

Wherever the French kings took up residence, at Orléans, Blois, or Paris, they maintained a large and elaborate court that included, among retainers of every kind, many musicians—not only trumpeters and drummers, virtuoso chamber musicians, and expert singers, but also some of the most distinguished composers of the period. After Ockeghem's death, Loyset Compère was surely the greatest musician to grace the court of Charles VIII, the king whose Italian campaigns gave such an important impetus to cultural exchange between the two countries. As we have seen, Josquin was in close contact with Louis XII, at least for a time, and Jean Mouton served the king as official court composer, a position he maintained during the first years of the reign of the handsome, dashing Francis I. But there were many other excellent composers at the French court during this period, among them Antoine de Févin (ca. 1480–1512), Johannes Prioris (fl. 1490–1512), Antoine de Longueval (died after 1523), Antonius Divitis (ca. 1475–after 1526), and Pierre Moulu (ca. 1480/90–ca. 1550).

Févin might well have been one of the greatest musicians of his age had he not died in his mid-thirties. His charming and graceful music reveals him as an attractive follower of Josquin, among the first composers to cultivate extensively full-fledged parody technique in his Masses (including two, *Missa Ave Maria* and *Missa Mente tota*, based on motets by Josquin), and also the creator of sparkling and witty three-part arrangements of popular songs. If his transparent textures, filled with paired imitations and fragments of dialogue between parts of the chorus, sometimes seem facile, he nevertheless seldom lost sight of his ideal: a clear and elegant formal musical design. Févin's parody Masses probably predate by only a few years several others written at the French court, notably two by Févin's colleagues Mouton and Divitis, perhaps conceived in friendly competition and both based on Richafort's motet *Quem dicunt homines*. This concentration of works using new techniques of composition suggests that parody procedure grew up in the musical circles around the French kings. Its central importance in sixteenth-century music will be more fully considered in the following chapter.

One of Pierre Moulu's best known works, the *Missa Alma redemptoris mater* (which paraphrases the Marian antiphon), reveals a markedly constructivist tendency in his musical personality; it is composed so that it can be performed either as it stands or by omitting all the rests longer than a minim. His other best known work, the motet *Mater floreat florescat*, probably written and first performed for the triumphal entry into Paris in 1517 of the newly crowned wife of Francis I, Queen Claude, furnishes the only evidence that the composer was connected with the royal chapel. It pays tribute to the most celebrated musicians of France and names many of the composers from the court. Along with Févin and his brother Robert, Mouton, Divitis, and many others, Moulu praises Longueval, Lourdault, and Prioris. Antoine de Longueval (or, to give him his French name, Jean à la Venture) is remembered today chiefly as the composer of a Passion—actually a series of fairly chordal motets telling the Passion story in words drawn from the four Evangelists and incorporating chant formulae—which in the sixteenth century was mistakenly thought to be a work by Obrecht, tribute indeed to the skill of the royal composer. Jean Braconnier may have taken his nickname, "Lourdault" (meaning clown, lout, or blockhead), from a chanson with that incipit; it fits what we know of his musical personality as expressed in his raucous, witty songs. Johannes Prioris, on the other hand, is a somewhat more serious and old-fashioned composer who did not exploit the new imitative techniques to nearly the same extent as his colleagues. His best known work, the lovely song-motet *Dulcis amica Dei*, like his delicate chansons, does not sound very different from older Burgundian music, and his Requiem Mass resembles in many ways that by his illustrious predecessor, Ockeghem.

Moulu's motet also mentions Antoine Brumel (ca. 1460–ca. 1520), a sometime Parisian (he served as *maître des enfants* and canon at the cathedral of Notre Dame for a few years just before the turn of the century) who had spent his earlier years in various French cities—Chartres, Laon and Lyons—before moving to Ferrara late in his life. Primarily a composer of sacred music, Brumel for the most part took Josquin as his model. The younger composer's use of imitation, duets, and dialogue passages, however, does not always display the same fertile imagination as his master, a point made by Glareanus, who compared a *Missa de Beata Virgine* by each composer, much to Brumel's detriment. While Brumel proved his skill at the craft of composition in works like the *Missa Et ecce terraemotus* for twelve voices, a musical oddity that is nevertheless not without aesthetic value, his counterpoint, like Févin's, is often merely facile. The long passages that move in parallel tenths and the sections where the text is simply declaimed on repeated notes show that Brumel wished to write a clear and simple sort of music. Like the more contrapuntally rigorous Mathieu Gascongne, who probably came to the French court during the reign of Francis I from Cambrai, Brumel may himself have served as model for those musicians in the 1520's and 1530's who established a specifically French musical style, more lucid and direct than the rich polyphony of the Netherlanders.

We have already seen that the small city states of northern Italy were able to attract the greatest musicians of the time by offering them artistic stimulation and enlightened patronage. But the continuing prosperity of each court depended on uncertain political conditions, and fortunes rose and fell continually during the fifteenth and sixteenth centuries. The brilliance of Milan's musical establishment was shortlived; it scarcely survived Galeazzo Maria Sforza's murder in 1476. Music in Florence suffered at the end of the fifteenth century with the rise of the puritanical reformer Savonarola and the expulsion of the Medici family. The great musical days of Venice were yet to come. Almost all of the records of the small but unusually civilized court of Urbino have been lost. And Mantua was too poor to compete on the international scene, in spite of the lively intelligence and determination of its patroness, the Marchesa Isabella d'Este. During the period 1480–1520, the goddess of musical fortune smiled most warmly on the court of Ferrara, especially under the leadership of Duke Hercules d'Este I and his successor Alfonso I. To their city, they invited a host of great musicians, among them Obrecht, Josquin, Brumel, Collinet de Lannoy, Johannes Ghiselin (called Verbonnet), and Johannes Martini. Ghiselin (who seems also to have worked for a time at the French court) enjoyed a wider international reputation than Martini—Petrucci, for example, published many of Ghiselin's motets and chansons and devoted a whole volume solely to his Masses—but Martini held a place of honor at the Ferrarese court, as principal composer for many years. Both Ghiselin and Martini wrote in a style similar in many respects to that of Agricola and Obrecht. Their layered polyphony betrays a predilection for cantus-firmus technique, and their textures are often shot through with short nervous motives or longer running passages. But both composers also made extensive use of imitation, and some of their work, like Ghiselin's predominantly chordal motet *O gloriosa domina*, shows that they appreciated the rhetorical effect of syllabic text setting.

As brilliant as Ferrara, but not certainly more notable in spite of being the center of Christianity, the Papal chapel in Rome carried on its long and distinguished tradition of excellence under the pontificates of Innocent VIII (1484–92); the infamous Alexander VI (1492–1503), born Rodrigo Borgia; Pius III (1503), who reigned for less than a month; Julius

II (1503–13), born Giuliano della Rovere, who established the Cappella Giulia (named for him) in St. Peter's as an organization distinct from the Sistine choir; and the great patron of the arts, Leo X (1513–21), born Giovanni de' Medici. Apart from Jósquin and Prioris, the best composers in the chapel included Gaspar van Weerbecke (ca. 1440–after 1517), a Flemish composer of unusually Italianate music who came to Rome from Milan and interrupted his service at the Vatican for about ten years (1489–1500) to return to Milan briefly and to serve in the chapel of the Burgundian duke, Philip the Handsome; Marbriano de Orto (d. 1529), who also left Rome for Philip's service; and Elzéar Genet (ca. 1470–1548), called Carpentras after his home town in southern France, who may more properly belong in the following chapter along with other members of the post-Josquin generation. Carpentras published most of his music at his own expense during his last years, as we know from a series of contracts between him and his printers, fascinating documents that supply many details about the printing business at the time.

If the dream of a Burgundian empire as a buffer state between France and the Holy Roman Empire had died with Charles the Bold in 1477, the musical distinction of the duke's chapel lived on, under both Philip the Handsome, Emperor Maximilian's son, and Marguerite of Austria, during the years she ruled as regent for her nephew, the future Emperor Charles V. We have already seen that Marguerite took special notice of the aging Josquin, living in retirement in the village of Condé. More directly involved with daily musical events at her and Philip's courts were Pierre de la Rue, Agricola, and the two alumni of the Papal chapel, Orto and Weerbecke. Other notable centers of musical activity in the Netherlands included the confraternity of Our Lady (the *Illustre Lieve Vrouwe Broederschap*) in 's-Hertogenbosch, a society of clerics and musicians who numbered the composers Mattheus Pipelare and Nicolaes Craen among their members; and the church of Our Lady in the great commercial city of Antwerp, which employed Obrecht and also, as their organist from about 1515 to 1516, the lesser master Benedictus de Opitiis.

BIBLIOGRAPHICAL NOTES

Editions of the complete works of many of the composers discussed in this chapter have been published or are in the course of publication in the series *Corpus Mensurabilis Musicae*, issued by the American Institute of Musicology—for example, Brumel, ed. Barton Huston (*CMM* 5), Johannes Ghiselin-Verbonnet, ed. Clytus Gottwald (*CMM* 23), Matthaes

Pipelare, ed. Ronald Cross (*CMM* 34), Elzéar Genet (Carpentras), ed. Albert Seay (*CMM* 58), and others. Examples of Franco-Flemish music of about 1500 may also be found in various volumes of the series *Das Chorwerk*, ed. Friedrich Blume (Wolfenbüttel, 1929–   ), and in Albert Smijers, ed., *Van Ockeghem tot Sweelinck* (Amsterdam, 1939–52, 6 vols.).

On sacred music of this period, see Edgar H. Sparks, *Cantus Firmus in Mass and Motet, 1420–1520* (Berkeley and Los Angeles, 1963). For a selection of motets, and a discussion of the French royal chapel and the Papal chapel, see Edward E. Lowinsky, ed., *The Medici Codex of 1518*, 3 volumes, *Monuments of Renaissance Music*, vols. 3–5 (Chicago and London, 1968). On the Burgundian court and a selection of chansons sung there, see Martin Picker, *The Chanson Albums of Marguerite of Austria* (Berkeley and Los Angeles, 1965). The first two of Petrucci's early anthologies of secular music have been published in modern editions by Helen Hewitt, as *Harmonice Musices Odhecaton A* (Cambridge, Mass., 1942), and *Ottaviano Petrucci, Canti B, numero cinquanta, Venice, 1502, Monuments of Renaissance Music*, vol. 2 (Chicago and London, 1967). On chansons about 1500, see also James Haar, ed., *Chanson and Madrigal, 1480–1530* (Cambridge, Mass., 1964). On the symbolism of Franco-Flemish music, see Willem Elders, *Studien zur Symbolik in der Musik der alten Niederländer* (Bilthoven, 1968).

On Agricola, see his *Opera Omnia*, ed. Edward R. Lerner (*CMM* 22), and Lerner, "The 'German' Works of Alexander Agricola," *Musical Quarterly*, 46 (1960). On Obrecht, see his *Werken*, ed. Johannes Wolf, 7 vols. (Amsterdam and Leipzig, 1912–21; repr. 1968), and an alternative *Opera Omnia*, ed. Marcus van Crevel (Amsterdam, 1959–   ). See also Otto Gombosi, *Jacob Obrecht* (Leipzig, 1925), and Arnold Salop, "Jacob Obrecht and the Early Development of Harmonic Polyphony," *Journal of the American Musicological Society*, 17 (1964). On Compère, see his *Opera Omnia*, ed. Ludwig Finscher (*CMM* 15), and Finscher, *Loyset Compère* (Rome, 1964).

Volume I of Isaac's *Choralis Constantinus* ed. E. Bezecny and W. Rabl, was published in *Denkmäler der Tonkunst in Oesterreich* (*DTO*), Jahrgang 5, vol. 10 (Vienna, 1898); Volume II, ed. Anton von Webern, in *DTO*, Jahrgang 16, vol. 32 (Vienna, 1909); and Volume III, ed. Louise Cuyler (Rochester, 1948). The five Mass Ordinaries appended to Volume III have also been edited by Cuyler (Ann Arbor, 1952). Other Masses have been edited by Martin Staehelin in Heinrich Isaac, *Messen, Musikalische Denkmäler*, vol. 7 (Mainz, 1970). Isaac's secular works were edited by Johannes Wolf in *DTO*, Jahrgang 14, vol. 28 (Vienna, 1907), with a supplement in *DTO*, Jahrgang 16, vol. 32. On Isaac's life, see Frank A. D'Accone, "Heinrich Isaac in Florence," *Musical Quarterly*, 49 (1963). His complete works are in the process of publication, ed. Edward R. Lerner (*CMM* 65).

Some of Pierre de la Rue's music may be found in modern editions in Smijers, *Van Ockeghem;* Picker, *Chanson Albums;* and *Das Chorwerk,* vols. 11 and 91. On La Rue's motets, see Nigel Davison, "The Motets of Pierre de la Rue," *Musical Quarterly,* 48 (1962).

Jean Mouton's complete works are in the process of being published by Andrew Minor as *CMM* 43.

part three

The High Renaissance:
1520-1560

SEVEN

THE POST-JOSQUIN GENERATION

The geography of music changed in the course of the sixteenth century. Some cities and courts where music had been cultivated most intensively lost their leading position, some preserved their reputations, and some that had never been famous for musical activities became major centers. Political events affected these changes but seem not to have determined them. Italy, for example, maintained its cultural richness and diversity in the face of overwhelming difficulties, even though the relative importance of its various cities shifted. Divided by many rival factions and apparently unable to unite in a common cause, Italy became Europe's battleground. The terrible sack of Rome by the mercenaries of Charles V in 1527 destroyed the city but not its musical traditions; the Papal chapel continued as one of the chief cultural institutions of the continent. Venice, in spite of its decreasing commercial importance and political power, enjoyed a burst of creative energy that was not to die down for several centuries. Willaert, Rore, Zarlino, the Gabrielis, and

Monteverdi, among others, helped to form a specifically Venetian musical tradition of great splendor. And Ferrara, never an important pawn in the game of international politics, maintained throughout the century its rich musical and literary culture. Milan, on the other hand, never regained its musical importance after it had been occupied by the French; and Florence became ever more provincial after the collapse of the republic in 1529 and the imposition on the city of the Medici as hereditary grand dukes of Tuscany. In the north, the French, largely unsuccessful in the politics of war, nevertheless continued to support a court chapel of great brilliance. Despite religious persecution in the Netherlands and religious strife in the Germanic countries, the Holy Roman Emperors, first Maximilian I and then Charles V, employed some of the best musicians of the time. And, especially after Albert V became Duke of Bavaria in 1550, Munich established itself for the first time as an international musical capital. Great patrons and enlightened policies towards the arts seem to have affected the status of music in the various cities and courts of Europe much more than political or economic trends.

Wherever they worked, many of the leading composers in the years between the death of Josquin and the maturity of Lasso and Palestrina—from about 1520 until mid-century or a bit later—took up and developed the techniques of composition that Josquin and his contemporaries had first explored. But new techniques and new genres were also invented, and new factors transformed the sound of music in this generation. The process of writing new compositions by parodying old ones became for many composers a regular technical resource. Musicians intensified their quest for ways to express the meaning as well as the form of the words they set. An autonomous instrumental music grew up, not dependent in any way on literary associations or on the dance. And the religious revolution that split Europe into two warring camps had far-reaching effects on music.

The second quarter of the sixteenth century also witnessed the rise and development of various national styles in music. This trend was to affect profoundly the physiognomy of sixteenth-century music, and ultimately it successfully challenged the hegemony of the Franco-Flemish pan-European musical language that had been the lingua franca for over a hundred years. For the first time, for example, it was possible to differentiate clearly between Netherlandish and Parisian chansons, and between French and Flemish sacred music; and lieder and madrigals became the predominant secular forms in the Germanic countries and Italy respectively. Moreover, Spain and England could boast of superb composers whose music did not quite fit into the central tradition of the rest of western Europe.

Nevertheless, a mainstream of Franco-Flemish music, led by

Adrian Willaert, Jacob Clemens non Papa, and Nicolas Gombert, can still be discerned cutting its channel through the first half of the sixteenth century, although its course grew ever more sluggish. To call the second quarter of the sixteenth century "the age of Willaert, Gombert, and Clemens non Papa" would be to acknowledge the central place that these three leading composers and their Franco-Flemish contemporaries occupy in the history of music in the Renaissance. They form an important group of northern musicians who carried on the traditions of Josquin and his colleagues. But the label seems to exclude many features peculiar to the period with which these masters had little or nothing to do. While characterizing music between 1520 and 1560 as the "age of pervading imitation" encompasses more than the individual achievements of three great musicians, doing so ignores the importance of text expression, among other things, and the growth of national dialects. Nor can the quarter century (and more) be considered by musicians as the "age of the Reformation," crucial as the religious schism was to political and intellectual trends for the remainder of the century; that label bypasses the most important repertory of compositions and neglects the most significant changes in the history of musical style. The apparently neutral phrase "the post-Josquin generation," then, describes the salient features of the age more accurately than might first be apparent, especially if the foremost achievements of the generation are seen to have been the way composers worked out the implications of the new imitative techniques, the manner in which they continued Josquin's endeavors to embody in their music the essence of the texts they set, and the skill with which this group of cosmopolitan musicians enhanced and developed local musical traditions wherever they worked in western Europe.

While changes in style and technique altered the sound of music in the second quarter of the sixteenth century, the rise and development of music printing drastically transformed the way music was distributed and the audience it reached. During the second half of the fifteenth century various attempts were made to devise a satisfactory method for including music in books, either by printing the staves and writing in the notes by hand or by preparing entire compositions on metal blocks or woodcuts. Movable type, however, turned out to be the most practical technique, and it was used for the first collection of part music, the anthology of secular songs called *Harmonice Musices Odhecaton A,* printed by Ottaviano Petrucci in Venice in 1501. Petrucci sent each page through his presses twice, once for the staves and once for the notes; this was a difficult process because of the careful alignment required, but he succeeded in overcoming the technical problems brilliantly, and the great elegance of his many volumes has set a high standard for music publishers ever since. Certainly none of the other Italian printers of the early sixteenth century who issued music books could rival the quality of Petrucci's press work, not even Andrea Antico, the only other publisher of the first quarter of the century to bring out a substantial number of volumes.

In the second quarter of the sixteenth century, music began to be printed by single impression. Type pieces made up of small fragments of the staff already combined with the notes were assembled by a type-setter into a composite so that each page needed to be sent through the presses only once. This was the technique used by Pierre Attaingnant in Paris beginning in the late 1520's, and it dominated music printing until the mid-eighteenth century. Attaingnant died about 1551, though his firm continued to be run by his widow for a few years. In the meantime, however, music printing in Paris had been taken over by Nicolas du Chemin and the firm of Le Roy and Ballard. In the provincial city of Lyons Jacques Moderne began his publishing business in the 1530's. In the Netherlands, Tielman Susato of Antwerp and Pierre Phalèse of Louvain both published large quantities of music from the 1540's onwards. Antwerp was the home, too, of the publishing house established by the composer Hubert Waelrant and the printer Jean Laet in 1554, and also of the famous publisher Christopher Plantin, who issued several volumes of music in the second half of the century. Venetian printers dominated the Italian scene at mid-century, especially the two rival firms of Gardane, begun by an émigré Frenchman, and Scotto, run by the same family for generations. Germany, where printing had been invented, was very active in the field of music almost from the beginning of the century, and the many distinguished publishers there included Peter Schoeffer the Younger, Nicolas Faber of Leipzig, Christian Egenolph of Frankfurt, Georg Rhaw of Wittenberg, Melchior Kriesstein of Augsburg, and Hieronymus Formschneider, Johannes Petreius, and Berg and Neuber, all from Nuremberg.

NICOLAS GOMBERT

Nicolas Gombert (ca. 1500–ca. 1556), master of the choirboys in the chapel of Emperor Charles V from about 1526 to about 1540, was one of the most brilliant composers of his day. His historical position is neatly summed up by the German theorist Hermann Finck, who wrote that Gombert, the student of Josquin, showed the musicians of his time how to write in a new style that avoided pauses and was filled with harmony and with imitations. And, in fact, Gombert's ten Masses (almost all of them parodies of motets or chansons), more than 160 motets (the majority for four or five voices), and some sixty chansons present the most classical formulation of the style of pervading imitation.

One of the great contrapuntists of the sixteenth century, Gombert wrote melodic lines built in long arching phrases filled with ingenious syncopations that keep the motion flowing gracefully forward while avoiding obvious metrical stresses and that often forego elaborate melismas except on the last stressed syllable of a phrase. Gombert's carelessness in planning these floating lines with little regard for the placement of text accents shows that he valued musical design over expression. But his music is not bland. On the contrary, his delight in unexpected, sometimes harsh dissonances constitutes one of the hallmarks of his style and gives to some of his part-writing its delightfully gritty quality. In his setting of the Responsory for Easter Sunday, *Expurgate vetus fermentum*, for instance, even the opening point of imitation (Example 7–1), with its exposition of two motives, one for each half of the opening phrase of text, includes several pungent appoggiaturas and instances where a suspension sounds simultaneously with its note of resolution. The motet follows the conventional form for Responsories, ending both its *partes* with the same text and music (aBcB). Gombert also used this formal device in other motets, though more often in those that are based on Biblical rather than strictly liturgical texts, and which generally eschew Willaert's favorite scaffolding devices of cantus firmus and canon.

Gombert's formal procedures, typical for Franco-Flemish composers of the post-Josquin generation, may clearly be seen in his setting of Psalm 129, *Beati omnes* (Example 7–2). Even though the composer made no attempt to arrange the musical details of his melodic lines to accommodate the text he sets—even the first words, "Beati omnes," are consistently misaccentuated—it is in fact the form of the psalm that determines the form of the music. Each clause of the text is set to a separate phrase of music identified by its own distinct and individual melodic material:

> *Beati omnes qui timent Dominum,*
> Blessed is everyone who fears the Lord,

> *qui ambulant in viis eius.*
> who walks in his ways!

> *Labores manuum tuarum quia manducabis:*
> You shall eat the fruit of the labor of your hands;

> *beatus es, et bene tibi erit.*
> you shall be happy, and it shall be well with you.

EXAMPLE 7–1. Nicolas Gombert, *Expurgate vetus fermentum,* mm. 1–11.
Used by permission of the American Institute of Musicology.

EXAMPLE 7–2. Gombert, *Beati omnes*, mm. 1–47. Used by permission of the American Institute of Musicology.

In the first phrase the point of imitation is laid out in a leisurely "classical" manner. Successive voices enter with their significant melodic material only after two or three bars, sufficient time to grasp clearly the relationship of each new voice to the whole. No clear-cut cadence separates the second from the first phrase. Instead, Gombert devises for "qui timent Dominum" a second short motive (mm. 13ff) which serves as a bridge passage. The following music for "qui ambulant," with its characteristic rising fourth and close time interval of imitation, thus overlaps the end of the first phrase. Similarly, no full cadence brings the forward motion to a halt at the end of the second phrase. Gombert makes clear that one sentence of the text has ended and another begun by cutting down the texture and by making the point of imitation on "Labores manuum tuarum" almost as leisurely in its layout as the initial exposition. And all of the next points, on "quia manducabis," "beatus es," and "et bene tibi erit," are also run together. The final phrase of the excerpt, on "et bene tibi erit," broadens out, in keeping with its formal position just before an important new section and in order to reflect the benign, spacious sentiments of its words; each voice states the text and the music associated with it at least twice.

In this motet—and in many other compositions by members of the post-Josquin generation—the music flows smoothly along without obvious seams or clearly demarcated points of articulation. The character of the imitation that pervades the texture changes according to its position in the larger musical design or according to the form or meaning of the words. Some points need abundant time to state their melodic material, while some are very compressed; in some points each voice imitates the others exactly, while in some an initial characteristic interval or even a more or less vague general shape suffices to establish the identity of the significant motives. Neither the order of entries nor the time interval between statements of a theme is ever fixed. The details of texture and layout can be arranged and re-arranged in an infinite number of ways. The texture or mood rarely changes abruptly from section to section. Composers continued to interrupt the complex polyphony from time to time with homorhythmic chordal passages that give special emphasis to individual words and phrases, but the music of the Franco-Flemish composers of the post-Josquin generation is seldom dramatic. In fact, many of the motives they devised for a single composition bear at least a general family resemblance to one another. None of the points of imitation in Example 7–2, for instance, is built from memorable melodic lines that resonate obsessively in the mind's ear. But what may at first seem to be a lack of melodic invention is often merely the result of the composer's evident intention to maintain musical decorum. In much of the music by Gombert, Clemens, and Willaert, Josquin's ideal of clarity, elegance, balance, and symmetry was replaced by the desire to create a continuous and placid flow of sound, not well articulated formally but held together by all possible permutations of the technique of imitation.

Gombert based a Mass on his own motet *Beati omnes*, and a comparison of the two works reveals some of the procedures composers of his generation commonly adopted in applying the new technique of parody to their works. In writing parody Masses, composers appropriated the entire substance of the polyphonic work they took as a model, not just a single melodic line set out as a cantus firmus. The composer elaborated the borrowed composition by taking from it individual phrases and motives, or sometimes merely rhythms, chords, or chord progressions, and subjecting them to free variation. In some passages the composer took over the pre-existing polyphony with hardly any changes, but in other passages he recomposed the original music almost completely, extending and elaborating the musical material, combining the melodic lines in entirely new ways, giving new emphasis to motives hardly touched in the original, ignoring or underplaying motives that had been given great attention in the model, reversing or otherwise changing the order in which the themes appear, or using them in altogether new contexts.

The first of the three acclamations in Kyrie I from Gombert's *Missa Beati omnes* (Example 7–3), for instance, duplicates almost exactly the opening point of imitation from his motet. Some of the melodic details are changed—in the superius, for example, a few intervals are filled in by stepwise motion, and two repeated quarter notes are combined into one half note—and the end of the phrase has been adjusted to take into account the fact that the Mass reduces the motet's five voices to four, but the music remains essentially unaltered. The second acclamation, on the other hand, beginning in m. 12, gives great attention to a motive hardly touched in the model, Gombert's alternative setting of the words "qui timent Dominum" which served as a bridge passage between the first and second phrases of the motet (Example 7–2, mm. 13–16). He recomposed and extended the original material to make an entirely new point of imitation on the same motive, a technique he also applied to the third acclamation of Kyrie I (mm. 19ff), which is based on the music set to the words "qui ambulant in viis eius" in the motet (Example 7–2, mm. 17–22). In the three acclamations of the Christe section of the Mass, Gombert used music he originally composed for "Labores manuum tuarum," "quia manducabis," and "beatus es," and in Kyrie II he picked out three motives from the second half of the motet's *prima pars*. In other words, in the Kyrie of this parody Mass built on one of his own motets, Gombert took up some but not all of the model's most important motives, in the order in which they originally appeared, and either quoted them fairly literally or else recomposed them completely.

Certain conventions about the use of borrowed material in the overall construction of Masses soon grew up and were frequently but not invariably observed. More often than not, Masses take up motives in

EXAMPLE 7–3. Gombert, *Missa Beati omnes, Kyrie I.* Used by permission of the American Institute of Musicology.

motives

1. the order in which they were presented in the model. The beginning of the model usually opens each major division of a parody Mass; all five movements of Gombert's *Missa Beati omnes,* for example, begin with the motet's initial point of imitation. Often, too, the first section of the

2. *secunda pars* of a model begins important subdivisions of a parody Mass. Gombert, for example, started the second main section of the Gloria and the second of his two Agnus Dei by parodying the opening point of imitation from the *secunda pars* of his motet, and the same material is reworked towards the middle of the Credo as well (though it appears there at the words "et resurrexit," which occur midway through a section for only three voices). Moreover, the final cadence of the model

3. often concludes each movement of the Mass cycle, a convention Gombert followed in the Gloria, Credo, and Agnus Dei of his *Missa Beati omnes,* but not in the Kyrie or Sanctus movements. In some sixteenth-century parody Masses, though not in the *Missa Beati omnes,* all of the

4. motives with which the composer chose to work appear in the Kyrie movement, which thus becomes a thematic repository for the rest of the

parody conventions

5. Mass; and in some Masses the composer occasionally reworked musical material originally identified with words that are related in one way or another to that particular passage of the Mass text, thus creating a literary as well as a musical association between the Mass and its model.

Some of the procedures composers had adopted in the fourteenth and fifteenth centuries resembled parody, and yet the fully worked-out technique of the sixteenth century reflects an entirely new attitude towards the task of basing a composition on pre-existing music; sixteenth-century parody technique could only have come about after the establishment of novel compositional methods. We have seen that later fifteenth-century composers began to enrich the textures of their cantus-firmus compositions by bringing in from time to time other voices from the polyphonic models they used. Parody technique simply extended that practice. Moreover, composers in the later fifteenth century built their melodies out of motives; Agricola, for example, differs from his predecessors in the way he unified his polyphonic texture motivically. The emergence of parody technique brought the first stage in the history of the musical motive to its logical conclusion. Most importantly, full-fledged parody technique depended on the new method of simultaneous, as opposed to successive, composition and on the new practice of constructing music from inter-locked phrases in which each individual voice need not be a self-contained linear entity. Composers did not have to lay out their pieces beforehand over a cantus firmus. Instead they worked with all strands of the polyphonic complex at once to create four or more equal and independent melodic lines. Individual voices could drop in and out of the texture at will. Even though composers continued to write music over cantus firmi, they came to depend more and more on the greater flexibility of parody procedures, better adapted to the new situation in which motives constituted the basic building blocks of composition. The history of parody technique in the sixteenth century, and its changing conventions, has yet to be written. It seems to have begun with the Mass and to have become a central feature of sixteenth-century settings of the divine service, but it also came to be applied to every other genre of music—madrigals, chansons, and instrumental compositions, as well as motets.

ADRIAN WILLAERT

Parody was an extremely important technique new to the composers of the post-Josquin generation. But the sound of their music was even more strongly affected by another feature of their compositions. Composers of the early sixteenth century became increasingly aware of the rhetorical and expressive possibilities in writing music that fits exactly the words it sets and that can embody not merely their external form, but also their intrinsic meaning. Following Josquin's lead, musicians everywhere in western Europe came to be more and more conscious of the virtues of a perfect union between melody and text. This development took place in all genres of music, but in none so strikingly as in the Italian madrigal. And few composers were as sensitive to the demands of poetry as Adrian Willaert (ca. 1490–1562), the Netherlandish chapel-master at St. Mark's in Venice. His mastery of musical declamation was recognized by his contemporaries, and perhaps no one has explained his position in the history of text setting better than the German theorist Gaspar Stocker, who wrote in his treatise on text underlay, dating from about 1570, that

> recently, Adrian Willaert seems to have begun, and happily so, a new music, in which he does away altogether with the liberties taken by the older composers. He so strictly observes well-defined rules that his compositions offer the singer greatest pleasure and no difficulties at all as far as the words are concerned. All modern composers follow him now. As Josquin appears to be the leader of the older school of music, so Adrianus stands out as the summit, the father, leader and creator of the new style which is now being generally imitated.

Stocker seems to be referring especially to Willaert's collection of motets and madrigals published in 1559 under the title *Musica Nova* (combining both genres in one set of part books was quite unusual in the sixteenth century, and that fact itself singles the collection out for special attention). Indirect evidence suggests that the anthology had in fact been issued for the first time in the mid-1540's with the title *La Pecorina*, in honor of Polissena Pecorina, a virtuoso soprano famous in Venice for her interpretation of Willaert's music; and most of the compositions in the volume were probably written in the late 1530's and early 1540's, a conjecture that gives us an approximate idea of the date by which Willaert had perfected the art of joining poetry to music.

Willaert's *Musica Nova* of 1559 contains twenty-seven motets, many of them settings of Old Testament texts or liturgical sequences, and twenty-five madrigals, all but one of them set to sonnets by Petrarch. Included in the collection are a few compositions for four or for seven voices, but most require five or six voices, numbers that were rapidly becoming standard. In keeping with the exalted tone of the poetry and the composer's own temperament, Willaert's expressiveness in these madrigals is usually quite restrained. A passage like that shown in Example 7–4, the beginning of *I piansi, hor canto,* is slightly exceptional in the clear way in which it depicts a typical Petrarchan antithesis,

EXAMPLE 7–4. Adrian Willaert, *I piansi, hor canto,* mm. 1–13. Used by permission of the American Institute of Musicology.

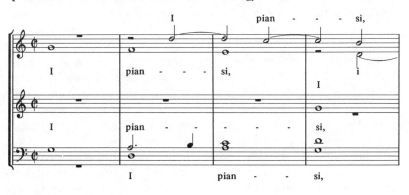

first weeping (by its slow tempo, long note values, relatively low register, and series of suspensions) and then singing (by its quicker note values, melismas, and high register), in a "madrigalism" of the sort that later came to be derided as naive. Nevertheless, the example demonstrates very well Willaert's intention of projecting the meaning of the text at the same time that he took care never to misaccentuate a word, but built into his melodic lines the tonic accents of phrases and even of sentences. Often predominantly syllabic, with many repeated notes on which the poetry is simply declaimed, Willaert's melodic lines in his madrigals gain in word projection and emphasis what they lack in sweep and breadth (which latter characteristics are more clearly associated with his motets). The "new" element in Willaert's *Musica Nova*, then, consists in the first place in the careful way the composer treated the words, even in the midst of the quietly flowing rivers of sound that characterize so much of the music by composers of the post-Josquin generation.

The motets from this seminal publication are among Willaert's best. Among other things, they reveal the artistic tension that underlies much of the composer's sacred music, the unresolved conflict between freely composed music conceived entirely from the composer's imagination and based on interlocked phrases, and those motets built over strict cantus firmi, especially those combining that old-fashioned technique with Willaert's favorite device of canon. Willaert's setting of a part of the Beatitudes (Matthew 5: 3–12), *Beati pauperes spiritu* (Example 7-5), exemplifies the newer style; it is free of borrowed material and the composer took the greatest care to observe the natural text accents. It also typifies Willaert's style in general, with its relatively dark sonorities (the superius, for example, never rising above c″); its thick seamless flow of sound seldom interrupted by reduced forces or by full cadences that stop the motion completely; its fairly regular harmonic rhythm and chordally oriented counterpoint; and its floating, non-metrical melodies that stress "down beats" only at cadences or when the first beat of a "measure" coincides with a word accent.

In its treatment of thematic material the passage resembles many in Willaert's output; to call it an example of pervading imitation, though, is surely an oversimplification. All voices take up the motive Willaert invented for "Beati pauperes," a motive which in its various transformations permeates the series of parallel statements that make up the text of the entire motet ("Blessed are the poor in spirit . . . ," "Blessed are the meek . . . ," "Blessed are those who mourn . . . ," and so on). On the other hand, the remainder of the first phrase, "quoniam ipsorum est regnum caelorum" ("for theirs is the kingdom of heaven"), is scarcely imitated at all beyond a few entries on "quoniam" that exhibit the same general shape, and a tendency to write repeated notes for "ipsorum." In this motet and in many others, Willaert preferred a steady, unbroken flow of polyphony rather than clearly separated sections that are each carefully identified by individually differentiated themes. Willaert gave *Beati pauperes* a discernible shape by the recurring motive that sets "Beati," and by breaking into a chordal section in triple meter at the end—after all the parallel statements have been made—for the final exclamation, "gaudete et exsultate, quoniam merces vestra copiosa est in caelis" ("rejoice and be glad, for your reward is great in heaven"). Willaert's brilliant setting of *Alma redemptoris mater* is no more obsessively imitative than

EXAMPLE 7-5. Willaert, *Beati pauperes*, mm. 1–21. Used by permission of the American Institute of Musicology.

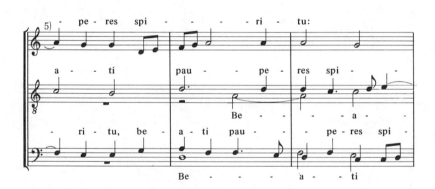

Beati pauperes, even though all parts share the themes of the paraphrased Marian antiphon that appears in canon between the next-to-top and the next-to-bottom voices. The music of this motet pours out with a continuity, ease, and homogeneity of sound that belies the presence of the old-fashioned "Netherlandish artifice" on which the work is based; but the scaffolding technique gives firm anchorage to the melodic lines that float above, beneath, and between the two canonic voices.

Willaert's career and his music demonstrate how fruitfully Italian and Netherlandish cultures interacted in the sixteenth century. Without the influence of Italian humanism, for example, Willaert might not have involved himself so deeply in the quest for a perfect marriage between poetry and melody. And without Willaert the history of music in six-teenth-century Italy would certainly be much different, for he was with-out doubt the most influential of the three great Franco-Flemish composers of the post-Josquin generation. His official position as chapel-master at St. Mark's in Venice and his unofficial position as teacher to Italy's most talented younger men allowed him to gather together an international circle of friends, students, and admirers whose influence on the Italian music of the time can scarcely be overestimated—men like Cipriano de Rore, Andrea Gabrieli, Gioseffo Zarlino, Annibale Padovano, Jachet Brumel, Jacques Buus, Marc'Antonio Cavazzoni, Gioseffo Guami, Claudio Merulo, Girolamo Parabosco, Nicola Vicentino, and many others. Willaert himself had studied with Jean Mouton in Paris, where he seems to have taken a law degree, and so he transmitted directly the heritage of Josquin and his circle to the Italian peninsula.

As a composer Willaert reflects the universality so admired during the Renaissance. He excelled in every genre. His parody Masses (many of them based on Mouton's motets) are among the finest of their kind. As we have seen, his motets best reveal his musical personality, and his madrigals show him to be extraordinarily sensitive to the natural accents of the words he set and deeply involved with the new search for musical expression. His chansons display the contrapuntal inventiveness and complexity of the best Netherlandish masters. His ricercars and fantasias for instrumental ensemble weave a virtually seamless web of pervading imitation. His arrangements for solo voice and lute of Verdelot's mad-rigals furnish important evidence of the differing ways in which ap-parently *a cappella* polyphonic music could be performed and instruct us, therefore, in the freedoms open to musicians in the Renaissance. His famous chromatic "duo," *Quid non ebrietas,* recently revealed to be a quartet, explores the furthermost reaches of chromaticism and thus shows him to be fully cognizant of the avant-garde tendencies of his time, if only in this isolated experiment. By applying the traditional rules of musica ficta to *Quid non ebrietas* and following Willaert's own hints in carrying his signed accidentals as far as G♭ and C♭, the musician bold enough to add F♭'s, B♭♭'s, E♭♭'s, and A♭♭'s to the written music will proceed around the complete cycle of fifths, a voyage that is necessary in order to land finally on an octave instead of the seventh that the notation most improbably seems to suggest. This setting of an epistle by

Horace identifies Willaert, then, as a musician alive to the new humanistic currents in Italy and the fascination of musicians there with chromatic experimentation and neo-classical learning. And Willaert's psalm
settings for double choirs (so-called *cori spezzati*), published in 1557, are
important landmarks in the history of this technique of antiphonal singing
even though they are not the first examples of their kind, as scholars had
previously supposed. The two galleries facing each other in St. Mark's
facilitate performance by two choirs—the practice came to be associated
especially closely with Venetian church music—but polychoral singing is
now known to have been widespread in northern Italy during the earlier
sixteenth century, and so Willaert merely furnished excellent models to
follow rather than inventing a completely new procedure.

CLEMENS NON PAPA AND OTHERS

Whereas Willaert and Gombert were both famous men, working
in centers of artistic activity that brought them to the attention of musicians everywhere in western Europe, the third great Netherlandish composer of the post-Josquin generation, Jacob Clemens non Papa (ca. 1510–
ca. 56/58), led a relatively obscure life as a church musician in his native
country. (His nickname, by the way, seems to have been intended to
distinguish him not from Pope Clement VII, who had died in 1534, but
from an obscure poet, Jacobus Papa, who worked for a time in the same
city, Ypres, as did the musician.) An enormously prolific composer,
Clemens wrote fifteen parody Masses plus a Requiem based on Gregorian
melodies, fifteen Magnificats, more than 230 motets (the majority for four
or five voices), 159 *Souterliedekens,* and about ninety chansons. A fluent
exponent of the style of pervading imitation, Clemens often extended his
motets based on short Biblical texts to great lengths by repeating his
principal thematic material over and over again, or by writing long
ostinati or chains of melodic sequences. He composed in a wide range of
styles. On the one extreme, his *Souterliedekens* are models of unpretentious simplicity. In them Clemens presented folk or popular tunes in
the middle of his three voices, adapting them to Dutch translations of
the Psalter intended to be sung in the home or at social gatherings.
    On the other extreme, Clemens departed radically from his usual
diatonic harmonic style in a handful of extremely chromatic motets that
seem to reveal his hidden sympathies with the religious reformers of
his time. Clemens, the composer-publisher Hubert Waelrant, and a few
other Netherlandish composers expressed their unorthodox beliefs by
means of a "secret chromatic art." In a passage like that shown in

Example 7–6 from Clemens's motet on the resurrection of Lazarus, *Fremuit spiritu Jesu,* initiated singers could, by following the rules of musica ficta, produce a beautiful and daringly chromatic reading of the music. (By omitting the accidentals a somewhat awkward and conventionally diatonic but perfectly acceptable version will result.) Such an obscure and enigmatic practice accords well with the mystical and arcane tendencies in the Netherlandish art and thought in both the fifteenth and the sixteenth centuries. As Lowinsky writes, the secret chromatic art of Clemens and his contemporaries expresses the "idea pervading all manifestations of the time—literary, artistic, philosophical—that the world offers two faces to man: one esoteric, full of significance and profound truth, accessible only to the initiate; the other exoteric, moving on a level of common understanding, open to the many, the vulgar."

EXAMPLE 7–6. Jacob Clemens, *Fremuit spiritu Jesu,* mm. 1–14. Used by permission of Columbia University Press.

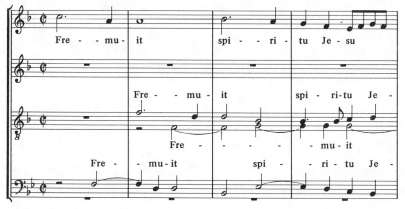

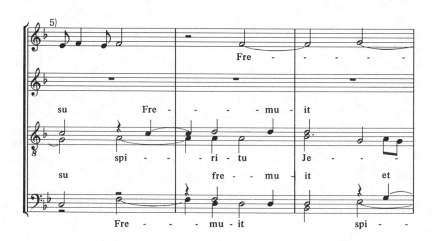

Willaert, Gombert, and Clemens non Papa were the greatest of the Netherlandish composers of the post-Josquin generation, but they were by no means the only northern European musicians whose works deserve to be studied and performed today. A second group of three men stands out for the brilliance of their music, the eminence of their reputations among their contemporaries, and the distinction of their careers: Thomas Créquillon (died ca. 1557), Gombert's colleague and successor at the court of the Emperor Charles V; Jean Richafort (ca. 1480–1547/48), sometime composer to the French king; and Pierre de Manchicourt (ca. 1510–1564), who died in Madrid while serving King Philip II. In varying ways the Masses, motets, and chansons by these three composers reflect their musical inheritance from Josquin and their dedication to the new

manner of pervading imitation. Other northern musicians, French as well
as Flemish, followed the example of their predecessors and sought em-
ployment in Italy, where they spent most of their lives and ended by
completely assimilating themselves into the foreign culture. Indeed, some
of them were instrumental in establishing a specifically Italian style of
composition, especially in the madrigal. Notable among these Italianized
northerners were Jacques Arcadelt (ca. 1504–after 1567), the Frenchman
Philippe Deslouges, called Verdelot (died before 1552), Jacques Buus
(died ca. 1564), and the brilliant madrigalist Cipriano de Rore (1516–65).
Besides these major figures of the post-Josquin generation, numerous
minor masters helped keep alive Netherlandish musical traditions everywhere in western Europe, among them Cornelius Canis, Johannes Guyot
(called Castileti), Andreas de Silva (who might, however, have been a
Spaniard), Jacob Vaet, and a number of men who are easily confused with
one another because of the similarity of their names (the so-called
Doppelmeister): Benedictus Appenzeller, who should not be mistaken
either for the German Benedictus Ducis or the earlier Flemish composer
Benedictus de Opitiis; the so-called "wolf pack," especially Johannes Lupi
and Lupus Hellinck; Jachet Berchem and Jachet of Mantua (whose real
name was Jacobus Collebaude); and the three men who are called "Maistre
Jean" in the musical sources of the time, Giovanni Nasco (who may have
been Italian), Jean Lecocq (also called "Gallus" and therefore possibly
a Frenchman), and Jhan Gero.

BIBLIOGRAPHICAL NOTES

Willaert's complete works, ed. by Hermann Zenck and Walter Gerstenberg, are in the process of publication by the American Institute of Musicology (CMM 3). On Willaert and his music, see Armen Carapetyan,
"The Musica Nova of Adriano Willaert," Journal of Renaissance and
Baroque Music, 1 (1946); Erich Hertzmann, Adrian Willaert in der welt-
lichen Vokalmusik seiner Zeit (Leipzig, 1931); René Lenaerts, "Notes sur
Adrien Willaert, maître de chapelle de St. Marc à Venise de 1527 à
1562," Bulletin de l'Institut historique belge de Rome (Rome, 1935);
Lenaerts, "Voor de biographie van Adriaen Willaert," Mélanges Charles
van den Borren (Antwerp, 1945); J. S. Levitan, "Adrian Willaert's Fa-
mous Duo 'Quidnam ebrietas,' " Tijdschrift der Vereeniging voor Neder-
landsche Muziekgeschiedenis, 15 (1938); Edward E. Lowinsky, "Adrian
Willaert's Chromatic 'Duo' Re-examined," Tijdschrift voor Muziekweten-
schap, 18 (1956); Lowinsky, "A Newly Discovered Sixteenth-Century
Motet Manuscript at the Biblioteca Vallicelliana in Rome," Journal of the
American Musicological Society, 3 (1950); Lowinsky, "A Treatise on Text

Underlay by a German Disciple of Francisco de Salinas," *Festschrift Heinrich Besseler* (Leipzig, 1961); Lowinsky, "Problems in Adrian Willaert's Iconography," *Aspects of Medieval and Renaissance Music*, ed. Jan La Rue (New York, 1966); and Hermann Zenck, "Adrian Willaert's 'Salmi Spezzate,'" *Die Musikforschung*, 2 (1949).

Nicolas Gombert's complete works, ed. by Joseph Schmidt-Görg, are in the process of publication by the American Institute of Musicology (*CMM* 6). On Gombert and his music, see Hans Eppstein, *Nicolas Gombert als Motettenkomponist* (Würzburg, 1935); and Joseph Schmidt-Görg, *Nicolas Gombert, Kapellmeister Karls V: Leben und Werk* (Bonn, 1938).

Clemens non Papa's complete works, ed. by Karel Ph. Bernet Kempers, are in the process of publication by the American Institute of Musicology (*CMM* 4). On Clemens non Papa and his music, see Bernet Kempers, *Jacobus Clemens non Papa und seine Motetten* (Augsburg, 1928); Bernet Kempers, "Bibliography of the Sacred Works of Jacobus Clemens non Papa," *Musica Disciplina*, 18 (1964); Bernet Kempers, "Jacobus Clemens non Papa's Chansons in their Chronological Order," *Musica Disciplina*, 15 (1961); Edward E. Lowinsky, *Secret Chromatic Art in the Netherlands Motet* (New York, 1946; repr. 1967); and Joseph Schmidt-Görg, "Die Messen des Clemens non Papa," *Zeitschrift für Musikwissenschaft*, 9 (1926–27).

On parody technique, see René Lenaerts, "The 16th-Century Parody Mass in the Netherlands," *Musical Quarterly*, 36 (1950); Lewis Lockwood, "'Parody' as Term and Concept in 16th-Century Music," *Aspects of Medieval and Renaissance Music*, ed. Jan La Rue (New York, 1966); and Lockwood, "A View of the Early Sixteenth-Century Parody Mass," *Twenty-fifth Anniversary Festschrift (1937–1962)* (Queens College of the City University of New York, Department of Music, 1964).

On music printing in the sixteenth century and on the work of Pierre Attaingnant in particular, see Daniel Heartz, *Pierre Attaingnant, Royal Printer of Music* (Berkeley and Los Angeles, 1969). Bibliographies of the works printed by the following publishers have also been made: Nicolas du Chemin (in *Annales musicologiques*, vol. 1), Adrian Le Roy and Robert Ballard (by F. Lesure and G. Thibault, Paris, 1955), Jacques Moderne (by S. Pogue, Geneva, 1969), and Tielman Susato (by U. Meissner, Berlin, 1967). Most of the motets published by Attaingnant in a fourteen-volume series between 1534 and 1539 have been published in a modern edition by Albert Smijers and A. Tillman Merritt as *Treize livres de motets parus chez Pierre Attaingnant en 1534 et 1535* (Monaco, 1934–63); the fourteenth volume has appeared as *Quatorzième Livre de motets composés par Pierre de Manchicourt, parus chez Pierre Attaingnant (1539)*, ed. A. Tillman Merritt (Monaco, 1964). The complete works of Pierre de Manchicourt, ed. John D. Wicks, are in the process of publication by the American Institute of Musicology (*CMM* 55).

EIGHT

NATIONAL STYLES

FRANCE

Paris had retained its importance as a musical center for centuries, and the French royal chapel employed some of the greatest musicians of the fifteenth century, including Ockeghem. But it is not possible to speak of a distinctively French as opposed to a Franco-Flemish or Netherlandish style of music much before the second decade of the sixteenth century. In the late 1520's the Parisian music publisher Pierre Attaingnant began to issue vast quantities of music written mostly by composers living and working in and around Paris and cast in a style markedly different from that of the post-Josquin Netherlanders with their complex imitative polyphony. The two greatest French composers of the time, Claudin de Sermisy (ca. 1490–1562) and Clément Janequin (ca. 1485–ca. 1560), are associated above all with a new kind of chanson—the so-called

Parisian chanson of the 1530's and 1540's—the genre in which the elegant simplicity and rational spirit of the French musicians were best expressed.

Many of Claudin's chansons are graceful but quite straightforward lyrical miniatures with charming melodies that follow closely the rhythms of the words they set. Claudin harmonized his polished soprano lines with simple chords, or placed them in a polyphonically animated homophony, or else he elaborated the important melodic material by means of relaxed bits of imitation that make the texture varied and interesting. But it is the very simplicity of a song like Claudin's *Tant que vivray* (Example 8–1), set to a poem by Clément Marot, that makes its greatness so elusive and so difficult to explain. Such a chanson certainly reaches no great expressive heights, although its charm and ability to delight listeners are immediately evident. As in so many of Claudin's chansons, the words seem to control the flow of the music. They are set for the most part syllabically, with short melismas occurring only towards the ends of phrases to serve a purely decorative function. Moreover, the structure of each musical phrase exactly matches the formal details of the poetry.

EXAMPLE 8–1. Claudin de Sermisy, *Tant que vivray*, mm. 1–12. Used by permission of the American Institute of Musicology.

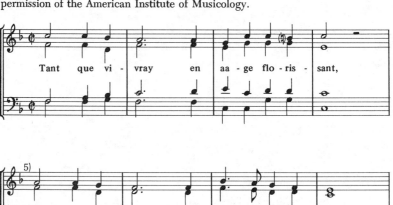

The pause on the fourth note of each of the first three phrases, for example, marks the caesura in the middle of the poetic line, and the characteristic opening rhythm, 𝅗𝅥 ♩♩, repeated at the beginning of each phrase, mirrors the dactyls of the poem. Some chanson melodies are virtually isorhythmic, so closely do they fit the patterned repetitive rhythms of the poetry. In spite of its imitative second half, *Tant que vivray* is unusually homorhythmic; in most Parisian chansons the texture is enlivened by more actively moving and independent inner parts. Moreover, most chansons in this repertory reveal more clearly than *Tant que vivray* that their counterpoint is based on a self-sufficient duet between superius and tenor, to which a harmonic bass and a complementary (and sometimes extraneous) altus have been added. Parisian composers, in other words, continued the older fifteenth-century Franco-Flemish traditions in the way they related individual lines to one another, even in these new compositions with their strikingly chordal textures; in *Tant que vivray*, though, Claudin did little more to emphasize this superius-tenor relationship than to move his scaffolding voices much of the time in parallel sixths.

Parisian composers in the second quarter of the sixteenth century no longer set their music to poems that followed the rigid formal and thematic conventions of the fifteenth-century *rhétoriqueurs*. Rondeaux, ballades, and virelais, for example, virtually never appear in any of the anthologies published by Attaingnant. Instead, the poems on which Parisian chansons are based follow no fixed rhyme scheme, although they are often strophic and their patterned repetitions are usually immediately intelligible. Often, as in *Tant que vivray*, the first several phrases of music are repeated to new text, and the last phrase or two of both words and music are also repeated, in order to round off the composition convincingly. Many Parisian chansons, for example, are organized according to the scheme AABCC, but that is only one of several similar groundplans commonly adopted. Like the formal schemes, the subject matter and diction of the poems chosen by Parisian composers also reflect a new freedom and a release from the strictness of late medieval traditions. The subject matter was more varied; it encompassed fulfilled as well as unrequited love, and comic as well as serious aspects of the amorous predicament. Many poems mix popular with courtly elements. Clément Marot, the leading chanson poet of the time, even edited anthologies of the song texts that were presumably those most frequently heard in the streets of Paris. And the poetic diction, less strained and artificial than in fifteenth-century chansons, took on a more relaxed, natural, sincere, and individual tone.

How different these Parisian chansons of the 1530's are from their contemporary Netherlandish counterparts can immediately be seen in comparing *Tant que vivray* with Clemens non Papa's five-voiced *Las je languis et si ne scay pourquoy* (Example 8–2), a chanson typical of those written by Clemens, Gombert, Willaert, Richafort, and Créquillon and published by Tielman Susato and other Flemish printers of the mid-sixteenth century. Without its words, *Las je languis* could well be mistaken for a motet, so pervading is its imitation and so dense its texture once all the voices have entered. In purely musical terms the secular nature of such a composition can be discerned only in matters of detail and emphasis: it is shorter, less serious, and somewhat more tuneful than many a motet, its phrases are concise and clearly defined, and its rhythms short-winded and inclined to regular emphasis (even though the implied meter often conflicts with the barlines of the modern edition).

   Not all Parisian chansons are as simple and lyrical as Claudin's *Tant que vivray*. French composers also wrote narrative chansons, many of them humorous and some as wittily indecent as Clément Marot's tale of an amorous priest, *Frère Thibault,* whose plans are foiled when his young lady friend gets stuck halfway through the latticework while attempting to enter his bedchamber. Marot's poem was set by Pierre Certon (died 1572), a musician somewhat younger than Claudin de Sermisy and Janequin, and the only other chanson composer of the time who can be considered a major figure. Like most narrative chansons, Certon's *Frère Thibault* alternates points of imitation based on short, precise motives with simple chordal passages which occasionally break into triple meter, changes of texture and technique designed to project the words and to underline their wit. Such procedures bear at least a slight family resemblance to those used in earlier chansons, like Compère's *Nous sommes de l'ordre de saint Babouin,* that also include *parlando*-style declamation and exploit imitation as the language of wit rather than of Netherlandish seriousness.

   Both highly productive, Claudin and Janequin between them wrote more than 400 chansons of various sorts—lyrical or narrative, relentlessly imitative, simply chordal, or in some in-between style of polyphonically animated homophony. Claudin excelled at composing delicate and sophisticated love songs, while Janequin's most characteristic works express the vivacious or irreverent side of the *esprit gaulois*. Quite extraordinary and in a class by themselves, though, are Janequin's long descriptive chansons, for which he is best known today. In the series of compositions that includes *La guerre, La chasse, Le chant des oiseaux, Les cris de Paris, Le caquet des femmes,* and others, he took up themes —the battle, the hunt, bird songs, street cries, and ladies' gossip—that allowed him to make a virtuoso display of their onomatopoeic possibilities. The harmonically static *La guerre,* for example, probably written to commemorate Francis I's victory at the battle of Marignano in 1515, imitates

EXAMPLE 8–2. Clemens, *Les je languis et si ne scay pourquoy,* mm. 1–12. Used by permission of the American Institute of Musicology.

trumpet fanfares, calls to arms, battle cries, cannon fire, and other war-like sounds. It became one of the best-known pieces of the entire century, copied by many other composers and arranged for keyboard or lute solo and for all varieties of instrumental ensemble. *Le chant des oiseaux,* on the other hand, includes a veritable ornithological garden of natural sounds. When the bird songs start, the harmonic rhythm slows down and the "counterpoint" becomes simpler. The series of slowly moving chords merely furnishes an unobtrusive frame for the rich jangle of fancifully elaborated animal noises that constitute the main point of this brilliantly amusing work.

How did the Parisian chanson style come about? Scholars have noted the superficial resemblance between frottole and chansons because of the chordal textures common to both. Any direct relationship between the two genres seems highly unlikely, however, since they grew up in such different ways, the one from a tradition of declaiming poetry over improvised, conventional chord progressions, and the other from a simplification of the complex superius-tenor-oriented polyphony of the northerners. Italian influence on the chanson, then, can only have come indirectly by way of its effect on the music of an earlier generation of Franco-Flemish musicians: Josquin des Prez and his contemporaries. Relatively few sources of the chanson survive for the years between Petrucci's three great anthologies from the opening years of the century —the *Odhecaton* (1501), *Canti B* (1502), and *Canti C* (1504)—and Attaingnant's publications of the 1530's and 1540's. But a handful of manuscripts and printed books do preserve a repertory of chansons by composers of this middle generation, musicians such as Ninot le Petit, Antoine Bruhier, Jean Mouton, and Antoine de Févin. This repertory suggests that there was a continuous tradition from the late fifteenth to the second quarter of the sixteenth century into which the Parisian chanson fits convincingly. The vogue for popular songs among the courtiers of Louis XII greatly influenced the character of secular music at his court. Composers there made many arrangements of popular tunes for three or four voices, either by putting the borrowed melody in the tenor and weaving imitative counterpoint around it, or by using the tunes as a source for freer points of imitation and chordal passages; and they wrote some chansons apparently free of borrowed material but resembling popular arrangements in their alternation of witty counterpoint and simple chords. It matters not whether Ninot le Petit's *Et la la la* (Example 8–3) is based on a borrowed popular melody. Such a chanson furnishes a link between the popular cantus-firmus chansons of the preceding generation and the narrative Parisian chanson. Moreover, some of the love songs by Mouton and Févin prefigure Claudin's most lyrical effusions, both in their simplicity and in their delicate beauty. In short, there is no need to look outside the northern countries to trace the genesis of the Parisian chanson.

Claudin, Janequin, and Certon were not the only composers whose chansons were printed by Pierre Attaingnant. Along with these major figures he published secular works by a host of minor masters as well, as did, after mid-century, the other two great Parisian publishing firms of

Nicolas du Chemin and Le Roy and Ballard. Among the most prolific of these Frenchmen were Pierre Cadéac, Pierre Cléreau, Jean Conseil, Jean Courtois, Garnier, Nicolle des Celliers d'Hesdin, Jacotin, Guillaume Le Heurteur, Jean L'Héritier, Jean Maillard, Mittantier, Passereau, Roger Pathie, Jean Rousée, Pierre Regnault (called Sandrin), Mathieu Sohier, Pierre Vermont the elder, and his relative, Pierre Vermont the younger. During the first half of the century there also grew up in France a school of provincial composers centered in Lyons, where Jacques Moderne published not only the works of composers from the capital city, but also compositions by musicians known chiefly through their association with him, among them Pierre Colin, the Florentine Francesco Layolle, Dominique Phinot, and Pierre de Villiers.

EXAMPLE 8–3. Ninot le Petit, *Et la la la,* mm. 1–12. Used by permission of the University of Chicago Press.

The chanson was not the only genre cultivated by Parisian composers of the second quarter of the sixteenth century, nor was it the only genre in which a distinctively French style grew up. Most features of the chanson were transferred directly to sacred music, and motets and Masses came to be written in France in the same simple rational manner as songs. Collections of French sacred music from the first half of the century include seven volumes of Masses (1532) and thirteen volumes of motets (1534–35) published by Pierre Attaingnant, and the so-called Medici Codex, a manuscript anthology of motets prepared in 1518 for the wedding of Lorenzo de' Medici, duke of Urbino, and Madeleine de la Tour d'Auvergne, daughter of one of Francis I's relatives. All these collections contain a miscellany of works by Frenchmen, Netherlanders, northerners active in Italy, and even some Italians—in short, motets and Masses from the musical mainstream and from its various tributaries. But if one isolates those compositions written by the Parisian chanson composers—Claudin's seventy-odd motets and thirteen Masses, for example—it will be seen that a distinctively French kind of sacred music did exist, quite different in its stylistic profile from the mainstream. French Masses, for example, built over Gregorian chants or parodying chansons, are generally brief and contrapuntally simple; their short-winded melodies usually set the text in declamatory style, with frequently faulty accentuation of words but without many melismas and without ever reaching great heights of expression. Claudin occasionally used structural canons in his motets, and in some (and this is true of motets by other Parisian composers of the time), he developed the melodic material by means of extended and elaborate counterpoint. But in general, Parisian motets, of which there are many of great charm and beauty, are distinguished for the condensation of their form, their easy, pleasing melodies, and the simplicity of their manner—just those features, in fact, that separate French chansons from their Netherlandish counterparts and from the music of the various other national schools of the sixteenth century.

ITALY

The Italian dialect of the pan-European musical language, like the French, can be heard in its purest form in the principal secular genre of the country, the sixteenth-century Italian madrigal. Like the earlier "frottola," the term "madrigal" has both a generic and a specific meaning. Most narrowly it refers to a poetic form new in the sixteenth century (though named for its fourteenth-century predecessor), a form distinguished by its irregularity and its freedoms. The most concise definition—that the madrigal is a canzone of one strophe—is accurate as far as it *madrigal verse form:*

goes. And indeed it is difficult to be much more precise. Usually each line of verse contains either seven or eleven syllables; stanzas mix both lengths in irregular combinations. The rhyme scheme is not fixed, although some madrigals end with a couplet. Nor does each stanza include a standard number of lines; there can be as few as six or as many as sixteen, although most madrigals have from ten to twelve lines. With reference to the music, the term "madrigal" in the sixteenth century encompasses settings of various forms of verse, especially those with relatively irregular structures—madrigals proper and canzone stanzas—but also sonnets, sestina stanzas, and even ballate. The poems are mostly of high literary quality, and in setting them, composers took pains to fit the music carefully to the words, in more or less rich polyphonic textures. Composers allowed themselves the freedom to utilize simple chordal textures as well as imitative polyphony in their madrigals, and they set the words in a variety of ways ranging from straightforward syllabic declamation to extended melismas; their choice of texture and technique depended more on the content of the poem than on its form, and more on rhetorical effect than on abstract formal principle. Since it is unlikely that music conceived for one set of words can with equal appropriateness fit a second set as well, madrigals are in principle through-composed. Certainly each stanza of a multi-stanza work invariably received new music, although composers frequently repeated individual musical phrases to different verses in order to give their compositions an easily intelligible form.

music

Unlike the madrigal, the frottola for most of its brief history made do with poetasters' verses of little literary merit, mere *poesia per musica*. Moreover, the patterned, song-like melodies of the typical frottola seem to have been devised for the ease with which they might fit any poetic line with the same number of syllables; in any case, the schematic musical formulas were invariably repeated to subsequent stanzas of text. But frottolists came more and more to prefer really good poems, especially those by Petrarch, the fourteenth-century poet whose influence so pervaded the sixteenth century. And when they set canzoni and verses similarly irregular in length, they had to modify the stereotyped and formulaic character of their music, as is evident in Example 4–5, Tromboncino's setting of Petrarch's canzone *Sì è debile il filo*. How different is Example 8–4, the beginning of Bernardo Pisano's imitative, almost motet-like version of the same poem, which he included in his volume of *Musica . . . sopra le canzone del Petrarcha*, published by Petrucci in 1520. Pisano's setting is almost a madrigal, and yet not quite, for he apparently intended the same music to be repeated for each stanza of the canzone. But the application of imitative polyphony to the poems of Petrarch certainly constituted an important step toward the early madrigal.

would be a madrigal, but strophic

EXAMPLE 8–4. Bernardo Pisano, Sì è *debile il filo,* mm. 1–12. Used by permission of the American Institute of Musicology.

To claim that the madrigal was born as a result of the application of Franco-Flemish polyphonic techniques to the native Italian frottola, however, would be overly simple. Rather, the impulse to the madrigal seems to have come from poetic as well as musical circles. The men who first cultivated the new genre were all deeply committed from the very beginning to the proposition that music should intensify our perceptions of the poetry it sets; they were therefore attempting to invent a music that enhanced poetry and revealed its inner meanings. Pietro Bembo (1470–1547), poet, Venetian nobleman and scholar, papal secretary in Rome from 1512 to 1520, and cardinal from 1539, was one of the most important influences in this movement. By praising and imitating the written Tuscan of Petrarch, Boccaccio, and Dante, he did more than anyone else to establish Italian as a literary language; Latin had been preferred by humanistic Italian writers throughout much of the neo-classical fifteenth century. In his analysis of Petrarch, Bembo stressed not only the poet's mastery of poetic technique and the propriety of his imagery but also the way he matched the sounds of words (as opposed to their meanings) with their effect on the reader. Bembo singled out two qualities especially that the sounds and rhythms of words can create: *piacevolezza* (roughly akin to "sweetness" or "grace") and *gravità* ("majesty" or "dignity"). His analysis of this poetry opened the way for musical settings in which more attention was paid to the way music can establish the reading of a poem. Composers could illustrate each word in a poem by simple and naïve word-painting—that is, by writing fast notes to set words like "running" or "flying," close imitation for "fleeing," pauses for "sighing" or "dying," and so on; or they could devise music that abstracted literary concepts to a greater extent, so that hard, harsh, or cruel words were set to music filled with minor chords, dissonances, suspensions, appoggiaturas, and unexpected harmonies, while merry, happy, serene, or contented words were set to major chords and consonant or sweet sounds. Moreover, by manipulating the rhythms and phrase structure of a madrigal, composers could emphasize individual words or sentences, declaiming some sections simply and extending others at great length, in order to interpret the content rather than the form of the poem.

Perhaps it is a paradox that the best of the earliest composers to write and publish Italian madrigals, the men who established the Italian national style in sixteenth-century music—Verdelot, Arcadelt, and Willaert—were all foreigners. The one exception to this anomalous situation was Costanzo Festa (died 1545), the first Italian musician of the century to command Netherlandish contrapuntal techniques as masterfully as the *oltremontani*. But perhaps the paradox does not really exist, and the mix of international elements was the inevitable result of the attempt to find a suitable musical language for the aesthetic ideals of the Petrarchist circles around Bembo, a language that had to be as rich, varied, and capable of infinite nuance as Franco-Flemish polyphony. If Festa, along with Verdelot, Arcadelt, and Willaert, did not quite create the madrigal—as we have seen, that honor should probably be given to the late frottolists like Andrea Antico or the Florentine Bernardo Pisano—they at least played the determining role in shaping its style and in bringing the madrigal to its first great peak of achievement. Several lesser native-born composers of madrigals should also be included in their circle, men like Francesco Corteccia (died 1571), Domenico Ferabosco (1513–74), Girolamo Parabosco (died c. 1557), and the Ferrarese Alfonso della Viola (ca. 1508–ca. 70).

Madrigals were written for a variety of reasons. Some were commissioned by noblemen who wanted music to honor the lady they loved (so-called "madonna madrigals"). Some were composed for specific entertainments, banquets, weddings, plays, and other festivities. After about 1540, Italian literary academies (small groups of poets, musicians, artists, and amateurs who met regularly to discuss intellectual and artistic subjects, to hear each other's words, and to witness musical performances) had madrigals written especially for them; the Accademia Filarmonica of Verona, founded in 1543, was the first academy to have well-developed musical interests. The madrigals composed for such groups were usually the most serious and intellectual. Some madrigals were doubtless composed for performance by professional groups during the normal course of events at a prince's court; and some, probably, were composed more as performer's music than as listener's music, to be sung by courtiers amusing themselves. Normally, madrigals were performed with one singer to a part, either *a cappella* or, as many contemporary documents show, with the participation of various instruments, either substituting for voices or doubling them.

  The speculation and discussions about the nature of music and poetry that led to the madrigal must have taken place in Rome, Venice, and Florence in the 1510's and 1520's, but the term did not appear on the title page of an anthology of music until 1530. Many of the earliest madrigals—from about 1530 until Festa's death in 1545—are simple and chordal. They are only slightly more complex polyphonically than frottole, although they differ in their formal organization and their freer melodic style; and they do not display any very new techniques for embodying in music the meaning of the poetry. Verdelot's *O dolce notte*, for instance, written to be performed during Act V of Machiavelli's play, *La Mandragola*, never departs from the lightly decorated homophonic texture with which it opens.

  Costanzo Festa's slightly more complex *Cosi suav'è'l foco* (Example 8–5) shows more clearly than many madrigals the interaction of Italian and northern cultures. It opens with a Josquin-like duet and continues with the superius singing in the manner of a frottola the phrase "et dolce il nodo" while the lower and faster-moving voices function as accompaniment; the second line of the poem, "Con che m'incendi amor," begins with a full-fledged point of imitation for all four voices. Arcadelt's madrigals tend to be written in a style not very different from the French chanson, a genre in which he was also expert. They are apt, for example, to be formally clear, since Arcadelt often repeated individual musical phrases, and their bland diatonic harmonies, their attractive melodies, simple suave polyphony, and transparent textures make them immediately appealing.

  Willaert was the composer among the first generation of madrigalists who first achieved a perfect union between words and

EXAMPLE 8–5. Costanzo Festa, *Cosi suav'è'l foco*, mm. 1–12. From *The Italian Madrigal*, by Alfred Einstein, translated by Alexander H. Krappe, Roger H. Sessions, and Oliver Strunk, Vol. III (copyright 1949 by Princeton University Press, Reissued 1971). Reprinted by permission of Princeton University Press.

music, although he avoided simple, syllabically set chordal passages on the one hand and extravagant rhetorical flourishes on the other. On occasion he could portray Petrarchan antitheses vividly, as we have seen in *I piansi, hor canto* (Example 7–4), even to the extent of violating melodic decorum. The superius of Example 7–4, for instance, fragmentary and containing an abrupt change of pace, makes no sense as a self-sufficient and autonomous melodic line; but once the words it sets are taken into account, its aptness is self-evident. More typically, Willaert's restraint in devising melodic lines that support and illuminate the verses —Einstein speaks of "a discreet inner rhetoric"—prevents him from depicting the poetic imagery with literal or vivid word painting or from breaking the even flow of sound. His setting of Petrarch's *Giunto m'ha*

Amor is more characteristic than *I piansi, hor canto* of the madrigals in
Musica nova, not only for the dense web of imitations and near imitations
within the lush harmonic framework, but also because it exemplifies the
convention he established of setting sonnets in two *partes*, the first reserved for the octave of the poem, the second for the sestet. The composer
did not project the meaning of *Giunto m'ha Amor* in any dramatic way—
the counterpoint is too thick for that—but his diction is so painstaking
that the individual melodic lines virtually sing themselves once the poem
has been mastered. And yet the music has a shape that follows the sense
rather than the form of the text. The points of articulation are often
planned according to the meanings of the words and not merely where
the lines of verse end. Willaert's madrigals do not dazzle the ears; they
are sober and highly refined interpretations of great poetry.

Willaert, Festa, and the other early madrigalists wrote some of
their compositions in a style of notation that began to appear in anthologies from about 1540 onwards, in which smaller note values were
used, with the common-time signature (C) replacing the more usual alla
breve (¢). These madrigals, called *madrigali a note nere* or *madrigali a
misura di breve*, are filled with lively rhythms and syncopations. They
are also sometimes known as *madrigali cromatici*, not because they require many accidentals, but because they are written with many *crome*,
or flagged seminiminims (transcribed in modern editions as sixteenth notes
or smaller). Seminiminims, heretofore used only in melismas, now had
their own syllables. From 1540 madrigals *a note nere* appeared both in
separate collections and in anthologies together with "normal" madrigals
with alla-breve time signatures.

By the second generation of sixteenth-century madrigalists, the
musicians who reached their maturity in the 1540's and 1550's, the
diverse elements of style had been completely amalgamated into a sensitive and expressive vehicle for enhancing fine poems. By 1560 native
musicians predominated, notwithstanding the fact that the most brilliant
madrigalist of all, Willaert's distinguished pupil Cipriano de Rore (1516–
1565), came from beyond the Alps. The "classical" madrigal style of the
mid-century and later is chiefly associated with men such as Andrea
Gabrieli (1510/20–86), Annibale Padovano (1527–75), Costanzo Porta (ca.
1529–1601), Francesco Portinaro (ca. 1520–after 1578), Vincenzo Ruffo
(1510–87), and Nicola Vicentino (1511–72).

Unlike his teacher, Cipriano de Rore did not shun extroverted
rhetorical devices. Indeed, he made of the madrigal a passionate and
personal vehicle capable of bringing out every nuance of the expressive
content of the poems he set. At the beginning of his career he seems to
have taken Willaert as his model. His early madrigals share some of the
same features as those by Willaert: above all, impeccable diction, but also
a penchant for relatively thick, continuous counterpoint, intensive if

inexact imitation, and overlapped cadences. Rore followed Willaert's example in composing Petrarchan sonnets in two *partes*, after the manner of sixteenth-century motets; even more ambitiously, he set as early as 1548 all the stanzas of Petrarch's canzone *Vergine bella* as a cycle of eleven madrigals, beginning a fashion for similar cycles that continued for the rest of the century. Rore deserves his place of honor in the history of the madrigal, however, less for his formal ambitiousness and ingenuity, or for his contrapuntal mastery (though that is very impressive), than for his profound skill in capturing and reflecting the changing moods of serious poetry—his mastery, in other words, of rhetoric. His polyphonic cunning notwithstanding, he could choose to compose a work such as *O sonno* (Example 8–6) almost entirely in homophonic textures. Rore makes palpable the image of sleep as the "placid son of humid shadowy

EXAMPLE 8–6. Cipriano de Rore, *O Sonno*, mm. 1–11. Used by permission of the American Institute of Musicology.

night" by chord spacing, control of range, and especially by his sensitive use of harmonic color. And even though Rore generally stayed within the bounds of the diatonic modal system, he could also use extreme chromaticism with stunning effect, as in the passage from *Da le belle contrade* shown in Example 8–7. The excerpt is not so much remarkable for the realism of the exclamation "T'en vai, haimé!" ("You go, alas"), nor for the

EXAMPLE 8–7. Rore, *Da le belle contrade*, mm. 30–52. Used by permission of the American Institute of Musicology.

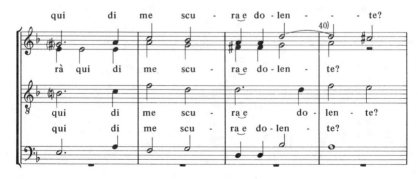

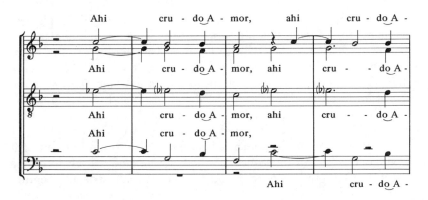

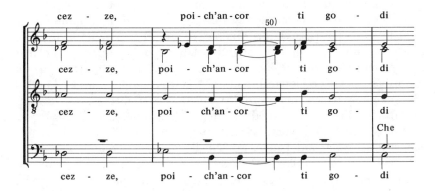

graphic depiction of "Sola mi lasci!" ("You are leaving me alone"), as for the series of striking chromatic sideslips: the C minor triad, for example, poignant and unexpected immediately following A major—a progression that makes the lover's cry, "Ahi crud'amor" ("O, cruel love") sound tangibly heartfelt and touching—or the incredible sweetness of the D-flat major triad on "dolcezze." In short, Rore exploited a wide range of techniques in his madrigals, from the strictest imitation to the plainest homophony, from bland diatonic to startlingly chromatic harmonies, and from simple syllabic declamation to florid melismatic display. But all of these devices were subservient to his central aim: to express the meaning of individual words and hence of the poem as a whole. This was the aspect of his musical personality that led composers and writers on music later in the century to identify him as the inventor of a "second practice" in contradistinction to the strict and musically autonomous polyphony of the Netherlands and of the Roman school led by Palestrina. Rore brought to a climax the "age of innocence" of the madrigal and proved to be the model whom the great virtuoso madrigalists of the late sixteenth century followed in forming their own styles. These were the composers who made up a third generation of madrigalists and who were to bring the Renaissance to an end—northerners such as Philippe de Monte, Giaches de Wert, and Orlando Lasso as well as the trio of famous Italians, Claudio Monteverdi, Luca Marenzio, and Carlo Gesualdo.

Besides serious madrigals, Italian musicians throughout the sixteenth century also cultivated lighter kinds of music. Roughly akin to present-day popular entertainments, villanelle, or *canzoni villanesche alla napoletana,* as they were first called, were presumably intended for the enjoyment of a wide spectrum of social classes in the various Italian cities. Certainly these lively but unpretentious pieces cannot be considered genuine folk art; for one thing, some of their composers also wrote refined and elevated madrigals. Villanelle or villanesche—the two terms seem to be used almost interchangeably in sixteenth-century sources—are generally quite simple three-part settings of popular verse in strophic forms, either in bare chordal style (so humble, in fact, that parallel fifths were readily tolerated) or in only slightly elaborated homophony. Thomas Morley somewhat rudely but not inaccurately described them as "a clownish musick to a clownish matter." Their Neapolitan origin, implied in the name by which they were first called, is confirmed by the volumes of canzoni villanesche issued in the 1530's, 1540's, and 1550's by Neapolitan composers such as Giovan Tommasso di Maio, Giovane Domenico da Nola, and Tommasso Cimello. Many of the poems are quite irreverent, and some follow the tradition of canti carnascialeschi by immediately identifying the characters singing as old ladies, blind beggars, German soldiers, stuttering Venetian noblemen, local citizens speaking in dialect, or members of some other group who can be used to illuminate the human comedy. Other poems, like *Madonna io non lo so,* set by Giovane Domenico da Nola, are slightly more refined lovers' laments. The fashion for villanelle soon spread from Naples northwards, and was taken up by composers as serious as Willaert (whose four-part arrangements of some of Nola's compositions, including *Madonna io non lo so,* place the Neapolitan's melody in the tenor), Baldissera Donato, and, somewhat later, Luca Marenzio.

Some of the variants of the villanella exploit local dialects or customs, such as the greghesca (in a mixture of Venetian and Greek), the giustiniana (in Venetian dialect; unrelated to the fifteenth-century poems of Leonardo Giustiniani), the moresca (incorporating Moorish elements), the todesche (in which a German accent is written into the poetry), and the bergamasca (in the dialect of Bergamo). Some, like the mascherate that were sung at masked balls and in processions, were presumably written for special occasions. Sixteenth-century title pages sometimes call similar pieces "villotte," but the term "villotta" should probably be reserved for the late fifteenth- and early sixteenth-century polyphonic arrangements in four parts of actual street songs and popular tunes, such as Compère's version of *Che fa la ramacina* or *Scaramella va alla guerra*. Similarly, a distinction should be made between the villanella and the late sixteenth-century canzonetta, a slightly more "respectable" if equally light-hearted genre cultivated by composers such as Giovanni Ferretti, Girolamo Conversi, and Giuseppe Caimo. (Given sacred words, the *canzonetta spirituale* was used in the service of the Counter Reformation late in the century.) And one should distinguish between villanelle and balletti, the dance songs written by Giovanni Giacomo Gastoldi. Beginning in the last quarter of the sixteenth century, these lighter forms had a great impact on music outside Italy. Thomas Morley's balletts are modelled on Gastoldi's, for example, and composers like Hans Leo Hassler and Johann Hermann Schein brought the villanella style to Germany in the late sixteenth and early seventeenth centuries.

GERMANY

Throughout the Middle Ages, polyphonic music in the Germanic countries remained peripheral to the mainstream. Even by the fifteenth century Germany still had not produced any composers equal in stature and accomplishment to the best of those in other western European countries. But in the late fifteenth and early sixteenth centuries Germany, like France and Italy, did develop a national style, especially in its secular music. Even though German composers about 1500 borrowed elements from Franco-Flemish music, they wrote lieder in a style essentially independent of secular genres in other countries; their most distinctive achievements, perhaps, were "Tenorlieder," songs in which the tenor states the principal melodic line, a simple but elegant tune addressed either to courtly circles (a so-called *Hofweise*) or to the educated classes (a *Gesellschaftslied*). The history of German lieder in the Renaissance divides neatly into four periods according to the groups of sources in which the songs are preserved: (1) several chansonniers from the second half of the fifteenth century, which include a number of mostly anonymous lieder along with chansons, song-motets, and instrumental music; (2) a group of printed anthologies and manuscripts from the 1510's, which contain songs written by Heinrich Isaac and his contemporaries, the best of whom were Heinrich Finck and Paul Hofhaimer; (3) anthologies published between 1534 and the mid-1550's, in which appear lieder by these men as well as composers of the following generation, of whom Ludwig Senfl was the most distinguished; (4) and finally, after the mid-1560's, collections which began to include German songs deeply influenced by foreign music, notably by Italian madrigals and villanelle.

The three best known of the late fifteenth-century chansonniers are the Lochamer Liederbuch (now in Berlin), assembled in or near Nuremberg between 1455 and 1460 and containing for the most part monophonic melodies, some of them parts of polyphonic compositions; the Schedelsches Liederbuch (now in Munich), written by Hartmann Schedel, a doctor and historian, during his student days in the 1460's in Leipzig, Padua, and possibly Nuremberg; and the Glogauer Liederbuch (now in Berlin), its three volumes prepared during the 1470's or 1480's, and possibly, therefore, the earliest example of a collection of music gathered together as a set of part books. Like most late fifteenth-century miscellanies, these manuscripts offer a selection of most of the kinds of music prevalent in Germany at the time. The Glogauer Liederbuch, for example, includes besides its seventy lieder 158 pieces with Latin text or incipit, sixty-one without text, three quodlibets, and one Italian and one Slavic song. Many of the Latin and textless compositions turn out to be Franco-Flemish chansons by Dufay, Binchois, Ockeghem, Busnois, and their contemporaries, although some of the Latin pieces are settings of hymns, sequences, responsories, and antiphons; and some of the textless pieces are very probably instrumental in conception. Among this latter group appears a series of compositions with fanciful titles: *Das yeger horn* ("The hunter's horn"), *Der fochss schwantcz* ("The fox's tail"), *Der kranch schnabil* ("The crane's beak"), *Der pfawin swancz* ("The peacock's tail"), *Der ratten schwancz* ("The rat's tail"), *Dy ezels crone* ("The ass's crown"), *Dy Katczen pfothe* ("The cat's paw"), *Dy krebis schere* ("The crab's claw"), and so on. Some of these were originally songs or motets, while others may well be dances, descriptive music, or at the very least compositions written for instrumental ensembles without any relationship to a text. The most distinctively German of the pieces in these anthologies are the lieder, such as the anonymous *In feuers hitz* from the Glogauer Liederbuch (Example 8–8), in which the simple song-like melody in the tenor is accompanied by three voices, which occasionally imitate it but mostly form two slightly faster-moving discants above it and a stable harmonic bass beneath it. Like many German lieder of the time, *In feuers hitz* uses the same music for each of its first two couplets and new music for the second quatrain, in a repetition scheme known as Bar form (consisting of two *Stollen* and an *Abgesang*—that is, AAB—for each strophe), one of the favorite formal designs of the earlier Minnesinger. The slightly awkward charm of the song depends partly on the way the composer has juxtaposed contrasting rhythms at different levels of perception; he not only contrasted the four-square duple meter of the tune with the triple meter of the other voices but also supplied in the faster moving altus, with its unexpected triplet figures, a lively rhythmic counterpoint to the main melody.

EXAMPLE 8–8. Anonymous, *In feuers hitz*, mm. 1–5. Printed by permission of the Bärenreiter-Verlag Cassel Basel Tours London, from *Das Erbe deutscher Musik*, vol. 4, Abteilung Mittelalter, vol. 1: "Das Glogauer Liederbuch, Erster Teil: Deutsche Lieder und Spielstücke," ed. Heribert Ringmann, rev. by Joseph Klapper (Cassel and Basel, 2/1954).

In the first decade of the sixteenth century, humanism made its influence felt on German music through the efforts of the poet and scholar Konrad Celtes (1459–1508). He encouraged his pupil Peter Treibenreif (or Petrus Tritonius, to call him by the Latin name he used in humanistic circles) to publish in 1507 specimen settings of the odes and epodes of Horace, made in order to help students learn the metrical patterns of classical Latin. Tritonius composed music for these Latin poems in simple four-part chords and metrically irregular rhythms that carefully observe the distinction between long and short syllables. As interesting and important as they are in the history of attempts by Renaissance musicians to understand precepts from the ancient world and to incorporate them into their own work, Tritonius's settings are simply too plain and bare to be in themselves significant artistically, and they had no great part in determining the character of German music later in the century. Such odes were regularly performed in Latin school dramas throughout Germany during the sixteenth century, however, and several important composers, including Hofhaimer and Senfl, experimented themselves with classical meters, even borrowing some of Tritonius's melodies.

In addition to humanistic settings of classical Latin poetry, monophonic song also flourished in Germany during the early sixteenth century because of the activities of the guilds of Meistersingers, self-conscious and pedantic groups of middle-class amateur musicians who modeled themselves on the noble medieval Minnesingers. They maintained organizations for the cultivation of singing and composing from about 1450 until about 1600 and devised elaborate rules for composing the rather stilted songs, many in Bar form and based on Biblical texts, that they sang to each other at contests held in their singing schools. The most famous of the Meistersingers, Hans Sachs (1494–1576), a cobbler in Nuremberg, wrote more than 6000 such songs, mostly set in notes of equal length, syllabically declaimed except for the more or less elaborate melismas, or *Blumen,* which decorate the beginnings of lines and important points of articulation.

After the Glogauer Liederbuch was completed in the 1470's or 1480's, no major collection of German polyphonic songs appeared until the second decade of the sixteenth century, when several anthologies were issued by various printers. Erhard Öglin of Augsburg published a collection of songs in part books in 1512, the first German music to be printed by movable type and the first to contain music entirely for four voices; a second volume, without date or publisher's name, may also have come from his shop. Peter Schöffer, son of one of Gutenberg's assistants, issued two volumes of lieder during the same period, the first in 1513 and a second undated collection probably a few years later. Arnt von Aich's Liederbuch, printed in Cologne and also undated, probably appeared towards the end of the same decade. These collections contain music by a host of minor composers, such as Jörg Brack, Heinrich Eytelwein, Malchinger, Adam Rener, Jörg Schönfelder, and Sebastian Virdung, as well as songs by two of the three most important lieder composers of the period, Heinrich Isaac and Paul Hofhaimer (1459–1537). The third great song writer, Heinrich Finck (1447–1527), is represented only in contemporary manuscripts and later printed sources. This generation of composers can be said to have consolidated the national style, following the models established in the late fifteenth-century manuscript chansonniers. While not abandoning the framework of the Tenorlied, these composers joined to it the technical features of the Josquin generation. Tenorlieder came to be written regularly in four rather than three parts; considerable imitation, especially at the beginning of each song and often also at the beginning of each of the very clearly differentiated phrases, underlined the greater equality of the voices (even though the altus was still often only a harmonic filler); and the superius often stated a melodic line almost as finely and carefully shaped as the tenor. Within their closely defined stylistic limits, German songs from the first quarter of the sixteenth century use a variety of musical techniques and set poetry that deals with a wide range of subject matter. The music of Isaac's famous *Innsbruck ich muss dich lassen,* for example, nostalgic and touching as the poem it sets, is written in as simple a style as can be found among these compositions; its elegant melodies are combined to make a series of chord progressions only lightly animated by rhythmic interplay. Some of the comic songs, on the other hand, such as Isaac's *Es het ein Baur ein Töchterlein* or Hofhaimer's *Greyner zanner,* are filled with coarse peasant humor as well as considerable contrapuntal artifice, including extensive imitation. Many German lieder are love songs, like Hofhaimer's *Ich klag und rew,* which combines chordal and imitative textures, and admirably demonstrates the superb craftsmanship of these composers.

Some fifteen or twenty years elapsed between the time the Öglin, Schöffer, and Arnt von Aich songbooks appeared and the publication of the next important German song books, those with music by the generation of composers following Isaac, Hofhaimer, and Finck, a period that saw some of the most decisive events of the Reformation in Germany. Johannes Ott, a Nuremberg book dealer and bibliophile (he owned at one time the Lochamer Liederbuch), gave a new impulse to the dissemination of secular music in Germany by editing *121 neue Lieder,* published by Hieronymus Formschneider in 1534; Ott prepared a second volume of 115 songs in 1544. Meanwhile, various other publishers and editors had begun to issue a number of important collections, notably the six volumes of *Gassenhawerlin, Reutterliedlein, Graszliedlein,* and so on, printed by Christian Egenolff in Frankfurt am Main in and about 1535; the five volumes of Georg Forster's *Frische teutsche Lieder,* published by Johannes Petreius of Nuremberg between 1539 and 1560; the *65 teutscher Lieder* printed by Peter Schöffer and Matthias Apiarius in Strasbourg about 1536; and a volume published in the same year by Formschneider, devoted chiefly to music by Heinrich Finck. These anthologies include music by earlier composers like Finck and works with French, Latin, and Italian texts, in addition to lieder by the newest composers, among them

Wilhelm Breitengraser, Arnold von Bruck, Sixt Dietrich, Lupus Hellinck, Stephan Mahu, Leonhard Paminger, Thomas Stoltzer, and the members of the so-called Heidelberg school—Jobst vom Brandt, Georg Forster, Lorenz Lemlin, Caspar Othmayr, and Stephan Zirler. Most important, these sources preserve for us many works by the best composer of German lieder during the second quarter of the sixteenth century, Ludwig Senfl (ca. 1486–1542/43), a Swiss who served Maximilian I until the emperor's death in 1519 and thereafter worked chiefly in Munich for Duke Wilhelm IV of Bavaria. In spite of the fact that German songs from the late fifteenth century to about 1560 have come down to us in neatly divided groups of sources, each separated from the others by a considerable interval of time, the character of the compositions changed only gradually over the years; in the history of the lied before 1560 there are no abrupt transformations of style. Composers of the early sixteenth century incorporated the new musical techniques they had learned from Josquin des Prez and his contemporaries, and Ludwig Senfl carried on in the tradition of his most important predecessors: Isaac, Hofhaimer, and Finck. Some of Senfl's songs are virtually indistinguishable in style from those by the earlier composers. Others, like *Ich stuend an einem morgen* (Example 8–9), one of several settings Senfl made of the same melody, do reflect new attitudes and techniques. It differs from the version by Isaac chiefly in its greater length and expansiveness and the greater floridness and complexity of Senfl's counterpoint. The initial point of imitation, for example, treats the principal melodic material more diffusely, and the sharply defined countersubject adds a complication not present in Isaac's setting. At the same time, Senfl's individual lines are so combined to create a more dynamic and predictable harmonic direction.

EXAMPLE 8–9. Ludwig Senfl, *Ich stuend an einem Morgen*, mm. 1–15. From *Sämtliche Werke, Band IV. Deutsche Lieder zu vier bis sieben Stimmen. II. Teil. Lieder aus Johannes Otts Liederbuch von 1534*, ed. Arnold Geering and Wilhelm Altwegg. Reprinted by permission of Möseler Verlag, Wolfenbüttel and Zürich.

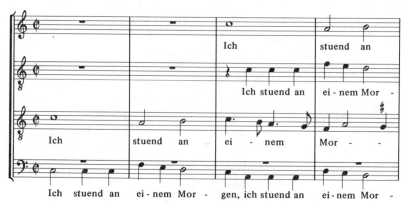

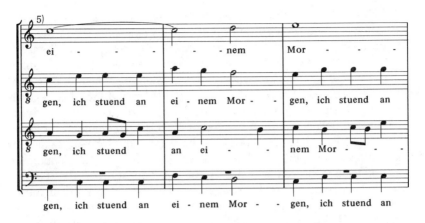

With Senfl's secular music the German national style of the Renaissance reached its high point and began its decline. From the mid-1560's to the end of the century, a number of composers, among them Ivo de Vento, Matthaeus Le Maistre, Leonhard Lechner, Jakob Regnart, Antonio Scandello, and the two greatest masters of the late sixteenth-century lied, Orlando Lasso and Hans Leo Hassler, published collections of songs in which foreign influence, especially that of the Italian madrigal and villanella, began to crowd out the native German elements. Without their words, many late sixteenth-century lieder could be mistaken for Italian compositions, but the best works, like Hassler's *Ach Schatz, ich thu dir klagen*, achieved a synthesis of the two styles. Like Thomas Morley, who played an analogous role in the history of English music, Hassler was especially attracted to the lighter Italian forms, and his balletti, modelled on those by Gastoldi, are filled with catchy tunes and lively dance rhythms.

Composers of sacred music in the Germanic countries during the fifteenth and sixteenth centuries cultivated a distinctively national style much less obviously than did composers of secular music, except of course in the congregational songs and other compositions that grew out of the religious schism, a repertory that will be treated separately. Musically speaking, Germany remained a provincial outpost of western Europe throughout much of the fifteenth century, and there even exist some examples of late fifteenth-century German organum in a style centuries out of date. On the other hand, there are also large manuscript anthologies of sacred music analogous to the Liederbücher of the period, like that prepared for Magister Nikolaus Apel of Leipzig (Leipzig, University Library, MS 1494), which contain vast quantities of Franco-Flemish as well as native German music written in a style not far different from the mainstream. By the turn of the century some German composers, like Hofhaimer and Finck, had reached a level of achievement at least equal to that of major composers in the rest of western Europe, and we have already seen that Isaac's *Choralis Constantinus*, composed for the German liturgy, was one of the great monuments of the High Renaissance.

During the second quarter of the sixteenth century, musicians, like other Germans, were faced with the necessity of declaring their religious sympathies, although their decision did not necessarily affect the style of their compositions. Many Protestant composers, like Sixt Dietrich, Benedictus Ducis, Adam Rener, and Balthasar Resinarius, supplied florid polyphony for the Catholic liturgy. And their music does not differ along sectarian lines from that by their Catholic contemporaries, such as Arnold von Bruck, Stephan Mahu, the great Ludwig Senfl (who had

Protestant sympathies), or Thomas Stoltzer, much of whose magnificent music was composed for the Hungarian royal court.

SPAIN

Franco-Flemish polyphony was widely performed in Spain throughout the fifteenth century, and many Flemish, French, and German musicians sang alongside native performers in Spanish cathedrals and chapels. Italy had close ties with Spain, especially with the kingdom of Aragon after Alfonso V of Aragon was declared king of Naples in 1442. It is no wonder, then, that Italian music came to be known in the Iberian peninsula and that some Spanish musicians lived and worked in Italy. The Spaniard Juan Cornago, for example, served both Alfonso and his son Ferrante in Naples, and he may have composed there his *Missa de la mapa mundi,* based on an Italian cantus firmus that refers to a map of the world. But a truly national musical style seems to have grown up in Spain, as in other western European countries, only at the end of the fifteenth century, especially in the music written during the reign of the so-called Catholic Monarchs, Ferdinand of Aragon and Isabella of Castile. Their wedding in 1469 ushered in an age of prosperity and political stability that enabled the arts in Spain to flourish; under Ferdinand and Isabella the Moors were expelled, the country was brought little by little under more direct control from Madrid, and its wealth and power grew immensely as a result of its vast empire in the New World, which Spain acquired because Ferdinand and Isabella rather fortuitously and unenthusiastically supported Christopher Columbus's voyages of exploration and discovery.

As befitted the defenders of Catholic orthodoxy and the founders of the Spanish Inquisition, Ferdinand and Isabella encouraged sacred music at their court. Juan de Anchieta, Francisco Peñalosa, and Pedro de Escobar are perhaps the best of the composers of Masses and motets from the time of the Catholic Monarchs, but a number of other musicians have left works that demonstrate a high level of musical activity and achievement, among them Alonso de Alva, Juan Escribano, Juan Ponce, and Martín de Rivaflecha.

But the largest and most characteristically Spanish repertory of music to survive from the age of Ferdinand and Isabella consists of the secular songs, chiefly romances and villancicos, that appear in five great manuscript cancioneros from the late fifteenth and early sixteenth centuries and in one later printed anthology. The largest source of all, the Cancionero Musical de Palacio, now in the library of the Royal Palace in Madrid, preserves the music performed in the household of the Duke of Alba, one of Spain's most powerful grandees. The bibliophile Ferdinand Columbus, son of the explorer, acquired the Cancionero de la Biblioteca Colombina for his library in Seville in 1534, although it was copied out at the end of the fifteenth century and includes the earliest compositions to be found in this group of sources. The Cancioneiro Musical e Poético da Biblioteca Pública Hortensia, copied in the sixteenth century and now kept at Elvas in Portugal, contains Spanish and Portuguese songs exclusively; they are all anonymous in the manuscript, but some are known to have been written by Juan del Encina and Pedro de Escobar. Barcelona, Biblioteca Central, MS 454, on the other hand, mixes Spanish secular music with sacred works by foreign and native-born composers. The Cancionero Musical in the Segovia Cathedral is an important source of Franco-Flemish Masses, motets, and chansons, although it also expands the repertory of villancicos and related pieces. Finally, the printed *Cancionero de Upsala,* published in Venice in 1556, also belongs with this group of manuscript anthologies, despite its late date, for some of its villancicos in two, three, four, and five parts (including one by Nicolas Gombert, the only composer named in the collection) were doubtless composed many years before its publication, and all of them fall squarely into the earlier tradition, even if some display an amount of imitation that argues for a later date of composition.

Most of the Spanish cancioneros, then, like their counterparts in other countries—French chansonniers and German Liederbücher—include various kinds of music and not simply Spanish secular songs such as villancicos and romances; compositions with Latin, French, and Italian texts by foreign composers such as Fogliano, Josquin, Robert Morton, Ockeghem, Tromboncino, and the Fleming Johannes Wreede (or Urrede) appear in these sources beside works with Castilian texts by native-born Spaniards, among them Alonso de Alva, Anchieta, Cornago, Escobar, Peñalosa, Ponce, and others. The best, and the best-represented, composer in the cancioneros is Juan del Encina (1468/69–ca. 1529), whose secular music all seems to have been written when he was a young man in the service of the Duke of Alba. Although Encina later spent many years in Rome, and his religious commitment was great enough for him to undertake a pilgrimage to the Holy Land in 1519 and to describe his travels in print, he never published any liturgical music; at least, none survives today. Eventually he returned to his native country, where he served as prior at León during the last decade of his life.

The villancico closely resembles the Italian frottola in musical style, even though its fixed and conventional repetition scheme is very similar to the French virelai or the Italian ballata. The music for one strophe of a villancico normally repeats according to the following pattern:

Estribillo (Refrain)	*Copla* (Stanza)		
	Mudanza		*Vuelta*
A	B	B	A

To be more precise, villancicos often follow the formula aB cd cd aB (in which each letter represents a single line of verse or a couplet, and the capital letter indicates a repetition of the same text as well as the same music—that is, a refrain), but the refrain that ends both the *estribillo* and the *vuelta* does not invariably appear. As in the frottola, the principal melody of a villancico, usually relatively simple and even tuneful, appears in the top voice. The bass provides solid harmonic support, and the one or two inner voices often seem to be little more than written out realizations of the harmonies implied by the bass. Escobar's *Coraçón triste, sofrid* displays the typical form and texture of the three-part villancico on a condensed scale, with a three-line *estribillo* and two couplets for the *mudanza;* Example 8–10 shows the music for the first two lines of the *estribillo.* Much of the effect of this relatively simple piece depends on

EXAMPLE 8–10. Pedro de Escobar, *Coraçón triste, sofrid,* mm. 1–11.

the composer's surprisingly sophisticated handling of rhythm, not only the way he carefully balanced long against short notes and introduced a disconcerting near-sequence at the end of the *estribillo*, but also his delightfully irregular phrase lengths.

Some villancicos have a more pronounced tonal (or at least chordal) focus than others; some, in fact, are nothing more than arrangements of one of those standard sets of chord patterns, like the Passamezzo Antico or the Folia, that underlay so much music for dancing and entertainment both in Spain and in Italy during the sixteenth century. For instance, Encina's *Oy comamos y bebamos* is based on the Folia, a sequence of chords best known today, perhaps, in its arrangement by Corelli in his Op. 5, No. 12.

None of the similarities between frottole and villancicos is so striking as the way both genres use harmonic patterns and progressions of chords in a tonally logical manner belying the traditional view that fifteenth- and sixteenth-century harmony consists of more or less fortuitous coincidences of melodic lines without much conscious or detailed planning. But there are also significant differences between the two genres. The villancico has a far greater range of expressive possibilities than the frottola. The patterned dance rhythms that give to many frottole their somewhat schematic character are rare in their Spanish counterparts, where the rhythms are apt to be more diversified and more subtle. And many villancicos establish a pathetic, contemplative, serious, or lyrical mood quite foreign to the nature of the frottola.

The overwhelming majority of Spanish songs in the cancioneros are villancicos, but composers also set a substantial number of romances, long narrative poems of many strophes. Since the strophes are almost always made up of quatrains, settings of romances usually consist of four phrases of music, presumably intended to be repeated over and over again. These simple sets of phrases functioned, in effect, either as formulae for declaiming the narrative poetry or as starting places for elaborate variation. It is not surprising that Spanish composers were so expert at writing sets of variations, in view of the multi-strophic romances on the one hand and villancicos based on traditional patterns of chords on the other.

Juan del Encina's romances and villancicos differ more in degree than in kind from those by his contemporaries. His establish their moods more sharply and succinctly than those by other composers; they are more charming, more moving, or more tuneful. His romance *Triste España sin ventura*, for instance, probably written to lament the death of Queen Isabella or her son, Prince Juan, is touching despite its utter simplicity. And *Gasajémonos de husía*, slightly more ambitious musically than the others, with its changes of texture and meter, compellingly invites the listener to abandon his cares and enjoy himself while he can. Both it and *Oy comamos* were composed for performance at one of the dramatic entertainments—*representaciones* or *eglogas*—that Encina had to provide for the household of the Duke of Alba. Encina wrote the plays, composed the music, supervised the productions at carnival and other times, and sometimes even acted in them. They are the starting point for all later Spanish secular drama.

Villancicos continued to be written throughout the sixteenth century, after the deaths of Ferdinand and Isabella and into the reigns of Charles V and Philip II. In addition, Spanish musicians cultivated the art of the Italian madrigal. Juan Vásquez (ca. 1500–ca. 1560), a distinguished composer unjustly neglected by scholars and performers today, wrote expertly in both genres. Joan Brudieu (ca. 1520–91), born a Frenchman, composed madrigals in both Italian and Catalan that can stand comparison with those by the major Italian and Franco-Flemish musicians of his time. And Mateo Flecha the younger (ca. 1520–1604) published in Prague in 1581 a volume of ensaladas by himself, his uncle Mateo Flecha the elder (ca. 1481–ca. 1533), and other musicians; it includes a number of witty masterpieces, comparable in their effect to Janequin's program chansons. Ensaladas are textual quodlibets filled with fragments of popular music, street songs, dramatic exchanges, and bits of satire that make them a clever and amusing reflection of the everyday life of their times.

Both Charles V and Philip II were extremely pious men, and they lavished great care on their choral establishments. Charles maintained throughout his life a chapel of Flemish clerics and musicians—it was called the *capilla flamenca* in Spain—though after 1526 he also kept a separate chapel of Spanish musicians. Philip took over the Spanish chapel, which included such eminent musicians during the 1540's and 1550's as Juan García de Basurto, Pedro de Pastrana, Francisco de Soto, and the great blind organist Antonio de Cabezón; eventually Philip also reestablished a Flemish chapel, which during the second half of the sixteenth century employed a number of outstanding composers, among them Nicolas Payen, Pierre de Manchicourt, George de la Hèle, and Philippe Rogier. But the greatest of all Spanish composers before Tomás Luis de Victoria never worked in the royal service. Cristóbal de Morales (ca. 1500–1553) spent all of his career in the service of the church, as did his most distinguished pupil, Francisco Guerrero (1527/28–99), whose music, all too little studied and performed today, makes him almost the equal of Morales and Victoria.

Born and educated in Seville, Morales served as *maestro de capilla* in the cathedrals of Avila and Plasencia before going to Rome to sing in the Papal chapel for ten years, from 1535 to 1545. When he came back to

Spain he served at the cathedrals of Toledo, Marchena (near Seville), and Málaga, where he died in 1553. Apparently an unusually pious man, an attribute not to be taken for granted among church musicians, Morales left very little secular music. His fame and distinction rest entirely on his sacred music: twenty-two Masses (more than any other major composer of the post-Josquin generation); sixteen Magnificats, which enjoyed unprecedented fame during his lifetime and afterwards; a set of Lamentations published posthumously; and more than eighty motets.

The great theorist, Juan Bermudo, who referred to Morales as "the light of Spain in music," wrote also of the "foreign music that today comes from the excellent Cristóbal de Morales, the profound Gombert, and the other outsiders"—acknowledgment that his Spanish contemporaries considered Morales a composer who carried on the traditions of Franco-Flemish polyphony, perhaps with an Italian accent derived from his years in Rome, where he sang alongside such masters of polyphony as Arcadelt and Costanzo Festa. Bermudo's assessment in fact comes close to the mark. Even if Morales did not meet or work with Gombert when he was a young man in Seville, his music nevertheless reveals certain affinities with that of the northern master. Especially his two volumes of Masses, which he had published at his own expense and under his personal supervision, show that Morales belonged in the mainstream of sixteenth-century polyphony. They and his other Masses include works using all of the compositional techniques prevalent at the time: parodies of Franco-Flemish motets, paraphrases and old-fashioned cantus-firmus arrangements of French and Spanish songs and Gregorian chants, and even one cycle of canons, a device Morales employed not infrequently in his other Masses and in his motets.

In short, Morales is one of the major figures of the post-Josquin generation, the equal in every way of Gombert, Clemens and Willaert. Like them he valued continuity and a compact dense texture over clearly articulated formal divisions and transparent sonorities; he tended to introduce imitation wherever he found an opportunity; he seldom interrupted the flow of polyphony for declamatory chordal passages; and withal, his polyphony is shaped and controlled by a strong sense of harmonic direction and logical chordal progressions. If in his Masses he reveals himself to be a devout polyphonist of an emotionally rather neutral cast, in some of his motets he shows a dramatic flair and a penchant for pungent, movingly expressive effects that are to be explained, perhaps, by his Spanish temperament. The telling suspensions, for example, at the beginning of one of his most famous motets, *Lamentabatur Jacob*, make palpable the sense of the text in a way that reminds the listener more of Josquin than of the more discreet and diffident Gombert. And if the texture of his well-known *Emendemus in melius* is almost unrelievedly continuous, the ostinato (one of his favorite devices) on "Memento homo quia pulvis es et in pulverem reverteris" ("Remember, man, that thou art dust, and unto dust shalt thou return") sets up a dramatic tension between the insistent and forbidding threat of judgment in the tenor and the appeal for mercy sung by the other voices.

ENGLAND

Two factors help to explain why a national musical style developed differently in sixteenth-century England than in other countries. In the first place, Franco-Flemish polyphony did not have the same impact on English music that it had on music in Germany and Italy. Whereas English musicians exerted a strong and immensely fruitful influence on the formation of an early Renaissance musical style during the first half of the fifteenth century, composers like Walter Frye and John Bedingham, active in the middle and late fifteenth century, wrote music that is virtually indistinguishable in style from that by their Franco-Flemish contemporaries. Nevertheless, continental influences appear not to have made many inroads at home, even though foreign musicians such as the Flemish lutenist Philip van Wilder and the Italian musicians Ambrose Lupo, viol player, and Dionisio Memo, organist, served at the English court from the time of Henry VIII on. When the pervadingly imitative music of the post-Josquin generation reached England, it did not effect any large-scale or basic changes in the national style, which by that time was already firmly fixed and which passed from one phase to another only gradually.

In the second place, the growth of a distinctively English style, unlike similar developments in other countries, had comparatively little to do with secular music, if the evidence of the surviving sources can be trusted. (So few English songbooks survive from the sixteenth century, however, that they may not reveal the true situation.) Several large manuscripts in the British Museum, among them the Fayrfax Book (MS Add. 5465), the Ritson Manuscript (MS Add. 5665), Royal Appendix MS 58, and King Henry VIII's Songbook (MS Add. 31922) preserve carols and court songs from the late fifteenth and early sixteenth centuries by Gilbert Banester, John Browne, William Cornysh the younger, Richard Davy, Robert Fayrfax, and others. The carols are written in a florid style quite unlike that of the earlier carol. A curious combination of monophony, imitative writing, syllabically declaimed lines of verse, and elaborately decorated melismas (or instrumental interludes) characterize this repertory. King Henry VIII's Songbook, dated only a few years later than the Fayrfax Book, includes, in addition to continental music, instrumental pieces (some of them in the same florid style as the songs in the earlier anthology), English court songs, and carols in a lively, attractive, and apparently indigenous style, by Cornysh, Fayrfax, King Henry himself, and many other composers. Except for the incompletely preserved *XX Songes* of 1530 (formerly believed to be the work of the distinguished publisher Wynkyn de Worde), which is the only printed collection of English polyphonic music from the first half of the sixteenth century, the four manuscripts listed above are the major sources of early sixteenth-century English secular music. After them and until the great vogue of madrigals and related pieces in the last quarter of the century, English songs were preserved only sporadically. The Oxford organist Thomas Mulliner arranged a few for keyboard and included them in the anthology he compiled after 1550. In 1571 the relatively minor composer Thomas Whythorne (author of a fascinating autobiography, the earliest in the English language) published a volume of his own songs. Other manuscripts are scattered throughout a number of libraries.

Thus the growth of a national musical style can best be seen in English church music, although in this sphere, too, the situation in Britain was more complex than in most other countries, for the effect of the Reformation on music was more widespread and more profound. Harrison (in the *New Oxford History of Music,* vol. III) neatly sums up the position of English church music at the beginning of the sixteenth century when he writes that "conservative design and florid style were the most characteristic features of English compositions from the death of Dunstable to the Reformation." In the several decades before and after 1500, large-scale choral music in England was generally written over a cantus firmus in highly decorative and ornate counterpoint, more often in five, six, or more parts than in four or fewer. The first section of John Browne's magnificent eight-part votive antiphon, *O Maria salvatoris Mater,* which opens the Eton Choirbook, furnishes an excellent sample of the rich tapestry of non-imitative counterpoint woven around a cantus firmus (in this case as yet unidentified) that typifies this repertory. Following the common practice of his time, Browne divided *O Maria* into clear-cut sections, many of them built up gradually from a few voices to a climactic passage for full choir. The luxuriant polyphony is well controlled, not only by the placement of tuttis, but also by important cadences that mark major points of articulation, by the inexorable progress of the cantus firmus, and by the simple harmonic schemes that underlie the dense, complex interplay of voices. The elaboration of this lucid structure by an intricate filigree of melodic and rhythmic detail produces an effect of great sumptuousness that Harrison has aptly compared with English Perpendicular architecture.

English composers of the late fifteenth and early sixteenth centuries set only a limited number of types of sacred pieces, each of which had a clearly defined place within the rituals of the church. Votive antiphons, like Browne's *O Maria,* are paraliturgical compositions, often addressed to the Virgin Mary, which were intended to be sung at services apart from the Mass and Office, such as evening celebrations before the Virgin's image in the Lady-chapel, or in some other votive chapel. Festal Masses, reserved for ceremonial occasions and roughly analogous to the Great Services of Anglican church music, were often based on cantus firmi appropriate to the liturgical occasion at which they were performed; like earlier English Masses, those from the sixteenth century often lack a polyphonic Kyrie and sometimes portions of the Credo are also omitted. Most English Magnificats, which formed the musical highpoint of the Office of Vespers, were written to be performed in *alternatim* manner. Besides votive antiphons, festal Masses, and Magnificats, English musicians also composed regular liturgical antiphons and simpler Mass settings (many of them intended for performance at Lady-Mass) as well as music written to replace parts of the chant during the liturgy, such as responds, hymns, Prosas, Alleluias, Sequences, and Passions.

The largest source of English church music from the turn of the century, the Eton Choirbook (Eton College, MS 178), which contains votive antiphons and Magnificats but no complete Masses, includes music by some of the finest composers of the late fifteenth century, such as John Browne, Richard Davy, William Horwood, Walter Lambe, and Robert Wylkynson, as well as compositions by slightly younger musicians such as William Cornysh (died 1523) and Robert Fayrfax (1464–1521). Fayrfax, one of the best of all the early Tudor composers, wrote music that is slightly less florid than that by his older colleagues in the Eton Choirbook, and in which imitation plays a greatly increased role. But, typically, the imitation in the verse from Fayrfax's *Magnificat "Regale"* shown in Example 8–11 is neither so consistent nor so important to the structure as it is in most compositions by Franco-Flemish musicians of Josquin's generation or just after; it is unmistakably English. Indeed, the style of the Magnificat verse resembles that of the main corpus of the Eton Choirbook because of its continuous full texture and its use of a cantus firmus (in this case a faburden to the Magnificat chant—that is, a melody that originated as a counterpoint to the plainsong). But Fayrfax made a greater effort than the older English composers to create a homogeneous texture by writing the same sorts of melodies and rhythms for each voice, and since his individual lines are less decorated with elaborate detail, his music has a plainer sound. Along with two Magnificats, about a dozen motets, and several secular songs, five of Fayrfax's Mass settings *a 5* survive complete, and they too reflect the composer's allegiance to a native tradition (slightly modified by his own personality and temperament). Aside from the *Missa O bone Jesu,* which makes some use of parody technique, they are all based on plainsong cantus firmi, which are, however, used quite differently in each work. In the *Missa O quam*

EXAMPLE 8–11. Robert Fayrfax, *Magnificat "Regale,"* mm. 1–12, from *Treasury of English Church Music*, edited by Denis Stevens and Peter le Huray. Used by permission of Blandford Press Ltd.

glorifica, for example, the chant appears but once in each movement, in the *Missa Regali ex progenie* twice, whereas the nine notes taken from an antiphon for the feast of St. Alban that form the scaffold of the *Missa Albanus* are repeated over and over again in the manner of an ostinato.

Until the Reformation, English composers based their music on Sarum chants, versions of plainsong adapted for the rituals of Salisbury Cathedral (hence called "Sarum"). The Sarum rite, which differed in many respects from the Roman liturgy, prevailed in Britain throughout the Middle Ages and the early Renaissance. It was abolished in 1547; thus the last composers to use these distinctively English forms of chant exclusively were those younger contemporaries of Fayrfax and Cornysh who died about mid-century, men like John Redford, the two Scottish priests Robert Carver and Robert Johnson, and Nicolas Ludford (ca. 1485–ca. 1557), whose most remarkable works are seven relatively short Lady Masses, one for each day of the week. These Masses, for three voices, include sections from the Proper as well as the Ordinary of the Mass; they are intended to be performed *alternatim;* and they are all based on a mysterious repertory of melodies called "squares," a word whose exact meaning is unknown, although scholars now suppose that "squares" were originally counterpoints to earlier plainsong cantus firmi.

The greatest musician by far among Ludford's contemporaries, and arguably the greatest of all English pre-Reformation composers, was John Taverner (ca. 1495–1545), whose magnificent music can be said to sum up developments in England during the first forty years of the sixteenth century, for it embodies most of the achievements of his contemporaries. Perhaps the most important feature of Taverner's music is his obvious desire to impose a rational control on its texture without foregoing entirely the earlier richness of sound created by constantly moving rhythms and by the melodic independence of individual voices. Thus in an apparent effort to achieve homogeneity of texture and clarity of structure, Taverner introduced into his larger and more elaborate music frequent imitations, melodic sequences, ostinatos, canons, and, in his shorter and simpler music, chordal passages and sections of antiphonal dialogue between parts of the choir. Yet he continued to write counterpoint in the florid English manner; indeed, much of his music is more florid than, say, the church music of Fayrfax. One verse of Taverner's *Magnificat in the Sixth Tone* for four voices (Example 8–12) illustrates the extent to which the composer sometimes integrated his texture by means of imitation. Although the cantus firmus does not share in the imitation at the beginning of the excerpt, by the end the other voices are almost entirely taken up with echoing the descending sequence stated by the tenor.

The complete regularity of both the imitation and the sequence in this example is slightly unusual in Taverner's work; more often he pre-

ferred to vary some of the intervals in the point of imitation or the pattern
of the sequence, perhaps, in order to veil slightly the clarity of his design,
or merely to enjoy the pleasures of asymmetry. Like Fayrfax, Taverner
made some use of parody in his *Missa Mater Christi*, but several of his
Mass settings are built over cantus firmi, all but one derived from plainsong. The one exception, *The Western Wind Mass*, is the earliest English
Mass setting based on a secular tune. (Actually, there are no other
English Masses based on secular melodies except for two that also use

EXAMPLE 8–12. John Taverner, *Magnificat in the Sixth Tone*, mm. 51–66,
from *Treasury of English Church Music.* Used by permission of Blandford
Press Ltd.

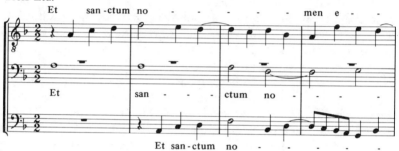

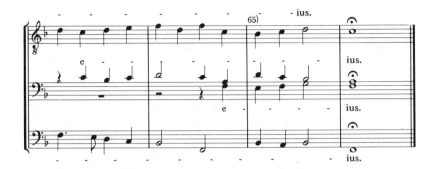

Western Wind, one by Tye and one by Shepherd.) The tune recurs nine times (eight times complete and the ninth truncated) in each movement, sung either by the treble (that is, superius), the tenor, or the bass part; thus, the Mass is, in effect, a gigantic set of variations.

The section of the Benedictus from Taverner's *Missa Gloria tibi trinitas* on the text "In nomine Domini" was apparently felt by some mid-sixteenth-century English musicians to be particularly appropriate to detach from its musical surroundings and to play independently on instruments. It appears, for example, in an organ arrangement in the Mulliner Book of about 1560–70. From that time onwards composers wrote new voices around the plainchant fragment that underlies that passage of Taverner's Mass—sometimes they even alluded to his version—and a whole repertory of *In nomine* pieces for viols and other instruments came into being; composers continued to write *In nomine* settings until the late seventeenth century.

Henry VIII, who made the definitive break with Rome in 1534 and suppressed the monasteries during the same decade, was conservative in liturgical matters and allowed florid Latin church music to flourish. On the other hand, Edward VI, who ruled from 1547 to 1553, came close to suppressing the English musical establishment altogether. During his years in power an English Prayer Book was approved which allowed few opportunities for elaborate polyphonic music; choral foundations and other important musical organizations were abolished; and many organs and liturgical books were destroyed. When Mary Tudor came to the throne in 1553, she restored the Roman rite with all its music, but neither she nor her Protestant half-sister, Elizabeth, who became Queen in 1558 and who finally confirmed the establishment of the Anglican Church as the state religion, could undo completely the damage that had already been done; thus church music in England was never fully brought back to its earlier thriving condition. From the 1540's onwards, the life of a church musician was uncertain and subject to numerous shifts of policy. But even after Elizabeth's accession Latin church music was not wholly forbidden: it could be sung in Chapels Royal, colleges, and public schools; hence it continued to be written and performed during the late sixteenth century, alongside elaborate Anglican anthems and services and simpler music designed for congregational participation.

The series of religious crises notwithstanding, a number of superb composers during the middle third of the century and just after managed to produce a distinguished body of sacred music. This group included William Mundy (died ca. 1591), Osbert Parsley (1511–85), Robert Parsons (died 1571), John Shepherd (ca. 1520/25–ca. 63), Christopher Tye (ca. 1500–1573), Robert White (died 1574), and the best of them all, Thomas Tallis (ca. 1505–85), gentleman of the Chapel Royal. During the lives of these men the Sarum rite was abolished and the interest in large-scale cantus-firmus Masses dwindled, although elaborate votive antiphons continued to be written during the last years of Henry VIII and into the reign of Mary, and a tradition of sacred music in English, especially anthems and services, came to be established. With the end of the Sarum rite, composers felt freer to set previously neglected sacred texts, such as psalms, in which they could express their own individuality more clearly than in the impersonal liturgical verses to which they had once felt restricted. Similarly, they turned to parts of the liturgy they had not cultivated before, like responds, hymns, and Lamentations. The set of Lamentations for Holy Week by Tallis is one of the greatest masterpieces of the entire Renaissance.

The greatest difficulty in briefly summing up Tallis's achievement stems from the bewildering variety of styles in which he wrote, a circumstance dictated at least partly by the changes in religious policy that took place during his lifetime. As a young man he continued the earlier English tradition and composed florid music that preserved the independence of individual voices to a much greater extent than did contemporaneous continental music. These first works of his maturity include not only extended votive antiphons but also the *Missa Salve intemerata virgo,* which makes use of parody technique. His grand seven-voiced festal Mass, based on a cantus firmus, the *Missa Puer natus est nobis,* may have been written to celebrate Queen Mary's marriage to Philip of Spain. During his middle years Tallis composed a number of strictly liturgical compositions in which, possibly for the first time, he used imitation as the chief structural principle. And during the reign of Elizabeth he wrote several mature motets in which the technique of pervading imitation became allied with a greater concern to associate the musical design with the words. If Tallis never became quite so "expressive" in an extroverted way as some late sixteenth-century continental composers, like Lasso and Victoria, he nevertheless took care to invent melodies that fit the syntax and the rhythms of the words, and he presented the points of imitation in an order that enabled their contrasting pace and shape to reflect something of the meaning of the text as a whole. The beginning of *Salvator mundi* (Example 8–13), a motet from the first book of Latin music printed in England, *Cantiones sacrae* (published by Tallis in 1575 in his old age, in collaboration with his much younger pupil, William Byrd), demonstrates his skill at handling imitative counterpoint in the "modern" manner. And the forty-voiced

EXAMPLE 8–13. Thomas Tallis, *Salvator mundi*, mm. 1–12, from *Treasury of English Church Music*. Used by permission of Blandford Press Ltd.

motet *Spem in alium*, a spectacular tour de force possibly commissioned for a great state occasion, shows a command of contrapuntal technique that belies the charge sometimes leveled against Tallis that his part writing is wooden and awkward. Finally, his Anglican services and anthems reflect his dutiful observance of the principles advocated by King Edward's musical advisers and other Protestants that the words should at all times be clearly audible. If an anthem like *O Lord, give thy Holy Spirit* mixes imitation and dialogue with its homophony, the music nevertheless preserves a simplicity of texture that does not obscure the clarity of the declamation.

BIBLIOGRAPHICAL NOTES

Modern editions of chansons and other French music of the sixteenth century include the following: H. M. Brown, ed., *Theatrical Chansons of the Fifteenth and Early Sixteenth Centuries* (Cambridge, Mass., 1963); Maurice Cauchie, ed., *Quinze chansons françaises du XVIe siècle* (Paris, 1926); Cauchie, ed., *Trente chansons de Clément Janequin* (Paris, 1928); Robert Eitner, ed., *60 Chansons zu vier Stimmen aus der ersten Hälfte des 16. Jahrhunderts, Publikationen älterer Musik*, 23 (Leipzig, 1899); Henry Expert, ed., *La fleur des musiciens de Pierre de Ronsard* (Paris, 1923); Expert, ed., *Florilège du concert vocal de la Renaissance* (Paris, 1928–29, 8 vols.); Expert, ed., *Les Maîtres musiciens de la Renaissance française* (Paris, 1894–1908, 23 vols.); Expert, ed., *Les Monuments de la musique française au temps de la Renaissance* (Paris, 1924–30, 10 vols.); François Lesure et al., *Anthologie de la chanson parisienne au XVIe siècle* (Monaco, 1953); L. Mairy, L. de la Laurencie, and G. Thibault, eds., *Chansons au luth et airs de cour français du XVIe siècle* (Paris, 1934); Albert Seay, ed., *Thirty Chansons for Three and Four Voices from Attaingnant's Collections, Collegium Musicum 2* (New Haven, Conn., 1960); and Seay, ed., *Pierre Attaingnant, Transcriptions of Chansons for Keyboard* (*CMM* 20; American Institute of Musicology, 1961). See also A. Smijers and A. T. Merritt, *Treize livres de motets parus chez Pierre Attaingnant en 1534 et 1535* (Monaco, 1934–63, 13 vols.); and Edward E. Lowinsky, *The Medici Codex of 1518*, 3 vols., *Monuments of Renaissance Music*, vols. 3–5 (Chicago and London, 1968). A group of chansons by Jacques Arcadelt has been edited by Everett Helm for the *Smith College Music Archives*, vol. 5. The complete works of Certon, ed. Henry Expert and Aimé Agnel, are in the process of publication (Paris, 1967–). The complete chansons of Clément Janequin have been edited by François Lesure and A. Tillman Merritt (Monaco, 1965–66). The complete works of Claudin de Sermisy, ed. Gaston Allaire and Isabelle Cazeaux, are in the process of publication by the American Institute of Musicology (*CMM* 52).

On French music in the first half of the sixteenth century, see Dénes Bartha, "Probleme der Chansongeschichte im 16. Jahrhundert," *Zeitschrift für Musikwissenschaft*, 13 (1931); Lawrence F. Bernstein, "Claude Gervaise as Chanson Composer," *Journal of the American Musicological Society*, 18 (1965); Bernstein, "The Cantus-Firmus Chansons of Tylman Susato," *Journal of the American Musicological Society*, 22 (1969); Bernstein, "*La Courone et fleur des chansons a troys:* A Mirror of the French Chanson in Italy in the Years between Ottaviano Petrucci and Antonio Gardano," *Journal of the American Musicological Society*, 26 (1973); Michel Brenet, *Musique et musiciens de la vieille France* (Paris, 1911); H. M. Brown, "The Chanson rustique: Popular Elements in the 15th- and 16th-Century Chanson," *Journal of the American Musicological Society*, 12 (1959); Brown, *Music in the French Secular Theater, 1400–1550* (Cambridge, Mass., 1963); Brown, "The Genesis of a Style: The Parisian Chanson, 1500–1530," *Chanson and Madrigal,* ed. James Haar (Cambridge, Mass., 1965); Caroline M. Cunningham, "Estienne du Tertre and the Mid-Sixteenth Century Parisian Chanson," *Musica Disciplina*, 25 (1971); Erich Hertzmann, "Trends in the Development of the Chanson in the Early 16th Century," *Papers of the American Musicological Society, 1940* (New York, 1946); Jean Jacquot, ed., *Musique et poésie au XVIe siècle* (Paris, 1954); François Lesure, "Autour de Clément Marot et de ses musiciens," *Revue de musicologie*, 33 (1951); Lesure, "Les Chansons à trois voix de Clément Janequin," *Revue de musicologie*, 44 (1959); Lesure, "Clément Janequin: Recherches sur sa vie et ses oeuvres," *Musica Disciplina*, 5 (1951); Lesure, *Poets and Musicians of the French Renaissance* (New York, 1955); and Jacques Levron, *Clément Janequin, musicien de la Renaissance* (Grenoble and Paris, 1948).

The standard book on the sixteenth-century Italian madrigal remains Alfred Einstein's magnificent *The Italian Madrigal* (Princeton, 1949, 3 vols.), which includes well-chosen selections from the entire century. A briefer introduction to the subject is Jerome Roche, *The Madrigal* (London, 1972). See also James Haar, "The 'Note Nere' Madrigal," *Journal of the American Musicological Society*, 18 (1965); Don Harran, "'Mannerism' in the Cinquecento Madrigal?," *Musical Quarterly*, 55 (1969); Harran, "Verse Types in the Early Madrigal," *Journal of the American Musicological Society*, 22 (1969); Dean T. Mace, "Pietro Bembo and the Literary Origins of the Italian Madrigal," *Musical Quarterly*, 55 (1969); Walter Rubsamen, "Sebastian Festa and the Early Madrigal," *Kongressbericht Kassel 1962* (Cassel, 1963); and H. Colin Slim, *A Gift of Madrigals and Motets* (Chicago and London, 1972, 2 vols.).

Editions of the complete works of the following important madrigal composers are in the process of publication by the American Institute of Musicology: Jacob Arcadelt, ed. Albert Seay (*CMM* 31); Costanzo Festa, ed. Alexander Main (*CMM* 25); Cipriano de Rore, ed. Bernhard Meier (*CMM* 14); Philippe Verdelot, ed. Anne-Marie Bragard (*CMM* 28); and Adrian Willaert, ed. Hermann Zenck and Walter Gerstenberg (*CMM* 3).

Collections of madrigals include Alfred Einstein, ed., *The Golden Age of the Madrigal* (New York, 1942); Gertrude P. Smith, ed., *The Madrigals of Cipriano de Rore for 3 and 4 Voices, Smith College Music Archives,* vol. 6 (Northampton, Mass., 1943); and Luigi Torchi, *L'Arte musicale in Italia* (Milan, 1897–1908, 7 vols.). A selection of villanelle appears in *Das Chorwerk,* vol. 8. Gastoldi's balletti for three voices are published in a modern edition in three volumes by W. Hermann (Berlin, 1927); those for five voices have been published by Michel Sanvoisin (Paris, 1968). The theatrical madrigals composed for intermedii in Florence in 1539 are published in Andrew C. Minor and B. Mitchell, *A Renaissance Entertainment: Festivities for the Marriage of Cosimo I, Duke of Florence, in 1539* (Columbia, Missouri, 1968). Those for the Florentine intermedii of 1589 appear in D. P. Walker, ed., *Les Fêtes du mariage de Ferdinand de Médicis et de Christine de Lorraine, Florence 1589* (Paris, 1963).

The most comprehensive books on German secular music in the fifteenth and sixteenth centuries are written in German; among them are Ernst Bücken, *Das deutsche Lied* (Hamburg, 1939); Hermann Kretzschmar, *Geschichte des neuen deutschen Liedes* (Leipzig, 1911); Günther Müller, *Geschichte des deutschen Liedes* (Munich, 1925); and Helmuth Osthoff, *Die Niederländer und das deutsche Lied (1400–1640)* (Berlin, 1938).

The Lochamer Liederbuch is published in a facsimile edition by Konrad Ameln (Cassel, 1925; new ed., 1972) and in modern editions by F. W. Arnold (*Jahrbuch für musikalische Wissenschaft,* 2, 1867), Konrad Ameln (the polyphonic music, Augsburg, 1929), E. Rohloff (the monophonic music, Halle, 1953), and Walter Salmen (*Denkmäler der Tonkunst in Bayern,* New Series, Sonderband 2, Wiesbaden, 1972). The secular music in the Schedelsches Liederbuch is included in Robert Eitner, *Das deutsche Lied des XV. und XVI. Jahrhunderts* (Berlin, 1876–80, 2 vols.). Much of the Glogauer Liederbuch appears in modern edition in *Das Erbe deutscher Musik,* vols. 4 and 8 (1936, 1937). The Horatian odes of Tritonius and others were published by Rochus von Liliencron, "Die Horazischen Metren in deutschen Kompositionen des 16. Jahrhunderts," *Vierteljahrsschrift für Musikwissenschaft,* 3 (1887). Some of Hans Sachs's Meistersinger melodies are in Georg Münzer, *Das Singbuch des Adam Puschman, nebst den Originalmelodien des M. Behaim und Hans Sachs* (Leipzig, 1907).

The Öglin Liederbuch of 1512 is published in *Publikation älterer praktischer und theoretischer Musikwerke,* vol. 9 (Berlin, 1880); the Peter Schöffer Liederbuch of 1513 in facsimile (Berlin, 1908), and a selection from it in modern edition in *Das Chorwerk,* vol. 29; and the Arnt von Aich Liederbuch in H. J. Moser and E. Bernoulli, eds., *Das Liederbuch des Arnt von Aich* (Cassel, 1930). The Liederbücher of the 1530's, 1540's and 1550's have been partially published in modern editions in various volumes of *Das Erbe deutscher Musik* and *Publikation älterer praktischer und theoretischer Musikwerke.* See also the facsimile edition of *Gassen-hawerlin und Reutterliedlin (1535),* ed. H. J. Moser (Augsburg and Co-logne, 1927), and various volumes of *Denkmäler der Tonkunst in Bayern* and *Denkmäler der Tonkunst in Oesterreich.* The Codex of Nikolaus Apel is published in *Das Erbe deutscher Musik,* vols. 32 and 33 (Cassel, 1956–60).

Heinrich Isaac's German music is published in *Denkmäler der Tonkunst in Oesterreich,* vols. 18 and 32; Hofhaimer's music in H. J. Moser, *Paul Hofhaimer* (Stuttgart and Berlin, 1929); and a selection of music by Heinrich Finck in *Publikation älterer praktischer und theoretischer Musikwerke,* vol. 8. The complete works of Ludwig Senfl, ed. E. Löhrer, O. Ursprung and others, are published in the 10-volume *Sämtliche Werke* (Wolfenbüttel and Zürich, 1937–72).

The series *Monumentos de la Música Espanola,* ed. Higini Anglès (Bar-celona, 1941–), includes, among other things, the Cancionero Musical de Palacio (vols. 5 and 10), the Cancionero musical de la Casa de Medin-aceli (vol. 8), and the complete works of Cristóbal de Morales (vols. 11, 13, 15, 17, 20, 21, and 24). The *Cancionero de Upsala* appears in a modern edition by R. Mitjana, J. Bal y Gay, and I. Pope (Mexico, 1944).

Two studies of Spanish music are Robert Stevenson, *Spanish Music in the Age of Columbus* (The Hague, 1960) and Stevenson, *Spanish Cathedral Music in the Golden Age* (Berkeley and Los Angeles, 1961).

Surveys of English music include Frank Ll. Harrison, *Music in Medieval Britain* (London, 1958); Denis Stevens, *Tudor Church Music* (London, 1961); and Peter le Huray, *Music and the Reformation in England, 1549–1660* (London, 1967). Secular music at Henry VIII's court is discussed in John Stevens, *Music and Poetry in the Early Tudor Court* (London, 1961).

On English composers, see Hugh Baillie, "Nicolas Ludford," *Musical Quarterly,* 49 (1958); H. B. Collins, "John Taverner's Masses," *Music and Letters,* 6 (1925); Dom Anselm Hughes, "An Introduction to Fayr-fax," *Musica Disciplina,* 6 (1952); Edwin B. Warren, "The Life and Works of Robert Fayrfax," *Musica Disciplina,* 11 (1957); H. B. Col-lins, "Thomas Tallis," *Music and Letters,* 10 (1929); and Paul Doe, *Tallis* (London, 1968). For discussions of the *In nomine,* see Robert Donington and Thurston Dart, "The Origin of the 'In nomine,' " *Music and Letters,* 30 (1949); and Denis Stevens, "The Background of the 'In nomine,' " *Monthly Musical Record,* 84 (1954).

The series *Musica Britannica* includes modern editions of the Mulliner Book (ed. Denis Stevens), King Henry's Songbook (ed. John Stevens), and the Eton Choirbook (ed. Frank Ll. Harrison). The 10-volume series *Tudor Church Music* (London, 1922–29) contains music by Taverner, Byrd, Gibbons, White, Tallis, and others. The series *Early English Church*

Music (London, 1962–   ) includes anthologies of Masses, Magnificats, and organ music, as well as volumes devoted to music by Mundy, Orlando Gibbons, Tomkins, Tallis, and others. A selection of representative examples of English church music appears in *Treasury of English Church Music*, vol. 1, ed. Denis Stevens, and vol. 2, ed. Peter le Huray (London, 1965).

NINE
INSTRUMENTAL MUSIC

The emancipation of instrumental from vocal music is one of the most important developments in the history of music between 1400 and 1600. A great deal of music was published during the century that was intended specifically for instruments, and even more is described as "apt for voices or instruments" on printed title pages. Moreover, a number of new instrumental forms were created or developed: the toccata, the ricercare, the canzona, the variation, and various dance types, for example.

Instrumental music during the sixteenth century may be divided into seven categories: (1) vocal music played by instruments, including a sizeable repertory of intabulations of chansons, madrigals, lieder, motets, and even Masses for solo keyboard or lute; (2) settings of pre-existing melodies, chiefly arrangements of plainchant for keyboard instruments; (3) variation sets, including ground basses and pieces built on recurring chord progressions; (4) ricercars, fantasias, and canzonas; (5) preludes, preambles, and toccatas for solo instruments, in a style that incorporated some idiomatic writing for the particular instrument in question; (6) dance music; and (7) songs composed specifically for lute and solo voice. Most of these genres were interchangeable as to medium; they include compositions for consorts of like instruments (viols, recorders, flutes, and so on) and mixtures of contrasting instruments, as well as music for solo instruments, both keyboards and plucked strings.

To judge from the surviving sources, instrumental music was cultivated more richly and more deeply in Italy than in any other country of western Europe during the sixteenth century. The earliest printed lute music, for example, was Italian: the volumes for solo lute, two lutes, and lute and voice by Francesco Spinacino, Joan Ambrosio Dalza, and Francesco Bossinensis published between 1507 and 1511. And Eustachio Romano's collection of duos, issued in Rome in 1521, was the earliest printed book devoted entirely to music for instrumental ensemble. While Andrea Antico's volumes of frottole arranged for keyboard (1517) and Marco Antonio Cavazzoni's *Recerchari, Motetti, Canzoni* of 1523 were not the first music for keyboard to be published—Arnolt Schlick's *Tabulaturen etlicher Lobgesang und Lidlein* (1512) preceded them by some years—they reveal the common performance practices of the period and show that Italians were in the forefront of new developments.

It was during the second quarter of the century, though, that instrumental music began to flourish in Italy. A great many Italian virtuoso lutenists published one or more collections of their own music, beginning with the greatest of them all, Francesco da Milano, whose first volume appeared in 1536, the same year as an anthology containing examples of music by him and by his distinguished contemporaries Pietro Paolo Borrono and Marco d'Aquila, among others. The same year, too, Adrian Willaert published his arrangements for solo voice and lute of an entire volume of madrigals by Philippe Verdelot, a collection that furnishes valuable insights into the way one great composer worked with music by another. From 1546 onwards a veritable avalanche of anthologies of lute music began to be issued, by Julio Abondante, Giovanni Maria da Crema, Marcantonio del Pifaro, Perino Fiorentino, and many others. Moreover, during the second quarter of the century, a number of composers—among them Adrian Willaert, Julio Segni, and Giuliano Tiburtino—published abstract instrumental music for whole and broken consorts—ricercars, fantasias, and duos—in greater quantity than ever before. And two composers of keyboard music, Jacques Buus and Girolamo Cavazzoni, both achieved prominence during the same period.

In like fashion the second half of the sixteenth century witnessed a bewildering amount of activity among instrumentalists and composers of instrumental music in Italy. The Gardane and Scotto families in

Venice, rival publishing houses, issued many volumes of music for lutes, keyboard instruments, and instrumental ensembles. In the 1580's and 1590's, Simone Verovio in Rome and Giacomo Vincenti in Venice published several series of canzonette along with arrangements of them for both lute and keyboard. Among the leading lutenists of the second half of the century were Vincenzo Galilei, Joan Pacolini, and Giovanni Antonio Terzi; and Andrea Gabrieli, Claudio Merulo, and Annibale Padovano, among others, distinguished themselves as composers of keyboard music. While the Italians were strangely reluctant to publish volumes of dances for instrumental ensemble—those by Francesco Bendusi in 1553 and Giorgio Mainerio in 1578 were the only ones issued in Italy during the century—a large number of composers wrote and published abstract instrumental music for whole and broken consorts (ensembles of like and dissimilar instruments, respectively), among them Adriano Banchieri, Andrea Gabrieli, Gioseffo Guami, Fiorenzo Maschera, Vincenzo Ruffo, and Ludovico Viadana.

Instrumental music got its start in France with the publishing activities of Pierre Attaingnant, who issued in the late 1520's and 1530's an important series of editions of music for keyboard and for lute and also, later, several sets of ensemble dance music. In the second half of the century, publication of instrumental music in France and Flanders was dominated by the firm of Pierre Phalèse in Louvain and Le Roy and Ballard in Paris, who both issued all manner of music for various plucked string instruments (lute, guitar, and cittern). Phalèse, along with Jacques Moderne of Lyons, Tielman Susato of Antwerp, and Nicolas du Chemin of Paris, also published sets of ensemble dances, a specialty of the French as much in the sixteenth as in later centuries. Their predilection for the dance explains why the major treatise on dancing in the century, Thoinot Arbeau's *Orchésographie* of 1589, is French. Aside from Attaingnant's series, keyboard music seems not to have been much cultivated in France, and abstract instrumental music—ricercars and fantasias, whether for lute or for ensembles—is rarer there than in other countries. On the other hand, a number of distinguished lutenists were active in France and Flanders, most notably the great Italian virtuoso Alberto da Ripa (Albert de Rippe), who worked at the French royal court, and Adrian le Roy and Guillaume Morlaye, both of whom wrote guitar music in addition to lute music.

In Germany, keyboard music flourished more than elsewhere. After Arnolt Schlick's tablature of 1512, a number of manuscripts from the first half of the century reveal what German organists and harpsichordists were writing, especially within that circle of musicians who looked to Paul Hofhaimer for their inspiration—Johannes Buchner of Constance, Leonhard Kleber, Johannes Kotter, and Fridolin Sicher. In the second half of the century a group of composers for the keyboard—Elias Nicolaus Ammerbach, Jakob Paix, Bernhard Schmid and others—decorated their works so heavily with quick runs and passage work that they have become known as "colorists."

Lute music from the first half of the sixteenth century was published in Germany by Hans Judenkünig, Hans Gerle, and Hans Newsidler. A great many German lutenists had their music printed during the second half of the century, among them Melchior Newsidler, Sebastian Ochsenkun, and Matthaeus Waissel; much of it consists of competent if unexciting arrangements of vocal music or dances. The Hungarian lutenist Valentin Bakfark, on the other hand, was one of the great virtuosi of the time. Curiously, relatively little music for instrumental ensemble was published in Germany until the last decade or two of the sixteenth century. For the most part, Hieronymus Formschneider's *Trium vocum carmina* of 1538—that is, instrumental pieces ("carmina") for three voices —contains vocal music with the text omitted. The vast collection of ensemble dances issued by Paul and Bartholomeus Hessen in 1555 is unfortunately preserved incompletely. Not until the very end of the century did abstract instrumental pieces and also dances for ensembles begin to appear in print, by Gregor Aichinger, Adam Gumpelzhaimer and Valentin Hausmann, among others.

Instrumental music in Spain is concentrated almost exclusively in the seven great vihuela tablatures of the sixteenth century—those by Luis Milán (1536), Luis de Narváez (1538), Alonso Mudarra (1546), Enriquez de Valderrábano (1547), Diego Pisador (1552), Miguel de Fuenllana (1554), and Esteban Daza (1576)—and on the volumes of keyboard music prepared by Luis Venegas de Henestrosa (1557), Antonio Valente, a Spaniard who worked in Naples (1576), and Hernando Cabezón, who published the music of his father, the great blind organist Antonio de Cabezón, in 1578.

Similarly, English instrumental music is rather scarce before the great "golden age" that began in the last decades of the sixteenth century. A handful of manuscript sources, chief among them the Mulliner Book, reveal that John Redford, Thomas Tallis, and John (not William) Blitheman were outstanding composers of music for the keyboard before William Byrd. But only toward the end of the sixteenth and the beginning of the seventeenth centuries did great quantities of instrumental music circulate widely in England—in the magnificent manuscript and printed anthologies of keyboard music (such as the Fitzwilliam Virginal Book, My Ladye Nevells Booke, and Parthenia), the collections of music for solo lute and for lute and voice (by John Dowland and his contemporaries), and music for consorts of viols and also broken consorts (such as the *Consort Lessons* by Thomas Morley of 1599).

INSTRUMENTAL PERFORMANCE
OF VOCAL MUSIC

That most vocal music in the sixteenth century was said to be "apt for voices or instruments" merely continues an older tradition; the central part of the repertory for all instruments continued to be arrangements of vocal music. Most sources offer no further details, but in a few volumes specific instrumentations are suggested. Already in 1533, for example, Pierre Attaingnant published two volumes of chansons in which some are marked as good for consorts of flutes or recorders, others as better for the one kind of instrument or the other. Treatises on ornamentation reveal that performances of polyphonic vocal compositions arranged for solo melody instrument (or voice) accompanied by lute (or keyboard) were common. And by the end of the sixteenth century and the beginning of the seventeenth, composers like Giovanni Gabrieli and Claudio Monteverdi were beginning more regularly to offer advice about instrumentation.

The largest repertory of vocal music arranged for instruments comprises the many volumes of intabulations of Masses, motets, and secular music for keyboard instruments, as well as lutes, vihuelas, guitars, citterns, and other plucked strings. The technique of intabulation remained essentially the same throughout the century. In an ideal arrangement, according to Adrian le Roy and Vincenzo Galilei, who both describe the process in treatises on lute playing, the performer takes over as much of the vocal music as the technique of his instrument allows, although in practice the arrangers sometimes omitted one voice or rearranged the part writing.

Virtually all sixteenth-century intabulators added ornamentation to the vocal models they arranged. They did so partly out of necessity— fast passagework helped to sustain the fragile sounds of the lute, vihuela, and harpsichord—and partly from a love of decoration that modern musicians do not always find tasteful. Most instrumentalists relied on stereotyped figuration patterns: runs, turns, and trills. The anonymous editor of Attaingnant's keyboard books adopted this technique in decorating Claudin de Sermisy's *Tant que vivray*, for instance, as a comparison of Example 9-1 with Example 8-1, the vocal original, makes clear. Earlier in the century, lutenists like Spinacino and Dalza maintained a steady eighth- or sixteenth-note motion in their intabulations, obscuring the contours of their models beneath an avalanche of endless and directionless scale fragments. Similarly, the German keyboard composers of the

EXAMPLE 9–1. Claudin de Sermisy, *Tant que vivray*, mm. 1–12, arranged for keyboard. Used by permission of the American Institute of ·Musicology.

last thirty years of the sixteenth century (Ammerbach, Schmid, Paix, and the other so-called "colorists") overwhelmed their models with mechanical decoration. Heavily ornamented intabulations from mid-century often restrict the number of stereotyped figuration patterns applied to any one section of a composition. Repeated wherever possible, these ornamental clichés form a superstructure, so to speak, over the given vocal piece, a network of motives completely independent of the original conception. Diego Ortiz employed this technique in his arrangements for viol and keyboard. And some of the greatest virtuosi of the century, like Valentin

Bakfark and Francesco da Milano, went further than lesser musicians in transforming the original composition into an idiomatic and virtuoso instrumental piece by means of a profusion of ever-varying runs, turns, and trills.

SETTINGS OF PRE-EXISTENT MELODIES

A few composers in the sixteenth century wrote counterpoints for melody instruments against a plainchant cantus firmus. Girolamo Parabosco, for example, included a *Da pacem* for four-part consort in the collection *Musica nova*, published in 1540; and Fernando de Las Infantas published in 1579 a collection of one hundred two- to eight-part canons over the cantus firmus *Laudate Dominum omnes gentes*. Some composers based their abstract instrumental music on melodic material borrowed from chant or from secular music, like Annibale Padovano, who published ricercars in 1556 based on chant melodies, and Vincenzo Ruffo, whose *Capricci* of 1564 incorporate music from madrigals and chansons. And German keyboard players, like Ammerbach in his *Orgel oder Instrument Tabulatur* of 1571, set Protestant chorales for the organ, the practice that was to culminate in Bach's great chorale preludes.

The largest category by far of instrumental settings of pre-existent vocal melodies, however, consists of liturgical organ music, arrangements of plainchants for use as a part of the divine service. Organists set not only parts of the Office hours (hymns, antiphons, psalm tones, and Magnificats) and the Proper of the Mass (Introits, Sequences, and hymns), but also complete Mass Ordinaries and single movements. Most of these pieces were designed for *alternatim* performance in which the sections for organ alone alternated with chant or polyphony sung by a chorus or soloists.

Many of these organ compositions doubtless reflect the practice of improvising keyboard movements based on chant during parts of the divine service. Some of the published music, therefore, is didactic in intent, meant to teach the young organist the techniques necessary for his profession. But some of the pieces—by Girolamo Cavazzoni, Andrea Gabrieli, Antonio de Cabezón, and others—are of the highest artistic caliber, among the best instrumental music of the entire century. The simplest technique for incorporating chant involves placing the borrowed melody, virtually unchanged, in any one voice (superius, alto, tenor, or bass) and writing counterpoints around it. Or else each phrase of the chant is treated as a point for imitation in the manner of vocal polyphony. But sixteenth-century composers also decorated the cantus firmus and enlivened it rhythmically, especially when it was placed in the top voice, using the paraphrase technique familiar from fifteenth-century hymn settings. Or else they transformed the chant by constructing a new melody based on its most characteristic features and then using the thematic material derived in this way for imitative entries and other contrapuntal manipulations.

The French organ music published by Attaingnant in 1531 relied mostly on cantus firmus technique, whereas German composers like Hofhaimer and Schlick were more adventurous in adapting imitative polyphony to their instruments. Girolamo Cavazzoni, whose music was issued in the 1540's, was one of the most skillful musicians in transforming chant into new melodic entities. His skill was matched by the later Italian keyboard composers—Andrea Gabrieli, Claudio Merulo, and their contemporaries—whose liturgical organ music includes a variety of techniques: strict cantus firmus, paraphrase, transformation, and imitation. And those techniques plus faburden appear in the English organ music by John Redford, Thomas Preston, Thomas Tallis, John Blitheman, and others, all predecessors of the great William Byrd.

The Italians and their Spanish counterparts, Antonio Valente, Bermudo, and especially Antonio Cabezón, developed a sophisticated and partly idiomatic keyboard style that is an important stage in the separation of instrumental from vocal styles of writing. Keyboard composers throughout the sixteenth century, especially those Italians and Spaniards who worked during its second half, began to take regular advantage of the freedom of a solo player to interrupt the polyphonic texture by adding or omitting notes, melodic lines, or chords at will; and this so-called *Freistimmigkeit* sometimes extended to sections written in an altogether freer toccata-like texture in which polyphony, chords, and runs (in one hand or divided between both) alternate, independent of any strict contrapuntal framework. Moreover, at times ornamental figures do not merely decorate an underlying simpler melodic line but become in themselves the principal thematic material; and these complementary motives are sometimes used to weave an elaborate web around the liturgical cantus firmus.

VARIATION SETS

Arrangements of polyphonic vocal compositions for solo keyboard and lute in which the top voice is decorated with figuration patterns, constitute, of course, variations of the original. Compositions based on ostinati are in effect sets of continuous variations on a given theme and rhythmic pattern. And settings of cantus firmi are, as it were, a single variation on a melody. These and other variation techniques were known during the Middle Ages. But full-fledged sets of variations, in which some elements of a relatively short, autonomous song or dance are preserved through a number of repetitions while other elements change, did not exist before the sixteenth century. Sets of variations began to be composed, apparently independently, in both Italy and Spain at about the same time. In England the practice began in the early sixteenth century but only really flourished later, while in Germany and France it never developed to the same extent as in the other western European countries.

Sixteenth-century composers treated the music to be varied in several different ways, sometimes changing from one to another technique from variation to variation. In some variations they preserved the original melody more or less intact, either in the top voice or in one of the lower voices, and changed the counterpoints or chords around the *cantus prius factus*. In some, the process of variation consisted of orna- ꞁ menting the melody itself with figuration patterns. And in some the orig- 2 inal melody disappeared and only its harmony and structure were 3 preserved.

As did settings of pre-existent melodies, sixteenth-century sets of variations for lute or keyboard used figuration patterns either to embellish a given melody or else to form motives which permeated the texture; or a combination of both techniques created a more or less free texture adapted to the exigencies of solo playing. Many sixteenth-century sets of variations were continuous; that is, they were based on a simple melodic formula, harmonic progression, or repeating bass in which no complete stop with double bar separated one statement from the next. The ground basses especially cultivated by the English fall into this category, as do the Italian song and dance formulas—the passamezzo basses, the Romanesca, the Ruggiero, the Folia, and so on. Other sets of variations, on the other hand, differentiated one unit from the next more clearly by pausing at the end of each segment, as in the English variations on popular songs, such as William Byrd's *Carman's Whistle, John Come Kiss Me Now,* and *Walsingham.* Moreover, variation technique in the sixteenth century included the practices of varying repeated strains of music and of writing variation suites. The former practice is exemplified by the English habit of writing out the repeated strains of pavanes and galliards (thus: A A' B B' C C'). The latter practice consists in its simplest form of a dance in duple meter followed by an "afterdance" based on the same melodic material but reworked in triple meter; eventually, longer sequences of dances were all unified by being based on the same thematic material.

Some of the dances in Joan Ambrosio Dalza's fourth book of lute music, published in 1508, are based on harmonic patterns; they are the earliest printed variation sets, all of the continuous sort. Other Italian lutenists did not begin to publish similar sets until the 1540's. Abondante (1546), Bianchini (1546), Gorzanis (1561), and others included dance pieces with varied sections, especially passamezzos, in their anthologies, and some wrote suites of dances in which each movement is built on the same melodic material. From the 1570's onwards, German keyboard players, too, began publishing passamezzo settings: Ammerbach (1571), Schmid (1577), Paix (1583), and others. The French, by contrast, restricted their use of variation technique to writing out repetitions of dance sections with added ornamentation, as in the keyboard dances published by Attaingnant in 1531.

Luis Milán ornamented repeated strains in the pavanes in his *El Maestro* (1536), but the great tradition of variation sets in Spanish vihuela and keyboard music did not begin until 1538 when Luis de Narváez included variations (called *diferencias*) on Gregorian hymns, villancicos, and romances in his *Delphin de musica*. Narváez was followed by the vihuelists Mudarra (1546) and Valderrabano (1547), the viol player Diego Ortiz, who included settings of various Italian grounds arranged for viol and keyboard in his *Trattado de glosas* (1553), and the great keyboard composer Antonio de Cabezón (1578), whose variety of approach and richness of invention made him one of the outstanding masters of the genre.

In England various ground basses, including several "dumps" and Hugh Aston's *Hornepype* (where the ground is actually in the tenor), were composed during the first half of the century; and passamezzo sets, like those in the Dublin Virginal Book, and variations on chants, like those in the Mulliner Book, showed that English composers were keeping abreast of continental developments. But it was not until the second half of the century that the variation flowered in England. Italian dance basses, varied repetitions in single and paired dances, cantus firmus settings of chants, and variation sets based on popular tunes all appear in great profusion in the virginal books of the late sixteenth and early seventeenth centuries, the most famous of which is the Fitzwilliam Virginal Book. And composers like John Bull, Giles Farnaby, Orlando Gibbons and, above all, William Byrd, carried the genre to its highest peak of perfection.

RICERCARS, FANTASIAS, AND CANZONAS

The terms "ricercare," "fantasia," and (in Spanish) "tiento" seem to have been used more or less interchangeably for an instrumental composition based neither on borrowed melodic material nor on a dance rhythm or a pre-formed scheme of any kind. Ricercars and fantasias came to be built on successive points of imitation by the middle of the sixteenth century, but they were by no means always imitative in their early history, and the terms do not presuppose any rigid formal plan. Canzonas, on the other hand, are compositions written in direct imitation of the intabulations of French chansons so common during the period; they are, therefore, more unified stylistically as a genre, even though composers during the seventeenth century transformed their character completely.

With the exception of France, where abstract instrumental music was not much cultivated during the sixteenth century, ricercars and fantasias were written everywhere in western Europe, but the nature of the genre changed drastically in the course of the century. The earliest sixteenth-century ricercars, those by Spinacino, Dalza, Francesco Bossinensis, and Vincenzo Capirola for lute, and Marco Antonio Cavazzoni for keyboard, are improvisatory in character. They mix sections that exploit the idiosyncracies of lute or keyboard—their penchant for runs, figuration patterns, and textures of varying density—with clichés borrowed from late fifteenth- and early sixteenth-century vocal music.

Formal symmetry—balanced phrases, paired imitative motives repeated in various octaves, cadential extensions, and short imitative sections—characterize the ricercars and fantasias by composers writing between about 1530 and 1545, especially the lutenists Francesco da Milano and Marco d'Aquila and the keyboard player Giacomo Fogliano, composers whose technique seems to have been influenced most decisively by the works of Josquin des Prez and his contemporaries.

From about 1540 onwards, ricercars and fantasias were more often than not based on the consistent use of points of imitation. This technique —constructing a composition by means of a series of expositions of themes that follow one another in succession—derived from the vocal style of the post-Josquin generation, and especially from the motet, even though ricercars and fantasias often concentrate on a smaller number of themes than do motets, and some are even monothematic. The new technique appeared for the first time in a collection for ensemble, *Musica nova* (1540), containing pieces by Adrian Willaert, Giulio Segni, Girolamo Parabosco, and others. But it soon dominated instrumental writing in Italy—by Girolamo Cavazzoni, Jacques Buus, Annibale Padovano, Andrea Gabrieli, Claudio Merulo, and many others—and in other countries: Spain (Cabezón, Bermudo, and others), Germany and eastern Europe (Bakfark, Drusina, Melchior Newsidler, and others), and eventually England (fantasias by Byrd, Bull, Gibbons, and others). Indeed, the imitative ricercare is precisely the kind of composition Thomas Morley described (in his *Plaine and Easie Introduction to Practicall Musicke* of 1597) in his famous definition of a fantasia as "the most principall and chiefest kind of musicke which is made without a dittie . . . that is, when a musician taketh a point at his pleasure, and wresteth and turneth it as he list, making either much or little of it according as shall seem best in his own conceit." The canzona as an independent instrumental genre developed later than the ricercare. The earliest canzonas for keyboard—those by Marco Antonio Cavazzoni (1523) and his son Girolamo (1542)—seem all to be based on thematic material actually drawn from French chansons. Models have not been found for all of the *canzoni francesi* published in the lute anthologies by Barberiis (1546 and 1547) and Rotta (1546), and so it is not clear whether they are intabulations of vocal pieces or compositions conceived for lute in imitation of chansons. It was not until the 1570's that the instrumental canzona was regularly cultivated, first by Nicola Vicentino and Marc'Antonio Ingegnieri and later by Fiorenzo Maschera, Claudio Merulo, and Giovanni Gabrieli, writing for instrumental ensemble, and by Andrea Gabrieli, Merulo, Pellegrini, and others, for keyboard.

Instrumental canzonas, like the vocal models on which they were originally based, are generally divided into clearly articulated sections, with strongly metrical themes (often beginning with the rhythm ♩ ♪ ♪). The sections are often contrasting (for example, an imitative section followed by a more chordal one, or a section in duple meter followed by one in triple), and canzonas are sometimes built on a simple repetition scheme (ABA, ABB, AABC, or the like).

PRELUDES, PREAMBLES, TOCCATAS, AND INTONATIONS

Early sixteenth-century ricercars, as we have seen, were often improvisatory pieces, apparently used to introduce performances of longer and weightier intabulations of vocal music. They thus resembled the preludes and preambles that appeared in early sixteenth-century lute books —those by Dalza (1508), Judenkünig (1523), Attaingnant (1529), and Gerle (1532 and 1533), for example. But whereas the ricercare came to be increasingly imitative and "learned," preludes preserved their improvisatory character. Filled with abrupt changes of texture, fast scale passages, and sections exploiting the idiosyncracies of lute or keyboard, they were the true successors of the fifteenth-century German keyboard preludes found in the Buxheim Organ Book and other manuscript sources.

In the second half of the sixteenth century the Italians excelled in composing in these free forms. Andrea and Giovanni Gabrieli's brief *intonazioni* mix chordal sections with those in which fast passagework is accompanied by chords. The longer and more elaborate toccatas by the Gabrielis, Annibale Padovano, and Claudio Merulo introduce imitative sections as well as passages in which figuration patterns are treated motivically in the midst of freer, more improvisatory textures. From the earliest years of the sixteenth century, these "free forms" for lute and keyboard were truly instrumental in style: they exploited techniques possible only on the instruments for which they were conceived, and were incapable of being adapted for voices because they were not written in a consistent polyphonic texture.

DANCE MUSIC

In the sixteenth century a vast quantity of dance music was published, much of it consisting of relatively straightforward harmonizations of simple tunes, or continuous variations on a set of chords or on a bass or soprano formula. Single dances included basse-dances, tourdions, branles of various kinds, allemandes, courantes, pavanes, galliards and passamezzos. Pavanes and galliards were often combined into related pairs, as were allemandes and courantes, allemandes and saltarellos, passamezzos and galliards, and passamezzos and saltarellos. And there were combinations of three or more dances into suites, although there seems to have been no conventional ordering of dance types; thus, Antonio Rotta in 1546 combined passamezzos with galliards and pavanes; Phalèse in 1570 published suites consisting of a passamezzo, a pavane, and a galliard; and Dominico Bianchini in 1546 followed a passamezzo with a pavane and a saltarello.

It is difficult to know the purpose for which published dance music was intended in the sixteenth century, whether for actual social dancing, for home entertainment, or as stylized artistic versions of more or less popular melodies. If the professional dance musician of the time had developed his ability to extemporize on tunes from a current repertory—to invent spontaneous sets of variations in the manner of today's jazz musicians—he would not have needed the elaborate polyphonic versions or the decorated arrangements for lute and keyboard that the printed books provided. At most an *aide memoire* would have sufficed. Perhaps, then, the printed dance music of the time was intended for amateurs to play at home, or as "neutral" versions to enlarge the professional's repertory. And some dances—notably those by the English keyboard composers—were artistic, highly refined, and stylized; they were never intended for the ballroom.

Whatever the purpose, dance music was published for every medium—for lute, keyboard, and ensemble—and in every country of western Europe. In France and Flanders the flow of dance music from the presses was especially copious. Pierre Attaingnant, Nicolas du Chemin, and the firm of Le Roy and Ballard (all of Paris), Jacques Moderne of Lyons, Tielman Susato of Antwerp, and Pierre Phalèse of Louvain published dances for every conceivable combination. Many Italian and German anthologies of lute and keyboard music contain at least one or two dances, but arrangements for instrumental ensembles were relatively rare in those countries. The voluminous, though incompletely preserved, collections of almost 500 ensemble dances made by Paul and Bartholomeus Hessen in 1555 partly make up for our ignorance about German ensemble dances from the early sixteenth century. These anthologies were in fact the earliest collections of ensemble dance music to be published in Germany. The first such collection printed in Italy—the *Opera nova de balli* by Francesco Bendusi—had appeared only two years previously, in 1553. The artistic highpoint of the century, though, was reached in the magnificent dances for keyboard by the English virginalists, above all those by John Bull, Orlando Gibbons, and William Byrd.

LUTE SONGS

Compositions for solo voice and lute or other plucked stringed instruments during the sixteenth century were, for the most part, arrangements of vocal pieces—frottole (those by Bossinensis, for example), lieder (Schlick), chansons (Attaingnant), madrigals (those by Verdelot arranged by Willaert), psalms (Morlaye), the lighter Italian forms (canzonettas and such by Antonelli, Fallamero, and Verovio, for example), and even, perhaps, English ayres (Dowland and Cavendish); most ayres, however, were probably conceived in the first instance for solo voice and lute. Some volumes contain music for one or more voices and one or more lutes (Adriansen's *Pratum musicum* of 1584, for example), and some for voice and keyboard (Verovio's *Diletto spirituale* of 1586). But at least one volume published in the sixteenth century (and there were probably more) contains music apparently conceived directly for lute and voice, or for lute alone. Adrian le Roy's third book of lute music (1552) contains arrangements of psalm tunes for which polyphonic originals have never been found. They may never have existed, for the music seems to have been conceived for only two real parts, melody and bass. Le Roy apparently added a bass beneath each tune, which he had taken from the 1549 Lyons edition of *Pseaulmes cinquante de David, mis en vers français par Clément Marot*. He then filled out the texture, not with two other polyphonic voices, but with chords, planned for their harmonic effect; with divisions including a good many stereotyped figuration patterns;

and with various formulas for ornamenting a given interval, for cadencing, and for arpeggiating or prolonging a triad. These proto-Baroque lute songs, then, mix elements of vocal counterpoint with features that are specifically instrumental.

BIBLIOGRAPHICAL NOTES

Instrumental music printed in the sixteenth century is listed and described in H. M. Brown, *Instrumental Music Printed Before 1600, A Bibliography* (Cambridge, Mass., 1965), which also includes a bibliography of modern editions. Jean Jacquot, ed., *La musique instrumentale de la Renaissance* (Paris, 1955), contains essays on various aspects of sixteenth-century instrumental music. On keyboard music in general, see Willi Apel, *The History of Keyboard Music to 1700*, transl. Hans Tischler (Bloomington, Indiana, 1972); and also Charles van den Borren, *The Sources of Keyboard Music in England* (London, 1913). Works dealing with organ music in particular include Gotthold Frotscher, *Geschichte der Orgelspiels und der Orgelkomposition* (Berlin, 1935, 2 vols.); Knud Jeppesen, *Die italienische Orgelmusik am Anfang des Cinquecento* (Copenhagen, 1943; 2nd rev. ed., 1960); Otto Kinkeldey, *Orgel und Klavier in der Music des 16. Jahrhunderts* (Leipzig, 1910); and Yvonne Rokseth, *La musique d'orgue au XVe et au début du XVIe siècle* (Paris, 1930). On lute music, see Otto Gombosi, ed., *Composizione di meser Vicenzo Capirola* (Neuilly-sur-Seine, 1955); Daniel Heartz, *Preludes, Chansons and Dances for Lute (1529–1530)* (Neuilly-sur-Seine, 1964); and Jean Jacquot, ed., *Le luth et sa musique* (Paris, 1958). Ensemble music is discussed in Dietrich Kämper, *Studien zur instrumentalen Ensemblemusik des 16. Jahrhunderts in Italien* (Cologne and Vienna, 1970). Thoinot Arbeau's treatise on dance, *Orchésographie* (Langres, 1589), is published in English translations by C. W. Beaumont (1925) and M. S. Evans (1948; repr. 1967); studies dealing with dance include Friedrich Blume, *Studien zur Vorgeschichte der Orchestersuite im 15. und 16. Jahrhunderts* (Leipzig, 1925); Frederick Crane, *Materials for the Study of the Fifteenth-Century Basse Dance* (Brooklyn, 1968); and Daniel Heartz, "The Basse Dance," *Annales musicologiques*, 6 (1958–63).

On musical instruments, see Anthony Baines, ed., *Musical Instruments Through The Ages;* and also several relevant chapters in *New Oxford History of Music*, vol. 3 (London, 1960) and vol. 4 (London, 1968). On instrumentation and arranging vocal music for combinations of voices and instruments, see H. M. Brown, *Sixteenth-Century Instrumentation: The Music for the Florentine Intermedii* (American Institute of Musicology, 1974).

TEN

THE MUSIC OF THE REFORMATION
AND THE COUNCIL OF TRENT

The challenges to the authority of the Roman Catholic Church in Germany, France, and England were among the most important events of sixteenth-century history. This series of dramatic confrontations had important consequences for music. The form music took in the service of the new religions depended in large part on the temperaments and personalities of the leaders of the several Protestant movements and on their attitude towards Catholic ceremony and elaborate ritual. While the puritanical John Calvin allowed only a restricted place for music in his city of God on earth, Martin Luther saw to it that the German countries under his spiritual leadership maintained a close connection with their rich musical past: a distinctively Protestant musical style evolved only very gradually in the Germanic countries. The effect on musical events of Martin Luther's unwittingly successful battle with the Catholics is important not so much for what it accomplished in purely musical terms as for what it presaged for the future.

Martin Luther was himself a very musical man. He was a great admirer of Netherlandish polyphony and of the works of Josquin in particular; he played the lute and the transverse flute; he took a keen personal interest in the role of music in the new liturgical ceremonies; and he even composed some of the melodies intended for congregational singing, among them one of the best known and most rousing of all Protestant chorales, *Ein feste Burg ist unser Gott*. Luther had no desire to abandon the musical heritage of Catholic Europe. He did not intend that his vernacular liturgy, the _Deudsche Messe_ of 1526, should completely replace Latin; and his enduring contribution to music—the encouragement of chorales, the simple strophic hymns sung by the congregation—was prompted more by his desire that all the people should be exposed to the educational and ethical powers of music than by an attempt to drive elaborate polyphony out of the church.

From a variety of sources and using a variety of techniques, Luther and his musical advisers collected a large repertory of sacred songs in the vernacular which were simple and tuneful enough for the common people to sing. Some were Catholic hymns with translated or newly created texts; some were old poems set to new music or vice versa; some were new versions of older pre-Reformation German songs; and some melodies were composed especially for the Lutherans to poems written for the purpose. They began publishing anthologies of sacred songs in the 1520's. In 1524 three collections with monophonic melodies appeared in print (the *Achtliederbuch* published by Jobst Gutknecht in Nuremberg, and two volumes called *Enchiridion,* both printed in Erfurt), along with Johann Walther's *Geystliche gesangk Buchleyn,* which contains polyphonic arrangements of the Lutheran tunes. Walther, who was a singer in the chapel of Frederick the Wise of Saxony, then for many years municipal cantor in Torgau, and finally (after Luther's death) chapel master of the Elector of Saxony in Dresden, deserves his place in music history less for the greatness of his musical achievement, perhaps, than because of his close association over a long period of time with Luther. In any case, there can be little doubt of his importance in shaping the new Lutheran music. Almost all of his polyphonic sacred songs in the *Geystliche gesangk Buchleyn,* one or two of them in Latin but most in German, state the Lutheran melodies in the tenor. Some of his songs are simple note-against-note settings, the first attempts at the sort of German chorale so well known from the works of later composers and especially J. S. Bach. Others (like Example 10–1) are more florid arrangements of the melodies, with freer counterpoints woven around the cantus firmus and some imitations before and between statements of the borrowed melodies.

In the two or three decades after 1524, numerous collections of monophonic hymns were published, similar in scope and purpose to the earliest anthologies. In 1526, Luther finished his proposals for a new German liturgy, the *Deudsche Messe*, based on the traditional service and partly adapting plainchant to the vernacular. In the 1530's and 1540's complete Protestant Psalters, in German and with single-line melodies, began to appear, influenced by the tradition of congregational psalm singing at the Cathedral of Strasbourg, for which Matthias Greiter, the principal singer there, had composed a number of melodies. And Protestant musicians also compiled some anthologies of polyphonic sacred songs, following the model established by Walther. Perhaps the most notable of these polyphonic anthologies is the *Newe deudsche geistliche Gesenge für die gemeinen Schulen*, printed by Georg Rhaw in Wittenberg in 1544 in order to give the students in German schools some understanding of church music and practice in performing it. The collection contains a cross-section of music in various German sacred song styles, by a wide variety of composers, among them Martin Agricola, Sixt Dietrich, Benedictus Ducis, Georg Forster, and Balthasar Resinarius, and even including some Catholics, such as Arnold von Bruck, Lupus Hellinck, Heinrich Isaac, Ludwig Senfl, and Thomas Stoltzer.

EXAMPLE 10–1. Walther, *Christ lag in Todesbanden*, mm. 1–10. Printed by permission of the Bärenreiter-Verlag Cassel Basel Tours London, from: Johann Walther, *Sämtliche Werke*, vol. 1: "Geistliches Gesangbüchlein Wittenberg 1551. Erster Teil: Deutsche Gesänge," ed. Otto Schröder. Cassel and Basel / St. Louis 1953.

In the 1560's and 1570's there seems to have been a reaction against congregational singing and simple German songs. Latin reasserted itself and more complex polyphony came once more to be written by composers like Jobst vom Brandt, Gallus Dressler, Matthaeus Le Maistre, and Jacob Meiland. In fact, throughout the latter half of the sixteenth century, Protestant composers continued to write music in Latin, and some Catholic composers did not disdain to set Protestant German texts. But by and large the later Protestant composers in Germany, like Seth Calvisius, Johannes Eccard, and Leonhard Lechner, concentrated on German verses, although Hans Leo Hassler, the Protestant organist to the Catholic banker Octavian II Fugger of Augsburg before he became municipal chapelmaster in Nuremberg and then organist to the Elector of Saxony, wrote in all sacred genres, Protestant as well as Catholic, in both German and Latin.

Of all the Protestant reformers, John Calvin of Geneva was the most severe in his condemnation of Catholic liturgy and ceremonial, including music. He prohibited his congregation from singing in church any texts not found in the Bible, and he even discouraged his followers from singing at home any music except *chansons spirituelles*, sacred (and sometimes polemic) contrafacta of worldly French chansons. Since he disapproved of polyphony in church because he felt it detracted from an easy understanding of the words, the settings of rhymed metrical translations from the Book of Psalms issued in Geneva were restricted to a single line of music. (Psalm settings in four or more parts, most of them simple but some in elaborated polyphony, were nevertheless composed by French-speaking Protestant musicians in the course of the century.) In restricting the place of music in public worship, Calvin was following the example set by the earlier Swiss Protestant, Ulrich Zwingli, who, although he was a cultivated musician himself, was determined to keep music out of church services; Zwingli even sanctioned the destruction of Swiss organs.

When Calvin was banished from Geneva in 1538 he sought refuge in Strasbourg, and there he heard the congregational psalm singing led by Matthias Greiter. This inspired Calvin to take up his own earlier proposals in favor of the practice, and as early as 1539 he published *Aulcuns pseaulmes et cantiques mys en chant* (Strasbourg: Knobloch), a small collection of psalm translations, some by the French poet Clément Marot and some by Calvin himself, set to melodies partly derived from those composed by Greiter and his German colleagues in Strasbourg. Shortly after Calvin's return to Geneva in 1541 he set to work to organize religious music in the community and, not surprisingly, placed much emphasis on the importance of congregational psalm singing.

It is not a little ironic that the sober Calvin made such extensive use of psalm translations by the elegant and worldly poet Marot, who had originally prepared them for the Catholic court of Francis I. But after Marot escaped religious persecution in France by fleeing to Geneva, the Council there was unwilling to support him while he completed his translations, and the job was taken over by Théodore de Bèze, whose complete Psalter was not finished until 1562. An undistinguished musician, Guillaume Franc, who later published a Psalter for the use of the Protestant church in Lausanne, began preparing the music for Marot's translations, but his job was soon taken over by Louis Bourgeois, the musician chiefly responsible for composing and arranging the melodies in the Genevan Psalter. Bourgeois adapted chanson melodies as well as plainchants and other earlier tunes to the psalm translations, in which the originally irregular verse forms of the Bible had been turned into regularly recurring strophes so that they resembled hymns, at least in form if not in content. Even though Calvin disapproved of polyphonic settings of psalm tunes, Bourgeois published not only a collection of simple note-against-note settings, the *Pseaumes cinquantes de David roy et prophète* (Lyons: Godefroy and Marcelin Beringen, 1547), but also more elaborate contrapuntal versions free of any borrowed melodic material. Of the many other polyphonic arrangements of the Marot-Bèze Psalter utilizing the tunes of Franc and Bourgeois, the most influential were those by the Frenchman Claude Goudimel. After his conversion to Protestantism in 1560, Goudimel set the entire collection twice. The two versions, one published in Paris in 1564 by Le Roy and Ballard and the other in Geneva in 1565, are both for four voices. Goudimel wrote the earlier collection in a slightly embellished chordal style, with the borrowed melodies mostly in the top voice, but in the later versions he returned to the earlier practice of placing the psalm tunes in the tenor, and he harmonized them with simple chords. Like the Dutch *Souterliedekens* (1540) that Clemens non Papa had composed and published over twenty years earlier, Goudimel's psalm settings were intended for domestic use; they respected, in other words, Calvin's strictures against polyphony inside the church.

In England, policy with regard to church music was in an almost constant state of flux throughout much of the century after Henry VIII's definitive break with Rome in 1534. Some Protestant extremists argued that music should be banned from church services, but the suggestion was never seriously taken up. As in Germany, Latin motets and settings of liturgical texts continued to be written by some of the same musicians who composed anthems and services in the vernacular. And, like Protestant communities in other countries, the Anglicans gradually developed a body of simple music fit for congregational singing. The first attempts at setting metrical psalm translations to music were made during Henry's reign. But Myles Coverdale's *Goostly psalmes and spirituall songs*, published in 1539 or 1540 and containing psalm translations and sacred songs supplied with monophonic tunes based on plainchant and German chorales, was suppressed by the king, who did not favor the Lutheran cause.

As early as 1544 Archbishop Cranmer, possibly with the help of the Protestant musician John Merbecke, published the Litany in English with the traditional chants adapted to the vernacular in a syllabic setting. A second version of the service, published during the same year, contains settings of the chants for five voices, as they were sung—or so the volume states—in the king's chapel. Shortly after Edward VI became king, the first Book of Common Prayer was prescribed for all services. John Merbecke issued his *Booke of Common Praier noted* in 1550, in which he ingeniously arranged the traditional chants and composed new monophonic music in a mixture of measured time values and rhythmically free recitation to produce a collection of melodies that fit their English words very well indeed. But Merbecke's Anglican chant fell out of use as soon as a second Book of Common Prayer was introduced in 1552, although it has been revived and is now sung in many Anglican churches.

During Edward VI's reign the first translations of the psalter by Thomas Sternhold and John Hopkins were published without music. Some expatriate English Protestants, who had fled to the continent from their native country during the revival of Roman Catholicism under Mary, issued an Anglo-Genevan Psalter in 1556 with music that was much indebted to the Calvinist melodies. But in spite of the various attempts in the 1540's and 1550's to set the psalms to music, the English Psalter did not take its more or less definitive shape until the early years of Elizabeth's reign, when John Day of London published *The Whole Book of Psalms* in 1562; it was based on the Sternhold-Hopkins translations and contained single-line melodies prepared by an unknown musician.

From the 1560's onwards, psalters and collections of Protestant songs began to be issued for domestic and congregational use in ever greater numbers, among them *Certaine notes set forthe in foure and three partes*, published by Day in 1560, which includes English contrafacta of Latin music written earlier in the century along with newly composed music for the Anglican service; and Archbishop Matthew Parker's *The Whole Psalter translated into English metre*, printed in 1567 or 1568 with nine settings for four voices by Thomas Tallis, which was never placed on sale. Among the other anthologies of simple Protestant music issued during the latter half of the sixteenth and the first half of the seventeenth centuries, several contain psalms intended either to be sung *a cappella* or with instrumental accompaniment. Richard Alison's *The Psalmes of David in Meter* (1599), for example, explains that the preexisting tune was "to be sung and plaide upon the Lute, Orpharyon,

Citterne or Base Violl, severally or altogether, the singing part to be either Tenor or Treble to the Instrument, according to the nature of the voyce or for fowre voyces." That is, the tune alone could be sung either in the soprano or the tenor octave and accompanied by an instrument (Alison supplies tablature for both lute and cittern), or else his four-voiced arrangements, with the tune in the soprano, could be sung *a cappella*.

Catholic reaction to attacks on the authority of the Church and a genuine and long-standing desire to reform its abuses prompted the Pope to call the Council of Trent, which met from 1545 to 1563. Towards the end of their deliberations, which dealt with many aspects of the liturgy, the cardinals finally took up the role of music in sacred services. They discussed the question in 1562 and 1563 and appointed a commission consisting of eight cardinals, of whom Carlo Borromeo and Vitellozzo Vitelli were the central figures, which met in Rome in 1564 and 1565 to study the problem further and to implement the suggestions of the Council within the papal organization in the city of Rome. At the beginning of their deliberations on music, Cardinal Otto von Truchsess von Waldburg, Bishop of Augsburg and Protector of Germany, had asked his private chapelmaster, Jacobus de Kerle, to compose settings of ten devotional Latin poems, the *Preces speciales pro salubri generalis concilii*, which were regularly performed at the Council's prayer sessions. And Waldburg and the Italian prelates compared sacred music by the leading composers of their respective countries: Orlando di Lasso from Munich and Palestrina and Francesco Rosselli from Rome. The belief that the cardinals were saved from banning polyphony altogether from the liturgy by the timely intervention of Emperor Ferdinand I is based on evidence that is highly ambiguous, to say the least; and the charming fable that church music was saved for all time by the performance before the cardinals of Palestrina's *Missa Papae Marcelli*, after angels had dictated it to him, has absolutely no foundation in fact.

The Council did not issue specific directives for practical reform but rather, in keeping with the nature of an ecumenical council, it formulated a general policy which the cardinals expected would be implemented at local levels. The consensus of opinion that emerged from their discussions centered around two important matters: the corruption of the liturgy caused by the introduction into it of secular elements, and the difficulty of understanding the words that convey the meaning of sacred ritual if they are obscured by florid polyphony. The liturgy, which in the past had sometimes been neglected, should be maintained properly, according to the cardinals, and profane music (presumably including Masses built on secular compositions) should be banished from the services. Moreover, composers should make certain that the sacred texts they set polyphonically were clearly audible at all times and therefore comprehensible to the congregation. To this end the Commission of Cardinals in 1565 tested various Masses for their intelligibility. Very likely they listened to a Mass especially written for the occasion by Vincenzo Ruffo, and possibly also to a chromatic Mass by Nicola Vicentino; Borromeo is known to have asked Vicentino to write such a work, but the composer's response is unknown and no Mass by him survives. We do not know what else they heard. Their final rulings stressed once again how important it was that the sacred texts be heard and understood even when enhanced by music; the Commissioners encouraged the correct accentuation of Latin and warned against excessive melismas.

The deliberations of the Council of Trent and its subsequent Commission of Cardinals made explicit the ideals of the Counter-Reformation and gave strong support to the objections against florid polyphony that had been raised again and again over the years. Doubtless the reformers influenced the development of church music in succeeding generations. But they did not succeed in effecting basic or radical changes in musical style. Even after the Council, composers still based their Masses on madrigals and chansons when the spirit moved them, for example; and elaborate counterpoint continued to be written even by those late-sixteenth-century composers who paid lip service to the aims of the reformers in their title pages, prefaces, and dedications.

BIBLIOGRAPHICAL NOTES

On Protestant music in Germany, see Konrad Ameln, *Luthers Kirchenlieder in Tonsätzen seiner Zeit* (Cassel, 1934); Ameln, Christhard Mahrenholz, and W. Thomas, eds., *Handbuch der deutschen evangelischen Kirchenmusic* (Göttingen, 1932–); Friedrich Blume, *Geschichte der evangelischen Kirchenmusik* (2nd ed., Cassel, 1965); Christhard Mahrenholz, *Das evangelische Kirchengesangbuch* (Cassel, 1950); Mahrenholz, *Luther und die Kirchenmusik* (Cassel, 1937); H. J. Moser, *Die evangelische Kirchenmusik in Deutschland* (Berlin, 1954); Paul Nettl, *Luther and Music* (Philadelphia, 1948); Basil Smallman, *The Background of Passion Music* (London, 1957); and Johannes Zahn, *Die Melodien der deutschen evangelischen Kirchenlieder* (Berlin, 1899–1910, 3 vols.).

On Calvin and the French Huguenots, see H. P. Clive, "The Calvinist Attitude to Music, and its Literary Aspects and Sources," *Bibliothèque d'humanisme et renaissance,* 19 (1957) and 20 (1958); Orentin Douen, *Clément Marot et le psautier huguenot* (Paris, 1878–79, 2 vols.); Charles Garside, Jr., "Calvin's Preface to the Psalter: A Re-Appraisal," *Musical Quarterly,* 37 (1951); Garside, *Zwingli and the Arts* (New Haven, 1966); Théodore Gérold, *Psaumes de Clément Marot avec les mélodies* (Strasbourg, 1919); Gérold, *Les plus anciennes mélodies de l'Église Protestante de Strasbourg* (Paris, 1928); Pierre Pidoux, *Le Psautier huguenot du 16e siècle* (Cassel, 1962); Waldo S. Pratt, *The Music of the French Psalter of 1562* (New York, 1939); and R. R. Terry, *Calvin's First Psalter (1539)* (London, 1932).

On Protestant music in England, see E. H. Fellowes, *English Cathedral Music* (London, 1941); Percy Scholes, *The Puritans and Music in England and New England* (2nd ed., New York, 1962); and especially Peter le Huray, *Music and the Reformation in England, 1549–1660* (London, 1967).

On the Council of Trent and the early Counter-Reformation, see Lewis H. Lockwood, "Vincenzo Ruffo and Musical Reform after the Council of Trent," *Musical Quarterly*, 43 (1957), and also Lockwood, *The Counter-Reformation and the Masses of Vincenzo Ruffo* (Venice, 1967).

part four

The Late Renaissance:
1560-1600

ELEVEN

PALESTRINA, LASSO, VICTORIA, AND BYRD

In his *Istitutioni harmoniche,* first published in 1558, the theorist Gioseffo Zarlino described his contemporaries, especially his teacher Adrian Willaert, as men who had brought music to a new state of perfection. In his praise of their genius, Zarlino implied that musicians of his time summed up the achievements of their predecessors and that they could not go much further without challenging basic premises about the nature of musical style. Zarlino's views can be defended and even enlarged to take into account the successors of Willaert, Gombert, and Clemens non Papa, that is, the greatest figures of the late Renaissance, Palestrina, Lasso, Victoria and Byrd. Their music can be seen as the logical outcome of trends set in motion earlier; it is written in a style that refines even to a state of perfection the techniques developed by composers during the first half of the sixteenth century.

But such a view not only simplifies the character of these four great musicians, it also distorts the distinguishing features of late sixteenth-century music by placing too little emphasis on the variety of kinds of music written during that time. In the final chapter of this book I shall argue that the intense concern of musicians for text expression, especially in the madrigal, led to the dissolution of the kind of polyphonic fabric that had been regarded as an ideal during most of the sixteenth century. Investigations into the nature of music in the ancient world helped to bring about the invention of opera and monody in Italy, and produced *musique mesurée à l'antique* in France. We have already seen that some musicians by the late sixteenth century had become specialists in composing instrumental music; that is, they concentrated on constructing autonomous forms in sound of a sort not heard before in western Europe. And even in perfecting the "classical" style of the Renaissance without dramatically stressing music's ability to express human emotions, Palestrina inspired a whole school of Roman composers whose sobriety and decorum can be contrasted with the extravagances of some of their more flamboyant contemporaries.

In short, it is not so easy to perceive a mainstream of music during the late sixteenth century as it is for the earlier part of the Renaissance, partly because so much more music survives from the later period, and also because so many conflicting styles co-existed and composers expressed such different attitudes and points of view.

From about 1560 to 1600, Italy continued to be the country where most of the significant innovations took place. Whereas foreigners, especially Netherlanders, held almost all the important musical positions in Italy during the first half of the century, by the second half Italian musicians trained by Adrian Willaert and his contemporaries had taken over the direction of musical life in most Italian cities. The Gabrielis, Baldissera Donato, Francesco and Gioseffo Guami, Claudio Merulo, Annibale Padovano, and eventually, of course, the great Claudio Monteverdi all lived and worked in Venice, and Giovanni Matteo Asola and Costanzo Porta were in nearby cities in the Veneto. Roman musicians, besides Palestrina and the superb madrigalist Luca Marenzio, included Felice and Giovanni Francesco Anerio, Giovanni Animuccia, Paolo Bellasio, Ruggiero Giovanelli, Cristofano Malvezzi, Giovanni Maria Nanino, and Paolo Quagliati. In Naples, Carlo Gesualdo, prince of Venosa, and Pomponio Nenna were among the foremost composers, along with the northerner, Giovanni de Macque. Though a Netherlander, Giaches de Wert, brought fame and brilliance to the courts of Mantua and Ferrara, a number of distinguished Italians also took an active part in the musical activities in those cities, among them Giovanni Giacomo Gastoldi, Luzzasco Luzzaschi, Benedetto Pallavicino, and Salomone Rossi. Vincenzo Galilei worked in Florence, Alessandro Striggio in Mantua and Florence, Vincenzo Ruffo in Milan, Adriano Banchieri in Bologna, Orazio Vecchi in Modena, Marc'Antonio Ingegnieri in Cremona. Some of the greatest non-Italian composers of the time, including Lasso, Victoria, Giaches de Wert, and Philippe de Monte, had much of their education or their earliest musical experiences in Italy, or else they spent much of their later life there. Even William Byrd, who never left England, could not escape the influence of the Italians. And, as we have seen, German musicians of the late sixteenth century wrote in a highly Italianate style, a state of affairs that continued into the seventeenth century with composers such as Schütz, Scheidt, and Schein.

To single out from among all these men four composers as the most important of their time may seem an intolerably arbitrary procedure. To be sure, if it suggests that the quartet of virtuoso madrigalists—Gesualdo, Marenzio, Monteverdi, and Wert—were not magnificent composers of great historical importance, or that men like Philippe de Monte and the Spaniard Francesco Guerrero were not musicians of the first rank, then to focus attention on so few figures may mislead the unwary. And yet Palestrina, Lasso, Victoria, and Byrd, perhaps to a greater extent than any of their contemporaries save the madrigalists, wrote music that transcends the limitations of their age; moreover, they conveniently illustrate the diversity of temperament and approach so characteristic of their time. That Palestrina should be included among the great composers of the late Renaissance hardly needs justification, since his music has been regarded by generations of musicians as the quintessence of the period. If today, with our greater historical perspective, we have modified that opinion somewhat, his music nevertheless embodies the *ars perfecta* more convincingly than that by anyone else. Victoria, who may have been Palestrina's student, added to his Roman training a passionate Spanish temperament. Lasso, the Franco-Flemish composer who passed much of his youth is Italy before spending most of his mature years at the Bavarian court in Munich, was the great virtuoso of the four. He was the master of every style, genre, and technique, as befitted his cosmopolitan career; and his music shows off the brilliant, expressive, and even experimental sides of the late Renaissance. William Byrd shared with Lasso the astounding fluency to command every technique and genre of his time, but he differs from his great contemporaries in at least two important ways: his music reflects the English independence from developments on the continent; and he, more obviously than the others, stands at the beginning as well as at the end of a period of history, for he not only incorporated into his own music the achievements of his predecessors, but he also ushered in the most brilliant musical era his country had ever known, during the later years of Elizabeth I and the reigns of James I and Charles I.

GIOVANNI PIERLUIGI DA PALESTRINA
Rome

Giovanni Pierluigi (ca. 1525–94), called Palestrina after the town of his birth, was a man of his time insofar as his music reflects the ideals of the Counter-Reformation and, especially, the desire of the reformers to encourage a spiritual quality completely detached from secular concerns. But our perception of Palestrina's place in music history, and ultimately even our conception of his music, has been highly colored by his reputation in later times. He passed on to his students and followers in Rome his techniques of writing superbly well-controlled and transparent counterpoint and his ideals of serenity and balance. In turn, music by him and his pupils served church musicians everywhere in western Europe during the seventeenth, eighteenth, and nineteenth centuries as models for their own compositions written in a *stile antico* that still seems intrinsically "sacred" to many people. Even by the time Monteverdi was called upon to defend his stylistic innovations in the foreword to his fifth book of madrigals, printed in 1607, he understood the sort of music written by Palestrina to be different from his own; it was a *prima prattica,* a "first practice" of "pure" counterpoint, more fit for the church than his own *seconda prattica,* which was more emotional, more expressive, and altogether freer of contrapuntal restrictions, and therefore more appropriate for chamber music and the theater. By the eighteenth century the Viennese composer Johann Joseph Fux had distilled Palestrina's style and written rigid rules for imitating it in his treatise *Gradus ad Parnassum,* which generations of students have learned to regard as the book containing the sacred tenets of sixteenth-century counterpoint. And after Giuseppe Baini's pioneering biography of Palestrina, first published in 1828, many musicians in the nineteenth and twentieth centuries have considered Palestrina the greatest musician of the Renaissance, whose music offers the clearest examples of modal counterpoint, uncontaminated by harmonic planning.

If some of these views can be shown to be naive or overly simple —Palestrina's counterpoint is in fact carefully regulated by harmonic progressions, for example, and Fux's rules give a distorted picture of standard sixteenth-century practice—the popular image of Palestrina nevertheless contains more than a little truth. His "objective" and rather impersonal style did stem from his desire to refine to their utmost techniques used by earlier composers, and thus it can be said to reflect a state of perfection. The spiritual quality so often noted in his music seems to derive from his overriding concern for balance and moderation. His compositions invariably take into account the proper accentuation of words, and often even their meaning, but without heightening their rhetoric so emphatically that the continuous flow of polyphony is broken. To ensure that the stream of counterpoint remained even and uninterrupted, he controlled his dissonances rigorously and invented melodies that introduce neither abrupt or disturbing leaps nor sudden changes of direction or pace. And the clarity of his textures is always maintained by the care with which he worked out imitative entries and antiphonal dialogues, leaving plenty of air and space and never producing the thick, almost impenetrable tangle of polyphony sometimes found in works by composers of the post-Josquin generation.

Unlike most of the other great composers of the Renaissance, Palestrina never left his homeland, Rome and its environs. He was educated as a choirboy at Santa Maria Maggiore in Rome, but at about 19, in 1544, he returned to the town of his birth, Palestrina, some forty-five miles away, to take up his first position as organist and singer at the cathedral there. The Bishop of Palestrina at that time was Cardinal Giovanni Maria del Monte, who was elected Pope and took the name Julius III in 1551; shortly thereafter he called the young composer back to Rome to become master of the Julian Chapel (the Cappella Giulia), which sang at services in St. Peter's. For the rest of his life Palestrina worked for one or another church or institution in Rome—the Papal Chapel (the Cappella Sistina), St. John Lateran, Santa Maria Maggiore, or the Roman Seminary, founded after the Council of Trent to educate young men for the priesthood. During several brief periods he was in charge of concerts given at the villa of Cardinal Ippolito d'Este in Tivoli. At least twice he was tempted to leave Rome: both the Duke of Mantua and Emperor Maximilian II of Vienna tried to lure him away, but Palestrina asked such a high salary that the invitations came to nothing.

Palestrina was not a priest. Indeed, his period of service at the Sistine Chapel ended because he was married, contrary to the rules of the organization. These had been ignored by Julius III in his eagerness to promote his young protégé, but Pope Paul IV insisted that Palestrina and the other married members of the chapel resign, albeit with a pension. So far as we know, Palestrina was only once tempted to become a priest, when he was in his mid 50's and shortly after his wife, two sons, and two brothers died in the plagues of the late 1570's that almost killed him as well. In 1581, after his first wife's death, he took minor orders, although not vows of celibacy; but he had a sudden change of heart and married the widow of a furrier. For at least a decade after his second marriage, he assisted his wife in managing her fur business, in addition to fulfilling his responsibilities as a church musician and composer. In short, the spirituality of his music should not mislead us into romantic notions about his life.

In his desire to refine the polyphonic fabric and purify it of all harsh or abrupt interruptions, Palestrina evolved so regular a set of compositional procedures that his style lends itself unusually well to systematic description. Knud Jeppesen, in an exceptionally definitive study of Palestrina and dissonance (London, 1946; reprinted New York, 1970), makes the point that a study of the nature of Palestrina's melodic lines forms the proper starting place for an understanding of the composer's style; and he describes a typically long-breathed melody by the composer as formed of gentle arches in which "the ascending and descending movements counterbalance each other with almost mathematical exactness." That is, Palestrina's elegant curves of sound, in which nothing disturbs the even flow of the line, consist mostly of stepwise motion with relatively few repeated notes and no large or unusual leaps. Indeed, except for minor sixths and octaves, he virtually never wrote skips of more than a fifth, and he almost invariably reversed the direction of the line immediately after intervals larger than a third. In compositions like the sparsely texted movements of Masses—the Kyrie, Sanctus, and Agnus Dei sections—these melodic lines often attain great length and freedom from obtrusive metrical regularity, since they are built from rhythmic units of changing length. In Mass movements with a greater density of text—the Glorias and Credos—and in many motets, on the other hand, Palestrina often wrote relatively short motives which alternate with long flowing lines and short declamatory passages.

In the Agnus Dei of Palestrina's *Missa Aeterna Christi munera* (Example 11–1a), a Mass that paraphrases an Office hymn, all intervals larger than a third are carefully recovered, and where series of thirds all move in the same direction, as in mm. 9–10 in the inner voices, the direction of the melody soon reverses itself to maintain the composer's typically placid sense of balance. The initial gentle curve of melody in the superius as well as the extended second phrase (mm. 11–21) are both inspired in the first place by the chant on which the polyphony is based (Example 11–1b). But to say that Palestrina modeled his melodic style on chant would be an exaggeration; and it should not be forgotten that the task assigned to him and Annibale Zoilo by Pope Gregory XIII in 1577, that of revising the chant books in the wave of post-Tridentine reforms—a task he never completed—consisted in large part of rewriting those passages that to a cultivated sixteenth-century ear seemed barbaric and improving the text setting according to the prevailing humanistic views of the late Renaissance.

EXAMPLE 11–1a. Giovanni Pierluigi da Palestrina, *Missa Aeterna Christi munera, Agnus Dei,* mm. 1–23.

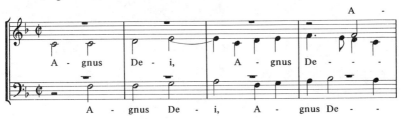

EXAMPLE 11–1b. The chant on which the Mass is based.

The Agnus Dei of Example 11–1 illustrates, too, another of the most striking features of Palestrina's music: the careful preparation and resolution of dissonances. The longer the note values, the more careful and discreet was Palestrina's preparation. Dissonant notes never have a value greater than a minim in the original notation (transcribed here as a quarter note, but in some modern editions as a half note), and they are never preceded by a note smaller in value. Palestrina introduced many of the long dissonances as consonant notes and then suspended them against a change of harmony, so that the dissonance and its resolution form 4–3 or 7–6 intervals with one of the lower voices (as in mm. 5, 9, 12, 15, 18, 21 and 22 of Example 11–1a). Dissonances also appear as passing notes on "weak" beats (that is, the second or fourth minim of a larger metrical unit). He treated smaller note values a bit more freely, although shorter dissonances usually occur either as passing notes or in one of a limited number of ornamental figures, such as turns or cambiatas. Except for suspensions, then, dissonances are almost entirely limited to normally unstressed beats. This well-regulated metrical plan increases the impression that a constant pulse underlies Palestrina's compositions, even though it is precisely the rhythmic irregularity of the details that brings the surface of his music to life and gives to his melodic lines their delicate vitality. While banishing harsh or unexpected clashes, he included just enough dissonance to avoid a saccharine sameness and to keep the motion flowing steadily forward.

Palestrina's counterpoint is controlled not only by the shape of his elegant melodic lines and careful handling of dissonance but also by his manner of using imitative techniques and by shrewd harmonic planning. He often built up his compositions by repeating entire passages, simply or with variants, or by adding new voices to the original material; or he used other rational devices, like invertible counterpoint or the transposition of whole points of imitation. The Agnus Dei in Example 11-1a, for instance, opens with a clear-cut point of imitation which he constructed by transposing the initial duet up a fourth for the third and fourth entries (mm. 4–8), while giving the original two voices new material. In spite of the imitations at the beginning of the second phrase (mm. 9–10), the "second theme" in the superius is subsequently treated more like a cantus firmus than a point to be imitated; it appears first in the bass (mm. 13–16), then overlapped in the tenor (mm. 16–18), and finally truncated in the bass (mm. 19–22), each time with new counterpoints written over or around it. The treatment of the melodic material—the initial transposition and the reiteration of the second theme—plays an important role in creating the clear tonal outlines of the movement: the first theme moves from V to I and its answer from I to IV (mm. 1–5), making an easy transition to the transposed entries which explore the subdominant area (mm. 6–9); the second theme returns to the tonic (m. 9ff), even though it quickly moves up to V, and Palestrina cadences on the dominant in m. 22; and the third phrase (after the excerpt quoted) is once again taken up with music centered around the tonic. Thus the overall plan, I–IV–I–V–I, is clearly organized and clearly tonal (though with a pattern different from later tonal schemes); even the vocabulary of chords, different as it is in many particulars from seventeenth- and eighteenth-century music, includes a surprisingly high percentage of progressions based on "tonal" scale degrees—that is, I, IV, and V in the tonic, subdominant and dominant "keys." For a presumably modal piece, this Mass section, like most of Palestrina's work, is remarkably susceptible to explanation in tonal terms.

The beginning of the Sanctus from Palestrina's magnificent *Missa Assumpta est Maria* (Example 11-2), a Mass that parodies one of his own motets, shows in a slightly more complex way how clearly his forms unfold. The first section (mm. 1–12) begins with a statement in four-part counterpoint of two principal motives (mm. 1–4), which is then transposed down a fifth and slightly rewritten (m. 5–8). The section continues with a shorter phrase (mm. 9–12) made up of the initial two motives in stretto, leading to the cadence on the fourth scale degree that ends the three-fold invocation, "Sanctus, sanctus, sanctus." The "Dominus Deus Sabaoth" is set as a declamatory passage that broadens out to a cadence (mm. 12–16); it is transposed down a fifth and rewritten (mm. 16–20), and Palestrina continued to work with the same material beyond the excerpt quoted in the example.

EXAMPLE 11–2. Palestrina, *Missa Assumpta est Maria, Sanctus,* mm. 1–21.

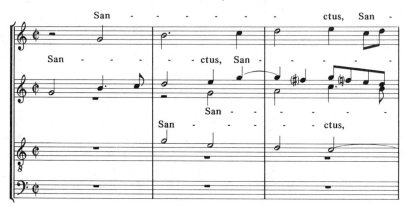

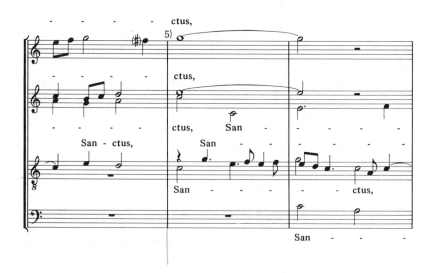

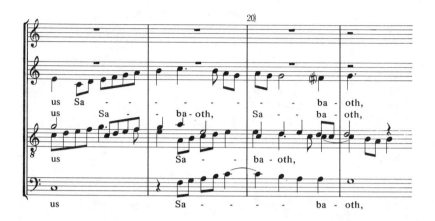

Many of Palestrina's compositions resemble these two fragments in growing from a short section of counterpoint that is then repeated, transposed, or slightly revised, or recomposed, always in a way that enhances the tonal organization of the entire work and that helps the listener to follow the musical thought as it occurs. From these two excerpts it also is clear that Palestrina did not always write points of imitation of the sort associated with Josquin and his immediate successors. Instead, he invented passages that introduce several motives simultaneously or play one or two voices off against the others, and he frequently wrote chordal sections, often placing them in antiphonal dialogue between sections of the choir. He was a master at manipulating sonorities and in grouping, spacing, and doubling chords; and his expertise shows itself in the ease with which his polyphonic textures sound clear and clean in performance.

Like most composers of the late sixteenth century, Palestrina scrupulously respected the syntax and accent patterns of the texts he set. He planned every voice within his polyphonic textures so that literary and musical accents coincide with an ease and naturalness that is the hallmark of a great composer. In highly contrapuntal music, of course, the words are not always clearly audible, and a work like the *Missa Papae Marcelli*—evidently conceived in the spirit of those Catholic reformers who urged that listeners be able to follow the words easily—is unusual in the amount of chordal declamation it contains. Example 11–3, the beginning of Palestrina's setting of *Surgam et circuibo civitatem*, from the Song of Songs, is more typical in showing the care with which Palestrina matched his musical motives with words in a polyphonic texture; the passage is slightly unusual, however, in that the opening ascending scale fragment seems to illustrate the sense of the text ("I will rise now and go about the city"). To be sure, discreet word-painting had long since become a standard part of every composer's technical equipment; but Palestrina seldom went to greater lengths than this to imitate the meanings of individual words, and he never disturbed the continuous stream of music in any dramatic way—by abrupt changes of pace or texture, for example—in order to insist on the priority of text over music. If some of his motets seem to fit the mood of their words beautifully—*Super flumina Babylonis* is melancholy, the eight-part *Jubilate Deo* joyous, and the held chords at the beginning of *O magnum mysterium* suggestive of awe and wonder—the reason is to be found less in the particular musical techniques used than in a number of intangible things (not least, perhaps, the subjective reaction of the modern listener). It is precisely Palestrina's reticence to display his heart on his sleeve, to disturb the placid surface of his works, that has created the impression that his music is impersonal and imbued with spiritual qualities.

Palestrina's diffidence with respect to text expression partly ex-

EXAMPLE 11–3. Palestrina, *Surgam et circuibo civitatem*, mm. 1–5.

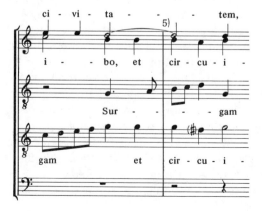

plains why he wrote so few madrigals. Perhaps, too, he was self-conscious about his role as a Roman church musician, a hypothesis suggested by the curious apology for having written secular music that he included in the dedication of his Song of Songs motets to Pope Gregory XIII in 1584, two years before the second of his two volumes of four-voiced madrigals appeared in print. The first volume, published in 1555, had revealed him to be a fine madrigalist in the tradition of Festa and Arcadelt, but hardly a pathbreaker. His two volumes of sacred madrigals (*madrigali spirituali*) in five voices, printed in 1581 and 1594, were doubtless more acceptable to the authorities in the reform-minded Rome of his time. Even though Palestrina did not write in the intense and personal manner of some of his contemporaries—his settings of Italian poems are by and large as sober and moderate in their expression as his motets—he nevertheless composed some fine madrigals, among them the unusually brilliant *Alla riva del Tebro* and one of the best known and most often arranged madrigals of the entire half century, *Vestiva i colli.*

Some critics have maintained that Palestrina's motets do not show him at his best, and that his 105 settings of the Mass Ordinary, in their ceremonial abstraction better suited to his reserved temperament, form the principal core of his work. Nevertheless, his motets contain superb music and reveal the breadth and variety of his moods and techniques. He composed more than 250 of them, preserved both in manuscript and printed sources. During his lifetime there appeared in print two volumes of four-voiced motets, five volumes for five or more voices (including the 1584 collection devoted entirely to settings from the Song of Songs), and several volumes containing music for particular liturgical functions (Lamentations for Holy Week, hymns, Magnificats, Offertories, and litanies).

Palestrina wrote most of his motets on themes of his own invention, without recourse to borrowed chants or other strict constructive devices, a procedure that left him free to plan each work according to a purely musical design or the dictates of the text or both. The sequence of musical events, the particular techniques he employed, and the formal proportions vary so much from motet to motet that it is impossible to generalize about his procedures beyond pointing out that almost all of his motets are based on imitative techniques modified in the various ways we have seen, with ample contrast furnished by more or less chordal passages. In general, each unit of text generates its own thematic material, and the successive points of imitation—with the declamatory passages judiciously placed to set them off—are arranged so that a listener can follow the process of musical thought clearly and easily. But within these limits Palestrina elaborated each motet in a new and different way. In his magnificent *Dum complerentur,* for example, the composer exploited opportunities to set the various parts of his six-voiced choir against one another in antiphonal dialogue largely made up of declamatory passages; in his equally splendid seven-voiced *Tu es Petrus,* by contrast, the even polyphonic flow is never interrupted by all the voices singing together in the same rhythm. The first part of his well-known *Sicut cervus* is taken up with a spacious exposition of three groups of themes, whereas the second part sets more lines of text and thus includes more and more varied melodic material and is altogether more condensed and faster paced. In *Super flumina Babylonis,* Palestrina exercised his penchant for repeating points of imitation with variations and revisions, so that the motet consists of a series of double expositions. In short, this vast repertory of freely composed motets exhibits an incredible diversity of forms and approaches; individual works repay close study, for each is unique and most in their way are masterpieces.

Some of the texts Palestrina set suggested their own repetition schemes. His responsories, for example, such as *Assumpta est Maria* and *Sancta et immaculata virginitatis,* both *a 6,* and *Fuit homo* and *Ascendo ad Patrem meum, a 5,* follow the liturgical pattern aBcB. Some of his settings of sequences, like the famous *Stabat mater,* ignore the double versicle structure of the sacred text, while others follow it more or less closely. In many of his motets, the composer did base his thematic material on chant; in *Veni Sancte Spiritus,* for example, he paraphrased the monophonic melody, distributing it among all his voices without stating it complete in any one, and thus merely borrowing its melodic ideas without influencing the details of the polyphonic structure. Some of his motets, like the six-voiced *Columna es immobilis* and *Cum ortus fuerit,* are built around canons, usually with extensive imitation between the scaffolding voices and the others, in order to weld the whole into a homogeneous texture.

The smaller liturgical works by Palestrina tend to be in a somewhat simpler style than his Masses and motets; they were evidently meant for everyday use in the service, or, as in the case of the Lamentations, which were regularly sung in the Papal Chapel during Holy Week, for occasions when more florid polyphony was not appropriate. Palestrina's litanies and his Lamentations are set for the most part in simple chords or slightly animated homophony. Except for the melismas that adorn the Hebrew letters beginning each section of the Lamentations, they resemble *falsobordoni,* the completely chordal harmonizations of psalm tones and other liturgical recitatives found especially in Spanish and Italian sources of the sixteenth century. Palestrina's Offertories are important historically since they and Lasso's similar collection are the earliest written in free motet style, without the use of borrowed chant. While not so simple as the litanies and Lamentations, they reveal

Palestrina at his most austere. Both the settings of hymns for the whole church year, *Hymnius totius anni,* and the series of Magnificats in each mode were intended for *alternatim* performance. Because Palestrina paraphrased the Gregorian tunes, each stanza is based on the same melodic material; thus the hymn settings afford an unusually convenient opportunity to study the variety of his techniques and approaches.

Palestrina's Masses contain some of his finest music. And they are as varied as his motets. They include some works built over cantus firmi, some that paraphrase chants, some built on canonic cycles, some that parody polyphonic motets, madrigals, or chansons, and some that are entirely free of borrowed material or constructive devices. Moreover, the Masses show, perhaps better than Palestrina's works in other genres, his stylistic development: the gradual perfection of his contrapuntal technique, and the simplification and greater homophony of his late works. Most of them were published in the thirteen volumes devoted to his Masses that appeared in print between 1554 and 1601, the last seven after his death. The Masses were not necessarily printed in the order in which they were composed; at best, the volumes present a very approximate chronological sequence, and the posthumous publications may have gathered together works written throughout the composer's long lifetime.

The *Missa Ecce sacerdos magnus,* however, is certainly an early work, for it opens Palestrina's first published collection, the *Missarum Liber Primus* (Rome: Dorico, 1554). It is an appropriate composition for such a place of honor, for it was almost certainly written to celebrate the elevation of the composer's patron, Julius III, to the pontificate; and, moreover, in basing each movement on a cantus firmus taken from a Gregorian antiphon for a Pope-confessor, it looks backward towards the past. Indeed, the work is so retrospective that Palestrina even combined music in three different mensuration signs for the last Agnus Dei, a technical trick more commonly found in music by much earlier composers. The borrowed melody appears in long notes in one of the inner voices, except in several sections where the superius sings it; the other voices mostly weave independent imitations around it; occasionally, as at the beginning of the Credo, the point to be imitated is derived from the scaffolding voice. While Palestrina could already write characteristically elegant arches of melody, which combine to form suave counterpoint, in this Mass the phrases are short-winded; hence the longer movements tend to sound more disjointed than in most of the composer's later works; control of architectonic features came with maturity. Palestrina built most of his other seven cantus-firmus Masses on plainsong tenors, except for one that takes up the *L'homme armé* tune and one based on the hexachord formula *Ut re mi fa sol la.*

Palestrina based a second Mass on the *L'homme armé* tune, but in that work as well as in many of his Masses derived from plainchant (about a third of his total output in the genre) he applied paraphrase technique. In forging a subject suitable for imitation from a plainsong, Palestrina usually stuck remarkably close to his model. Often, in fact, he retained all or almost all of the pitches of the chant, merely omitting a note or two of the original in order to make his theme more concise as he cast it in a distinctive rhythmic form; less often he embellished the original. We have already seen from his *Missa Aeterna Christi munera* (Example 11–1) how close the relationship between model and paraphrase could be. Moreover, in that Mass, as in many of Palestrina's paraphrased works, the model was deployed in a way that enhances the structure of the new composition. The Gregorian hymn *Aeterna Christi munera* consists of four phrases, the last of which repeats the first. Palestrina invariably used the melodic material in the order in which it appears in the hymn. He based the three sections of the Kyrie, for example, on successive phrases of the hymn. In the Sanctus he created the following refrain form:

	Sanctus	Pleni	Osanna I	Benedictus	Osanna II
phrase of model	1 and 2	3	4 (= 1)	2 and 3	4 (= 1)

In some of his other paraphrase Masses, like the *Missa Sanctorum meritis,* Palestrina chose to elaborate only one or two phrases from his model, allowing them to permeate the whole work. And in his nine Mantuan Masses—so called because they use versions of the chant sung at the church of Santa Barbara in Mantua—the composer set only the alternate verses in the Gloria and Credo movements. The remaining verses were to be sung as plainchant.

Five of Palestrina's Masses are constructed as cycles of canons. Each movement of the *Missa Ad fugam,* for example, consists entirely of double canons, two two-part canons superimposed on one another, except for the Pleni and Benedictus (both three-part canons) and the last Agnus (a three-part over a two-part canon). To relate the movements even more closely to one another, Palestrina based some of the canons on the same or similar thematic material.

Of Palestrina's six apparently free Masses, the *Missa Papae Marcelli,* designed to make the text as intelligible as possible, is by far the best known, though in its simpler way the *Missa Brevis,* a short work intended for everyday use in the service, is an equally attractive composition.

Almost half of Palestrina's Masses parody a polyphonic model, either one of his own motets or a madrigal, motet, or chanson by some earlier composer whom he admired or wished to emulate or better; among these are Domenico Ferabosco, Lupus Hellinck, Jachet of Mantua, Josquin, L'Héritier, Morales, Moulu, Richafort, Rore, and Verdelot. Palestrina's parody Masses are among his best works, and the superb six-voiced *Missa Assumpta est Maria* and *Missa Tu es Petrus*, both based on his own motets, are among his best parody Masses. In his *Missa Ascendo ad Patrem*, the composer's technique of adapting the music of his own motet to new textual and formal circumstances is unusually sophisticated. The beginning of the first Kyrie duplicates the beginning of the motet almost exactly, whereas its second half is less obviously modelled on Palestrina's setting of a second phrase of text in which the head of the motive has been changed and the music re-composed. The Christe elaborates motives from the middle of the motet's first part and the second Kyrie quite conventionally takes up themes from the beginning of the second part. Through much of the Gloria, Palestrina did not duplicate music from the motet literally, although its derivation from the motet's opening motives is ultimately clear. But neither his technique of parody, its great skill notwithstanding, nor the exquisite detail of his counterpoint completely explains Palestrina's genius, which resides as well in the incredibly impressive way he built individual phrases into gigantic structures of sound. His Masses especially are best studied in their entirety as architectonic wholes.

ORLANDO DI LASSO

　　In many ways Orlando di Lasso (1532–94) was very different from Palestrina, with whom he is often linked. Both Lasso's career and his music contrast strongly with those of the Italian composer. Whereas Palestrina spent his entire life in and around Rome, Lasso traveled widely; he was truly cosmopolitan. One of the last of the great Netherlanders (along with Philippe de Monte and Giaches de Wert), Lasso received much of his education in Italy, and Italian musicians played a decisive role in shaping his musical personality, although from his mid-twenties he lived and worked in Germany. Whereas Palestrina concentrated his attention almost exclusively on sacred music, Lasso displayed a dazzling virtuosity in mastering every style and genre of his time. His motets are often singled out by modern musicians as the most important segment of his *oeuvre* but he was equally skillful at writing Italian madrigals, French chansons, German lieder, and settings of the Mass Ordinary. And whereas Palestrina wrote a counterpoint distinguished for its sobriety and decorum, Lasso was passionately committed to the idea that music should heighten, enhance, and even embody the meaning of the texts he set. While this concern for expression distinguishes him from Palestrina and some of their contemporaries, it constituted one of the main preoccupations of many composers in the late sixteenth century; for them Lasso's music served as model and inspiration.

Lasso probably began his musical career as a choirboy at the church of St. Nicholas in his native town of Mons. His voice was so beautiful, or his musical talent so evident, that eventually he was kidnapped, presumably by Italian agents who constantly sought out promising young musicians to fill the choirs of their princely employers. For a decade during his formative years—from the age of twelve to about twenty-two or twenty-three—Lasso lived and worked in Italy. In the service of Ferdinand Gonzaga, viceroy of Sicily, the young composer traveled to Mantua and Milan; he also visited Naples and Palermo and became, at the incredibly early age of twenty-one, chapelmaster of St. John Lateran in Rome, a position he took over from Giovanni Animuccia and relinquished a scant year and a half later to Palestrina, whom he must have known during his service there. In 1554 or 1555, at the age of twenty-two or twenty-three, Lasso returned from Italy to Antwerp, where he lived for several years and where he published his first important works: a collection of seventeen motets printed by Jan Laet (the so-called "Antwerp Motet Book," 1556), and an anthology printed by Tielman Susato in 1555 that contains madrigals, villanesche, and chansons as well as motets, and includes the highly chromatic *Alma nemes* and the work on which it was modelled, Cipriano de Rore's *Calami sonum ferentes.*

In 1556, soon after Lasso's return to the Netherlands, he was called to Munich to serve at the court of Albert V, Duke of Bavaria, and he stayed there for the rest of his life, eventually becoming not only chapelmaster but also the respected and honored official court composer and friend to the ducal family. He was granted a patent of nobility by Emperor Maximilian II and made a Knight of the Golden Spur by Pope Gregory XIII. Duke Albert valued Lasso's music so highly that he had the composer's settings of the penitential psalms (*Psalmi Davidis penitentiales*) copied into magnificent choirbooks elegantly decorated by the court painter, Hans Mielich, with illustrations that include several portraying Lasso with his court musicians. And Duke Albert's son, who became Duke Wilhelm V after his father's death in 1579, encouraged the Munich printer Adam Berg to publish the *Patrocinium musices* (twelve volumes, 1573–1598), a sumptuously produced collection of sacred music, seven volumes of which were devoted entirely to music by Lasso. A number of letters by the composer survive, almost all of them addressed to Wilhelm. Written in an amusing mixture of Italian, Latin,

French, and German, they reveal Lasso to have been a man of strong temperament, quick and witty, and with a lively sense of humor occasionally darkened by moodiness. During the last several years of his life, this moodiness gave way to a deep depression that found expression in his final collection of twenty spiritual madrigals on morbidly religious texts, the *Lagrime di San Pietro*, posthumously published by Berg. After Lasso's death his two sons, Rudolph and Ferdinand, brought out the *Magnum opus musicum* (1619), a vast retrospective collection of his motets—516 for from two to twelve voices. (This collection unfortunately served as a basis for the incomplete modern edition of the composer's works: Lasso's sons did not always reproduce the best readings; they sometimes replaced the words Lasso set with others; and they adopted an ordering by number of voices, thus obscuring the chronology of the motets and hence an easy view of the composer's development.)

By the age of twenty-three, at the time the Antwerp Motet Book was published, Lasso had already formed for himself a fully mature and personal musical style, related both to older Netherlandish practices and to the new freedoms of Italian musicians. But if his desire to create a music generated by the words may be considered the single most distinctive feature of the Antwerp motets, their great variety—equally a hallmark of Lasso's work—should not be overlooked. The composer did not restrict himself to one compositional procedure or to a single approach to problems of form, style, and technique. *Creator omnium Deus,* for example, is built around a canon derived in part from Willaert's setting of the same text; an ostinato serves as scaffolding in *Fremuit spiritu Jesu,* a work that imitates some features of Clemens non Papa's motet on this text; and the final motet in the volume, *Da pacem Domine,* merely alludes to the Gregorian melody associated with this prayer for peace without presenting it complete in any one voice or paraphrasing each of its phrases. Most of the motets in the collection eschew borrowed material and constructive devices in order to leave the composer free to mold the music according to the shape and meaning of the text. Moreover, Lasso chose his texts from a number of different sources. Some of the Antwerp motets are taken from psalms, some from other parts of the Bible or from a liturgical service book. Some set newly written secular texts, like *Stet quicunque volet potens,* which celebrates the virtues of the quiet life and was possibly inspired by Lasso's return to Antwerp, and the three works honoring individuals: (1) the opening motet, *Deliciae Phoebi,* addressed to Antonio Perenotto, bishop of Arras and the man to whom Lasso dedicated the collection, (2) *Te spectant,* celebrating the English cardinal, Reginald Pole, and (3) *Heroum soboles,* praising the Emperor, Charles V. Most of the compositions in the Antwerp Motet Book make some use of imitative techniques, albeit in a way markedly different from the earlier Netherlanders (like Gombert, Willaert and Clemens non Papa) and from Palestrina. But Lasso's dependence on imitation as a formal procedure can easily be exaggerated, and some of these early motets, like *Heroum soboles*, consist largely of music in homophonic textures.

No single work, then, can be considered completely representative of Lasso's Antwerp Motet Book, and yet a closer study of a composition like *Gustate et videte* reveals at least some of the most important features of his style. This motet, which sets several verses from Psalm 34, achieved great fame in Lasso's own lifetime, though not for purely musical reasons. Rain and thunder threatened to curtail the Corpus Christi procession in Munich in 1584, but as Lasso and his musicians began to sing *Gustate et videte* the sun came out. Every year from then on Lasso's motet was performed during the procession, to ensure that the weather would be fine.

The motet opens (Example 11–4) with a point of imitation on "Gustate et videte" ("O taste and see") that resembles earlier Netherlandish counterpoint in its general layout and style, although Lasso's theme—with its obvious division into two motives, its clear rhythmic shape, and the easy natural way it fits the words—is more memorable than many by musicians of the post-Josquin generation. Continuing without a break, the music for "quoniam suavis est Dominus" ("that the Lord is good") consists of a passage without any imitations beyond the dotted rhythmic motive that sets the first word; instead, the contrapuntally animated chords work around to a B♭ major triad that beautifully embodies the sense of "suavis." After the important cadence in m. 20, the next section, on "Beatus vir qui sperat in eo" ("Happy is the man who takes refuge in him"), centered around a simple motive that fills in a fourth by stepwise motion, gradually works up from the initial syncopated imitation between bass and tenor II to the highpoint of the composition immediately preceding the cadence in m. 32, which divides the *prima pars* of *Gustate et videte* into two halves. The second half relaxes and gradually subsides in a series of phrases involving relatively little imitation.

Working within a continuing northern European tradition, in *Gustate et videte* and the other compositions of the Antwerp Motet Book, Lasso nevertheless departed in significant ways from the style of his predecessors. The degree to which Lasso's music is informed and controlled by the words on which it is based can scarcely be exaggerated. Almost every page of his works reveals particular compositional decisions that he made in order to heighten, illustrate, or embody a literary meaning. Short motives, suggested by the words and hence more often syllabic than melismatic, generate many of the thematic events in his motets, and these epigrammatic ideas, expanded and manipulated, take the place of the long gentle arches of melody so often found in Palestrina's music. Moreover, within any one work the sections vary widely in length, density, and style; their character is usually determined either by the literary context—the way each phrase fits the meaning and rhetoric of the entire text—or else by Lasso's conception of overall musical design. The latter consideration undoubtedly determined the unusually clear sectionalism of *Gustate et videte*, for example.

EXAMPLE 11–4. Orlando di Lasso, *Gustate et videte*, mm. 1–32.

In building individual phrases Lasso relied less on imitation as a structural device than did many of his contemporaries. In its place he generally preferred textures that depend for their effect on varied and imaginative choral groupings (one voice against three or more, semi-chorus against semi-chorus, or one group echoed by another); or he wrote a kind of non-imitative counterpoint that retains its clarity because of the careful shape of individual melodic lines; or he animated an essentially chordal texture by rhythmic imitations and other allusions of one voice to another. The importance of harmonic progressions directed towards tonal goals must also be considered in assessing Lasso's style. Neither Lasso nor his contemporaries had a technical vocabulary capable of explaining in detail the way each chord within a mode relates to its tonic, and we have still not devised a completely satisfactory method of dealing with the "tonal" implications of "modal" music. Yet Lasso's works plainly exhibit a sophisticated network of tonal relationships, including a highly developed sense of movement within a key and even modulation away from and back to a central point.

In at least one of his early works (*Prophetiae sibyllarum*, the series of twelve motets that invoke the Sibyls who in ancient times prophesied the coming of Christ), Lasso even made use of extreme chromaticism, writing in a technique that Lowinsky aptly describes as "triadic atonality." The Sibylline compositions go even further in their radical use of accidentals than *Alma nemes*, which, as we have seen, appeared in Lasso's first published collection. The opening nine measures of the introduction to the *Prophetiae* (Example 11–5), for instance, introduce all twelve semi-tones of the equal-tempered scale, and the chords of which they form a part stray so far from the G-Mixolydian "key" in which the movement ends that the listener loses all sense of tonal orientation. This remarkable cycle can only have come about as a result of Lasso's contact with the music of the Italian avant-garde, works by men like Nicola Vicentino, Rore, and others, whose chromatic expressionism was sanctioned by classical authority and the humanistic sentiments of the time. Lasso never again went so far in exploring chromatic musical space; these works of his young manhood remained isolated experiments as he turned his attention more and more to discovering the most effective means of heightening the impact of words by creating ever more vivid and expressive music.

EXAMPLE 11–5. Lasso, *Prophetiae Sibyllarum*, mm. 1–9. "Carmina Chromatico," text and music ed. Hans Joachim Therstappen in Friedrich Blume (ed.), *Das Chorwerk*, vol. 48 (Möseler Verlag, Wolfenbüttel and Zürich).

Lasso was astonishingly productive after his arrival in Munich in 1556. During his first dozen or so years there he wrote almost a third of his more than 500 motets. For many of them he chose texts that allowed him scope for personal expression: passages from the Psalms and the Song of Songs, for example, and Biblical excerpts that present tragic figures (Job, the Prodigal Son, and Rachel). But his motets cover a wide spectrum of moods, styles, and techniques. The antiphonal eight-voiced motets, like *Omnes de Saba venient, Confitebor tibi Domine, In convertendo Dominus,* and *Laudate Dominum* (all published in vol. 21 of his *Complete Works*), are as splendid and brilliant as any Venetian motets of the time. Some of the secular Latin compositions, like *Jam lucis orto sidere* (*Works*, XXI) and *Quod licet id libeat* (*Works*, XI), reveal the composer's robust sense of humor, while others show his more serious side, like his largely homophonic setting of Dido's lament from the

Aeneid, Dulces exuviae (*Works,* XI). A few motets· are built over cantus firmi. Lasso was especially fond of weaving his elaborate polyphony around an ostinato; in *Congregati sunt* (*Works,* IX), for example, the superius sings "Dissipa gentes quae bella volunt" five times, each time a tone lower, and then repeats the sequence; and in *Libera me, Domine* (*Works,* XV), the tenor sings "Respice finem" at various pitches and in the latter part in halved note-values. But mostly Lasso kept himself free from borrowed material and scaffolding devices, and instead conveyed the mood or the meaning of the text by adroitly inventing well-defined motives of contrasting character, sometimes but not always placed in imitative entries; by skillfully planning his compositions so that the rhythmic character and pace varied from section to section to reflect and enhance the rhetoric of the text; and by alternating and combining in a masterful and imaginative way imitative, non-imitative, homophonic, and antiphonal textures.

Lasso's settings of the seven penitential psalms, commissioned presumably by Duke Albert to counterbalance the frivolity of his court, are among the best and most famous motets from the composer's first decade in Munich. In the commentary written by Samuel Quickelberg, physician, humanist, and member of the Bavarian court, which appears in the magnificent manuscript that contains the psalm settings, Lasso's music is praised precisely for the beautifully apt way it enhances the somber texts. "One cannot know whether the sweetness of the emotions more adorns the plaintive melodies or the plaintive melodies the sweetness of the emotions," wrote Quickelberg. He called the sequence of compositions an excellent example of *musica reservata,* a somewhat mysterious term, the exact meaning of which scholars have ever since debated; most likely it refers to music that expresses its text, as Quickelberg's statement seems to suggest, though it may also refer to music intended for connoisseurs rather than a wider public, a definition that would also fit Lasso's psalms. His settings are all composed of many relatively short, self-contained sections. *De profundis clamavi,* for example, consists of \ten *partes* scored for from three to six voices. In some ways the most impressive of the lot dramatically in spite of its austerity, *De profundis* is exceptional in being built over a declamatory psalm tone used as cantus firmus. Even within this single relatively restrained work, though, Lasso was able to achieve a wide range of effects. The opening section (Example 11–6), for instance, exhibits one of Lasso's typical textures, consisting of word-generated melodic lines in which rhythmic imitation plays a greater role than pitch identity, and in which the nearly imitative counterpoint is controlled by a clearly focused series of harmonic progressions. The trio on "Quia apud Dominum" is a model of how to add two contrapuntal parts to a cantus firmus. Several sections set the cantus firmus in canon, either simply or in contrary motion. The "Gloria Patri" begins with a classical point of imitation derived from the scaffolding voice. And the final section, "Sicut erat in principio," begins with half-chorus pitted against half-chorus but ends with all voices joined together for an appropriately impressive close.

Just as the trio in *De profundis clamavi* sets a contrapuntal standard worth emulating, so the twelve duos, or *bicinia,* six with moralizing Latin texts and six without text (they were also called *fantasie* or *ricercari* in the original editions), which Lasso published in 1577 and which were reprinted many times in later years, can serve students today in the same way they served students in the sixteenth century: as models and exercises to be played and studied by young musicians learning counterpoint and also by aspiring instrumentalists and singers. Lasso's *bicinia* differ from the others in the century chiefly by being better; neither schoolmasterly nor pedantic, they contain some first-rate music.

During his last years, in the 1580's and the early 1590's, Lasso seems to have restricted his emotional range somewhat and emphasized the serious and even melancholy side of his musical personality. Many of his late motets draw their texts from the liturgy, a practice Lasso did not cultivate as much in his earlier years. His *Sacrae cantiones* of 1585, for example, consist chiefly of short offertories, among the best he wrote. His last collection of motets, the *Cantiones sacrae sex vocum* (Graz: Georg Widmanstätter, 1594), published during the year of his death, do not restrict themselves exclusively to items from the sacred service, but they, too, lack the fire and brilliance of much of his earlier work, replacing those qualities with a sobriety and austerity reminiscent in some ways of earlier Netherlandish music—that is, the tradition of Lasso's youth. It is true that some of the works in the volume, like *Heu quis armorum* (*Works*, XIX), which conjures up the day of the Last Judgment using largely homophonic textures in antiphonal combinations, seem just as emotive and vivid as the motets of his early and middle periods; and some, like *Lauda anima mea* (*Works*, XVII), include sections where the top two voices dominate the others to an extent that seems to prefigure early seventeenth-century monody. But most of these motets resemble the opening section of *Musica Dei donum*, the composer's panegyric to the art of music, which consists of short motives relatively lacking in contrast, woven into a thick and fairly seamless contrapuntal web. Lasso's motets of 1594 are the noble and dignified last testament of a serious old man who has put away the frivolities of his youth even while rediscovering his musical patrimony.

EXAMPLE 11–6. Lasso, *De profundis,* mm. 1–13.

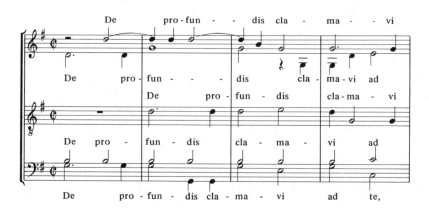

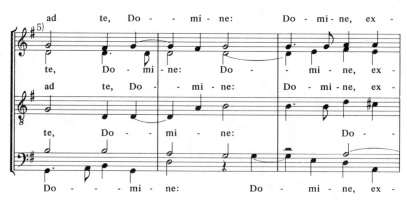

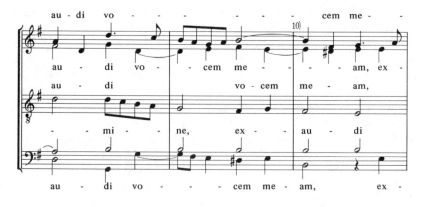

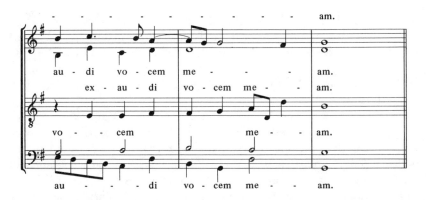

In addition to his magnificent motets, Lasso also wrote several compositions intended for special occasions during the liturgical year. His *Lectiones matutinae de nativitate Christi* (1575), meant to be sung at matins on Christmas morning, and his two sets of *lectiones* drawn from the book of Job (the first published in 1565 and the second in 1582) are among his most beautiful and impressive works, as are his settings of the Lamentations of Jeremiah (1585), performed during Holy Week. The Lamentations and the passages from Job are comparable in general mood and musical achievement to Lasso's settings of the penitential psalms, the prevailing homophony of the later set of *lectiones* notwithstanding. His hundred Magnificats, published in their entirety only after his death as a part of *Magnum opus musicum,* include some superb music. About half of the Magnificats are based on Gregorian chant, and most of the rest parody chansons, madrigals, or motets by Lasso, Rore, and others. Some are complete settings in polyphony of the entire canticle of the Blessed Virgin, while others follow the traditional pattern of alternation between verses composed polyphonically and others to be performed either as monophonic chant or as organ versets.

Lasso used parody technique much more often in his Masses than in his Magnificats. Almost all of his more than fifty Masses derive in one way or another from some pre-existent chanson, madrigal, or motet. But Lasso appears not to have been stimulated to ingenious feats by the challenge of recomposing older material, and for the most part he confined himself to extensive literal quotation only in the Kyrie, while merely alluding in the other movements to his model at the beginning, possibly the end, and sometimes at a few structurally important passages in the middle. Some of his Masses, especially the simpler ones of the *Missa brevis* variety, seem to have been written in the line of duty. They are perfunctory workaday compositions that were probably intended for unimportant daily services; they never reach the heights of his motets. But others of his Masses, like those on Sandrin's chanson *Doulce memoire,* Palestrina's madrigal *Io son ferito,* and Lasso's own motets *In te Domine speravi* and *Dixit Joseph,* are filled with felicitous details of counterpoint and text setting and display the composer's sure command in organizing large musical forms; they are as skillfully made as any of his other compositions.

Lasso was so astonishingly productive that his approximately 150 chansons seem an insignificant part, quantitatively at least, of his entire output. But they include some of the best works in this genre of the entire century. Stylistically, many of them resemble earlier French or Netherlandish chansons; or they use those traditions as a point of departure—yet another indication of Lasso's impressive ability to assimilate diverse elements into his own musical language. His many light, witty, and even licentious songs are especially close to the chanson tradition of the early sixteenth century. *Quand mon mary vient de dehors* (*Works,* XII), for instance, with its initial paired duets and its incisive homophony, is not very different from many of the chansons published by Pierre Attaingnant in the 1530's and 1540's, nor is the bawdy *Il estoit une religieuse* (*Works,* XII), with its blasphemous joke associating "Pater noster" and "Ave Maria," underlined by mock-pompous counterpoint and long melismas. What differences there are between the two repertories can be explained by Lasso's greater harmonic focus and motivic concentration and the sensitive way in which his music reveals both the form and the meaning of the poem it sets. Lasso built on earlier styles, too, for his more serious songs, working out his musical material with a finesse and imagination that produced a series of unique masterpieces. His famous *Susanne ung jour* (*Works,* XIV), one of the most widely distributed songs of the late sixteenth century and far better known than the earlier setting by Didier Lupi on which Lasso's is based, clothes the borrowed material in rich Netherlandish counterpoint. Lasso's equally well-known setting of Ronsard's *Bon jour mon coeur* (*Works,* XII), on the other hand, maintains a deceptively simple chordal texture almost throughout; but no Parisian composers of earlier times ever enhanced the rhetoric of a poem as directly as Lasso did, varying the rhythmic pace, determining the lengths of the phrases, and shaping the melodies according to the emphasis he wished to place on various words or phrases. In some compositions Lasso set French poetry in a musical style that combines rich harmonic effects, contrasting sections of counterpoint, word painting, and a constant insistence on expression and atmosphere—a style, in short, which recalls the Italian madrigal and represents a genuinely new contribution on Lasso's part to the history of the chanson. Even the opening few bars of *La nuict froide et sombre* (Example 11–7), one of the best of his Italianate French songs, suffice to show how far such music is from the emotional neutrality of many chansons.

EXAMPLE 11–7. Lasso, *La nuict froide et sombre,* mm. 1–15.

Similarly, some of Lasso's German lieder exhibit madrigalian traits, while others continue the older tenor song tradition (even to the extent of using either a pre-existent or a newly invented cantus firmus), or make extensive use of motet-like imitation, or borrow from the chanson the technique of fast syllabic declamation. Some lieder repeat themes or phrases according to the sense of the text, some contain no repetitions at all, and in others entire sections are repeated literally. In short, the composer's ninety-odd lieder show even more stylistic and formal variety than his works in other genres. Even the texts he chose to set differ widely in type one from another. Songs with sacred words are mixed in Lasso's collections of lieder with drinking songs, bawdy songs, comic narratives in several sections, and lyrical love songs.

The strain of slightly raucous humor, even licentiousness, that runs through Lasso's chansons and lieder appears also in some of his settings of Italian poetry. As late as 1581 he published a volume of villanelle, moresche, and other light pieces in which characters from the Neapolitan streets and the commedia dell'arte figure prominently (Giorgia, Lucia, Pantaleone, Zanni, and others). The collection contains, too, the well-known echo song for double chorus, O la, o che bon eccho (Works, X), as well as Matona mia cara, the villanella (or more properly, "todescha") with a text in a heavily accented Italian as though sung by one of the Emperor's German soldiers. The Bavarian court obviously enjoyed these playful, quasi-popular songs, which were performed at various entertainments there.

By and large Lasso's serious side came to the fore in his almost 150 madrigals, especially as he got older. The extroverted polyphony or animated homophony of his earlier madrigals—the first of them were published in 1555—gradually gave way to a more sober and dense counterpoint. The opening of Nessun visse giamai (Example 11–8), for instance, a late work first printed in 1584, does not immediately engage the listener by obvious madrigalisms or striking thematic material. Rather, each of the two phrases expands in full, chordally determined polyphony from the same simple rhythmic motive on one repeated pitch, which conveys so effectively the mood of sadness and resignation. Lasso came more and more to prefer those of Petrarch's poems written, like Nessun visse giamai, after the death of his beloved Laura; earlier, the composer more often chose Petrarch's sonnets "in vita di Madonna Laura." Petrarch, whose works were associated in the sixteenth century with more serious madrigal settings, seems to have remained Lasso's favorite poet throughout his life. The composer set a number of his poems, including several complete sestinas, but he also composed madrigals on poems by Ariosto, Tasso, Bembo, Sannazaro, and others. He neglected the new pastoral poems of Guarini in favor of sacred texts by the religious Petrarchists Gabriele Fiamma and Luigi Tansillo. Tansillo wrote the words for Lasso's cycle of seven-voiced madrigali spirituali, the Lagrime di San Pietro, a work of almost Baroque religious fervor, written, like Lasso's last motets, in an austere polyphony that seldom allows a place for elaborate melismas, and yet draws on a lifetime's experience to bring out the poetry's meaning by relatively simple but inexhaustibly subtle and inventive means.

EXAMPLE 11-8. Lasso, *Nessun visse giamai*, mm. 1-8.

It is virtually impossible to characterize succinctly Lasso's work as a whole. His mastery and the range of his capabilities were so great that his music is still only half understood. There are, for example, almost no completely satisfactory recordings of any of his works. To be sure, much of his polyphony is very difficult to control in performance; it is no easy task to bring out the subtlety and shapeliness of individual melodic lines within the typically dense mass of counterpoint. Unlike Palestrina's music, Lasso's does not virtually sing itself, for it lacks the ladcs

transparency of texture and grace so important to the Roman composer. But Lasso's compositions gain thereby in energy and "rugged power" (Gustave Reese's phrase). If one characteristic feature should be emphasized more than any other, it is that he derived his inspiration chiefly from the words he set, allowing them to generate most of the musical details in his works. More than any of the other great composers of the late sixteenth century except the virtuoso madrigalists, Lasso understood that the words were to be master of the music.

TOMÁS LUIS DE VICTORIA

Francisco Guerrero was the only one of the three greatest Spanish polyphonists of the sixteenth century who was educated and worked entirely in Spain. Tomás Luis de Victoria (ca. 1548–1611), on the other hand, like Cristóbal de Morales before him, spent many years in Rome, and his music reflects the contact he had with Palestrina and his circle. Born near Ávila, Victoria received his early education at Segovia under Bartolomé Escobedo. At about the age of nineteen he was awarded a grant by Philip II in order to pursue his studies in Rome. He enrolled there in the Collegium Germanicum (a Jesuit college founded to counteract Lutheran tendencies among German youth), which was under Spanish direction at the time Victoria entered it. Palestrina served as chapelmaster at its sister institution, the Collegium Romanum, during those years, and the young Spaniard may have learned from him. After his studies were completed, Victoria held positions at several Roman churches and at the Collegium Romanum, and eventually he became chapelmaster at the Collegium Germanicum, where he stayed from 1573 to 1578. In 1575 he was ordained as a priest. Ultimately he decided to return home after so many years abroad. He entered the service of the Empress Maria, sister of Philip II and widow of Maximilian II. She retired to a convent in Madrid in 1584, and Victoria remained with her, working at the convent from 1586 until his death in 1611.

As we have seen, Spain had a rich and flourishing musical culture during the sixteenth century. Aside from the great international figures, the country supported a number of lesser composers—Rodrigo Ceballos, Bernardo Clavijo del Castillo, Juan Esquivel de Barahona, the two Mateo Flechas (uncle and nephew), Juan Navarro, and Juan Vasquez, to name but a few—whose music is so fine that it deserves to be studied and performed even today. But of them all only Victoria can be compared with Palestrina, Lasso, and Byrd for the stature of his achievement, in spite of the fact that the Spaniard was neither very prolific (at least not by comparison with the other great musicians, who composed an incredibly large number of masterpieces) nor very wide-ranging in his outlook. About twenty Masses, about forty-five motets, and a number of other compositions with specific liturgical functions—Magnificats, Offices for the Dead and for Holy Week (including superb Lamentations and two dramatic Passions), and a series of hymns for the complete church year—make up his complete works. He wrote no madrigals or other secular music of any kind, and this restriction of genre provides a key to his musical personality. His music is devout, pious, and intense. "He had no other aim," Higini Anglès wrote in the *New Oxford History of Music*, "than to sing of the Cross and the mysteries of the Redemption, using means uncontaminated by profane art." Actually, however, Victoria's compositions are "contaminated" by techniques associated with secular music to the extent that these techniques support and enhance the deeply felt views expressed in the sacred texts he chose to set. He never composed a sacred work on a secular cantus firmus (although one of his Masses parodies Janequin's *La Guerre*). But his motets are imbued with the notion that music must reveal and intensify literary meanings, an idea derived at least in part from the humanistic predilections of Italian musicians and worldly churchmen, and worked out first and most enthusiastically in the madrigal. In his concern with text expression Victoria resembles Lasso, although the Spaniard's style is closer to Palestrina's. Like Palestrina, Victoria wrote a music distinguished for its clarity and internal logic. But Victoria was willing to disturb the even flow of counterpoint; to emphasize a word or a phrase he would tolerate an "ungraceful" leap of a major sixth, for example, which Palestrina would have avoided, or he would allow a strong melodic line to proceed on its way without immediately reversing its direction to preserve a sense of careful balance. In fact, it is no exaggeration to say that Victoria showed a genuinely dramatic flair in the way he set sacred texts.

Victoria's motets are all so finely made and so perfectly fitted to their words that it is difficult to know which of them represent him at his best or most typical. Many choice passages come immediately to mind. The beautifully balanced chordal opening of *O quam gloriosum*, for example, soon rises to its high point before sinking down to the cadence; the passage vividly conveys the sense of the words, "O how glorious is the kingdom where all the Saints rejoice with Christ." In the same motet, stunning bursts of imitative rising scale passages erupt beneath the sustained line of the superius at the word "gaudent" ("they rejoice"). The spacious opening imitation of the Christmas motet *O magnum mysterium* (Example 11–9) is skillfully fitted together so that none of the

EXAMPLE 11–9. Tomás Luis de Victoria, *O magnum mysterium*, mm. 1–19.

joins show; the new music sung by the upper two voices at the entrance of the lower two voices forms a perfect foil for the last member of the phrase, the partially sequential cadencing material (mm. 15ff) derived from the second part of the opening melody. Victoria varied the rhythmic pace and texture of *O magnum mysterium* to bring out the rhetoric of the words; the slow, chordal salutation to the Virgin, "O beata Virgine," for example, contrasts very effectively with the preceding imitative counterpoint and with the conventional but nevertheless impressive shift to triple meter that follows almost immediately afterwards on "Alleluia." Victoria showed off his contrapuntal skill in constructing a canon between the two top voices of the five-voiced *Resplenduit facies ejus* (and several other five-voiced motets). And he made symbolism palpable in *Iste Sanctus* when he introduced a Gregorian cantus firmus in long notes at the words "for he was founded upon a sure rock."

But Victoria's art consists of more than striking passages in isolation and demonstrations of contrapuntal skill. Individual phrases fit into their proper place within a larger context, and technical feats are subordinated to the composer's expressive intent. *O vos omnes*, a relatively short and contrapuntally uncomplicated motet of great emotional impact and intensity, serves well to demonstrate Victoria's mastery at shaping entire movements. To be sure, the formal outlines of the composition are quite conventional: since the text is a responsory—taken from the Lamentations of Jeremiah: "All ye that pass by, behold and see if there be any sorrow like unto my sorrow"—the music repeats according to the scheme aBcB. The motet seems to grow from the single pitch D, sung first by the tenor and then doubled by the altus (Example 11–10). The voices enter one by one without imitating each other. The opening words ("All ye that pass by") are set relatively neutrally as two balanced phrases, the first ending on a chord other than the tonic (III in D-Dorian), the second cadencing (with a VII^6–I formula) on the tonic.

Some of the emotional impact of the work comes from its superb details, especially those in the refrain. The descending tetrachord on "si est dolor" (a motive already suggested in the first phrase of the motet) calls forth suspensions, and their frequency and their level of dissonance increases sharply on "similis" (Example 11–11). Indeed, the train of suspensions starting in m. 21 with the pungent interplay between the "forbidden" interval C sharp to F, takes as long as three measures to resolve. The declamatory motive on "sicut dolor meus," rising a minor second and then falling back to its original pitch, is extraordinarily poignant, despite its simplicity and adherence to convention. (Victoria frequently expressed sorrow by motives similarly involving a minor second.) Introduced by empty fifths, the motive is stated three times, each time being reworked with different harmonies.

EXAMPLE 11–10. Victoria, *O vos omnes,* mm. 1–10.

EXAMPLE 11–11. Victoria, *O vos omnes,* mm. 17–33.

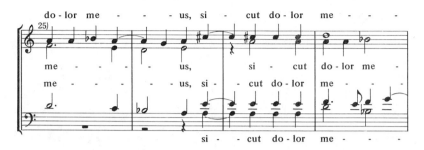

Even more striking than these details, though, is the effect Victoria achieved by recomposing the phrase "attendite et videte" ("behold and see") the second time it appears. The first time, he began the phrase with a straightforward declamatory motive on "attendite," mostly on one pitch and scored as a dialogue between a trio of voices and the solo superius, and followed by a tutti on "et videte" (Example 11–12a). When the phrase reappears (Example 11–12b) it is recomposed in a higher range (at the beginning the roles of the voices are reversed, the solo superius being answered by a trio) and extended; and the music for "dolorem meum" reworks—one might almost say "develops"—material from the first phrase. The effect of these changes gives the second exhortation much greater intensity, if not greater urgency, and makes the refrain that follows more than the last member of a conventional repetition scheme; it is a moving dénouement, made necessary by the previous buildup. In *O vos omnes*, Victoria gave musical coherence to the structure not merely by following a traditional formal pattern, nor by concentrating his attention on the few central motives that permeate the entire motet, nor by carefully balancing each phrase against the others (a procedure in which the role of tonality should not be underestimated), though he did all those things; the most important element in the coherence of the motet stems from its dramatic credibility.

In addition to his relatively small but very fine corpus of motets for from four to six voices, Victoria also wrote a series of sacred works for

EXAMPLE 11–12. Victoria, *O vos omnes.*

(a) mm.11-16

(b) mm.34-51

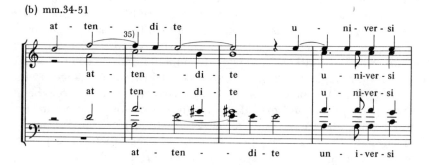

two or three antiphonal choruses, including several Masses, Magnificats, Marian antiphons, and sequences. Neither so concentrated nor so intensely expressive as his motets for single choir, Victoria's antiphonal compositions generally proceed in a fairly relaxed imitative polyphony frequently interspersed with purely chordal passages—a style similar to that of most polychoral music of the late sixteenth century. If Victoria did not strive for great depth of feeling in these works, neither did he attempt the spectacular and colorful effects achieved by the best Venetian composers of the time. Victoria's antiphonal works are solemn and ceremonial. The *Missa pro victoria,* based on Janequin's *La Guerre,* is exceptional not only in being his sole work built on a secular model but also in its exploration of a *concertante* style with many repeated notes and short time-values, more characteristic of the virtuoso northern Italian musicians (even then in the process of forging a new Baroque style) than of the sober Roman circle of composers around Palestrina. When they were first published, many of these antiphonal works were supplied with an organ part that duplicates all the voices of the first chorus as literally as the limitations of the instrument permit; when the other choruses sing, the organ remains silent. Perhaps Victoria intended precisely the particular sonority that the published music indicates. More likely the existence of the printed organ accompaniment reflects a widespread performing convention of the time. If organists had the option to double singers whenever they wished, they would have needed to prepare such parts for themselves; the printed version saved them time and trouble, and ensured them an accompaniment free from errors. It may even be that Victoria's organ parts for Chorus I imply instrumental support or doubling for Choruses II and III as well.

Victoria's twenty Masses include some that paraphrase plainchant (like the *Missa Ave maris stella* and the *Missa de Beata Virgine*) and some that parody motets by other great composers of the time (like those on Guerrero's *Simile est regnum coelorum* and Palestrina's *Surge propera*, and the *Missa Gaudeamus*, which is based on Morales's *Jubilate Deo*). But more than half of the composer's Masses parody his own motets— *Ascendens Christus*, *O magnum mysterium*, *O quam gloriosum*, *Quam pulchri sunt*, *Trahe me post te*, and others. In reworking his own music for use in a new context, Victoria seems neither to have followed a single set of rules mechanically nor to have developed a fixed convention that applies equally well to all his works. Instead, he chose those passages from his motets that seemed to him most appropriate for recomposition (or for a particular section of the new work); sometimes he quoted them quite literally; at other times he reworked them almost beyond recognition. Nowhere in his *Missa O quam gloriosum*, for example, does he quote the splendid opening phrase of his own motet on which the Mass is based. He focused his attention on the subsequent points of imitation in the model, and especially on the three that dominate the three sections of the Kyrie movement. The "Christe" section, for instance, duplicates the final phrase of the motet. Victoria preserved his original polyphony except for minor adjustments and the addition of a new imitative line in the altus at the very beginning. The same musical material appears again at the end of the first half of the Credo and at the end of the first section of the Sanctus, as well as during the opening section of the Gloria, where it comes in and out of focus, at it were, barely recognizable and imbedded in newly-written polyphony. Victoria's technique of parodying pre-existent music, in short, is highly sophisticated, reflecting the refinement and change that any procedure undergoes after a half century or more of common use.

That Victoria failed to cite the magnificent opening phrase of *O quam gloriosum* in his Mass based on the motet suggests that he felt the passage to be too highly charged, expressive, or vivid, or merely too intimately connected with its original text to serve appropriately as a part of the solemn and traditional ritual of the Mass Ordinary. In fact, Victoria seldom set the words of the Mass dramatically. Occasionally he introduced a madrigalism, and he frequently gave special attention to the passages traditionally singled out for emphasis (like "Et incarnatus est," "Crucifixus," and "Et resurrexit" in the Credo) by setting them in contrasting textures. But in general, his Masses, with their impeccable diction and reserved and sober counterpoint, show off his conservative, Palestrinian side. If they are not filled with so many sweeping melismas and long gentle arches of melody as those by the Roman composer, they often are marked by a concision in declamatory and imitative passages that allowed neither for extensive elaboration of the musical material nor for illustrating the words. A fervent, mystical, intense musician, Victoria showed in his Masses that he understood, too, the virtue of economy of means and that he was one of the great masters of the "strict" contrapuntal style of the late Renaissance.

WILLIAM BYRD

Rather than concentrating his efforts on a single style or on one kind of music, William Byrd (1543–1623), like Orlando di Lasso, displayed a multi-faceted musical personality. The range and versatility of Byrd's achievement, as well as the superb quality of individual compositions, distinguish him from his contemporaries. He excelled in almost every genre cultivated in the England of his time: Latin Masses and motets, English anthems and services, songs and madrigalian compositions, and music for viol consort and for keyboard instruments. At the same time, the character of Byrd's work and his chronological position make him a pivotal figure in the history of English music. He was both the last great composer in the rich tradition of Catholic polyphony in Britain and the first of that "golden age of music" which began in the middle years of Elizabeth I's reign. His Latin church music embodies the final perfect union between the native tradition and the contrapuntal techniques that flourished in Italy and the Netherlands earlier in the century. His English church music, including his verse anthems—a genre that seems to have sprung up full-blown from the composer's own fertile imagination—ushers in a period of great creativity during the seventeenth century by musicians like Orlando Gibbons, Henry and William Lawes, William Child, and Matthew Locke. Elements from an older English song tradition combine in his consort songs and other polyphonic songs and madrigals with new techniques introduced into England from Italy; his secular works stand at the head of that amazing development during the reigns of Elizabeth I and James I that produced so many fine madrigals and related compositions by Thomas Morley, Thomas Weelkes, John Wilbye, among others, and lute ayres by musicians such as John Dowland, Thomas Campion, Philip Rosseter, and John Danyel, a development that started with the publication of a collection of Italian madrigals in translation, *Musica Transalpina,* edited by Nicholas Yonge and printed by Thomas

East in 1588. And Byrd's fantasias for viol consort and his pavans, galliards and sets of variations for virginals and other keyboard instruments have an honored place in the incredibly rich repertory of Elizabethan and Jacobean instrumental music. They herald that astonishing burst of activity in the late sixteenth and seventeenth centuries that brought forth compositions for lute, cittern, bandora, and other plucked stringed instruments by Anthony Holborne, John Dowland, Francis Cutting, Francis Pilkington, Robert Johnson, and many others, for viol consort by composers such as Alfonso Ferrabosco the younger and other members of his family, Thomas Lupo, Richard Deering, John Cooper (or Giovanni Coperario, as he preferred to call himself), John Jenkins, and Orlando Gibbons; and for keyboard instruments by John Bull, Orlando Gibbons, and a host of only slightly less important virginalists, among them Thomas Tomkins, Giles Farnaby, and Peter Philips.

Byrd spent most of his professional life playing the organ for the Chapel Royal. He was appointed to it in 1570 (though he may not have joined it until 1572) as a young man in his late twenties, after having worked as organist at Lincoln Cathedral for almost ten years, and he continued to serve the court until he died some fifty years later in 1623. To judge from the texts he chose to set, many of them grave, penitential, or supplicatory, he was a sober and pious man. He remained a Catholic throughout his life, in a Protestant country hostile to his religion. Although he had difficulties from time to time with the authorities about his deeply held beliefs, he obviously felt secure enough to compose and even publish music for the Catholic liturgy, and his views prevented him neither from holding an important position in the Anglican church nor from providing compositions for its services.

One early commentator wrote that Byrd was "bred up to music under Tallis," although just when or where the young Byrd could have studied with the older master is unclear. Certainly the two shared the position as organist in the Chapel Royal; and until Tallis's death in 1585 they shared, too, a monopoly to print music in England, a privilege that turned out to be not quite so profitable as the two musicians might have hoped, and which Byrd eventually assigned to Thomas East of London. The first volume the two composers published under their license was the *Cantiones Sacrae* of 1575, to which each of them contributed seventeen motets. (Denis Stevens has made the ingenious suggestion that the number was suggested by the fact that the collection appeared in the seventeenth year of Elizabeth's reign.) These thirty-four motets were the first Latin church music to be printed in England, and the earliest of the two composers' works to be published. The music in the publication, and especially the compositions by the thirty-two-year-old Byrd, must have astonished musicians in London, who would have appreciated the new subtlety and flexibility displayed in the handling of imitative techniques and in the manipulation of texture, the new expressiveness of the melodies, and the new freedom Byrd enjoyed in choosing texts for apparently personal rather than strictly liturgical reasons.

Tallis seems to have included in the *Cantiones Sacrae* some works that he wrote a number of years earlier. It is not surprising, then, that his choice of texts and his treatment of imitation reflect slightly older practices. His contribution to the anthology, however, includes some of his best works, like the highly expressive *In jejunio* and the adroitly canonic *Miserere nostri.*

Early English composers who made extensive use of imitative techniques tended to lay out their points in perfectly symmetrical patterns. In the 1575 *Cantiones Sacrae,* Byrd adopted a more flexible procedure and introduced successive voices irregularly so that he could spin out his contrapuntal lines in a complex and interesting manner. In *Domine secundum actum meum* (Example 11–13), Byrd's setting of a respond from the Office of the Dead, the initial exposition takes up two sharply defined motives: the declamatory "Domine" and another, separated from the first by rests, on "secundum actum meum" involving an upper neighbor note. The shape of both themes, clearly, is suggested by the words. In order to "develop" them independently, a process that continues throughout the typically expansive thirty-two-measure opening section, Byrd staggered the entrances of the voices in asymmetrical sequence. That he derived his plan for doing so from a similar motet by Alfonso Ferrabosco the elder, *Domine, non secundum peccata mea,* does not, as

EXAMPLE 11–13. William Byrd, *Domine secundum actum meum,* mm. 1–10. Copyright by Stainer & Bell Ltd. All Rights Reserved. Reprinted by permission of Stainer & Bell, London.

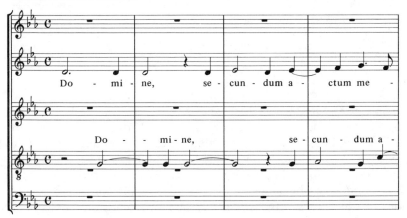

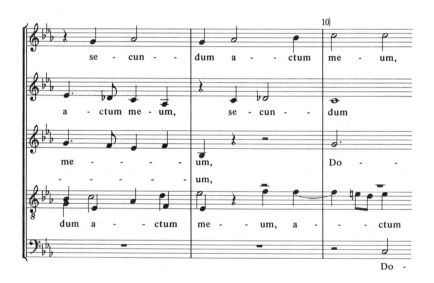

Joseph Kerman has convincingly shown, challenge the notion that Byrd broadened the horizons of British music in the 1570's by developing freer and more flexible methods of writing imitative counterpoint than had previously been heard. Many of his motets, for example, are unusually long, allowing him full scope to work over his themes and to show them off in various combinations; and a number of his works proceed as a series of expositions with two, or occasionally even three, subjects. One or two of the 1575 motets employ canon in a systematic way, and one, *Diliges Dominum*, is written for eight voices in two choirs (although some of the six-voiced compositions more fully exploit antiphonal effects). But in spite of Byrd's preoccupation with contrapuntal technique, the most important voices in his motets—those that most clearly reveal the underlying structure as the music proceeds—are apt to be soprano and bass. The polarity of voices is of course especially evident in those works written almost entirely in a homophonic texture, like *Emendemus in melius*, one of the finest motets in the whole collection.

For a few of the motets in the 1575 *Cantiones Sacrae*, Byrd chose texts of a traditional kind which he treated in a traditional way; there is one respond, *Libera me*, built over a cantus firmus, for example, and a canonic antiphon, *Miserere mihi Domine*, with cantus firmus. One motet, *Laudate, pueri*, is nothing more than a previously composed fantasia for viols, to which selected psalm verses have been added. Many of the texts in the anthology do not have a regular place in the liturgy, and most of the responds are handled freely, without borrowed material, in imitative polyphony. As we have seen, continental composers earlier in the century had begun to choose motet texts for apparently personal rather than liturgical reasons, but Byrd departed radically from English practice in doing so. His inclination to set whatever words attracted him, regardless of their role in the service, suggests that he wished his music to support and enhance texts he selected, whether they were from Scripture, hymns, prayers, or parts of the liturgy. He made his attitude explicit in the preface to his *Gradualia* of 1605, where he wrote, "In sacred words . . . there is such a profound and hidden power that to one thinking upon things divine and diligently and earnestly pondering them, all the fittest numbers occur as if of themselves." Eschewing madrigalisms and other extroverted sorts of word illustration, Byrd nevertheless invented themes and musical structures tied as closely to their words as any devised by the other great exponents of text expression in the late sixteenth century, Lasso, Victoria, or the virtuoso madrigalists of Italy.

Byrd published two further volumes of *Cantiones Sacrae*, one in 1589 for five voices and the other in 1591 for five and six voices. These later sets of motets, as long and expansive as those in the 1575 collection, contain even fewer strictly liturgical works. In them Byrd confirmed his predilection for choosing texts from strong personal preference or belief. Kerman has even convincingly argued that the large number of motets from the 1589 and 1591 *Cantiones Sacrae* that deal with the Babylonian captivity or the coming of God, or that beg not for mercy but for liberty, reflect the composer's deep concern over the plight of the recusant (Catholic) community in Protestant England. Certainly the music seems to have been inspired by Byrd's response to the words, a stylistic trait even more apparent in the later than the earlier collections. His later motets also span a wider range of textures and styles; Byrd makes greater use of chromaticism and antiphonal effects, for example, and he writes livelier and more varied rhythms.

Whereas the *Cantiones Sacrae* are largely independent of the liturgy, Byrd's two volumes of *Gradualia* (first published in 1605 and 1607, and both re-issued in 1610) contain the most important collection of Mass and Office Propers since Isaac's *Choralis Constantinus*, a claim that takes into account the less complete sets of music for the divine service that began to be published on the continent, and especially in Italy, after the Council of Trent. In the *Gradualia*, which Byrd himself described as his "swan song" (although he was only in his early sixties when the volume was published, and he was to live almost twenty years longer), the composer included more than 100 motets, mostly settings of Introits, Graduals, Alleluias, Offertories and Communions for the principal feasts of the Catholic church year. As befits music used within the ritual, the motets in the *Gradualia* are relatively short and concise; the service does not allow time for the elaborate and leisurely contrapuntal developments of which Byrd was so fond in the *Cantiones Sacrae*. But the music in the *Gradualia* is not less fine because it is more succinct. On the contrary, the composer maintained a consistently high standard of excellence throughout the volume. Perhaps the best known composition in the collection is Byrd's lovely *Ave verum corpus*, but it would be misleading to regard it as typical, since Byrd made use of all the diverse techniques at his command, and since the individual motets ought to be considered in the wider context of the complete setting of the Proper for the occasion.

Precisely why Byrd assembled two volumes of music intended for the Roman Catholic liturgy has never been satisfactorily explained, and we do not know who might have been allowed to sing the motets in the *Gradualia*. Public celebration of the Catholic Mass was forbidden under both Elizabeth and James—at least one person was arrested for owning the *Gradualia* in 1605—and even quite large groups of recusants were not likely to have sung on a regular basis complex three- to six-voiced polyphony during their semi-secret services. It is difficult to imagine, too, circumstances that would have been appropriate for performances of Byrd's three settings of the Mass Ordinary, compositions that survive only in copies with their title pages missing, perhaps significantly, so that we do not know the year they were published (though a case can be made for supposing they came out between about 1592 and 1595). Byrd's Masses for three, four, and five voices are all free of borrowed material or any scaffolding devices, although they do make limited use of head motives. Byrd built up these magnificent structures from imitative polyphony handled freely and flexibly in his finest mature manner. But his Masses are literally incomparable, for no continental composers invented a textural complexity quite the same as that which characterizes Byrd's music as English, and no other British composers of his generation wrote polyphonic settings of the Ordinary of the Mass.

In spite of his deeply held religious beliefs, Byrd wrote some of his finest music for the Anglican church, including his two complete Services, that is, settings of the morning and evening canticles (in Byrd's time the Venite, Te Deum, Benedictus, Magnificat, and Nunc Dimittis) and the Communion Service (Kyrie, Creed, and sometimes Sanctus), which together form the central ritual of the English church. They are the Anglican counterparts of his Catholic Masses. Byrd's Short Service, like all so-called "short" Services, is written largely in the note-against-note counterpoint that Archbishop Cranmer recommended to Henry VIII as the only appropriate style for church music; in Byrd's setting the two sides of the choir, *decani* and *cantoris,* answer each other without overlapping. On the other hand, his Great Service ("great" because written in elaborated florid counterpoint) fully explores all possible combinations of its two five-voiced choirs. The rich density of its frequently imitative texture helps to explain why this is one of the greatest works in the Anglican tradition.

Byrd also composed anthems—in effect, English motets. Whereas some of them appeared only in manuscripts, many were printed in three miscellaneous collections that were issued during his lifetime: *Psalmes, Sonets and Songs* (1588), *Songs of Sundrie Natures* (1589), and *Psalmes, Songs and Sonets* (1611). As their titles imply, these anthologies contain a variety of types of music by Byrd: settings of psalms, full and verse anthems, secular and sacred songs for solo voice accompanied by a consort of viols (so-called "consort songs"), one or two genuine madrigals along with a greater number of works that are better called simply "polyphonic songs," two instrumental fantasias, and even one setting in Italian of a stanza by Ariosto.

Byrd gave equal importance to all the lines in the three- and four-voiced compositions in his miscellany of 1589; they are "classical" examples of late Renaissance imitative polyphony, some with simultaneous expositions of two subjects and other contrapuntal artifices. But most of the works for five and six voices in the volumes from 1588 and 1589 (and some of the six-voiced compositions of 1611) were conceived for a single singer (or sometimes two), whose relatively simple melodies are contrasted with a complex contrapuntal web of melodic lines originally intended to be played by a consort of viols, even though they are supplied with texts in the printed volumes (probably to take advantage of the new market for madrigals). As Byrd wrote in the epistle to the reader from the 1588 collection, "Heere are divers songs, which being originally made for Instruments to expresse the harmonie, and one voyce to pronounce the dittie, are now framed in all parts for voyces to sing the same." These consort songs, which include metrical psalms as well as moral and courtly poems (many of them cast in strophic form), are not written as solos with subordinated accompaniment. Instead, the voice shares the musical interest with the viols; it is as though a sung cantus firmus were imposed on a viol fantasia. The beginning of *Susanna fair* (Example 11–14), Byrd's setting of a translation of the chanson *Susanne ung jour*, which was so popular with continental composers, shows the typical stylistic features of the composer's consort songs. The well-shaped vocal line, with its impeccable diction and carefully planned climax, does not obviously express the meaning of the text; the emotionally neutral cast of the melody enabled Byrd with greater ease to repeat it literally to set subsequent stanzas of the poem. The composition proceeds in uninterrupted flowing counterpoint with no abrupt changes or contrasts to make of it a dramatic event. In his consort songs Byrd concentrated on elements of musical design and formal structure rather than on rhetorical display or vivid text expression.

A tradition of instrumentally accompanied solo songs had existed in England at least since the choirboy plays and court entertainments of the 1550's and 1560's; Philip Brett has published a wide selection of them as vol. 22 of *Musica Britannica*. Byrd, however, was the chief composer to carry the tradition forward. The lute ayres of Dowland and Campion share some of the traits of the consort songs, however, at least in their strophic orientation, though the textures of the two genres are totally different. In addition, the small repertory of seventeenth-century "cries" by Thomas Weelkes, Orlando Gibbons, and others—extended viol fantasias on which a collection of street cries and songs of itinerant vendors are superimposed more or less randomly—constitute a special sub-category of music derived in style from consort songs. Byrd evidently resisted the well-nigh overwhelming tide of madrigal writing that swept England after the *Musica Transalpina* of 1588. He continued to cultivate his intricate, finely wrought, continuous counterpoint in which an uninterrupted flow is more important than a dramatic presentation of the text. Only very occasionally, as in *This sweet and merry month of May*, did Byrd ever approach the madrigalian attitude as expressed, for example, in the works of Thomas Morley, Thomas Weelkes, and John Wilbye.

Many of the metrical psalms in Byrd's three miscellaneous volumes were conceived for solo voice and viols in the manner of consort songs.

EXAMPLE 11–14. Byrd, *Susanna fair,* mm. 1–16. Copyright by Stainer & Bell Ltd. All Rights Reserved. Reprinted by permission of Stainer & Bell, London.

Two carols in the 1589 collection, *From Virgin's womb* and *An earthly tree,* contrast a verse for solo voice or duet and viols with a burden for full choir. And the 1589 anthology includes an Easter anthem, *Christ rising again,* in which sections for two solo singers and viols alternate with sections for full choir, making it the first "verse" anthem. Each of the three volumes contains, as well, some anthems for unaccompanied choir ("full" as opposed to "verse" anthems). Some of these in the 1611 collection, like *Retire my soul* and *Arise, Lord, into thy rest,* are superb examples of Byrd's contrapuntal and expressive skill; they are among his finest works.

Byrd's instrumental music, which set new artistic standards for his contemporaries, consists for the most part of fantasias, dances, variation sets, and cantus firmus settings (including *In nomines*), for solo keyboard (harpsichord, virginals, or organ) or for instrumental ensemble (chiefly consorts of viols but presumably also groups of recorders or other appropriate instruments). The viol music is preserved mostly in manuscript miscellanies of textless part music (anthologies which may include a high proportion of motets and secular vocal compositions without their words) and the virginal music in a series of important keyboard collections, the most famous of which is the enormous *Fitzwilliam Virginal Book,* containing nearly 300 pieces copied out by a Catholic, Francis Tregian, while he was in prison for his religious (and political) beliefs from 1609 to 1619. Other keyboard sources include the elegantly written *My Ladye Nevell's Booke,* dated 1591 and containing Byrd's works exclusively; a number of other manuscript books copied out by or for private individuals; and one important printed anthology, *Parthenia, or the Maydenhead of the First Musicke that ever was printed for the Virginalls,* published in 1612 or 1613 (the title involves a pun on the Greek word, *parthenos,* for "virgin," which was repeated and carried further in a companion volume, *Parthenia In-violata,* containing songs and dances for virginals with bass viol). *Parthenia* offers music by three of the most distinguished virginalists —Byrd, John Bull, and Orlando Gibbons.

Almost half of Byrd's viol music is made up of cantus firmus settings in three, four, and five voices, apparently mostly early works, in which the composer has added suave imitative counterpoint around a simple statement of a plainsong hymn, Miserere, or the *In nomine* melody so beloved of English composers of the sixteenth and early seventeenth centuries. Byrd's few dances for viols—a five-voiced pavan, and a six-voiced pavan–galliard pair that are thematically linked—show how skillfully he could work out an intricate texture in music which is structurally simple (consisting normally of three short strains, each repeated) and basically homophonic; and his two grounds for viol consort, including the well-known five-voiced *Browning* (on a tune also known as *The leaves be greene*), display his ingenuity in devising constantly renewed counterpoints against the same repeated melody. His viol fantasias are written in the rich and rather dense imitative texture of much of Byrd's other music; we have seen that one could be transformed into a motet with very little adjustment. Byrd does, however, sometimes divide his fantasias into clearly articulated sections, and several include passages of dance-like music.

In Byrd's keyboard music, which was written largely in the same forms as his viol music, fantasias and other abstract musical forms are far out-weighed by dance movements (especially the magisterial pavan–galliard pairs that he stylized and brought into the realm of high art music) and long, brilliantly developed sets of variations (many of them, like *Go from my window*, *Gypsies' Round*, and *John come kiss me now*, based on simple folk or popular tunes). An alignment of the first two bars from several variations on *The Woods so Wild* (Example 11–15) amply demonstrates Byrd's inventiveness in devising figuration patterns to fit within the melodic and harmonic framework suggested by the tune, but excerpts cannot illustrate the expert way he formed complete pieces from disparate units by controlling the pace of each voice and building to an impressive climax. Perhaps the greatest pleasure, though, in hearing Byrd's keyboard music (indeed, music by any of the English virginalists) comes from perceiving the sumptuous and imaginative ways he put together a rich texture and then varied it, often by applying and manipulating one stereotyped figuration pattern for each unit of the structure. It is a kind of music to be savored in its details.

EXAMPLE 11–15. Byrd, *The Woods So Wild*, beginnings of five variations.

Byrd did not write every kind of instrumental music cultivated in England in his time. He has left us no lute music, no ayres, and no music for the favorite English combination of lute, pandora, cittern, two viols, and flute—the "broken consort" that Thomas Morley, for example, exploited in his *Consort Lessons* of 1599. Nevertheless, there were few composers of the late Renaissance who were so broad in their interests and achievements as William Byrd. He would have been memorable for his Latin or English church music alone, or for his consort songs or virginal music. As it is, his extraordinary accomplishments in virtually every genre earned for him a place of distinction even during England's golden age of music.

BIBLIOGRAPHICAL NOTES

Palestrina's complete works are available in two editions, the earlier made by F. X. Haberl, F. Espagne, and others and published in 33 volumes (Leipzig, 1862–1907), the second made by R. Casimiri, L. Virgili, K. Jeppesen, and L. Bianchi, in 31 volumes (Rome, 1935–65). The best-known study of Palestrina in English is Knud Jeppesen, *The Style of*

Palestrina and the Dissonance (London, 1946; repr. 1970). See also H. K. Andrews, *An Introduction to the Technique of Palestrina* (London, 1958); Karl Gustav Fellerer, *Der Palestrinastil und seine Bedeutung in der vokalen Kirchenmusik des 18. Jahrhunderts* (Augsburg, 1929); Fellerer, *Palestrina* (2nd rev. ed., Düsseldorf, 1960); Robert Marshall, "The Paraphrase Technique of Palestrina in his Masses Based on Hymns," *Journal of the American Musicological Society*, 16 (1963); and Jerome Roche, *Palestrina* (London, 1971).

The incomplete edition of Lasso's works, ed. F. X. Haberl and A. Sandberger in 21 volumes (Leipzig, 1894–1927), has been continued by Wolfgang Boetticher in a new series, of which 10 volumes have appeared to date (Cassel, 1956–). The standard biography of Lasso is Boetticher, *Orlando di Lasso und seine Zeit* (Cassel, 1958). See also Boetticher, *Aus Orlando di Lassos Wirkungskreis* (Cassel, 1963); Charles van den Borren, *Roland de Lassus* (Brussels, 1943); Kenneth Levy, "*Susanne un jour*, The History of a 16th-Century Chanson," *Annales musicologiques*, 1 (1953); Edward E. Lowinsky, *Das Antwerpener Motettenbuch Orlando di Lassos und seine Beziehungen zum Motettenschaffen der niederländischen Zeitgenossen* (The Hague, 1937); and Adolf Sandberger, *Beiträge zur Geschichte der bayrischen Hofkapelle unter Orlando di Lasso*, of which only vols. 1 and 3 were published (Leipzig, 1894–95).

The complete works of Victoria were published by Felipe Pedrell in 8 volumes (Leipzig, 1902–13; repr. 1965). On Victoria's life and works, see Raffaele Casimiri, *Il Vittoria: nuovi documenti per una biografia sincera di Tommaso Ludovico de Victoria* (Rome, 1934); Hans von May, *Die Kompositionstechnik T. L. de Victorias* (Berne, 1943); Felipe Pedrell, *Tomás Luis de Victoria Abulense* (Valencia, 1918); and Robert Stevenson, *Spanish Cathedral Music in the Golden Age* (Berkeley and Los Angeles, 1961).

Edmund H. Fellowes, *William Byrd* (London, 1936), remains the best monograph on the composer, although it is by now out of date in some details. Fellowes's pioneering work also led him to edit *The Collected Works of William Byrd* (London, 1937–50, 20 vols.), an edition that is now in the process of being re-issued with revisions (and some volumes completely re-edited) by Thurston Dart, Philip Brett, and others. Byrd's keyboard music has been edited by Alan Brown as volumes 27 and 28 of the series *Musica Britannica*. H. K. Andrews, *The Technique of Byrd's Vocal Polyphony* (London, 1966) is a detailed investigation of the composer's compositional technique.

The section on Byrd owes much to the following studies by Joseph Kerman: "Byrd's Motets: Chronology and Canon," *Journal of the American Musicological Society*, 14 (1961); "The Elizabethan Motet: A Study of Texts for Music," *Studies in the Renaissance*, 9 (1962); *The Elizabethan Madrigal* (New York, 1962); "On William Byrd's *Emendemus in Melius*,"

Musical Quarterly, 49 (1963); and "Byrd, Tallis, and the Art of Imitation," in *Aspects of Medieval and Renaissance Music: A Birthday Offering to Gustave Reese*, ed. Jan LaRue (New York, 1966). On particular aspects of the composer's work, see also Philip Brett, "The English Consort Song, 1570–1625," *Proceedings of the Royal Musical Association*, 88 (1961–62); Brett, "Word-Setting in the Songs of Byrd," *Proceedings of the Royal Musical Association*, 98 (1971–72); and James L. Jackman, "Liturgical Aspects of Byrd's *Gradualia*," *Musical Quarterly*, 49 (1963).

General studies of English music during the period that provide stimulating ideas and guides to further reading include Morrison C. Boyd, *Elizabethan Music and Musical Criticism* (Philadelphia, 2nd ed., 1962); Bruce Pattison, *Music and Poetry of the English Renaissance* (London, 1948); and Walter L. Woodfill, *Musicians in English Society* (Princeton, 1953).

Both the *Fitzwilliam Virginal Book* and *My Lady Nevell's Booke* have been reprinted by Dover Publications, New York.

TWELVE

THE END OF THE RENAISSANCE

NEO-CLASSICAL EXPERIMENT

No matter how great the achievement of Palestrina, Lasso, Victoria, and Byrd, their work did not reflect everything that went on in music between 1560 and 1600, nor can it explain the radical change in style which took place at the turn of the century. It is in Italy, especially in the madrigal and the lyric genres that grew out of it, that the disintegration of Renaissance techniques and ideals can be seen most clearly and that the new Baroque style developed its firmest roots. But even within Italy the situation was complex, and elements of continuity and change existed side by side at the end of the sixteenth century. In addition to highly expressive settings of lyric poetry in a genuinely new style requiring the services of virtuoso singers to do them full justice, for example, some composers wrote madrigals that scarcely differ in aesthetic outlook from

those of the preceding generation; others put together sequences of
3. simple, tuneful pieces to form narrative or quasi-dramatic madrigal
4. comedies, or composed light and entertaining canzonette, balletti, balli,
5. and the like. Some composers of sacred music took Palestrina as their
model and continued to write carefully regulated and expressively neutral
counterpoint well into the seventeenth century and even beyond. In
Venice the two Gabrielis and their contemporaries refined the technique
6. of combining voices and instruments into splendid polychoral concertos.

Among the most interesting and important intellectual developments of the late sixteenth century was a fascination with music of the
ancient world. In Italy, discussion about Greek and Roman music led on
the one hand to various experiments in tuning and temperament, and on
the other to the invention of opera and monody. In France, similar discussions inspired the foundation of Baïf's Académie de poésie et musique
and created a new style, *musique mesurée à l'antique*, which had a great
influence on French music of the emerging Baroque era. As early as the
first decade of the sixteenth century, as we have seen, the German composer Tritonius, under the influence of the humanist Konrad Celtes, had
published settings of Horace designed to help students learn classical
meters. But more general and widespread study of the music of the
ancients did not take place until later in the century, long after classical
influence had made a strong impact on the other arts. The nature of
classical studies in music was different from studies in other fields, since
very few specimens of actual Greek music were known, and they could
probably not be deciphered. Scholars were thus forced to speculate
about the true nature of Greek music on the basis of theoretical treatises,
some of which began to be generally known only toward the middle of
the sixteenth century.

D. P. Walker, whose series of articles on musical humanism in the
sixteenth and early seventeenth centuries is the most complete résumé to
date of the ideas about Greek musical thought current during the
Renaissance, makes clear how universal the interest in Greek music was.
Almost all sixteenth-century treatises pay at least lip service to the Greeks,
and many writers made a serious attempt to understand the character of
Greek music. Surprisingly enough, in spite of the lack of classical sources,
sixteenth-century scholars all arrived at very much the same general conception of ancient music, even though there were important details about
which they differed. Quite aside from these details, though, they were in
basic disagreement about the extent to which modern music ought to be
reformed according to ancient precepts. Some humanists, like Franchino
Gafori, Giovanni Artusi, Francisco Salinas, and Domenico Pietro Cerone,
took a purely scholarly interest in Greek music. Others, like Pontus de
Tyard, Vincenzo Galilei, Girolamo Mei, and Giovanni Battista Doni, be-

lieved modern music to be vastly inferior and wished to change it radically. Still others, including Gioseffo Zarlino, Heinrich Glareanus, Nicola Vicentino, and perhaps most of the more humanistically inclined composers, took a middle position: sixteenth-century music, they thought, had reached a new state of perfection, but it could be improved still more, since it was in certain ways inferior to that of the Greeks.

A great deal of sixteenth-century speculation and discussion about ancient music centered on a variety of theoretical problems, among them the nature of the Greek diatonic, chromatic, and enharmonic genera and of the various tuning systems proposed by ancient theorists, and the way quantitative Greek and Latin meters could best be adapted to the accentual prosody of French and Italian poetry. Nicola Vicentino, for example, described the Greek genera in his treatise *L'antica musica ridotta alla moderna prattica* (published in 1555, partly as a result of his defeat in a public debate on the subject), and he explained how to demonstrate them on his invention, the *arcicembalo*, a harpsichord with six manuals capable of dividing the octave into thirty-one parts. Vicentino also furnished specimens of his own compositions, including some that illustrate the enharmonic gender and use microtones (indicated by dots over the notes). Andrea Gabrieli wrote choruses for the first performance in Italian of a Greek tragedy, Sophocles's *Oedipus rex*, translated by Orsatto Giustiniano on the occasion of the opening of the neo-classical Teatro Olimpico in Vicenza in 1585. Gabrieli tried to match exactly in his music the ancient meters. However important historically, the task defeated him artistically. In the long run, such experiments with prosody and speculation about genera, modes, and tuning systems had only an indirect influence on the mainstream of music. Some stylistic innovations, like the rise of chromaticism in the sixteenth-century madrigal, can be linked to humanistic study (see, for example, Lasso's *Prophetiae sibyllarum* or even the highly chromatic works in Vicentino's fifth book of five-voiced madrigals, published in 1572), but the more historically oriented experiments, like those reported in Vicentino's treatise, had no far-reaching practical consequences.

The avenue of approach that proved most fruitful to composers, right from the beginning of discussions about Greek music, was the exploration of means for connecting the music more closely with the text to which it was set. Many mid-sixteenth-century theorists were concerned that their music could not produce the powerful psychological and sometimes even miraculous effects on listeners that Greek music was supposed to have been capable of producing. Writers on music described the miracles said to have been worked by Orpheus, Amphion, Arion, Timotheus, and various other Greek musicians. Zarlino, for example, noted that although ancient music was imperfect, the ancient musicians were able to arouse in the human soul many different kinds of emotions. They could move the soul to anger and then change that anger to gentleness and docility. They could also induce sadness, joy, and other similar passions. Their ability to move men, he wrote, is all the more incredible, since modern music is incapable of producing such effects.

Vincenzo Galilei, Florentine lutenist and father of the famous scientist, was extreme in his condemnation of modern music and in his support of Greek music, especially because the ancient musicians appeared to have acknowledged fully the power of words. The noblest and most important part of music is the conception of the soul expressed by means of words, Galilei wrote, and modern musicians had made reason a slave of their appetites in pretending that the way in which all the parts of a polyphonic composition come together is more important than expression. His treatise, *Dialogo della musica antica et della musica moderna*, published in 1581, apparently sets down the sentiments of the circle of musicians, poets, and scholars around Count Giovanni de' Bardi in Florence, who met from the late 1570's to the early 1590's to discuss music in Greek culture, among many other things. The radical stance of the Camerata, as this informal group of intellectuals called themselves, and especially their insistence that the words need to be declaimed in order to convey their emotion and that emotional power can only be gained by abandoning elaborate polyphony and returning to some sort of texture reminiscent of Greek monody, resulted eventually in the invention of opera and early Baroque monody. The two professional singers in the group, Jacopo Peri and Giulio Caccini, both explored ways of composing music that communicates the feelings expressed in the text immediately and directly to the listener. Theirs was the most radical solution of the late sixteenth and early seventeenth centuries to the challenge of writing expressive music. In using *basso continuo* texture and writing in a newly declamatory melodic style, they abandoned completely the polyphonic ideals of the Renaissance; indeed, their music leads us into the emerging Baroque era.

To a much greater extent than in Italy, literary figures in France led the discussions about music in the ancient world. Active interest in the subject dated from mid-century and centered around the group of poets known as the Pléiade, with Pierre de Ronsard their greatest representative. Ronsard's colleague, Joachim du Bellay, outlined the group's aims in his important treatise, *La Deffence et illustration de la langue françoyse* (1549), in which he urged poets to imitate classical forms and meters. As a model of collaboration between the arts, Ronsard included in his *Amours* of 1552 an appendix with ten musical settings by some of the best musicians of the time: Clément Janequin, Pierre Certon, and Claude Goudimel as well as the lesser known humanist-composer, Marc-Antoine de Muret. The ten chansons were so conceived that all 150-odd sonnets in the collection could be sung to one or another of them. In Ronsard's preface to his *Mellanges de chansons* (1560) and in his *Abrégé de l'art poétique françoys* (1565), the poet set down his vision of a new union of poetry and music that was intended to revive the ideal state of the arts in ancient times. Ronsard's ideas, many of them derived from Plato, stressed the ethical and moral quality of music. Whether or not he and his collaborating poets and musicians really succeeded in bringing the arts closer together is questionable—the issue is still being debated by scholars —but it is clear that Ronsard succeeded in creating a mystique about the arts in the ancient world, a climate of opinion which welcomed neo-classical postures without imposing any specific technical prescriptions on composers; and most of the best French musicians of the time set Ronsard's poetry to music in a variety of styles, among them Guillaume Costeley, Pierre Cléreau, Anthoine de Bertrand, and Claude Le Jeune, as well as the great Orlando di Lasso.

One of the members of the Pléiade, Jean-Antoine de Baïf, in co-operation with an obscure musician named Joachim Thibaut de Courville, *joueur de lyre du roi*, went further than anyone else in attempting to establish a firm connection between music and poetry and to rediscover the effects of ancient music, by devising both "vers et musique mesurés à l'antique." They worked out an accentual version in French of the metrical patterns of Greek and Latin poetry and invented a kind of music in which long syllables were set by long notes and short syllables by short notes. Baïf's Académie de poésie et musique, founded in 1570 partly with the royal support of Charles IX, had an elaborate set of statutes. The chief function of the Académie was to give concerts of musique mesurée at Baïf's house, and to educate young musicians as well as listeners in the new art. Baïf's secrecy—neither the *auditeurs* who paid for the concerts nor the *musiciens* who played in them were to reveal what went on—prevents us from knowing in detail precisely what these performances of the new music were like (although much of it was eventually published, albeit some years after the event). Baïf obviously wished to impose his views about music, especially those about its ethical power and those regarding good prosody, on the intellectual elite of France. The Académie in its original form did not survive for more than a year or two, but the in-fluence of its work continued to make itself felt for many decades to come; it extended even to the strophic *airs de cour* of the early seventeenth century.

The most distinguished musician associated with Baïf's enter-prise was Claude Le Jeune (ca. 1525/30–1600), a superb composer whose works are unjustly neglected today. A Protestant, Le Jeune took so active a part in the religious debate in France that he had to flee Paris in 1590, and his works were only saved from destruction through the efforts of his good friend and collaborator in Baïf's circle, the important composer Jacques Mauduit (1557–1627). The best-known example of *musique mesurée* is probably Le Jeune's setting of *Revecy venir le printemps* (Example 12–1), in which the stark chordal texture is skillfully enlivened with brief melismas. Like most compositions in this style, Le Jeune's chanson alternates between refrain (called *rechant*) and stanzas (called *chants*). The close relationship between poetic meter and musical rhythm gives the composition its most distinctive feature and explains why barlines cannot be added regularly without distorting the music's character.

EXAMPLE 12–1. Claude Le Jeune, *Revecy venir le printemps*, Rechant and beginning of Chant.

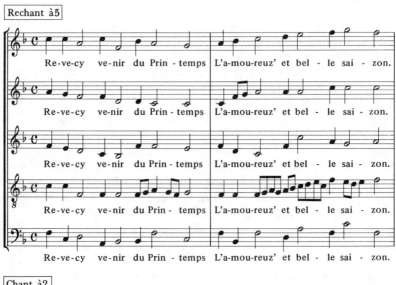

But Le Jeune also composed more conventional polyphonic chansons, like his exquisite setting of Ronsard's *Rossignol mon mignon*. And his activity as a composer also led him to collaborate with Nicholas de la Grotte, Henry III's organist, on the occasion of the marriage of the Duc de Joyeuse, one of the king's favorites, with the queen's half-sister in 1581. It was on the same occasion that the *Balet comique de la royne* was performed—the first *ballet de cour* and the first time in France that drama, music, and dancing had been combined. That Baïf was not called on to contribute to this entertainment, organized by the court violinist Balthasar de Beaujoyeulx, can probably be explained by court intrigue; Baïf was certainly interested in extending his ideas to take in dance and drama, and as early as 1573 he supposedly had in readiness a ballet with music by Courville and Le Jeune in which even the dancing was *mesuré à l'antique*.

THE VIRTUOSO MADRIGALISTS

Vast quantities of madrigals were composed and published during the second half of the sixteenth century in a bewildering variety of styles. Musicians set epic, lyric, pastoral, dramatic, and even moral or philosophical poetry to music, for performances by virtuosi at courts, dilettanti in academies, amateurs at home, or for splendidly festive occasions such as princely weddings and banquets. Poetry by Petrarch continued to be set throughout the second half of the century, along with excerpts from Lodovico Ariosto's semi-heroic, semi-comic, very humane epic, *Orlando Furioso*, and from the gentle Arcadian verses of Jacopo Sannazaro. But more and more composers were attracted to the gloomier, more mannered and emotional work of Torquato Tasso, including excerpts from his pastoral play *Aminta* and his epic *Gerusalemme liberata*, and to the poetry of Tasso's fellow Ferrarese, Giambattista Guarini, whose brilliantly artificial pastoral, *Il Pastor fido*, became the literary rage of the *fin de siècle*. The small city-states of Italy vied with one another to procure for themselves the best available musicians, and musical courtiers and critics alike valued novelty highly; fashions changed rapidly in the madrigal. To some extent, then, I am following sixteenth-century criteria in singling out four composers—Giaches de Wert, Luca Marenzio, Carlo Gesualdo, and Claudio Monteverdi—as representatives of their time, because in my opinion they wrote the newest and best madrigals, even though many other musicians during the same period, needless to say, were also composing excellent music. But I have chosen them, too, because their works reveal more clearly than most by their contemporaries the change in style which gradually took place during the last decades of the sixteenth century, the new aesthetic attitudes and techniques that signal the transition from the Renaissance to the Baroque era.

Giaches de Wert (1535–96) was the oldest of these "virtuoso madrigalists" and the only Netherlander among them, for, as we have seen, native-born Italians had finally taken back command of the musical life in their own country. Wert spent most of his mature working life at Mantua, in the service of the Gonzaga family, where he could also be in close contact with the musical circles at the Este court in Ferrara; Mantua and Ferrara formed an axis around which many of the most significant events in the history of the late sixteenth-century madrigal turned. Indeed, Wert's connection with Ferrara was very close, for after his wife had first cuckolded him and then deserted him he fell in love with a Ferrarese court lady, Tarquinia Molza, who returned his love. Their affair became known, Molza was banished to Modena, and Wert was temporarily disgraced. The musical significance of this tragic series of events in the composer's life stems from the fact that Tarquinia Molza was one of three or four virtuoso sopranos whose performances in Ferrara brought them fame throughout all of Italy, and who inspired a number of composers to take their prowess into account in writing madrigals for them. Wert, Marenzio, Luzzasco Luzzaschi, and even Gesualdo, among many others, created textures in some of their works in which two, three, or four high parts, clearly intended for the "ladies of Ferrara," are set off in one way or another from the two or more lowest voices.

Wert's secular music—eleven books of madrigals for five voices, one volume for four, a collection of light *canzone villanelle*, and a handful of madrigals printed in various miscellaneous collections—makes up the largest part of his complete works. The first three books of five-voiced madrigals contain his youthful compositions, written before he came to Mantua. Books 4–6, published in 1567, 1571, and 1577, during his first twenty-odd years at the Gonzaga court, reveal him in his maturity as a composer of madrigals similar in many ways to those by Cipriano de Rore, his fellow Netherlander who had worked in Ferrara until a few years before Wert's arrival in Mantua in 1565. In Wert's compositions, as in Rore's, technical artifice was by and large subservient to text expression. Dense imitative counterpoint, homophony, splendid polychoral dialogue, choral declamation, simple diatonic or highly chromatic melodic lines—these as well as various other textures and styles were all brought into play as the occasion demanded, following the sense of text rather than any abstract musical design.

In Wert's last five books of five-voiced madrigals, published between 1581 and 1595, the composer showed a markedly increased willingness to underscore literary meaning at the expense of polyphonic decorum. In his late "mannered" works, lyric, dramatic, and pathetic texts all receive highly individual settings that sometimes threaten the stability of the polyphonic fabric. This change in his style during the 1580's and 1590's was partly signalled by a shift in his taste for poetry, away from his earlier favorites—Petrarch, Ariosto, and the mid-sixteenth-century Petrarchist Luigi Tansillo—and towards the greater emotionalism of his colleagues in Ferrara, Torquato Tasso and Giambattista Guarini. Wert was the first composer to set stanzas from Tasso's epic *Gerusalemme liberata*—he may even have done so at the poet's request—and they demonstrate Wert's new manner very well. For example, in *Giunto alla tomba* (Example 12–2), Tancredi's lament at the tomb of Clorinda, the low-pitched, gloomy declamation of the opening (in the parlando style Wert came more and more to use for narrative passages) contrasts so strikingly with the melismatic madrigalism of "sgorgando un lagrimoso rivo" ("gushing forth a river of tears") that the listener's sense of continuity is threatened; and the affective leaps downward on "in un languido oimè" ("with a languishing 'alas' ") violate older ideals of melodic elegance as thoroughly as they embody the meaning of the words. Changes of pace like that between the first and second phrases of *Giunto alla tomba* occur in various other madrigals from Wert's seventh book, either to enhance the drama or merely to illustrate a word or a clause. His setting of Petrarch's sonnet *Solo e pensoso*, for example, moves at the beginning in generally slow notes that aptly fit the opening lines, "Thoughtful and alone, I pace the most deserted fields with slow and dragging steps," but the music soon picks up speed and never returns to its first tempo. The expressive—one is tempted to say "expressionistic"—nature of Wert's music for *Solo e pensoso* is evident, too, from the character of the opening melodic line (Example 12–3), which covers a range of almost two octaves. Beside this intense, artfully distorted theme—this parody of a classically proportioned Renaissance melody—the gentle arches of a Palestrina seem tame indeed.

EXAMPLE 12–2. Giaches de Wert, *Giunto alla tomba*, mm. 1–26. Used by permission of the American Institute of Musicology.

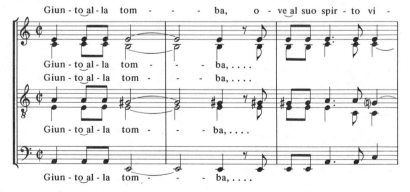

EXAMPLE 12–3. Wert, *Solo e pensoso,* opening line in the bass. Used by permission of the American Institute of Musicology.

Wert's eighth book of five-voiced madrigals (1586) is filled with compositions that offer unusually good opportunities for virtuoso display; the volume was dedicated to the Duke and Duchess of Ferrara, and much of it was apparently written for the superb performers at their court. Book 9 (1588) opens with a madrigal, *Or si rallegri il cielo,* composed for the coronation of Vincenzo Gonzaga as fourth duke of Mantua; the volume contains other examples as well of Wert's splendid official manner, most of them intended for the duke's singers in Mantua. Book 10 (1591) was dedicated to the duke's mistress, and many of the madrigals in it may be settings of poems written by her and her circle of friends and sung by them at her residence, the Palazzo del Tè on the outskirts of Mantua. Both the poetry and its courtly music are slightly lighter in tone than most of Wert's other works; the composer evoked the atmosphere of the canzonetta and the balletto while using the more elaborate techniques of the madrigal. Nearly half of Book 11 (1595), Wert's swan song, is devoted to compositions originally conceived for theatrical performances, a genre Wert had had to cultivate assiduously during his career at the Mantuan court. It opens with *Ah, dolente partita* (Example 12–4), on a passage from Guarini's play, *Il pastor fido,* and Einstein has described it as an "aria in advance of its time," doubtless because the top line carries much of the burden of presenting the principal melodic material; since it was intended for the theater, it may well have been performed the first

time by a solo singer accompanied by instruments. In all four of the last
madrigal books, Wert favored pastoral rather more than dramatic or
pathetic poetry, and by the second half of the 1580's he had all but
abandoned complex imitative counterpoint as his normal texture. Passages
in imitation still occur, of course, but they are often quite short and they
seldom predominate. Instead, Wert more often pitted duos, trios, or other
sections of the ensemble against one another in dialogue, or wrote chordal
passages in which the top voice naturally stands out. His constantly
changing textures, his sensitive use of harmonic progressions for expressive purposes, and his melodic lines filled with written-out *passaggi*
(ornamental runs and turns) make these late madrigals exciting, highly
colorful, "baroque" compositions. As Einstein wrote, "The later Wert is
no longer Rore's successor; he is the contemporary of Marenzio, Gesualdo,
and the young Monteverdi and one of the forerunners and founders of the
music of the seventeenth century."

EXAMPLE 12–4. Wert, *Ah, dolente partita*, mm. 1–22. Used by permission
of the American Institute of Musicology.

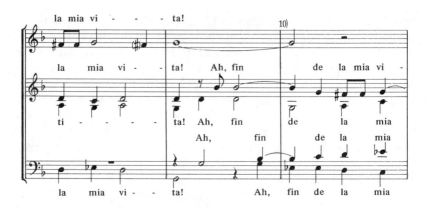

The second of the four virtuoso madrigalists, Luca Marenzio (1553–99), spent most of his life in Rome—he went there from his native village near Brescia when he was in his mid-twenties, if not before—but during the course of his life he had contact with various other centers of music in Italy, notably Ferrara and Mantua (through his patron, Cardinal Luigi d'Este) and Florence (where he collaborated with Cristofano Malvezzi, Alessandro Striggio, and others in composing music to celebrate the wedding of Grand Duke Ferdinand I de' Medici to Christina of Lorraine in 1589), and he worked for King Sigismund III in Poland for several years. Just as Wert excelled throughout much of his life at the dramatic and pathetic madrigal, so Marenzio must be considered the genius of the lyrical and pastoral manners, the "Schubert of the madrigal," as Denis Arnold has aptly called him. It might even be argued that Marenzio wrote the most refined and elegant madrigals of the entire century. Then as well as now, his earliest works—brilliant, playful and sensuous—are his best known. They are better known now than his later works because only his first three books for five voices have been published in their entirety in modern times (although a new edition of his complete works has been announced); they were better known then because he burst upon the Roman scene in 1580 with astonishing success, a success that may be partly explained by the fact that he had no real competition as a madrigalist in Rome, and partly because his works filled a genuine need in Roman society for music that could be sung by cultivated amateurs (as opposed to the professional virtuosi for whom many of the northern Italian musicians composed). But his fame was more than merely local; his madrigal books were re-issued again and again—his first book *a* 5, for example, was reprinted at least nine times by 1610—and his works quickly spread throughout all of Europe. A number of his compositions even appeared in translation in the first volume of madrigals printed in England, Yonge's *Musica Transalpina* of 1588, and they had an important influence on the development of the English madrigal.

Marenzio was extraordinarily prolific. Besides a single book of madrigals for four voices (rather an anachronism by 1585), he published nine books for five voices (ten including his *madrigali spirituali* of 1584), six books for six voices, a collection of serious madrigals for four, five and six voices (printed in 1588 and composed in a manner very different from his former style, to paraphrase his own dedication to the volume), and five books of villanelle for three voices, as well as a number of individual works in miscellaneous collections. His first publication, *Il primo libro de madrigali a cinque voci*, was printed in Venice by Angelo Gardano in 1580. Within five years, Marenzio had published twelve volumes altogether and had become one of the best and best known madrigalists of his time.

Like all the late sixteenth-century madrigalists, Marenzio adapted his compositional techniques to fit the sense of the particular poem he was setting, so that each work is individual to a high degree, making generalizations unusually unreliable. Still, two characteristics of his style should be emphasized in considering his earlier works: his brevity and conciseness, and his penchant for depicting graphically as many of the concrete details of a poem as he could, qualities that do not explain the polish and effectiveness of his music but help to distinguish his madrigals from those by his contemporaries. The first trait is evident even in the first several phrases of his setting of Petrarch's sonnet *Zefiro torna* (Example 12–5a). Within twenty measures, four different textures appear: the initial dialogue among the voices on the simple descending motive for "Zefiro torna" ("The west wind returns"); the homophony of "e'l bel tempo rimena" ("and the beautiful weather comes back"); the imitation, or rather the repetition at different pitches of a brief motive (consisting of an ornamented ascending second) over a sequential descending scale in the bass, on the words "e i fiori e l'erbe" ("and the flowers and the grass"); and the animated homophony (harmonizing a continuation of the sequential bass pattern) leading to a cadence on "sua dolce famiglia" ("his sweet family"). Each half-line gets its separate treatment, and even though the first line is repeated with some variants and the two halves of the second line are related by the bass pattern, there is no lengthy discourse or extensive thematic manipulation. Each literary conceit is given a characterization that is as economical as it is telling and vivid, then the composer moves on. The poem contrasts the life and vitality of nature in the spring with the lover's bitter sense of loneliness, deprived of his beloved. The turning point is depicted in an instant by a few bold strokes (Example 12–5b). The series of suspensions on "Ma per me, lasso, tornano i più gravi sospiri" ("but for me, alas, the deepest sighs come back") include no unusually harsh dissonances (and for once the word *sospiri*—"sighs"—is not realistically illustrated by a rest before it begins). Nevertheless, Marenzio immediately captured the essence of the text by his abrupt change in pace and texture. The result, of course, is a composition broken up into small segments, a work that violates the earlier concern to maintain an uninterrupted flow of polyphony. In writing what Einstein has called "a symphonic structure in the service of the text," Marenzio pushed almost to its breaking-point the ideal of a continuous polyphonic fabric that had been cultivated by musicians throughout the fifteenth and sixteenth centuries.

EXAMPLE 12–5. Luca Marenzio, *Zefiro torna.*

(a) mm.1-22

(b) mm.74-90

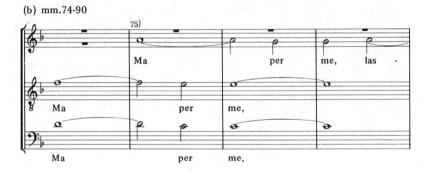

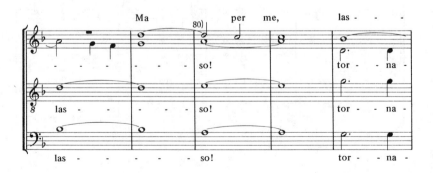

Marenzio's habit of musical word-painting, of graphically illustrating individual words or clauses, followed naturally from his desire to be brief and to the point and to characterize instantly and vividly the mood or meaning of the text. Example 12–6 furnishes an unusually clear sample of the lengths to which he was prepared to go. The passage comes from *Dolorosi martir*, which, together with *Liquide perle* and *Tirsi morir volea* (an erotic dialogue by Guarini and a favorite text of late sixteenth- and early seventeenth-century composers), is perhaps the most stunning and most modern of the compositions in Marenzio's first book of madrigals for five voices. In the Elizabethan translation in *Musica Transalpina*, the first lines of *Dolorosi martir* read:

> Dolorous mournful cares, ruthless tormenting,
> Hateful gyves, cursed bondage, sharpest endurance
> Wherein both nights and days my heart ever venting,
> Wretch, I bewail my lost delight and pleasure.

Example 12–6 includes the music for the last clause of the second line and all of the third and fourth lines. Marenzio not only heightened the sentiment, "Wretch, I bewail," by writing a poignantly chromatic progression; he also depicted at least four words and phrases literally by means of "madrigalisms." "Aspre catene" (literally, "bitter chains" rather than the "sharpest endurance" of the translation) is set to an inordinately long chain of suspensions. "Night" is set by two blackened notes (the triplet in m. 19 in modern notation), an example of so-called *Augenmusik* ("eye music"), in which the notation suggests a pun that is not audible (such as blackened notes for grief or night, two white semibreves, o o , for

EXAMPLE 12–6. Marenzio, *Dolorosi martir*, mm. 14–25.

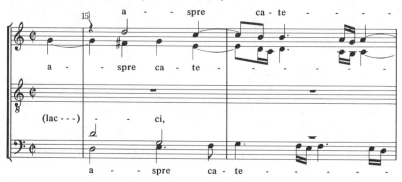

"eyes," and so on). In a famous passage from another madrigal, Petrarch's
O voi che sospirate, Marenzio illustrated the line "muti una volta quel
suo antico stile" ("change once his ancient style") by means of a somewhat
less literal madrigalism: "ancient style" suggested to the composer the
recent researches into the diatonic, chromatic, and enharmonic genera of
the Greeks, hence he set the line with a strikingly chromatic series of
chords involving enharmonic equivalents (and therefore, by the way,
implying equal temperament). Marenzio's extravagant pictorialism may
well be as naive as some critics claim, but it is an integral part of the
style of these delightful, playful, voluptuous compositions, which are
nothing if not highly sophisticated evocations of extraordinarily subtle,
refined poetry.

But lest Marenzio be seen only as the most brilliant, if slightly
superficial, member of the quartet of virtuoso madrigalists, his late works,
too, should be considered, even if they are not all yet available in modern
editions. He wrote of the change in his style that took place during the
last decade or so of his life in the dedication to his *Madrigali a quattro,
cinque, et sei voci* of 1588, explaining that the compositions included in
the volume were "composed in a manner very different from my former
one in that through the imitation of the words and the propriety of the
style I have sought a sort of melancholy gravity [*mesta gravità*] that will
perhaps be prized the more highly by connoisseurs." It may be that he
underwent a spiritual crisis (possibly influenced by the ideas of the
Counter-Reformation), a reaction against the delightful frivolities of his
youth—certainly he began to prefer texts expressing hopelessness and
melancholy and even longing for death. Or perhaps the change resulted
from a more purely musical response to the artistic climate of his time,
an answer to Tasso's complaint that modern music was decadent: as
Einstein has pointed out, Tasso asked for precisely that quality of *gravità*
that Marenzio claims in his dedication. Whatever the cause, the result
—to judge from three of the most easily accessible examples of Marenzio's
late works: *Fiere silvestre*, published in Einstein's useful anthology, *The*

Golden Age of the Madrigal (New York, 1942); *O fere stelle,* published
in the third volume of Einstein's *The Italian Madrigal;* and his long six-
voiced madrigal cycle, *Giovane donna,* edited by Denis Arnold for the
Pennsylvania State Music Series—was a repertory of works more austere
in their contrapuntal orientation and less immediately charming and
pictorial, more chromatic and with better integrated excursions into dis-
tant tonal areas, more continuous and less fragmented in their structure,
and altogether more intense than any of his earlier works. They deserve
to be better known and more easily available to interested musicians.

Carlo Gesualdo, Prince of Venosa (ca. 1560–1613), in some of his
madrigals went even further than Wert and Marenzio in transforming
Renaissance polyphony into something strange and new for the sake of
expression. But then the melancholy and temperamental Gesualdo was a
man of excess, a member of the high Neapolitan nobility and the central
figure in one of the most notorious scandals in sixteenth-century music
history. He was also, and most importantly, a distinguished musician,
although even his reputation as a composer has fluctuated wildly over the
centuries, from the scathing denunciation by Burney in the eighteenth
century to his adulation as a cult figure by Aldous Huxley and Stravinsky
in our own times. If his influence was neither wide nor lasting—his work
affected most directly a small group of Neapolitans (who may have influenced him as much as he influenced them), among them Giovanni de
Macque, Scipione Dentice, and his presumed teacher, Pomponio Nenna,
and he made a striking impression in Ferrarese musical circles in the
1590's—his music does nevertheless exemplify in extreme form that body
of late sixteenth-century music in which the older styles and ideals of the
Renaissance were rapidly breaking down; he can neither be dismissed as
a mere aberration nor patronized as a noble dabbler in the arts.

The major scandal in his life happened in 1590, when he murdered
his wife, whom he caught in adultery. Always a gloomy, eccentric, and
rather wilful man, Gesualdo seems to have increased in emotional in-
stability after the event. In 1594 he married again. His new wife,
Leonora d'Este, niece of Alfonso I, Duke of Ferrara, brought the Neapolitan prince into contact with the brilliant Ferrarese court, where he lived
for several years and where he had particularly close ties with Luzzasco
Luzzaschi, a composer most famous for his madrigals for one, two, and
three sopranos with written-out keyboard accompaniment, the first such
compositions in the history of music. Gesualdo and Luzzaschi may have
laid plans for an ambitious aesthetic program to renew the Ferrarese
madrigal—Luzzaschi's preface to his sixth book of five-voiced madrigals
(1596) is clearly intended to be a manifesto of the composer's musical
hopes for the future—but in 1596, after travelling for a time, Gesualdo
returned to the small town of Gesualdo near Naples and never again
paid an extended visit to the north.

Gesualdo's first two books of five-voiced madrigals, published in Ferrara in 1594 but written before he arrived there to claim his second wife, show him to have been a gifted if rather conventional composer as a young man. Books 3 and 4 (published in 1595 and 1596) reflect the influence of the Ferrarese musicians. In them he began to reveal his mature musical personality and to demonstrate how far he was to go in fragmenting textures, juxtaposing drastically contrasting elements within a very short space of time, and increasing the harmonic and melodic intensity of his music by means of strikingly chromatic progressions. All this he did in his search for heightened expression. The individual brief sections of *Ecco morirò dunque* (Example 12–7), from his fourth book, for instance, are fragmented, so that "Ecco" is divided from "morirò dunque" and "Ne fia" from "che pur rimire." The harmonic surprises of the first few measures, created by the chromaticisms, are in the end perhaps no more startling than the unconventional chords, chord spacings, and part writing of the last four measures of the example.

Many of the poems Gesualdo set are undistinguished as literature; he took relatively few texts from the major poets favored by other late

EXAMPLE 12–7. Carlo Gesualdo, *Ecco morirò dunque*, mm. 1–12. © 1958 by Ugrino Verlag, Hamburg. By the kind permission of VEB Deutscher Verlag für Musik, Leipzig.

sixteenth-century composers, although he did write some madrigals on poems by Guarini and quite a few on texts given him by his friend and fellow neurotic, the Ferrarese poet Torquato Tasso. *Ecco morirò dunque* illustrates Gesualdo's paradoxical attitude towards the poems he chose. Example 12–7 reproduces half of the first part of the madrigal. The second half repeats the same text with the same music recomposed, re-scored to include the bass (which had been silent for the entire first state-ment), and extended at the end. Gesualdo, like his contemporaries, was intent on devising a music derived from the words; but he also wished to shape his music as he pleased, by repeating clauses or whole lines of verse at will. That is why in general he preferred brief poems which he could rework at his pleasure; also why he was not above mutilating the verses he set, as he did to Guarini's *Tirsi morir volea* by simply omitting the entire ending.

Within a period of ten years at the end of his life, five volumes of Gesualdo's music appeared: two volumes of motets (the *Sacrae Cantiones* of 1603), and his responsories for Holy Week, and Books 5 and 6 of five-voiced madrigals, all printed in Gesualdo in 1611 under the direct supervi-sion of the composer. A single collection of six-voiced madrigals, unfortunately incompletely preserved, was published posthumously in 1626. His sacred music is somewhat more traditional than his madrigals—the polyphony is less chromatic and flows more continuously—but his motets are deeply felt and highly expressive, and the responsories are im-bued with techniques worked out first in his secular compositions. The last two volumes of five-voiced madrigals, Books 5 and 6, contain the music that has established Gesualdo's reputation for waywardness and disequilib-rium. Example 12–8, the beginning of his most famous work, *Moro lasso*, from Book 6, explains why. The extreme chromaticism and fairly slow pace of the first and third phrases, with their progressions of only distantly related chords, contrast drastically with the faster pace and the diatonic close imitation of the second phrase, with its melodic material partly consisting of written-out ornamental figures. As in *Ecco morirò dunque*,

Gesualdo proceeded to repeat the entire first section of *Moro lasso* before going on, recomposing it by rearranging the same musical elements at different pitches and by writing new points of imitation. He managed, barely, to keep his polyphonic structures from disintegrating completely into separate and unrelated clauses and to give his harmonic progressions, tending at times towards "floating atonality" (Lowinsky's phrase), coherence and direction. But it is difficult to see how anyone could have extended or developed his techniques or carried them further. In Gesualdo's music, even more clearly than in Wert's and Marenzio's, the Renaissance had come to an end.

EXAMPLE 12–8. Gesualdo, *Moro lasso*, mm. 1–22. © 1958 by Ugrino Verlag, Hamburg. By the kind permission of VEB Deutscher Verlag für Musik, Leipzig.

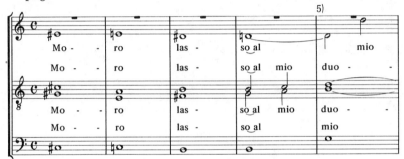

Marenzio, and to a lesser extent Wert and Gesualdo, often worked
1. with short, well-defined motives rather than building up long arches of
melody; instead of restricting themselves to evenly paced, smoothly flowing lines, the three composers gave to some of their voices the sorts of
2. highly decorated runs and trills that had become a part of the improvisational arsenal of virtuoso singers; Gesualdo, and sometimes Wert and
Marenzio, occasionally came close to harmonic chaos because they over-
loaded some of their music with so many chromatic notes, chords, and
3. progressions; and all three composers disrupted the continuous flow of
polyphony by juxtaposing short sections in contrasting textures and styles

in an effort to increase the immediate emotional impact of their madrigals on the listener. And yet all of them kept at all times to at least a semblance of the traditional polyphonic fabric. It was left to Claudio Monteverdi (1567–1643) to take the fatal plunge and add an obligatory *basso continuo* part for keyboard or chitarrone accompaniment to six of the madrigals in his fifth book (1605), as well as an optional *basso seguente* (a bass line composed of the lowest sounding notes, regardless of the voices singing them) to the rest of the compositions in that volume. Doubtless the chordal instrument was intended to hold together even the most fragmented texture, but that was surely not the sole reason for the innovation. The regular addition of a *basso continuo* (from the sixth book onwards) was merely a symptom that Monteverdi, the youngest of the virtuoso madrigalists, was in the process of forging an essentially new Baroque style.

Monteverdi's first book of five-voiced madrigals was published in 1587, when the composer was twenty years old and still living in his native Cremona; it is filled with passages that remind the listener of canzonette in their playfulness, their frequent three-part textures, and their evocation of pastoral moods (hardly surprising in view of the fact that Monteverdi had published an entire volume of pieces in the lighter genre three years previously). In many of their details these earliest madrigals by Monteverdi resemble those by Wert, Marenzio, contemporary Venetians like Andrea Gabrieli, or other northern Italian masters. Books 2 and 3, issued in 1590 and 1592, came out during Monteverdi's first three years in Mantua, long before he had become *maestro di cappella;* Wert was still the leading musician there and Monteverdi sang and played the viol under his direction. Einstein has called Books 2 and 3 "transitional" in style, by which he presumably meant that Monteverdi's fourth and fifth books, published in 1603 and 1605 after he had lived in Mantua for some years and had absorbed the influence of the brilliant musical life there and in neighboring Ferrara, contain examples of the most fully mature and individual manner the composer developed for the polyphonic madrigal (as opposed to those requiring *continuo*). Certainly the earlier books include some superb music, like the atmospheric, naturalistic, and justly famous *Ecco mormorar l'onde*; the magnificent settings of Tasso's poetry which make up almost half of Book 2; and the brilliant virtuoso settings (probably intended for the "ladies of Ferrara") of Book 3. But equally certainly it is best to turn to Books 4 and 5 for the clearest impression of Monteverdi's strengths as a madrigalist of the late Renaissance.

Examples 12–9 and 12–10, the first sections of the madrigals which open Books 4 and 5, both based on poems by Guarini, *Ah dolente partita* (compare Wert's version of the same passage in Example 12–4) and *Cruda*

Amarilli, can furnish us with at least a preliminary notion of Monteverdi's style. By 1603, attenuated textures in polyphonic music and a central concern for text expression can surely be taken for granted. In these examples, as in many of the compositions in the first five madrigal books, Monteverdi worked with small, well-defined motives. Some, like the motive setting "Ah, fin de la mia vita" in Example 12–9, closely resemble those used by Marenzio and the other virtuoso madrigalists. Some, like that setting "ahi lasso" in Example 12–10, incorporate written-out ornamental turns, runs, or trills into the very nature of the motive, a mannerism that became an important feature of Baroque melodic style. And some motives are starkly declamatory, like that setting "Ah dolente partita" in Example 12–9; one of those extraordinarily effective passages too simple for anyone but a great composer to have written, it is nothing more, really, than a recitation formula on two notes, depending for its immensely telling effect on the obvious and easy device of two suspensions. There are a number of similarly declamatory phrases in Monteverdi's first five books, from the chanted passages of *Sfogava con le stelle* of Book 4, in which the words are set beneath a single chord and meant to be sung in unmeasured speech rhythm, to the declaimed narrative or dramatic passages in almost every one of the works in Book 5 and to the sorts of formulas, such as that setting "Ah, dolente partita," which have real thematic or motivic significance. Einstein described these quasi-recitatives as examples of monody "beating against the bars of its cage," an anthropomorphic image suggesting the straining of the composer's polyphonic madrigals towards a more thoroughly Baroque style.

One of the things genuinely new in Monteverdi's works is the constructive and combinative way he worked with his brief motives. In a number of madrigals Monteverdi superimposed various parts of the poem (and the motives associated with them) to make a complex and rather dense texture, but one basically different from the dense imitative polyphony of earlier generations. The opening of *Ah, dolente partita* is an example of such a rich mixture of diverse poetic lines. Musically it might be described as a free fantasia on four themes: the declamatory two-voiced "Ah, dolente partita," which recurs four times (all but once with both voices intact) as a kind of cantus firmus; the simple descending motive on "Ah, fin de la mia vita"; and the two different declamatory motives on "Da te part'e non moro?" and "E pur io provo la pena de la morte." In *Cruda Amarilli*, on the other hand, the constructivist element involves controlled repetition: the opening phrase is immediately repeated in a slightly varied transposition, and the repetition of the second line (for three voices) preserves the essential features of the first statement (for five voices), but in compressed form. The first five books of madrigals include many similar examples, as well as passages in invertible counterpoint, expositions with two subjects, varied transpositions, and other such devices for achieving textural and structural coherence in a highly volatile context.

EXAMPLE 12–9. Claudio Monteverdi, *Ah, dolente partita,* mm. 1–31.

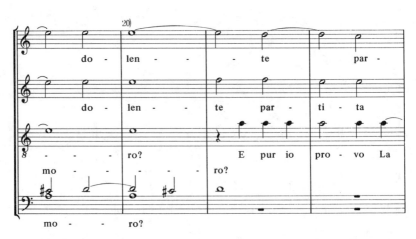

EXAMPLE 12–10. Monteverdi, *Cruda Amarilli,* mm. 1–14.

Harmony, as well as melody and counterpoint, is treated in a distinctive way in Monteverdi's madrigal books. Even Palestrina and Lasso, whose counterpoint is chordally oriented and tonally coherent, surely thought of the triad as the meeting place of converging polyphonic lines. But in Monteverdi's *Cruda Amarilli* (Example 12–10, m. 13) the triad has to have been conceived as a separate, independently existing entity, for the superius enters after a rest on an unprepared dissonance and then leaps to another dissonance. This is the famous passage that elicited such a vehement protest from the conservative Bolognese theorist Giovanni Maria Artusi that Monteverdi felt he had to reply and promised, in a short preface to Book 5, that he would write a treatise to be called "The Second Practice, or the Perfections of Modern Music." He never had time to finish his written defense, but his brother, Giulio Cesare Monteverdi, expanded on his few remarks in a slightly more informative foreword to Claudio's *Scherzi musicali* of 1607. In it, Monteverdi makes clear his distinction between "first practice" and "second practice." First practice "considers the harmony not commanded, but commanding, not the servant, but the mistress of the words." He goes on to explain that compositions in which purely musical principles predominate over text expression had been written by Ockeghem, Josquin, Pierre de la Rue, Mouton, Créquillon, Clemens non Papa, Gombert, and others; he might have added Palestrina and his Roman followers (Giovanni Bernardino and Giovanni Maria Nanino, Felice and Giovanni Francesco Anerio, Ruggiero Giovanelli, and Giovanni Animuccia) as well as the composers who continued to write "Renaissance polyphony" well into the seventeenth century. With this style of composition Monteverdi contrasts the second practice, which "considers harmony not commanding, but commanded, and makes the words the mistress of the harmony." This famous slogan of those who put expression above contrapuntal rules—*l'oratione sia padrona del armonia e non serva*—was hardly a new sentiment in 1607. Cipriano de Rore, fifty years before, would surely have subscribed to it, even though Rore never went to the extremes in rending the polyphonic fabric that Monteverdi and his colleagues and contemporaries were prepared to tolerate. Indeed, Monteverdi names Rore as the first exponent of the second practice, whose followers he lists as Ingegneri, Marenzio, Wert, Luzzaschi, Peri, and Caccini.

After Book 5 there was a gap of almost ten years before Monteverdi published another volume of madrigals. By the time Book 6 appeared in 1614, Monteverdi was already *maestro di cappella* at the basilica of St. Mark's in Venice, and he had composed his Mantuan operas, *L'Orfeo* (performed in 1607 and published in 1609) and *L'Arianna* (performed in 1608; only Ariadne's lament survives, separately and also in an arrangement for five voices in Book 6 of the madrigals). These works, as well as his Venetian madrigals, published in Books 7 (1619), 8 (1638), and, posthumously, 9 (1651); his Venetian operas, *Il Ritorno d'Ulisse in patria* (performed in 1641) and his great masterpiece, *L'Incoronazione di Poppea* (performed in 1642); and his gorgeous sacred music, composed both in Mantua and in Venice, belong outside the subject of this book. By the time Monteverdi died in 1643, even the first stages of the Baroque era had already come to a close.

Wert, Luzzaschi, and Monteverdi all worked in Mantua or Ferrara during important periods of their lives. The brilliant musical culture there strongly affected, too, the compositions of the Neapolitan, Gesualdo, and even touched the Roman, Marenzio. The artistic ferment and high artistic standards at those two courts had a profound influence on the character of the late sixteenth-century madrigal, and hence on the disintegration of Renaissance style. Mantua and Ferrara were at least as important in determining the shape of things to come as Florence, where opera and monody were born. But if, with hindsight, we can see that those centers led the way in encouraging the exploration of new techniques and new means of expression, the contemporary observer of the Italian scene would have been aware of many other fine composers in those and other cities whose music did not challenge older ideals quite so directly. And some of those musicians, too, influenced the nature of early Baroque music.

In Venice, for example, musical activities were as lively, as elegantly presented, and as influential in their own time and later as in any other Italian city. But the circle of Venetian madrigalists after Willaert and Rore seem to have intended their works more for "entertainment and delight" (Jerome Roche's phrase) than for serious expression. Andrea

Gabrieli (ca. 1520–86), only a few years older than Rore, wrote superb convivial, amatory, and pastoral madrigals, as well as some intended for great festival occasions; moreover, his greghesche and giustiniane are as light, frothy, and inconsequential as his few neo-classical choruses (such as those for the first performance of *Oedipus rex* in Vicenza) are serious in their attempt to recapture the spirit if not the techniques of the ancient world. Detailed word painting and straining after expressive effect were less important to him than choral sonority and harmonic color. His madrigals on themes of love are seldom overwrought, and his grand official manner is truly splendid. His brilliant nephew, Giovanni Gabrieli (ca. 1556–1612), the leading musician in Venice during the 1580's and 1590's, was apparently less interested in the madrigal than in the sacred music he wrote for the basilica of St. Mark's, where he served as organist. Both as a composer of sumptuous polychoral motets and grandiose imitative instrumental canzonas that were perfectly adapted to the tastes of the pleasure-loving Venetians, and as a distinguished teacher who numbered Michael Praetorius and Heinrich Schütz among his students, Giovanni helped to establish the "colossal Baroque" manner of the early seventeenth century, especially the *concertato* style with its colorful mixtures of voices and instruments.

In other Italian cities as well, musical life followed its own dynamics. For example, Rome, appropriately for the capital city of Christendom, preserved its conservative image as the stronghold of the *prima prattica*. In Modena and Bologna, composers like Orazio Vecchi (1550–1605) and Adriano Banchieri (1567–1634) wrote madrigal comedies, cycles of madrigals organized loosely around a dramatic plot. Madrigal comedies were not meant to be acted, as Vecchi makes clear in the preface to his *L'Amfiparnaso* (1597), where he writes that "this spectacle is observed with the mind, which it enters through the ears, not the eyes." Most of the plots are comic, with just enough serious moments to offer a bit of welcome contrast. Madrigal comedies are filled with characters from the commedia dell'arte, stereotyped figures like the braggart, the lecherous old doctor, the moneylender, and the clever servant, or with provincials and foreigners, like Sicilians and Germans, whose accents can be parodied. Many of them mock features of everyday life, like stuttering, or the chattering of women as they wash their clothes (as in Alessandro Striggio's *Il cicalamento delle donne al bucato*, the earliest madrigal comedy, published in 1567); and some imitate natural sounds, like the barking of dogs in Vecchi's *Veglie di Siena* (1604) or the cuckoo, owl, cat, and dog in Banchieri's *Festina nella sera del giovedi grasso* of 1608 ("An entertainment for the evening before mardi gras"), who sing a *contrappunto bestiale* against a mock-liturgical cantus firmus.

Madrigal comedies, as delightful as they are, added few new features to the repertory of techniques available to the late sixteenth-century composer of Italian secular music. Venetian madrigals and concertato motets include some of the greatest music of the late Renaissance; they are based on compositional procedures conservative for their times—systematic imitation and antiphonal textures, for example—although they strongly influenced the character of music in the seventeenth century. Such considerations lead us to the conclusion that descriptive terms like "Renaissance" or "Baroque era"—oversimple but useful, and even necessary—imply ways of looking at complex situations by emphasizing elements of change while ignoring things that continue in the same tradition or change but little. Many of the innovations of the late sixteenth and early seventeenth centuries had their roots in even earlier practices. Composers at least since the late fifteenth century were concerned to write a kind of music that reflected the words it set. The highly ornamented melodic style of the early Baroque era stems at least in part from composers' attempts to curb the improvisational excesses of late sixteenth-century virtuoso singers by writing into their music precisely the notes they wished sung. And even the new *basso continuo* texture grew out of the habit, almost certainly a common practice even during the early years of the sixteenth century, of having a lute or keyboard instrument double the parts in at least some vocal ensembles. There are other elements of continuity as well between the sixteenth and seventeenth centuries. The Baroque era did not begin overnight, nor did it wipe away in an instant every trace of the lingering Renaissance.

BIBLIOGRAPHICAL NOTES

On French and Italian neo-classical experiments at the end of the sixteenth century, see H. M. Brown, "How Opera Began: An Introduction to Jacopo Peri's *Euridice* (1600)," *The Late Renaissance: 1525–1630*, ed. Eric Cochrane (London, 1970); Henry Kaufmann, *Nicola Vicentino (1511–76): Life and Works* (American Institute of Musicology, 1965), along with Kaufmann's edition of Vicentino's complete works, also published by the American Institute of Musicology (*CMM* 26), and Edward E. Lowinsky's edition of a facsimile of Vicentino's treatise, *L'antica musica ridotta alla moderna prattica* (Cassel, 1959); Kenneth J. Levy, "Costeley's Chromatic Chanson," *Annales musicologiques*, 3 (1955); Lowinsky, *Tonality and Atonality in Sixteenth-Century Music* (Berkeley and Los Angeles, 1962); Claude V. Palisca, "Girolamo Mei, Mentor to the Florentine Camerata," *Musical Quarterly*, 40 (1954); Palisca, "Vincenzo Galilei and Some Links Between 'Pseudo-Monody' and Monody,"

Musical Quarterly, 46 (1960); Palisca, *Girolamo Mei, Letters on Ancient and Modern Music to Vincenzo Galilei and Giovanni Bardi* (American Institute of Musicology, 1960); Nino Pirrotta, "Temperaments and Tendencies in the Florentine Camerata," *Musical Quarterly*, 40 (1954); Leo Schrade, *La Représentation d'Edipo Tiranno au Teatro Olimpico (Vicence 1585)* (Paris, 1960); G. Thibault and L. Perceau, *Bibliographie des poésies de P. de Ronsard mises en musique au XVIe siècle* (Paris, 1941); Julien Tiersot, "Ronsard et la musique de son temps," *Sammelbände der internationalen Musikgesellschaft*, 8 (1906–7); D. P. Walker, "Musical Humanism in the 16th and Early 17th Centuries," *Music Review*, 2 (1941) and 3 (1942); Walker, "The Aims of Baïf's *Académie de Poésie et de Musique*," *Journal of Renaissance and Baroque Music*, 1 (1946); Walker, "The Influence of *Musique mesurée à l'antique*, Particularly on the *Airs de cour* of the Early Seventeenth Century," *Musica Disciplina*, 2 (1948); Walker and François Lesure, "Claude Le Jeune and Musique mesurée," *Musica Disciplina*, 3 (1949); Walker, "Some Aspects and Problems of *Musique mesurée à l'antique*," *Musica Disciplina*, 4 (1950); Walker, ed., *Claude Le Jeune: Airs (1608)* (American Institute of Musicology, 1951); and Yates, *The French Academies of the Sixteenth Century* (London, 1947). The *Balet comique de la royne* has been published in a facsimile edition (Turin, 1962), and in an English translation by Carol MacClintock (American Institute of Musicology, 1972).

Both Einstein, *The Italian Madrigal*, and Roche, *The Madrigal*, deal with the virtuoso madrigalists. A complete edition of the music of Luca Marenzio has not yet been published, although one has now been announced (New York, 1975–   ). Six books of his five-voiced madrigals were published by Alfred Einstein, in *Publikationen älterer Musik*, vols. 4 and 6 (Leipzig, 1929–31), and selections have appeared in L. Virgili, ed., *Luca Marenzio. Madrigali a 4 e 5 voci* (Rome, 1952), and F. Mompellio, *Luca Marenzio. Madrigali a 5 e 6 voci* (Milan, 1953). Hans Engel edited Marenzio's villanelle (Cassel, 1928) and wrote the most extensive monograph on the composer to date, *Luca Marenzio* (Florence, 1957). The only book on Marenzio in English is Denis Arnold's brief but useful *Marenzio* (London, 1965).

Wert's complete works, ed. Carol MacClintock, are in the course of publication by the American Institute of Musicology (*CMM* 24). On the composer's life and works, see MacClintock, *Giaches de Wert, Life and Works* (American Institute of Musicology, 1966).

On Gesualdo, see Glenn Watkins, *Gesualdo: The Man and his Music* (London, 1973). His complete works have been edited by Glenn Watkins and Wilhelm Weismann in 10 volumes (Hamburg, 1957–66). Cecil Gray and Philip Heseltine, *Carlo Gesualdo, Musician and Murderer* (London, 1926), has been superseded by Watkins's book, but it can still be regarded as a good historical novel.

Claudio Monteverdi's works have been published by G. F. Malipiero in 16 volumes (Vienna, 1926–66). Two new editions are underway, one edited by Raffaello Monterosso (Cremona: Fondazione Claudio Monteverdi, 1970–   ), and the other edited by Bernard Bailly de Surcy (Paris and New York: Les Éditions renaissantes, 1972–   ). The best introduction to Monteverdi's music is still Leo Schrade, *Monteverdi, Creator of Modern Music* (New York, 1950). See also Henry Prunières, *La Vie et l'oeuvre de Claudio Monteverdi*, translated into English by M. D. Mackie (London, 1926); H. F. Redlich, *Claudio Monteverdi: Life and Works* (London, 1952); and *The Monteverdi Companion*, ed. Nigel Fortune and Denis Arnold (London, 1968).

On Giovanni Gabrieli, see Egon Kenton, *Life and Works of Giovanni Gabrieli* (American Institute of Musicology, 1967). Gabrieli's complete works are in course of publication, ed. Denis Arnold, by the American Institute of Musicology (*CMM* 12). Selected madrigal comedies have been published in *Capolavori polifonici del secolo XVI*, ed. B. Somma (Rome, 1939–47), and in L. Torchi, *L'Arte musicale in Italia* (Milan, 1897–1908, 7 vols.).

INDEX OF NAMES

375